JOURNAL OF AN OVERLAND EXPEDITION IN AUSTRALIA

by

LUDWIG LEICHHARDT

FROM MORETON BAY TO PORT ESSINGTON,
A DISTANCE OF UPWARDS OF 3000 MILES, DURING THE
YEARS 1844-1845

Table of Contents

PREFACE..6

INTRODUCTION..6

CHAPTER I...11

CHAPTER II..24

CHAPTER III...39

CHAPTER IV...57

CHAPTER V..77

CHAPTER VI...95

CHAPTER VII..109

CHAPTER VIII..126

CHAPTER IX...149

CHAPTER X..167

CHAPTER XI...187

CHAPTER XII..202

CHAPTER XIII...222

CHAPTER XIV...242

CHAPTER XV..260

3

PREFACE

In preparing this volume for the press, I have been under the greatest obligations to Captain P. P. King, R. N., an officer whose researches have added so much to the geography of Australia. This gentleman has not only corrected my manuscript, but has added notes, the value of which will be appreciated by all who consider the opportunities he has had of obtaining the most correct information upon these subjects, during his surveys of the coasts parallel to my track.

To S. A. Perry, Esq., Deputy Surveyor General, I am extremely indebted for the assiduous labour he has bestowed in draughting my map. I shall ever remember the friendly interest he expressed, and the courteous attention with which he listened to the details of my journey.

From the Rev. W. B. Clarke, in addition to the unvaried kindness he has evinced towards me since my arrival in Australia, I have received every assistance which his high scientific acquirements enabled him to give.

I take this opportunity of publicly expressing my most sincere thanks to these gentlemen, for the generous assistance they have afforded me on this occasion, and for the warm interest which they have been kind enough to take in the success of my approaching enterprise.

LUDWIG LEICHIHARDT.
SYDNEY,
September 29th, 1846.

INTRODUCTION

ORIGIN OF THE EXPEDITION
PARTY FORMED
LEAVE SYDNEY FOR BRISBANE
PARTY ENLARGED
OUTFIT AND STORES.

On my return to Moreton Bay, from an exploratory journey in the country northward of that district, which had occupied me for two years, I found that the subject of an overland expedition to Port Essington on the North Coast of Australia, was occupying much attention, as well on the part of the public as on that of the Legislative Council, which had earnestly recommended the appropriation of a sum of money to the amount of 1000 pounds, for the equipment of an expedition under Sir Thomas Mitchell, to accomplish this highly interesting object. Some delay was, however, caused by the necessity of communicating with the Secretary of State for the Colonies; and in the mean time it was understood that Captain Sturt was preparing to start from Adelaide to proceed across the Continent. From the experience which I had gained during my two years' journeyings, both in surmounting the difficulties of travelling through a broken mountainous country, and in enduring privations of every sort, "I was inspired with the desire of attempting it," provided I could be assisted in the expense that would necessarily be incurred for the outfit, and could find a few companions who would be contented with animal food, and willingly and patiently submit to the privation of flour, tea, and sugar, and resign themselves to my guidance.

I had well considered this interesting subject in all its bearings, and had discussed it with many of my acquaintances at Brisbane and its neighbouring district; who were generally of opinion that it was practicable, under the plan I had marked out: but with others, particularly at Sydney, I had to contend against a strong but kindly meant opposition to my journey. Some, who took more than a common interest in my pursuits, regretted that I should leave so promising a field of research as that which offered itself within the limits of New South Wales, and in which they considered I had laboured with some success during the last two years. Others considered the undertaking exceedingly dangerous, and even the conception of it madness on my part; and the consequence of a blind enthusiasm, nourished either by a deep devotion to science, or by an unreasonable craving for fame: whilst others did not feel themselves justified in assisting a man who they considered was setting out with an intention of committing suicide. I was not, however, blind as to the difficulties of the journey which I was determined to undertake; on the contrary, and I hope my readers will believe me to be sincere, I thought they would be many and great--greater indeed than they eventually proved to be; but, during my recent excursions through the Squatting districts, I had so accustomed myself to a comparatively wild life, and had so closely observed the habits of the aborigines, that I felt assured that the only real difficulties which I could meet with would be of a local character. And I was satisfied that, by cautiously proceeding, and always reconnoitring in advance or on either side of our course, I should be able to conduct my party through a grassy and well watered route; and, if I were so fortunate as to effect this, I felt assured that the journey, once commenced, would be finished only by our arrival at Port Essington. Buoyed up by this feeling, and by confidence in myself, I prevailed against the solicitations and arguments of my friends, and commenced my preparations, which, so far as my own slender means and the contributions of kind friends allowed, were rather hurriedly completed by the 13th August, 1844.

As our movements were to be comparatively in light marching order, our preparations were confined more to such provisions and stores as were actually necessary, than to anything else. But I had frequently reason to regret that I was not better furnished with instruments, particularly Barometers, or a boiling water apparatus, to ascertain the elevation of the country and ranges we had to travel over. The only instruments which I carried, were a Sextant and Artificial Horizon, a Chronometer, a hand Kater's Compass, a small Thermometer, and Arrowsmith's Map of the Continent of New Holland.

In arranging the plan of my journey I had limited my party to six individuals; and although many young men volunteered their services, I was obliged to decline their offers, and confine myself to the stated number, as it was intimately connected with the principles and the means on which I started.

On leaving Sydney, my companions consisted of Mr. James Calvert; Mr. John Roper; John Murphy, a lad of about 16 years old: of William Phillips, a prisoner of the Crown; and of "Harry Brown," an aboriginal of the Newcastle tribe: making with myself six individuals.

We left Sydney, on the night of the 13th August, for Moreton Bay, in the steamer "Sovereign," Captain Cape; and I have much pleasure in recording and thankfully acknowledging the liberality and disinterested kindness of the Hunter's River Steam Navigation Company, in allowing me a free passage for my party with our luggage and thirteen horses. The passage was unusually long, and, instead of arriving at Brisbane in three days, we were at sea a week, so that my horses suffered much for food and water, and became discouragingly poor. On arriving at Brisbane, we were received with the greatest kindness by my friends the "Squatters," a class principally composed of young men of good education, gentlemanly habits, and high principles, and whose unbounded hospitality and friendly assistance I had previously experienced during my former travels through the district. These gentlemen and the inhabitants of Brisbane overloaded me with kind contributions, much of which, however, to avoid any unnecessary increase to my luggage, I found myself compelled to decline or leave behind; so that I had to forego the advantage of many useful and desirable articles, from their being too cumbersome for my limited means of carriage, and therefore interfering with the arrangements for my undertaking.

My means, however, had since my arrival been so much increased, that I was after much reluctance prevailed upon to make one change,--to increase my party; and the following persons were added to the expedition:--Mr. Pemberton Hodgson, a resident of the district; Mr. Gilbert; Caleb, an American negro; and "Charley," an aboriginal native of the Bathurst tribe. Mr. Hodgson was so desirous of accompanying me that, in consideration of former obligations, I could not refuse him, and, as he was fond of Botanical pursuits, I thought he might be useful. Of Mr. Gilbert I knew nothing; he was in the service of Mr. Gould, the talented Zoologist who has added so much to our knowledge of the Fauna of Australia, and expressed himself so anxious for an opportunity of making important observations as to the limits of the habitat of the Eastern Coast Birds, and also where those of the North Coast commence; as well as of discovering forms new to Science during the progress of the journey, that, from a desire to render all the service in my power to Natural History, I found myself obliged to yield to his solicitations, although for some time I was opposed to his wish. These gentlemen equipped themselves, and added four horses and two bullocks to those already provided.

Perhaps, of all the difficulties I afterwards encountered, none were of so much real annoyance as those we experienced at first starting from Brisbane. Much rain had fallen, which filled the creeks and set them running, and made the road so boggy and soft as to render them almost impassable. It took us the whole day to transport our party, cattle, and provisions over the river, and the operation was not concluded before sunset; but, as it was a fine moonlight night, I determined to start, however short my first stage might be. Fortunately, my friends had lent me a bullock dray to convey a portion of our stores as far as Darling Downs; but, having purchased a light spring cart, it was also loaded; and, flattering myself that we should proceed comfortably and rapidly, I gave orders to march. After much continued difficulty in urging and assisting our horses to drag the cart through the boggy road, we arrived, at about one o'clock in the morning, at Cowper's Plains, about ten miles from Brisbane.

I now found my cart an impediment to our movements; but, as it had been an expensive article, I did not despair of its becoming more useful after passing the boggy country. A few days afterwards, however, an accident settled the question; the horses ran away with it, and thereby the shaft was broken, and the spring injured, so that I was compelled to leave it; which I then did most cheerfully, as it is always easier to man to yield to necessity, than to adopt an apparently inconvenient measure by his own free will. The load was removed to pack-horses, and we proceeded with comparative ease to Mr. Campbell's station, enjoying the hospitality of the settlers as we passed on, and carrying with us their best wishes.

I was fortunate in exchanging my broken cart for three good travelling bullocks, and afterwards purchased five draft-bullocks, which we commenced to break in for the pack-saddle; for I had by this time satisfied myself that we could not depend upon the horses for carrying our load. Neither my companions nor myself knew much about bullocks, and it was a long time

9

before we were reconciled to the dangerous vicinity of their horns. By means, however, of iron nose-rings with ropes attached, we obtained a tolerable command over their movements; and, at last, by dint of habit, soon became familiar with, and even got attached to, our blunt and often refractory COMPAGNONS DE VOYAGE.

By a present from Messieurs Campbell and Stephens of four young steers and one old bullock, and of a fat bullock from Mr. Isaacs, our stock of cattle consisted now of 16 head: of horses we had 17: and our party consisted of ten individuals. Of provisions--we had 1200 lbs. of flour: 200 lbs. of sugar: 80 lbs. of tea: 20 lbs. of gelatine: and other articles of less consideration, but adding much to our comfort during the first few weeks of our journey. Of ammunition--we had about 30 pounds of powder, and 8 bags of shot of different sizes, chiefly of No. 4 and No. 6. Every one, at my desire, had provided himself with two pair of strong trowsers, three strong shirts, and two pair of shoes; and I may further remark that some of us were provided with Ponchos, made of light strong calico, saturated with oil, which proved very useful to us by keeping out the wet, and made us independent of the weather; so that we were well provided for seven months, which I was sanguine enough to think would be a sufficient time for our journey. The result proved that our calculations, as to the provisions, were very nearly correct; for even our flour, much of which was destroyed by accident, lasted to the end of May, the eighth month of our journey; but, as to the time it occupied, we were very much deceived.

Our riding-saddles and pack-saddles were made of good materials, but they were not fitted to the horses' backs, which caused a constant inconvenience, and which would not have happened, had my means allowed me to go to a greater expense. So long as we had spare horses, to allow those with sore backs to recover, we did not suffer by it: but when we were compelled to ride the same horses without intermission, it exposed us to great misery and even danger, as well as the risk of losing our provisions and stores. Our pack-saddles had consequently to be altered to the dimensions of the bullocks; and, having to use the new ones for breaking in, they were much injured, even before we left Mr. Campbell's to commence our journey. The statements of what a bullock was able to carry were very contradictory; but in putting 250 lbs. upon them the animals were overloaded; and my experience has since shown me that they cannot, continually day after day, carry more than 150 lbs. for any distance. The difficulties which we met with for the first three weeks, were indeed very trying:--the loading of bullocks and horses took generally two hours; and the slightest accident, or the cargo getting loose during the day's journey, frequently caused the bullocks to upset their loads and break the straps, and gave us great trouble even in catching them again:--at night, too, if we gave them the slightest chance, they would invariably stray back to the previous camp; and we had frequently to wait until noon before Charley and Brown, who generally performed the office of herdsman in turns, recovered the ramblers. The consequences were that we could proceed only very slowly, and that, for several months, we had to keep a careful watch upon them throughout the night. The horses, with some few exceptions, caused us less trouble at the commencement of our journey than afterwards, when our hobbles were worn out and lost, and, with the exception of one or two which in turns were tethered in the neighbourhood of the camp in order to prevent the others from straying, they were necessarily allowed to feed at large. It may readily be imagined that my anxiety to secure our horses was very great, because the loss of them would have put an immediate stop to my undertaking.--But I hasten to enter on the narrative of our journey.

CHAPTER I

LEAVE THE LAST STATION
FOSSIL REMAINS
DARLING DOWNS
ENTER THE WILDERNESS
WATERLOO PLAINS
THE CONDAMINE
HEAVY RAINS
CHARLEY'S MISCONDUCT
MURPHY AND CALEB LOST
KENT'S LAGOON
COAL
MURPHY AND CALEB FOUND AGAIN.

It was at the end of September, 1844, when we completed the necessary preparations for our journey, and left the station of Messrs. Campbell and Stephens, moving slowly towards the farthest point on which the white man has established himself. We passed the stations of Messrs. Hughs and Isaacs and of Mr. Coxen, and arrived on the 30th September, at Jimba, [It is almost always written Fimba, in the Journal; but I have corrected it to Jimba.--(ED.)] where we were to bid farewell to civilization.

These stations are established on creeks which come down from the western slopes of the Coast Range--here extending in a north and south direction--and meander through plains of more or less extent to join the Condamine River; which--also rising in the Coast Range, where the latter expands into the table-land of New England--sweeps round to the northward, and, flowing parallel to the Coast Range, receives the whole drainage from the country to the westward of the range. The Condamine forms, for a great distance, the separation of the sandstone country to the westward, from the rich basaltic plains to the eastward. These plains, so famous for the richness of their pasture, and for the excellency of the sheep and cattle depastured upon them, have become equally remarkable as the depositaries of the remains of extinct species of animals, several of which must have been of a gigantic size, being the Marsupial representatives of the Pachydermal order of other continents.

Mr. Isaacs' station is particularly rich in these fossil remains; and they have been likewise found in the beds and banks of Mr. Hodgson's and of Mr. Campbell's Creeks, and also of Oaky Creek. At Isaacs' Creek, they occur together with recent freshwater shells of species still living in the neighbouring ponds, and with marly and calcareous concretions; which induces me to suppose that these plains were covered with large sheets of water, fed probably by calcareous springs connected with the basaltic range, and that huge animals, fond of water, were living, either on the rich herbage surrounding these ponds or lakes, or browsing upon the leaves and branches of trees forming thick brushes on the slopes of the neighbouring hills. The rise of the country, which is very generally supposed to have taken place, was probably the cause of the disappearance of the water, and of the animals becoming extinct, when its necessary supply ceased to exist. Similar remains have been found in Wellington Valley, and in the Port Phillip District, where, probably, similar changes have taken place.

The elevation of Darling Downs--about 1800 to 2000 feet, according to the barometrical observations of Mr. Cunningham--renders the climate much cooler than its latitude would lead one to suppose; indeed, ice has frequently been found, during the calm clear nights of winter. During September and October, we observed at sunrise an almost perfect calm. About nine o'clock, light westerly winds set in, which increased towards noon, died away towards evening, and after sunset, were succeeded by light easterly breezes; thunder-storms rose from south and south-west, and passed over with a violent gust of wind and heavy showers of rain; frequently, in half an hour's time, the sky was entirely clear again; sometimes, however, the night and following day were cloudy.

The plains, as we passed, were covered with the most luxuriant grass and herbage. Plants of the leguminosae and compositae, were by far the most prevalent; the colour of the former, generally a showy red, that of the latter, a bright yellow. Belts of open forest land, principally composed of the Box-tree of the Colonists (a species of Eucalyptus), separate the different plains; and patches of scrub, consisting of several species of Acacias, and of a variety of small trees, appear to be the outposts of the extensive scrubs of the interior. There are particularly three species of Acacias, which bestow a peculiar character on these scrubs: the one is the Myal (A. pendula)--first seen by Oxley on Liverpool Plains, and afterwards at the Barwan, and which exists in all the western plains between the Barwan and Darling Downs--whose drooping foliage and rich yellow blossoms render it extremely elegant and ornamental. The second, the Acacia of Coxen, resembles the Myal (without its drooping character), its narrow lanceolate phyllodia rather stiff, its yellowish branches erect. The third, is the Bricklow Acacia, which seems to be identical with the Rose-wood Acacia of Moreton Bay; the latter, however, is a fine tree, 50 to 60 feet high, whereas the former is either a small tree or a shrub. I could not satisfactorily ascertain the origin of the word Bricklow [Brigaloe, GOULD.], but, as it is well understood and generally adopted by all the squatters between the Severn River and the Boyne, I shall make use of the name. Its long, slightly falcate leaves, being of a silvery green colour, give a peculiar character to the forest, where the tree abounds.

Oct. 1.--After having repaired some harness, which had been broken by our refractory bullocks upsetting their loads, and after my companions had completed their arrangements, in which Mr. Bell kindly assisted, we left Jimba, and launched, buoyant with hope, into the wilderness of Australia.

Many a man's heart would have thrilled like our own, had he seen us winding our way round the first rise beyond the station, with a full chorus of "God Save the Queen," which has inspired many a British soldier,--aye, and many a Prussian too--with courage in the time of danger. Scarcely a mile from Jimba we crossed Jimba Creek, and travelled over Waterloo Plains, in a N. W. direction, about eight miles, where we made our first camp at a chain of ponds. Isolated cones and ridges were seen to the N. E., and Craig Range to the eastward: the plains were without trees, richly grassed, of a black soil with frequent concretions of a marly and calcareous nature. Charley gave a proof of his wonderful power of sight, by finding every strap of a pack-saddle, that had been broken, in the high grass of Waterloo Plains.

Oct. 2.--Bullocks astray, but found at last by Charley; and a start attempted at 1 o'clock; the greater part of the bullocks with sore backs: the native tobacco in blossom. One of the bullocks broke his pack-saddle, and compelled us to halt.

Oct. 3.--Rise at five o'clock, and start at half-past nine; small plains alternate with a flat forest country, slightly timbered; melon-holes; marly concretions, a stiff clayey soil, beautifully grassed: the prevailing timber trees are Bastard box, the Moreton Bay ash, and the Flooded Gum. After travelling seven miles, in a north-west direction, we came on a dense Myal scrub, skirted by a chain of shallow water-holes. The scrub trending towards, and disappearing in, the S. W.: the Loranthus and the Myal in immense bushes; Casuarina frequent. In

13

the forest, Ranunculus inundatus; Eryngium with terete simple leaves, of which the horses are fond; Prasophyllum elatum, sweetly scented. A new composite with white blossoms, the rays narrow and numerous. Sky clear; cumuli to the S. W.; wind from the westward. Ridges visible to the N.N.E. and N.E. At the outskirts of the scrub, the short-tailed sleeping lizard with knobby scales was frequent: one of them contained six eggs. We camped outside of the scrub, surrounded by small tufts of the Bricklow Acacia. Droves of kangaroos entered the scrub; their foot-paths crossed the forest in every direction.

The thermometer, before and at sunrise, 32 degrees; so cold that I could not work with my knife, away from the fire. At sunset, a thick gathering of clouds to the westward.

Oct. 4.--Cloudy sky; thermometer 50 degrees at sunrise; little dew; 64 degrees at eight o'clock.

We travelled about eleven miles in a S. W. and S. S. W. direction, skirting the scrub. During the journey, two thunder-storms passed over; one to the southward beyond the Condamine, the other to the north and north-east over the mountains. The scrub is a dense mass of vegetation, with a well defined outline--a dark body of foliage, without grass, with many broken branches and trees; no traces of water, or of a rush of waters. More to the southward, the outline of the scrub becomes less defined, and small patches are seen here and there in the forest. The forest is open and well timbered; but the trees are rather small. A chain of lagoons from E. by N.--W. by S.; large flooded gum-trees (but no casuarinas) at the low banks of the lagoons. The presence of many fresh-water muscles (Unio) shows that the water is constant, at least in ordinary seasons.

The scrub opens more and more; a beautiful country with Bricklow groves, and a white Vitex in full blossom. The flats most richly adorned by flowers of a great variety of colours: the yellow Senecios, scarlet Vetches, the large Xeranthemums, several species of Gnaphalium, white Anthemis-like compositae: the soil is a stiff clay with concretions: melon-holes with rushes; the lagoons with reeds.

At night, a thunder-storm from south-west. Our dogs caught a female kangaroo with a young one in its pouch, and a kangaroo rat.

Oct. 5.--We followed the chain of lagoons for about seven miles, in a west by south direction; the country to our right was most beautiful, presenting detached Bricklow groves, with the Myal, and with the Vitex in full bloom, surrounded by lawns of the richest grass and herbage; the partridge pigeon (Geophaps scripta) abounded in the Acacia groves; the note of the Wonga

14

Wonga (Leucosarcia picata, GOULD.) was heard; and ducks and two pelicans were seen on the lagoons. Blackfellows had been here a short time ago: large unio shells were abundant; the bones of the codfish, and the shield of the fresh-water turtle, showed that they did not want food. A small orange tree, about 5-8 minutes high, grows either socially or scattered in the open scrub, and a leafless shrub, belonging to the Santalaceae, grows in oblong detached low thickets. Chenopodiaceous plants are always frequent where the Myal grows. The latitude of our camp was 26 degrees 56 minutes 11 seconds.

Oct. 6.--Was fully occupied with mending our packsaddles and straps, broken by the bullocks in throwing off their loads.

Oct. 7.--In following the chain of lagoons to the westward, we came, after a few miles travelling, to the Condamine, which flows to the north-west: it has a broad, very irregular bed, and was, at the time, well provided with water--a sluggish stream, of a yellowish muddy colour, occasionally accompanied by reeds. We passed several gullies and a creek from the northward, slightly running.

The forest on the right side of the river was tolerably open, though patches of Myal scrub several times exposed us to great inconvenience; the left bank of the Condamine, as much as we could see of it, was a fine well grassed open forest. Conglomerate and sandstone cropped out in several sections. Mosquitoes and sandflies were very trouble-some. I found a species of snail nearly resembling Succinea, in the fissures of the bark of the Myal, on the Box, and in the moist grass. The muscle-shells are of immense size. The well-known tracks of Blackfellows are everywhere visible; such as trees recently stripped of their bark, the swellings of the apple-tree cut off to make vessels for carrying water, honey cut out, and fresh steps cut in the trees to climb for opossums. Our latitude was 26 degrees 49 minutes. The thermometer was 41 1/2 at sunrise; but in the shade, between 12 and 2 o'clock, it stood at 80 degrees, and the heat was very great, though a gentle breeze and passing clouds mitigated the power of the scorching sun.

Oct. 8.--During the night, we had a tremendous thunder-storm, with much thunder and lightning from the west. The river was very winding, so that we did not advance more than 7 or 8 miles W.N.W.; the Bricklow scrub compelled us frequently to travel upon the flood-bed of the river. Fine grassy forest-land intervened between the Bricklow and Myal scrubs; the latter is always more open than the former, and the soil is of a rich black concretionary character. The soil of the Bricklow scrub is a stiff clay, washed out by the rains into shallow holes, well known by the squatters under the name of melon-holes; the composing rock of the low ridges was a clayey sandstone (Psammite). Sky cloudy; wind north-east; thermometer 80 degrees at 2 o'clock; the sunshine

15

plant (Mimosa terminalis) was frequent on the black soil; a Swainsonia; an Anthericum, with allium leaf and fine large yellow blossoms; and another species with small blossoms, (Stypandra).

Oct. 9.--Commenced with cloudy weather, threatening rain. It cleared up, however, about 10 o'clock, and we had a very warm day. We followed the course of the river for some time, which is fringed with Myal scrubs, separated by hills with fine open forest. Finding that the river trended so considerably to the northward [It seems that NORTHWARD here is merely miswritten for WESTWARD.--(ED.)], we left it at a westerly bend, hoping to make it again in a north-west direction. Thus, we continued travelling through a beautiful undulating country, until arrested by a Bricklow scrub, which turned us to the south-west; after having skirted it, we were enabled to resume our course to W.N.W., until the decline of day made me look for water to the south-west. The scrubs were awful, and threatened to surround us; but we succeeded in finding a fine large lagoon, probably filled by the drainage of the almost level country to the north-east. No water-course, not the slightest channel produced by heavy rains, was visible to indicate the flow of waters. Occasionally we met with swampy ground, covered with reeds, and with some standing water of the last rains; the ground was so rotten, that the horses and bullocks sunk into it over the fetlocks. The principal timber trees here, are the bastard box, the flooded-gum, and the Moreton Bay ash; in the Myal scrub, Coxen's Acacia attains a very considerable size; we saw also some Ironbark trees.

The tracks and dung of cattle were observed; and this was the farthest point to the westward where we met with them. Kangaroos seemed to be very rare; but kangaroo rats were numerous. Black-fellows were very near to us last night; they very probably withdrew upon seeing us make our appearance.

Oct. 10.--Cloudy; wind northerly; thermometer at 2h. 30m. P. M. 88 degrees. At about 1 1/2 or 2 miles distance, in a north-west direction from our last camp, we came to a fine running creek from the north-east, which we easily crossed; and, at about one mile farther, reached a creek--which, at this time of the year, is a chain of lagoons--lined on both sides by Bricklow scrub, which occupied a portion of its limited flats in little points and detached groves. This vale was one of the most picturesque spots we had yet seen. An Ironbark tree, with greyish fissured bark and pale-green foliage, grows here, and Sterculia heterophylla is pretty frequent amongst the box and flooded-gum, on the rising ground between the two creeks. Farther on, the country opened, the scrub receded; Ironbark ridges here and there, with spotted gum, with dog-wood (Jacksonia) on a sandy soil, covered with flint pebbles, diversified the sameness. The grass was beautiful, but the tufts distant; the Ironbark forest was sometimes interspersed with clusters of Acacias;

16

sometimes the Ironbark trees were small and formed thickets. Towards the end of the stage, the country became again entirely flat, without any indication of drainage, and we were in manifest danger of being without water. At last, a solitary lagoon was discovered, about 30 yards in diameter, of little depth, but with one large flooded gum-tree, marked, by a piece of bark stripped off, as the former resting-place of a native; the forest oak is abundant. Here I first met with Hakea lorea, R. Br., with long terete drooping leaves, every leaf one and a-half to two feet long--a small tree 18--24 minutes high--and with Grevillea mimosoides, R. Br., also a small tree, with very long riband-like leaves of a silvery grey. We did not see any kangaroos, but got a kangaroo rat and a bandicoot.

Oct. 11.--Travelling north-west we came to a Cypress-pine thicket, which formed the outside of a Bricklow scrub. This scrub was, at first, unusually open, and I thought that it would be of little extent; I was, however, very much mistaken: the Bricklow Acacia, Casuarinas and a stunted tea-tree, formed so impervious a thicket, that the bullocks, in forcing their way through it, tore the flour-bags, upset their loads, broke their straps, and severely tried the patience of my companions, who were almost continually occupied with reloading one or other of the restless brutes. Having travelled five miles into it, and finding no prospect of its termination, I resolved upon returning to our last camp, which, however, I was not enabled to effect, without experiencing great difficulty, delay, and loss; and it was not until the expiration of two days, that we retraced our steps, and reached the lagoon which we had left on the 11th. We had lost about 143 pounds of flour; Mr. Gilbert lost his tent, and injured the stock of his gun. The same night, rain set in, which lasted the whole of the next day: it came in heavy showers, with thunder-storms, from the north and north-west, and rendered the ground extremely boggy, and made us apprehensive of being inundated, for the lagoon was rapidly rising: our tent was a perfect puddle, and the horses and cattle were scarcely able to walk.

Within the scrub there was a slight elevation, in which sandstone cropped out: it was covered with cypress-pine, and an Acacia, different from the Bricklow. The Bottle-tree (Sterculia, remarkable for an enlargement of the stem, about three feet above the ground,) was observed within the scrub: the white Vitex (?) and Geigera, SCHOTT., a small tree, with aromatic linear-lanceolate leaves, grew at its outside, and in small groves scattered through the open forest. Fusanus, a small tree with pinnate leaves, and Buttneria, a small shrub, were also found in these groves.

Many pigeons were seen; the black cockatoo of Leach (Calyptorhynchus Leachii) was shot; we passed several nests of the brush-turkey (Talegalla Lathami, GOULD). Charley got a probably new species of bandicoot, with

17

longer ears than the common one, and with white paws. We distinguished, during the rain, three different frogs, which made a very inharmonious concert. The succinea-like shells were very abundant in the moist grass; and a limnaea in the lagoon seemed to me to be a species different from those I had observed in the Moreton Bay district, The thermometer at sunset 62 degrees (in the water 68 degrees); at sunrise 52 degrees (in the water 62 degrees).

On the 15th October, the wind changed during the afternoon to the westward, and cleared the sky, and dried the ground very rapidly.

Oct. 17.--The ground was too heavy and boggy to permit us to start yesterday; besides, three horses were absent, and could not be found. Last night, Mr. Roper brought in three ducks and a pigeon, and was joyfully welcomed by all hands. Charley had been insolent several times, when I sent him out after the cattle, and, this morning, he even threatened to shoot Mr. Gilbert. I immediately dismissed him from our service, and took from him all the things which he held on condition of stopping with us. The wind continued from the west and south-west.

Oct. 18.--Towards evening Charley came and begged my pardon. I told him that he had particularly offended Mr. Gilbert, and that I could not think of allowing him to stay, if Mr. Gilbert had the slightest objection to it: he, therefore, addressed himself to Mr. Gilbert, and, with his consent, Charley entered again into our service. John Murphy and Caleb, the American negro, went to a creek, which Mr. Hodgson had first seen, when out on a RECONNOISSANCE to the northward, in order to get some game. John had been there twice before, and it was not four miles distant: they, however, did not return, and, at nine o'clock at night, we heard firing to the north-east. We answered by a similar signal, but they did not come in. I sent Mr. Hodgson and Charley to bring them back. If they had simply given the bridle to their horses, they would have brought them back without delay; but probably both got bewildered.

The latitude of this lagoon, which I called Kent's Lagoon, after F. Kent, Esq., is 26 degrees 42 minutes 30 seconds. We tried to obtain opossums, during the clear moonlight night, but only caught the common rabbit-rat.

Our horses go right into the scrub, to get rid of the little flies, which torment them. The weather is very fair; the regular westerly breeze, during the day, is setting in again: the dew is very abundant during clear nights: the morning very cold; the water of the lagoon 8 degrees to 10 degrees warmer than the air.

We have regularly balanced our loads, and made up every bag of flour to the weight of 120 pounds: of these we have eight, which are to be carried by four bullocks. The chocolate and the gelatine are very acceptable at present, as so little animal food can be obtained. The country continues to be extremely boggy, though the weather has been fine, with high winds, for the last four days. Tracks of Blackfellows have been seen; but they appear rare and scattered in this part of the country. Though we meet with no game, tracks of kangaroos are very numerous, and they frequently indicate animals of great size. Emus have been seen twice.

Thermometer at sunset 65 degrees 7 minutes (75 degrees in the water); at a quarter past one, 90 degrees. South-westerly winds.

Oct. 19.--During the night, north-easterly breeze; at the break of day, a perfect calm; after sunset easterly winds again. Thermometer at sunrise 51 degrees (60 degrees in the water); a cloudless sky. Mr. Hodgson and Charley, whom I had sent to seek John and Caleb, returned to the camp with a kangaroo. I sent them immediately off again, with Mr. Roper, to find the two unfortunate people, whose absence gave me the greatest anxiety. Mr. Roper and Mr. Gilbert had brought one pigeon and one duck, as a day's sport; which, with the kangaroo, gave us a good and desirable supper of animal food. During the evening and the night, a short bellowing noise was heard, made probably by kangaroos, of which Mr. Gilbert stated he had seen specimens standing nine feet high. Brown brought a carpet snake, and a brown snake with yellow belly. The flies become very numerous, but the mosquitoes are very rare.

On a botanical excursion I found a new Loranthus, with flat linear leaves, on Casuarina, a new species of Scaevola, Buttneria, and three species of Solanum. Mr. Hodgson brought a shrubby Goodenia; another species with linear leaves, and with very small yellow blossoms, growing on moist places in the forest; two shrubby Compositae; three different species of Dodonaea, entering into fruit; and a Stenochilus, R. Br. with red blossoms, the most common little shrub of the forest.

Mr. Gilbert brought me a piece of coal from the crossing place of the creek of the 10th October. It belongs probably to the same layer which is found at Flagstone Creek, on Mr. Leslie's station, on Darling Downs. We find coal at the eastern side of the Coast Range, from Illawarra up to Wide Bay, with sandstone; and it seems that it likewise extends to the westward of the Coast Range, being found, to my knowledge, at Liverpool Plains, at Darling Downs, and at Charley's Creek, of the 10th Oct. It is here, as well as at the east side, connected with sandstone. Flint pebbles, of a red colour, were very abundant at Charley's Creek, and in the scrub, which I called the Flourspill, as it had made such a heavy inroad into our flour-bags. The flat on which we encamp, is composed of a mild clay, which rapidly absorbs the rain and changes into

19

mud; a layer of stiff clay is about one foot below the surface. The grasses are at present in full ear, and often four feet high; but the tufts are distant, very different from the dense sward at the other side of the Range. As we left the Myal country of the Condamine, we left also its herbage, abounding in composite, leguminous, and chenopodiaceous plants, with a great variety of grasses.

Oct. 20.--This morning, at half-past nine o'clock, Messrs. Roper, Hodgson, and Charley, returned with John Murphy and Caleb. They had strayed about twelve miles from the camp, and had fairly lost themselves. Their trackers had to ride over seventy miles, before they came up to them, and they would certainly have perished, had not Charley been able to track them: it was indeed a providential circumstance that he had not left us. According to their statement, the country is very open, with a fine large creek, which flows down to the Condamine; this is the creek which we passed on the 10th Oct., and which I called "Charley's Creek." The creek first seen by Mr. Hodgson joins this, and we are consequently still on westerly waters.

Thermometer, at sunrise, 54 degrees (in the water 64 degrees); at eight o'clock 64 degrees. Strong easterly and northerly winds during the last two nights. It becomes calm at a quarter past three, with the rise of Venus.

Mr. Calvert brought an edible mushroom out of Flourspill Scrub.

The Loranthus of the Myal grows also on other Acacias with glaucous leaves. A bright yellow everlasting is very fine and frequent.

Oct. 22.--I left Kent's lagoon yesterday. In order to skirt the scrub, I had to keep to the north-east, which direction brought me, after about three miles travelling through open forest, to Mr. Hodgson's creek, at which John Murphy and Caleb had been lost. The creek here consists of a close chain of fine rocky water-holes; the rock is principally clay, resembling very much a decomposed igneous rock, but full of nodules and veins of iron-stone. I now turned to the northward, and encamped at the upper part of the creek. To-day I took my old course to the north-west, and passed a scrubby Ironbark forest, and flat openly-timbered forest land. I came again, however, to a Bricklow scrub, which I skirted, and after having crossed a very dense scrubby Ironbark forest, came to a chain of rushy water-holes, with the fall of the waters to the north-east. The whole drainage of a north-easterly basin, seems to have its outlet, through Charley's Creek, into the Condamine.

On the banks of Hodgson's Creek, grows a species of Dampiera, with many blue flowers, which deserves the name of "D. floribunda;" here also were Leptospermum; Persoonia with lanceolate pubescent leaf; Jacksonia (Dogwood); the cypress-pine with a light amber-coloured resin (Charley

20

brought me fine claret-coloured resin, and I should not be surprised to find that it belongs to a different species of Callitris); an Acacia with glaucous lanceolate one-inch-long phyllodia; and a Daviesia; another Acacia with glaucous bipinnate leaves; a white Scaevola, Anthericum, and a little Sida, with very showy blossoms. Spotted-gum and Ironbark formed the forest; farther on, flooded-gum.

Pigeons, mutton-birds (Struthidia), are frequent, and provided us with several messes; iguanas are considered great delicacies; several black kangaroos were seen to day.

The weather very fine, but hot; the wind westerly; thermometer at sunset 74 degrees (84 degrees in the water.)

Oct. 23.--At the commencement of last night, westerly winds, the sky clear; at the setting of the moon (about 3 o'clock a.m.), the wind changed to the north-east; scuddy clouds passing rapidly from that quarter; at sunrise it clears a little, but the whole morning cloudy, and fine travelling weather.

We travelled in a north-westerly direction, through a Casuarina thicket, but soon entered again into fine open Ironbark forest, with occasionally closer underwood; leaving a Bricklow scrub to our right, we came to a dry creek with a deep channel; which I called "Acacia Creek," from the abundance of several species of Acacia. Not a mile farther we came on a second creek, with running water, which, from the number of Dogwood shrubs (Jacksonia), in the full glory of their golden blossoms. I called "Dogwood Creek." The creek came from north and north-east and flowed to the south-west, to join the Condamine. The rock of Dogwood Creek is a fine grained porous Psammite (clayey sandstone), with veins and nodules of iron, like that of Hodgson's creek. A new gum-tree, with a rusty-coloured scaly bark, the texture of which, as well as the seed-vessel and the leaf, resembled bloodwood, but specifically different; the apple-tree (Angophora lanceolata); the flooded-gum; a Hakea with red blossoms; Zierea; Dodonaea; a crassulaceous plant with handsome pink flowers; a new myrtaceous tree of irregular stunted growth, about 30 feet high, with linear leaves, similar to those of the rosemary; a stiff grass, peculiar to sandstone regions; and a fine Brunonia, with its chaste blue blossoms, adorn the flats of the creek as well as the forest land. The country is at present well provided with water and grass, though the scattered tufts of Anthistiria, and the first appearance of the small grass-tree (Xanthorrhaea), render its constancy very doubtful. The winding narrow-leaved Kennedyas, Gnaphaliums in abundance; Aotus in low bushes.

No game, except a kangaroo rat, pigeons, ducks, and mutton-birds. Mr. Phillips brought a crawfish from the creek: it had just thrown off its old shell. Fresh-water muscles plentiful, though not of the size of those of the

21

Condamine. A small rat was caught this morning amongst our flour bags; it had no white tip at the tail, nor is the tail so bushy as that of the rabbit-rat: probably it was a young animal.

Oct. 24.--The creek being boggy, we had to follow it down for several miles to find a crossing place. Even here, one of the horses which carried the tea, fell back into the water, whilst endeavouring to scramble up the opposite bank, and drenched its valuable load. We now travelled through a country full of lagoons, and chains of water-holes, and passed through several patches of cypress-pine, until we came to another creek with rocky water-holes, with the fall to the eastward, probably joining Dogwood Creek, from which we were not four miles distant. Fine grassy flats accompanied the creek on its left, whilst a cypress-pine forest grew on its right bank. The latitude of our yesterday's camp was 26 degrees 26 minutes 30 seconds and, to-day, we are only four miles more to the westward. The country is still so flat and so completely wooded--sometimes with scrubs, thickets, Acacia, and Vitex groves, sometimes with open Ironbark forest intermingled with spotted gum-- that no view of distant objects can be obtained. Several Epacridaceous shrubs and species of Bossiaea and Daviesia reminded me of the flora of the more southern districts.

Oct. 25.--We travelled about twelve miles in a north-westerly direction, our latitude being 26 degrees 15 minutes 46 seconds. The country in general scrubby, with occasional reaches of open forest land. The rosemary-leaved tree of the 23rd was very abundant. An Acacia with spiny phyllodia, the lower half attached to the stem, the upper bent off in the form of an open hook, had been observed by me on the sandstone ridges of Liverpool Plains: and the tout ensemble reminded me forcibly of that locality. The cypress-pine, several species of Melaleuca, and a fine Ironbark, with broad lanceolate, but not cordate, glaucous leaves, and very dark bark, formed the forest. An arborescent Acacia, in dense thickets, intercepted our course several times. Bronze-winged pigeons were very numerous, but exceedingly shy.

The stillness of the moonlight night is not interrupted by the screeching of opossums and flying squirrels, nor by the monotonous note of the barking-bird and little owlet; no native dog is howling round our camp in the chilly morning: the cricket alone chirps along the water-holes; and the musical note of an unknown bird, sounding like "gluck gluck" frequently repeated, and ending in a shake, and the melancholy wail of the curlew, are heard from the neighbouring scrub.

Oct. 26.--Our journey was resumed: wind in the morning from the west; light clouds passing rapidly from that quarter.

Messrs. Hodgson and Roper, following the chain of ponds on which we had encamped, came to a large creek, with high rocky banks and a broad stream flowing to the south-west. We passed an Acacia scrub, and stretches of fine open Ironbark forest, interspersed with thickets of an aborescent species of Acacia, for about four miles in a north-west course, when we found ourselves on the margin of a considerable valley full of Bricklow scrub; we were on flat-topped ridges, about 80 to 100 feet above the level of the valley. After several attempts to cross, we had to turn to the N. N. E. and east, in order to head it, travelling through a most beautiful open Ironbark forest, with the grass in full seed, from three to four feet high. Following a hollow, in which the fall of the country was indicated by the grass bent by the run of water after heavy showers of rain, we came to fine water-holes, about five miles from our last camp.

At the other side of the valley, we saw distant ranges to the north-west and northward. The scrub was occasionally more open, and fine large bottle-trees (Sterculia) were frequent: the young wood of which, containing a great quantity of starch between its woody fibres, was frequently chewed by our party. Fusanus was abundant and in full bearing; its fruit (of the size of a small apple), when entirely ripe and dropped from the tree, furnished a very agreeable repast: the rind, however, which surrounds its large rough kernel, is very thin.

Oct. 27.--During last night a very strong, cold, westerly wind.

After travelling about 3 1/2 miles north, we were stopped by a Bricklow scrub, which compelled us to go to the east and south-east. I encamped, about three miles north-east by north from my last resting place, and examined the scrub: it was out of the question to cross it. Mr. Gilbert shot three black cockatoos and a bronze-winged pigeon.

Oct. 28.--During the night it was very cold, though no wind was stirring. In the morning we experienced an easterly breeze. Travelling to the eastward and east by south, I found that the water-holes outside of the scrub at which we were encamped, changed into a creek with rocky bed, having its banks partly covered with cypress-pine thickets. I crossed it about three miles lower down, and, finding the Ironbark forest sufficiently open, turned to the northward; scarcely three miles farther, we came to another creek of a character similar to that of the last, which I suppose to be one of the heads of Dogwood Creek. The blue Brunonia was again frequent; the grass five feet high, in full ear, and waving like a rye field. The soil, however, is sandy and rotten, and the grass in isolated tufts. We encamped about four miles north-east from our last camp.

CHAPTER II

PARTY REDUCED BY THE RETURN OF MR. HODGSON AND CALEB
MEET FRIENDLY NATIVES
NATIVE TOMB
THE DAWSON
VERVAIN PLAINS
GILBERT'S RANGE
LYND'S RANGE
ROBINSON'S CREEK
MURPHY'S LAKE
MOUNTAINOUS COUNTRY
EXPEDITION RANGE
MOUNT NICHOLSON
ALDIS'S PEAK
THE BOYD.

Nov. 3.--For the past week, the heat was very oppressive during the day, whilst, at night, it was often exceedingly cold; for two or three hours before dawn, and for an hour after sunset, it was generally delightful, particularly within the influence of a cheerful cypress-pine fire, which perfumes the air with the sweet scent of the burning resin.

It had now become painfully evident to me that I had been too sanguine in my calculations, as to our finding a sufficiency of game to furnish my party with animal food, and that the want of it was impairing our strength. We had also been compelled to use our flour to a greater extent than I wished; and I saw clearly that my party, which I had reluctantly increased on my arrival at Moreton Bay, was too large for our provisions. I, therefore, communicated to my companions the absolute necessity of reducing our number: all, however, appeared equally desirous to continue the journey; and it was, therefore, but just that those who had joined last, should leave. Mr. Gilbert, however, who would, under this arrangement, have had to retire, found a substitute in Mr. Hodgson, who had perhaps suffered most by additional fatigues; so that he and Caleb, the American negro, prepared for their return to Moreton Bay. Previous, however, to their departure, they assisted in killing one of our steers, the meat of which we cut into thin slices, and dried in the sun. This, our first experiment--on the favourable result of which the success of our expedition entirely depended--kept us, during the process, in a state of great excitement. It succeeded, however, to our great joy, and inspired us with confidence for the future. The little steer gave us 65lbs. of dried meat, and about 15lbs. of fat. The operation concluded, we took leave of our companions; and although our material was reduced by the two horses on which they returned, Mr.

24

Hodgson left us the greater part of his own equipment. The loss of the two horses caused us some little inconvenience, as it increased the loads of the animals. The daily ration of the party was now fixed at six pounds of flour per day, with three pounds of dried beef, which we found perfectly sufficient to keep up our strength.

Whenever it was necessary to delay for any time at one place, our cattle and horses gave us great trouble: they would continually stray back in the direction we came from, and we had frequently to fetch them back five, seven, and even ten miles. Mr. Hodgson's horses had returned even to the camp of the 21st October, and three days were required to find them and bring them back. These matters caused us considerable delay; but they were irremediable. On the 30th October, towards evening, we were hailed by natives, from the scrub; but, with the exception of one, they kept out of sight. This man knew a few English words, and spoke the language of Darling Downs; he seemed to be familiar with the country round Jimba; and asked permission to come to the camp: this, however, I did not permit; and they entered the scrub, when they saw us handle our guns, and bring forward two horses to the camp. On the 3rd of November they visited us again, and communicated with us, behaving in a very friendly way: they pointed out honey in one of the neighbouring trees, assisted in cutting it out and eating it, and asked for tobacco; it was, however, impossible to make any presents, as we had nothing to spare. They particularly admired the red blankets, were terror-struck at the sight of a large sword, which they tremblingly begged might be returned into the sheath, and wondered at the ticking of a watch, and at the movement of its wheels. The greater part were young men of mild disposition, and pleasing countenance; the children remained in the distance, and I only saw two women.

According to their statements, the scrub extends to the Condamine.

The scrub was crossed in every direction by tracks of wallabies, of which, however, we could not even get a sight. The glucking bird--by which name, in consequence of its note, the bird may be distinguished--was heard through the night. They live probably upon the seeds of the cypress-pine; the female answers the loud call of the male, but in a more subdued voice.

A Gristes, about seven inches long, resembling the one described in Sir Thomas Mitchell's journey, but specifically different from it, was caught in the water-holes of the creek, which I called "Dried-beef Creek," in memorial of our late occupation.

A Goodenoviaceous shrub, a pink Hibiscus, and a fine prostrate Sida, were found between the camp of the 27th October and Dried-beef Creek.

Nov. 4.--Having previously examined and found a passage through the scrub, we travelled through it for about eight miles on a north by west course. The head of Dried-beef Creek, was found to be formed by separate water-holes, in a slight hollow along the scrub; and, when these disappeared, we were moving over a perfectly level land, without any sign of drainage, but occasionally passing isolated holes, now for the greater part dry. On our left, our course was bounded by a dense Bricklow scrub; but, on our right, for the first four miles, the country was comparatively open, with scattered Acacias; it then became densely timbered, but free from scrub. Farther on, however, scrub appeared even to our right. A natural opening, which had recently been enlarged by a bush fire, enabled us to pass into a dense Ironbark and cypress-pine forest; and then, bearing a little to the right, we came on a slight watercourse to the northward, which rapidly enlarged as it descended between ranges, which seemed to be the spurs of the table land we had just left.

Nov. 5.--We observed the tomb of a native near our camp. It was a simple conical heap of sand, which had been raised over the body, which was probably bent into the squatting position of the natives; but, as our object was to pass quietly, without giving offence to the aborigines, we did not disturb it. It is, however, remarkable that, throughout our whole journey, we never met with graves or tombs, or even any remains of Blackfellows again; with the exception of a skull, which I shall notice at a later period. Several isolated conical hills were in the vicinity of our camp; sandstone cropped out in the creek, furnishing us with good whetstones.

After travelling about four miles in a north-west direction, through a fine open undulating country, we came to, and followed the course of, a considerable creek flowing to the westward, bounded by extensive flooded gum-flats and ridges, clothed with a forest of silver-leaved Ironbark. Large reedy lagoons, well supplied with fish, were in its bed. Our latitude was 26 degrees 4 minutes 9 seconds.

Nov. 6.--The arrangement for loading our cattle enabled me at last to mount every one of my companions, which was very desirable; for the summer having fairly set in, and no thunder-storms having cooled the atmosphere since we left the Condamine, the fatigue of walking during the middle of the day had become very severe. From Jimba we started with a few horses without load, which only enabled us to ride alternately; but, as our provisions gradually decreased in quantity, one after the other mounted his horse; and this day I had the pleasure of seeing everybody on horseback.

We travelled along the valley of the river about ten miles, in a west-northerly course; our latitude of this day being 26 degrees 3 minutes 44 seconds Fine box and apple-tree flats were on both sides of the creek, now deserving the appellation of a "River," and which I called the "Dawson," in acknowledgment of the kind support I received from R. Dawson, Esq., of Black Creek, Hunter's River. At the foot of the ridges some fine lagoons were observed, as also several plains, with the soil and the vegetation of the Downs, but bounded on the northward by impenetrable Bricklow scrub. In a watercourse, meandering through this scrub, sandstone cropped out, in which impressions of fossil plants were noticed by me. It was interesting to observe how strictly the scrub kept to the sandstone and to the stiff loam lying upon it, whilst the mild black whinstone soil was without trees, but covered with luxuriant grasses and herbs; and this fact struck me as remarkable, because, during my travels in the Bunya country of Moreton Bay, I found it to be exactly the reverse: the sandstone spurs of the range being there covered with an open well grassed forest, whilst a dense vine brush extended over the basaltic rock. The phenomenon is probably to be explained by the capability of the different soils of retaining moisture, and, at the same time, by taking into account the distance of the localities from the seacoast. I called these plains "Calvert's Plains," after my companion, Mr. Calvert. Farther to the westward we passed over open ridges, covered with Bastard-box and silver-leaved Ironbark: the former tree grows generally in rich black soil, which appeared several times in the form of ploughed land, well known, in other parts of the colony, either under that name, or under that of "Devil-devil land," as the natives believe it to be the work of an evil spirit.

Nov. 7.--The first two hours of the day were cloudy, but it cleared up and became very hot; the atmosphere was hazy and sultry; cumuli with undefined outlines all round the horizon: wind from south-west and south. I travelled west by north about eight miles, along the foot of Bastard-box and silver-leaved Ironbark ridges. The country was exceedingly fine; the ground was firm; the valley from two to three miles broad, clothed with rich grass, and sprinkled with apple-tree, flooded-gum, and Bastard-box; the hills formed gentle ascents, and were openly timbered. The water-holes seemed to be constant; they are very deep, densely surrounded by reeds, and with numerous heaps of broken muscle-shells round their banks. Scrub was, however, to be seen in the distance, and formed the dark spot in the pleasant picture. Game became more frequent; and last night every body had a duck. As we were pursuing our course, Mr. Gilbert started a large kangaroo, known by the familiar name of "old man," which took refuge in a water-hole, where it was killed, but at the expense of two of our kangaroo dogs, which were mortally wounded. As we were sitting at our dinner, a fine half-grown emu walked slowly up to us, as if curious to know what business we had in its lonely haunts; unfortunately for us, the bark of our little terrier frightened it; and, although one of my Blackfellows shot after it, it retired unscathed into the neighbouring thicket. Mr. Roper killed a Rallus, which Mr. Gilbert thought to be new. The high land from which we came, appears at present as a distant range to the south-east. Fine-grained sandstone, with impressions of leaves, was again observed, and a few pieces of silicified wood. A Thysanotus with fine large blossoms now adorns the forest. The native carrot is in seed; the Eryngium of Jimba, and a leguminous plant, prostrate with ternate leaves and bunches of yellow flowers, were frequent; several beautiful species of everlastings were occasionally seen, and the little orange-tree of the Condamine grew in the scrub.

Nov. 8.--We followed the Dawson for about eight miles lower down. About four miles from our camp, it is joined by a fine chain of ponds from the north-east. The flats on both sides are covered by open Bastard-box forest, of a more or less open character. In the rainy season, the whole valley is probably covered with water; for we frequently observed the marks of torrents rushing down from the hills; and, along the foot of the ridges, ponds and lagoons were frequent. The heat of summer had already burnt up a great part of the grasses; and it was only in the immediate neighbourhood of the river that there was any appearance of verdure. The bed of the river became drier, and changed its character considerably. Charley stated, that he had seen a large plain extending for many miles to the south-west, and a high mountain to the north. Several emus, pigeons, and ducks were seen. Mr. Calvert found concretions of marl in the creek. John Murphy caught a great number of crawfish. For the first time since leaving the Condamine, we were visited by a thunder-storm. Cumuli generally during the afternoon, with wind from the W.N.W; during the night it usually clears up.

Nov. 10.--The country along the river changed, during the last two stages, considerably for the worse. The scrub approached very near to the banks of the river, and, where it receded, a disagreeable thicket of Bastard-box saplings filled almost the whole valley: fine lagoons were along the river, frequently far above its level; the river itself divided into anabranches, which, with the shallow watercourses of occasional floods from the hills, made the whole valley a maze of channels, from which we could only with difficulty extricate ourselves. "I never saw such a rum river, in my life," said my blackfellow Charley.

The open forest was sometimes one large field of everlasting flowers with bright yellow blossoms; whilst the scrub plains were thickly covered with grasses and vervain. Almost all the grasses of Liverpool Plains grow here. Ironstone and quartz pebbles were strewed over the ground; and, in the valley, fine-grained sandstone with layers of iron-ore cropped out.

Large fish were seen in the lagoons; but we only succeeded in catching some small fish of the genus Gristes. Muscles continued to be frequent; and we saw the gunyas of the natives everywhere, although no native made his appearance.

It was here that I first met, growing on the scrubby hills, a species of Bauhinia, either shrubby or a small shady tree, with spreading branches; the pods are flat, of a blunt form, almost one inch in breadth, and from three to four inches long. The Bricklow seems to prevent the growth of almost all other vegetation, with the exception of a small shrub, with linear lanceolate aromatic leaves. An Acacia, with long drooping, almost terete leaves, grew along the river; and Crinums grew in patches amongst the everlasting flowers, on a sandy soil. Our latitude, of the 9th November, was 25 degrees 53 minutes 55 seconds; and that of the 10th, 25 degrees 47 minutes 55 seconds, at about eleven miles north-west from the camp of the 8th November.

Until the 14th of November, we travelled down the Dawson. In order to avoid the winding course of the river, and the scrub and thickets that covered its valley, which rendered our progress very slow, we had generally to keep to the ridges, which were more open. We several times met with fine plains, which I called "Vervain Plains," as that plant grew abundantly on them. They were surrounded with scrub, frequently sprinkled with Bricklow groves, interspersed with the rich green of the Bauhinia, and the strange forms of the Bottle-tree; which imparted to the scene a very picturesque character. From one of these plains we obtained, for the first time, a view of some well-defined ranges to the west-north-west. The general course of the river, between the latitudes of 25 degrees 41 minutes 55 seconds and 25 degrees 37 minutes 12 seconds, was to the northward; but, as it commenced to turn to the east, I was induced to cross it, and to follow my former direction to the northwest. Between those two latitudes, the river had commenced to run, which was not the ease higher up, notwithstanding it was formed by long reaches of water, upon which pelicans and ducks were abundant. Mr. Calvert and the black, Charley, who had been sent back to one of our last camping places, had, on returning, kept a little more to the north-east, and had seen a river flowing to the northward, and a large creek; both of which, probably, join the Dawson lower down. At that part of the river where it commences to run, its bed was more confined, and was fringed by Melaleucas and drooping Acacias.

Our provisions had been increased by an emu, which Charley shot; our remaining two kangaroo dogs also succeeded in catching an "old man" kangaroo on the Vervain Plains of the 14th November. I made it an invariable practice to dry the meat which remained after the consumption of the day's allowance, and it served considerably to save our stock of dried beef, and to lengthen the lives of our bullocks. The utmost economy was necessary;--for we were constantly exposed to losses, occasioned by the pack bullocks upsetting their loads; an annoyance which was at this time of frequent occurrence from the animals being irritated by the stings of hornets--a retaliation for the injuries done to their nests, which, being suspended to the branches of trees, were frequently torn down by the bullocks passing underneath.

A large turtle was seen; and Mr. Gilbert caught two fine eels in one of the lagoons. We had thunder-storms on the 12th and 13th of November: the morning is generally cloudy, the clouds come from the north-east and north, clearing away in the middle of the day; and the afternoon is exceedingly hot.

Nov. 14.--A dense scrub, which had driven us back to the river, obliged me to reconnoitre to the north-west, in which I was very successful; for, after having crossed the scrub, I came into an open country, furnished with some fine sheets of water, and a creek with Corypha palms, growing to the height of 25 or 30 feet. The feelings of delight which I experienced when, upon emerging from the more than usually inhospitable Bricklow scrub, the dark verdure of a swamp surrounding a small lake --with native companions (ARDEAANTIGONE) strutting round, and swarms of ducks playing on its still water, backed by an open forest, in which the noble palm tree was conspicuous--suddenly burst upon our view, were so great as to be quite indescribable. I joyfully returned to the camp, to bring forward my party; which was not, however, performed without considerable trouble. We had to follow the Dawson down to where the creek joined it; for the scrub was impassable for loaded bullocks, and, even on this detour, we had to contend with much scrub as we proceeded down the valley. It, however, became more free from scrub at every step, and opened out into flats of more or less extent on either side, skirted by hills, clothed with an open forest, rising into regular ranges. On my RECONNAISSANCE I crossed the Gilbert Ranges, which were named after my companion Mr. Gilbert, and came on waters which fall to the eastward, and join the Dawson lower down. From the summit of an open part of the range, I saw other ranges to the northward, but covered with Bricklow scrub, as was also the greater part of Gibert's Range. To the east, however, the view was more cheering; for the hills are more open, and the vegetation composed of the silver-leaved and narrow-leaved Ironbark trees and an open Vitex scrub. Several rocky gullies were passed, that were full of palm trees. The valley of Palm-tree Creek extends about nineteen miles from west to east The ranges which bound it to the south, I called "Lynd's Range," after my friend R. Lynd, Esq. Gilbert's Range bounds it to the northward: Middle Range separates the creek from the Dawson up to their junction. Several large swamps are within the valley; one of which, the small lake which first broke upon my view, received the name of "Roper's Lake," after one of my companions.

Nov. 17.--We went about nine miles up the valley, on a south branch of Palm-tree Creek, which derives its waters from Lynd's Range. The fine water-hole which I selected for our camp, was not only shaded by stately Coryphas and flooded gums, but the drooping Callistemon, the creek Melaleuca, and the Casuarina, gave to it the character of the rivers and creeks of the Moreton Bay district. It changed, however, into a shallow waterless channel, communicating with one of the large swamps which generally extend along the base of the hills. I rode up Lynd's Range, passing plains similar to those I have before mentioned, composed of black soil intermingled with fossil wood and decomposed sandstone, and densely covered with Burr, (a composite plant) and Verbena, and scattered tufts either of Bricklow, or of Coxen's Acacia, or of the bright green Fusanus, or of the darker verdure of Bauhinia, with here and there a solitary tree of a rich dark-green hue, from forty to fifty feet in height. From the summit I had a fine view down the valley of the Dawson, which was bounded on both sides by ranges. A high distant mountain was seen about N.N.E. from Lynd's Range, at the left side of the Dawson.

The water-holes abounded with jew-fish and eels; of the latter we obtained a good supply, and dried two of them, which kept very well. Two species of Limnaea, the one of narrow lengthened form, the other shorter and broader; a species of Paludina, and Cyclas and Unios, were frequent. The jew-fish has the same distoma in its swimming bladder, which I observed in specimens caught in the Severn River to the southward of Moreton Bay: on examining the intestines of this fish, they were full of the shells of Limnaea and Cyclas. Large specimens of helix were frequent on the Vervain Plains, but they were only dead shells. The fat-hen (Atriplex) and the sow-thistle (Sonchus) grew abundantly on the reedy flats at the upper end of the creek; Grewia, a prostrate Myoporum, and a bean with yellow blossoms, were frequent all over the valley. Atriplex forms, when young, as we gratefully experienced, an excellent vegetable, as do also the young shoots of Sonchus. The tops of the Corypha palm eat well, either baked in hot ashes or raw, and, although very indigestible, did not prove injurious to health when eaten in small quantities. In the vicinity of the swamps of Palm-tree Creek, I noticed a grass with an ear much resembling the bearded wheat: with the exception of the cultivated Cerealia, it had the largest seed I ever met with in grasses; even my Blackfellow was astonished at its remarkable size.

During the night we experienced a strong wind from the northward, and, during the afternoon, a gust of wind and rain from west and north-west; but no thunder.

Nov. 18.--Clouds gathered from the west and north-west, a few drops of rain fell, and a few low peals of thunder were heard; but, although charged with electric fluid, and, in appearance, threatening an approaching thunder-storm, no discharge of lightning took place. We were very much annoyed and harassed, during the evening and the early part of the night, by sand-flies and mosquitoes; but the clear night grew so cold, that these great enemies of bush comforts were soon benumbed. The latitude of the camp of the 18th November was 25 degrees 30 minutes 11 seconds.

Nov. 19.--No air stirring, night very cold and bright; dew heavy; the surface of the creek covered with vapour; the water very warm.

Having no apparatus for ascertaining the height of our position above the level of the sea, this very interesting fact could not be determined; but, from the cold experienced, at a period so near the summer solstice, the elevation must have been very considerable.

We travelled during the day in a westerly direction over a level country, partly covered with reeds and fat-hen, and came to a broad sandy creek, which turned to the south-east and south. Having crossed it, we passed several large lagoons and swamps covered with plovers and ducks; and, at a short mile farther, came again on the creek, which now had a deep channel and a broad sandy bed lined with casuarinas and flooded-gum trees. I called this "Robinson's Creek." At its left bank, we saw a wide sheet of water, beyond which rose a range densely covered with scrub: I called them "Murphy's Lake and Range," after John Murphy, one of my companions.

I believe that Robinson's Creek is a westerly water; and, if so, it is very remarkable that the heads of Palm-tree Creek, which flows to the eastward, should be scarcely a mile distant; and that the interesting space, separating the two systems of waters, should be, to all appearance, a dead level.

I had descended--from a scrubby table land, the continuation of Darling Downs--into a system of easterly waters. I had followed down the Dawson for a considerable distance, and then, following up one of its creeks, found myself again on westerly waters. I could not decide, to my entire satisfaction, whether my views were right; for the country was difficult for reconnoitring; and I was necessarily compelled to move quickly on, to accomplish the object of my expedition: but it is a very interesting point for geographical research, and I hope, if I am not anticipated by other explorers, to ascertain, at some future period, the course of these creeks and rivers.

Nov. 20.--The first part of the night till the setting of the moon was very clear; after this it became cloudy, but cleared again at sunrise, with the exception of some mackerel-sky and stratus to the north-west. During the forenoon it was again cloudy, and a thunder-storm occurred at half-past two o'clock from the north-west and west-north-west, with little rain, but a heavy gust of wind.

In travelling to the westward, along Robinson's Creek, although two or three miles distant from it, we passed two lakes, one of which was a fine, long, but rather narrow, sheet of water, with swamps to the south-east. About six miles farther on, the country began to rise into irregular scrubby ridges; the scrub generally composed of Vitex intermingled with various forest trees. The small orange-tree, which we had found in blossom at the Condamine, was setting its fruit. Farther on, the dense Bricklow scrub compelled me to approach the banks of the creek, where we travelled over fine flats, but with a rather sandy rotten soil. The apple-tree, flooded-gum, silver-leaved ironbark, and the bastard-box grew on the flats and on the ridges. The creek was well provided with large water-holes, surrounded by high reeds.

We now entered a mountainous country; and the banks of the creek became sometimes very steep and broken by narrow gullies, rendering our progress slow and difficult. We had to wind our way through narrow valleys, and over ranges from which the descent was frequently very steep and dangerous. The latitude of our camp of the 21st November was 25 degrees 28 minutes 12 seconds; that of the 22nd was 25 degrees 25 minutes; that of the 23rd, about 32 miles west of Murphy's Lake, was 25 degrees 27 minutes 12 seconds. Here the ranges were, for the most part, openly timbered, with the exception of the higher points, which were generally covered with vine-brush; in one of which we found the nests of the brush turkey (Talegalla Lathami), and observed the bird itself. Some considerable stretches of beautiful country were now travelled over; the leading feature being low ridges, openly timbered with the silver-leaved ironbark, covered with an abundance of grass and herbs, and furnished with large lagoons; there was also a constant supply of water in the creek itself. On the banks of the latter, a species of Sterculia grows to a large size, and is one of the most pleasing and ornamental trees of the country; it is probably different from, although nearly allied to S. heterophylla. Very disagreeable, however, was the abundance of Burr and of a spear-grass (Aristida), which attached themselves to our clothes and blankets, and entered (particularly the latter) into the very skin. I have also to mention, that a yellow Villarsia was found on one of the lakes; which were generally surrounded by high sedges. We have not seen black swans since leaving Murphy's Lake; at which place we first saw a species of whistling duck, (Leptotarsis, GOULD.)

Appearances indicated that the commencement of the ranges was a favourite resort of the "Blackfellows." The remains of recent repasts of muscles were strewed about the larger water-holes, and, as I passed a native camp, which had only lately been vacated, I found, under a few sheets of bark, four fine kangaroo nets, made of the bark of Sterculia; also several bundles of sticks, which are used to stretch them. As I was in the greatest want of cordage, I took two of these nets; and left, in return, a fine brass hilted sword, the hilt of which was well polished, four fishing-hooks, and a silk handkerchief; with which, I felt convinced, they would be as well pleased, as I was with the cordage of their nets. It was to this spot that Mr. Pemberton Hodgson penetrated, when he afterwards followed my tracks, to ascertain the truth of the rumours, which had been carried by the blacks to Moreton Bay, of my having been either killed by the natives, or destroyed by a hurricane, which was said to have passed through the narrow valley of the confined creek.

The high mountain ranges, at the head of Robinson's Creek, which we observed from the tops of the hills, at the entrance into the mountainous country, bore W.N.W., and N.W. from the position I now occupied. We had a thunder-storm on the 21st November, followed by continued rain and a perfect calm During the night occasional showers of rain fell; at sunrise light fleecy clouds from W.N.W.: the nights, when clear, were very cold.

Until very lately we had all suffered severely from diarrhoea, which I could not account for, othewise than by attributing it to our change of diet. Fresh meat had almost invariably affected us; but after a time our continued exposure to the air, the regularity of our movements, and constant state of exertion, rendered us more hardy, and sharpened our appetites. Iguanas, opossums, and birds of all kinds, had for some time past been most gladly consigned to our stewing-pot, neither good, bad, nor indifferent being rejected. The dried kangaroo meat, one of our luxuries, differed very little in flavour from the dried beef, and both, after long stewing, afforded us an excellent broth, to which we generally added a little flour. It is remarkable how soon man becomes indifferent to the niceties of food; and, when all the artificial wants of society have dropped off, the bare necessities of life form the only object of his desires.

One of our bullocks had torn one of the flour-bags, and about fifteen pounds of flour were scattered over the ground. We all set to work, to scrape as much of it up as we could, using the dry gum leaves as spoons to collect it; and, when it got too dirty to mix again with our flour, rather than leave so much behind, we collected about six pounds of it well mixed with dried leaves and dust, and of this we made a porridge,--a mess which, with the addition of some gelatine, every one of us enjoyed highly.

No new insects, few new birds, and but few plants, attracted our attention. Mr. Gilbert's parrot, which he first met with on the downs, was very frequent; the glucking-bird and the barking-owl were heard throughout the moonlight nights. Several native dogs were killed, and their howling was frequently heard. Only one kangaroo had been shot since we left the Dawson, although their tracks were met with every where. Charley had taken several opossums; the presence of these animals generally indicates a good country. Quails were abundant, but not worth our powder; flocks of spur-winged plovers were living at the lakes and swamps, and a shy hornbill (Scythrops) was seen and heard several times. The nests of the white ant were rarely seen; but the soldier ant, and the whole host of the others, were every where. The funnel ant digs a perpendicular hole in the ground, and surrounds the opening with an elevated wall, sloping outwards like a funnel; the presence of this insect generally indicates a rotten soil, into which horses and cattle sink beyond their fetlocks. This soil is, however, by no means a pure sand, but is well mixed with particles of clay, which allow the ant to construct its fabric. In rainy weather this soil forms the best travelling ground, and is by no means so rotten as when dry.

Large hornets of a bright yellow colour, with some black marks, made their paper nests on the stems of trees, or suspended them from the dry branches; most of us were several times severely stung by them. When found near our encampment we generally destroyed them, by quickly raising a large fire with dry grass.

A species of Gristes was abundant in the water-holes, but it was of small size: the eels have disappeared.

Nov. 25.--We travelled about eight miles, north by west, ascending a spur, from which the waters flowed, both to the south-west and to the eastward, but both collecting in Robinson's Creek. Every time we turned to the westward we came on tremendous gullies, with almost perpendicular walls, whereas the easterly waters formed shallow valleys of a gently sloping character. The range was openly timbered with white-gum, spotted-gum, Ironbark, rusty-gum, and the cypress-pine near the gullies; and with a little dioecious tree belonging to the Euphorbiaceae, which I first met with at the Severn River, and which was known amongst us under the name of the "Severn Tree:" it had a yellow or red three-capsular fruit, with a thin fleshy pericarp, of an exceedingly bitter taste; the capsules were one-seeded. The gullies were full of bush-trees, amongst which the Bottle-tree, and the Corypha-palm were frequent. Pomaderris and Flindersia were in fruit and blossom. According to Mr. Gilbert, rock wallabies were very numerous. On a RECONNOISSANCE I traversed the continuation of the range, which I found to be of a flat, sandy, and rotten character, having, with the exception of the Blackbutt, all the trees and other characteristics of the sandstone country of Moreton Bay: Xylomelum, Xanthorrhaea, Zamia, Leptospermum, a new species of forest oak, which deserves the name of Casuarina VILLOSA, for its bark looks quite villous; Persoonia falcata, R. Br., a small tree about fifteen feet high, with stiff glaucous falcate leaves, and racemose inflorescence; a dwarf Persoonia, with linear leaves, the stringy-bark, and a species of Melaleuca along the creek. In my excursion I crossed the main branch of Robinson's Creek, and found the gullies of its right bank as steep and tremendous as those of the left. Water was very scarce. The whole country is composed of a fine-grained sandstone.

As the water-holes on the range are very few and distant from each other, they are frequented by the bronze-winged pigeons in great numbers. Mr. Gilbert shot eight of them, and Mr. Roper, John Murphy, and Charley, added to the number, so that we had a fine pigeon supper and breakfast, each having his bird--a rare occurrence in our expedition. A few drops of rain fell in the morning.

Nov. 26.--When we were waiting for our bullocks, four emus came trotting down the slope towards the camp. Messrs. Gilbert, Roper, Murphy, and Brown, having their horses ready, gave chase, and, after a dangerous gallop, over extremely rocky ground, succeeded, with the assistance of our kangaroo dog, Spring, in securing one of them. When Charley returned to the camp with the bullocks, he told us that he had found these emus walking amongst the bullocks, and that he had struck one of them with his tomahawk. On our road to the water, which I had found on my reconnoisance, about seven miles W.N.W., under a still higher range, rising at the right of Robinson's Creek, we started a herd of eight kangaroos, when our horsemen, assisted by Spring, were again successful in taking one of them.

Nov. 27.--A thunder-storm during the night, which passed, however, to the other side of the range. After a gust of wind of short duration, we had some very light showers; so light indeed, as not to interrupt our meat-drying process.

Proceeding on our journey, we ascended the range, and travelled between four and five miles on its level summit, which was covered with open forest, interspersed with thickets of Acacias and Casuarinas. From the extremity of the range we enjoyed a very fine and extensive view. Ranges of mountains with conspicuous peaks, cupolas, and precipitous walls of rock, were observed extending at various distances from west by north to north-west. The most distant range was particularly striking and imposing; I called it "Expedition Range," and to a bell-shaped mountain bearing N. 68 degrees W., I gave the name of "Mount Nicholson," in honour of Dr. Charles Nicholson, who first introduced into the Legislative Council of New South Wales, the subject of an overland expedition to Port Essington; and to a sharp peak N. 66 degrees W., the name of "Aldis's Peak," in acknowledgment of the kind assistance received from Mr. Aldis of Sydney. We then descended, with great difficulty into a broad valley, bounded on either side by fine slopes and ridges, openly timbered with silver-leaved Ironbark. On the small well-grassed flats along the watercourse, the flooded-gum and apple-trees grew to a considerable size.

The morning was cloudy, with occasional drops of rain; but it cleared up towards noon, and, near sunset, a wall of dark clouds rose in the west, over the ranges. Thunder-storms very generally come with westerly cloudy weather, with north-westerly, and northerly winds. We busied ourselves in extracting the oil from the skin of the emu: this operation was performed by suspending it on sticks before a gentle fire, the oil dripping from it into a shallow vessel. It is of a light amber colour, and is very useful in oiling the locks of our fire-arms; it has been considered a good anti-rheumatic, and I occasionally used it for that purpose.

Mr. Gilbert skinned the tail of the kangaroo to make a bag for holding fat; but it broke and ripped so easily when dry, as to render it unfit for that purpose. We used the skins of the kangaroos to cover our flour-bags, which were in a most wretched condition. Our latitude was 25 degrees 19 minutes 19 seconds.

Nov. 28.--Charley and Brown informed us that they had followed the watercourse, and had come to a broad river with precipitous banks, which would not allow any passage for our horses and cattle; they also stated that the watercourse on which we were encamped, became a rocky gully, and that it would be impossible to cross it lower down. From this information I supposed that a river, like the Robinson, rising in many gullies of the north-east ranges, and flowing in south-west direction was before us; I, therefore, decided upon heading it. It was, however, very difficult to find a leading spur, and we frequently came on deep and impassable gullies, surrounded by a dense thicket of cypresspine, and a great variety of shrubs peculiar to sandstone rock. After travelling about nine miles in a N. 15 degrees E. direction, we came to a subordinate range, and having found, in one of its watercourses, some tolerable grass and a fine water-hole, we were enabled to encamp. Mr. Roper and Charley, who had kept a little more to the left, reported that they had been on one of the heads of the Boyd, and had seen a fine open country to the westward, and south-west. The "Boyd" was so named in acknowledgment of the liberal support I had received from Benjamin Boyd, Esq.

Amongst the shrubs along the gullies, a new species of Dodonaea, with pinnate pubescent leaves, was frequent. Towards evening we had a thunderstorm from the westward.

Nov. 29.--In reconnoitring the country in the neighbourhood of the camp, I ascended three mountains, and ascertained that there are five parallel ranges, striking from north to south, of which the three easterly ones send their waters to the eastward; whereas the two westerly ones send theirs to the Boyd, the valley of which has a south-westerly direction. To the north of the Boyd, there is a steep mountain barrier, striking from east to west. All these ranges are composed of sandstone, with their horizontal strata, some of which have a very fine grain. Impressions of Calamites were observed in one of the gullies. We also saw two kangaroos. In the water-hole near our camp, there were numerous small brown leeches, which were very keen in the water, but dropped off as soon as we lifted our feet out of it. The hornets also were very troublesome. Recent bush fires and still smoking trees betokened the presence of natives; who keep, however, carefully out of sight. This country, with its dry scrubby ranges and its deep rocky gullies, seems to be thinly inhabited; the natives keeping, probably, to the lower course of Robinson's Creek and of the Boyd. The descent to the easterly waters is much more gentle; water remains longer in the deep rocky basins or puddled holes of its creeks, and the vegetation is richer and greener. Instead of the cypress-pine scrub, the Corypha-palm and the Casuarina grew here, and invited us to cool shaded waters; the Corypha-palm promised a good supply of cabbage. We had a thunder-storm from the southward, which turned from the range to the eastward. The two last days were cloudless and very hot; but, on the ranges, a cool breeze was stirring from the northward.

Nov. 30.--I wished to move my camp to a small water-hole about eight miles east by north, which I had found yesterday; but, though I kept more to the northward than I thought necessary, we were everywhere intercepted by deep rocky gullies. Losing much time in heading them, I ventured to descend one of the more practicable spurs, and, to my great satisfaction, my bullocks did it admirably well. The valley into which I entered was very different from these barriers; gentle slopes, covered with open forest of silver-leaved Ironbark, and most beautifully grassed, facilitated my gradual descent to the bottom of the valley, which was broad, flat, thinly timbered with flooded-gum and apple-trees, densely covered with grass, and, in the bed of the creek which passed through it, well provided with reedy water-holes. Before I ventured to proceed with my whole party, I determined to examine the country in advance, and therefore followed up one of the branches of the main creek, in a northerly direction. In proceeding, the silver-leaved Ironbark forest soon ceased, and the valley became narrow and bounded by perpendicular walls of sandstone, composed of coarse grains of quartz, rising out of sandy slopes covered with Dogwood (Jacksonia) and spotted-gum. The rock is in a state of rapid decomposition, with deep holes and caves inhabited by rock-wallabies; and with abundance of nests of wasps, and wasp-like Hymenoptera, attached to their walls, or fixed in the interstices of the loose rock. Through a few gullies I succeeded in ascending a kind of table-land, covered with a low scrub, in

38

which the vegetation about Sydney appeared in several of its most common forms. I then descended into other valleys to the eastward, but all turned to the east and south-east; and, after a long and patient investigation, I found no opening through which we could pass with our bullocks. Although I returned little satisfied with my ride, I had obtained much interesting information as to the geological character of this singular country.

CHAPTER III

RUINED CASTLE CREEK
ZAMIA CREEK
BIGGE'S MOUNTAIN
ALLOWANCE OF FLOUR REDUCED
NATIVES SPEAR A HORSE
CHRISTMAS RANGES
BROWN'S LAGOONS
THUNDER-STORMS
ALBINIA DOWNS
COMET CREEK
NATIVE CAMP.

Dec. 1.--I rode to the eastward from our camp, to ascertain how far we were from the water-hole to which I had intended to conduct my party. After having ascended the gullies, and passed the low scrub and cypress-pine thicket which surrounds them, I came into the open forest, and soon found our tracks, and the little creek for which I had steered the day before. This creek, however, soon became a rocky gully, and joined a large creek, trending to the east and south-east. Disheartened and fatigued, I returned to the camp, resolved upon following down the course of the Boyd to the south-west, until I should come into a more open country. On my way back, I fell in with a new system of gullies, south of the creek I had left, and east of the creek on which our camp was, and which I had called "The Creek of the Ruined Castles," because high sandstone rocks, fissured and broken like pillars and walls and the high gates of the ruined castles of Germany, rise from the broad sandy summits of many hills on both sides of the valley.

When I returned to the camp, Mr. Gilbert told me, that Mr. Roper and John Murphy had been on a mountain towards the head of the main creek, north-west from our camp, and that they had seen an open country before them. I therefore started, on the 2d December, with Mr. Gilbert to examine it. Our admiration of the valley increased at every step. The whole system of creeks and glens which join "Ruined Castle Creek," would form a most excellent cattle station. With the exception of the narrow gorge through which the

39

main creek passes to join the Creek of Palms [Mr. Arrowsmith is of opinion that such a junction is improbable, if the author is alluding to the creek, called Palm Tree Creek, which he fell in with about 60 miles to the S.E.--ED.] to the south-east, which might be shut by a fence not thirty yards long; and of the passable ranges to the north-west, which lead into a new country, and which form the pass seen by Roper and Murphy, it is everywhere surrounded by impassable barriers. Beautiful grass, plenty of water in the lower part of the creek, and useful timber, unite to recommend this locality for such a purpose. The creeks to the east and south-east are also equally adapted for cattle stations. After passing a stony ridge covered with spotted-gum, from which the remarkable features of the country around us--the flat-topped mountain wall, the isolated pillars, the immense heaps of ruins towering over the summits of the mountains--were visible, we descended a slope of silver-leaved Ironbark, and came to a chain of water-holes falling to the east. Travelling in a north-westerly direction, and passing over an openly timbered country, for about two miles, we came to the division of the waters, on a slight ridge which seemed to connect two rather isolated ranges. We followed a watercourse to the northward, which, at seven miles [In the original drawing the watercourse is not more than two miles long, according to Mr. Arrowsmith, so that seven miles must be a mistake.--ED.] lower down, joined an oak-tree creek, coming from the ranges to the eastward. Here water was very scarce; the banks of the creek were covered with Bricklow scrub; and a bush-fire, which had recently swept down the valley, had left very little food for our cattle: the blady-grass, however, had begun to show its young shoots, and the vegetation, on some patches of less recent burnings, looked green. Sterculia (heterophylla?) and the Bottle-tree, were growing in the scrub; and many Wonga-Wonga pigeons (Leucosarcia picata, GOULD.) were started from their roosting-places under the old trees in the sandy bed of the creek. We caught a young curlew; and Mr. Gilbert shot two Wonga-Wongas, and three partridge-pigeons (Geophaps scripta). The latter abound in the silver-leaved Ironbark forest, where the grass has been recently burned.

After having contended with scrubs, with swamps, and with mountains, we were again doomed to grapple with our old enemy, the silver-leaved Bricklow, and a prickly Acacia with pinnate leaves, much resembling the A. farnesiana of Darling Downs.

The most remarkable feature in the vegetation; however, was an aborescent Zamia, with a stem from seven to eight or ten feet high, and about nine inches in diameter, and with elongated cones, not yet ripe. In consequence of the prevalence of this plant, I called the creek "Zamia Creek." In the fat-hen flats, over which we travelled in following the watercourse to Zamia creek, I was surprised to find Erythrina, which I had been accustomed to meet with only

40

on the creeks, and at the outskirts of mountain brushes, near the sea-coast. The white cedar (Melia Azedarach) grows also along Zamia Creek, with casuarina, and a species of Leptospermum. On my return to the camp, I found that a party had been out wallabi shooting, and had brought in three; they were about two feet long; body reddish grey, neck mouse grey, a white stripe on each shoulder, black muzzle, and black at the back of the ear; the tail with rather long hair. The flying squirrel (Petaurus sciureus) which was not different from that of the Hunter; and a Centropus phasianellus, (the swamp pheasant of Moreton Bay), were shot.

Dec. 3.--We stopped at Ruined Castle Creek, in order to obtain more wallabies, which abounded among the rocks, and which appeared to be a new species: it approaches nearest to Petrogale lateralis of GOULD, from which, however, it essentially differs. Mr. Gilbert and all our best shots went to try their luck; they succeeded in killing seven of them.

The weather was cloudy, but it cleared up during the forenoon; in the afternoon rain commenced with a perfect calm; for the last three days easterly winds have prevailed, often blowing very strong at night.

In the rocky gullies, we found the following plants: a new species of Grevillea, having pinnatifid leaves with very long divisions, the blossoms of a fine red, and the seed-vessels containing two flat seeds, surrounded by a narrow transparent membrane; Leucopogon juniperinum and lanceolatum; a Dodonaea with long linear leaves and D. triquetra, were frequent.

Dec. 4.--I went with my whole party to Zamia Creek, the latitude of which is 25 degrees 5 minutes 4 seconds, and which is about sixteen miles west by north from our last camp.

Dec. 5.--We followed Zamia Creek about six miles down. It is very winding and scrubby; the rock on its banks is a clayey flagstone (Psammite); the upper strata are more clayey, and break in many small pieces. Several hills approached the creek; and a large mountain which I called Bigge's Mountain, in acknowledgment of the kind support of Frederic Bigge, Esq., was seen to the eastward. A large kangaroo started out of the creek, and was killed by our dogs; it appeared to be rather different from the common one, being remarkably light-coloured, with a white belly, black end of the tail, and the inside of the ear dark. We soon met with a fine reedy water-hole, with swarms of little finches fluttering about it; and, the place being suitable, I encamped for the night, and took the opportunity to repair some of our harness. The night was cloudy; the morning very fine; and the day very hot, with an occasional fresh breeze from the northward, which generally sets in about eleven o'clock. Thick cumuli came from the northward during the afternoon, but disappeared towards sunset.

41

Dec. 6.--After a fine night, we had a cold morning with heavy dew. From the hills near the camp, Mount Nicholson bore N. 30 degrees W. and Aldis's Peak due north; Bigge's Range was in sight to the eastward.

The horses had gone back to Ruined Castle Creek, about twenty-one miles distant; and the bullocks to our last camp, which, according to Charley, had been visited by the Blackfellows, who had apparently examined it very minutely. It was evident that they kept an eye upon us, although they never made their appearance. Our allowance of flour was now reduced from six pounds to five.

Dec. 7.--We travelled down Zamia Creek. The bed of the creek, though lined with many casuarinas, was entirely dry, and we did not reach a water-hole until we had travelled a distance of nine miles from the camp. Hoping that the supply of water would increase, I travelled on ward, leaving Mount Nicholson about six miles to the left. As we proceeded, the flats along the creek increased in size; and we entered a level country (which seemed unbounded towards the north-east) covered with silver-leaved Ironbark, box, and flooded-gum. We passed a large scrubby creek, coming from Mount Nicholson, and a considerable watercourse from Aldis's Peak. On the latter, we found a fine water-hole, at which we encamped. We started a great number of kangaroos; but, unfortunately, they all escaped. The whole country was full of game.

Whilst preparing to proceed on a RECONNOISSANCE of the neighbourhood, Charley, who had been sent for my horse, returned at full gallop, and told me that Blackfellows were spearing our horses. Fortunately Messrs. Gilbert and Calvert had just come in; and, mounting our horses, three of us hastened to the place where Charley had seen the Blacks, leaving the remainder of our party to defend the camp. We found one of our horses had been deeply wounded in the shoulder; but fortunately, the others were unhurt, and were grazing quietly. Charley saw two Blackfellows retreating into the scrub, but had seen a great number of them when he first came to the place. This event, fortunately not a very disastrous one, was so far useful, as it impressed every one with the necessity of being watchful, even when the Blackfellows were not suspected to be near.

The latitude of our camp was 24 degrees 54 minutes 19 seconds, and about seven miles from our last camp. Aldis's Peak bore N.W. by W., distant two miles and a half; and I found that it was surrounded by a dense scrub. After following Zamia Creek for some miles, I turned to the left, and travelled about north-north-west, when the scrub opened, and we came upon open ridges, and, at about a mile and a half from the river, found some fine lagoons. The ridges, which are spurs of Aldis's Peak and Expedition Range, disappear in the level country to the north-east. Farther on to the north-

north-west, I passed some fine plains, having the black soil, the vegetation, the dry creeks and watercourses, of Darling Downs. Thick scrub seems to extend all along the foot of the range, from Aldis's Peak to Mount Nicholson. Both these mountains are composed of basalt, containing numerous crystals of peridot.

Dec. 8.--I travelled with my whole party over the ground which I had reconnoitred yesterday, and had to go a considerable distance farther to find water. Along the scrubs there are generally chains of water-holes, which retain the water for a long time, and are soon filled by heavy thunderstorms; they are well puddled with clay, and, therefore, become dry almost exclusively by evaporation. Our camp was about eight miles N.N.W. from the last.

The feed was all parched up: the native carrot, which was so green when we passed Darling Downs, was here withered and in seed. Immense stretches of forest had been lately burned, and no trace of vegetation remained. Partridge-pigeons were very numerous, and the tracks of kangaroos and wallabies were like sheep-walks. Charley saw an emu; but an iguana and a partridge-pigeon were the only addition to our night's mess.

The sky was covered by a thin haze, occasioned by extensive bush fires. A fine breeze, which sprung up at eleven o'clock, from the northward, made travelling very agreeable. We enjoy no meal so much as our tea and damper at luncheon, when we encamp between twelve and two o'clock. It is remarkable how readily the tea dispels every feeling of fatigue, without the slightest subsequent injury of health.

Paludinas and Unios were very frequent in the water-holes. The silver-leaved Ironbark (Eucalyptus pulverulentus) was here coming into blossom. The whole vegetation seemed to feel the heat of an almost vertical sun; and, with the exception of the fresh green of the Vitex shrub, the silver-leaved Bricklow, and those patches of young grass which had been burnt about a month before--all nature looked withered. It was very hot from nine o'clock to eleven, when the cooling northerly breeze usually sets in.

Upon reaching the place of our next camp, Mr. Roper went to cut tent-poles, but, perhaps too intent on finding good ones, unfortunately lost his way, and wandered about the bush for about five miles before we were able to make him hear our cooees. Accidents of this kind happen very easily in a wooded country, where there is no leading range or watercourse to guide the rambler, or when sufficient care is not taken to mark and keep the direction of the camp.

Dec. 9.--The haze of yesterday cleared up at sunset, after having formed two threatening masses of clouds in the east and in the west, united by a broad belt of mare's tails across the sky. It became cloudy again, and prevented my taking observations during the night; the morning was cool and agreeable, clearing up about eleven o'clock; the northerly wind stirring, as usual. Proceeding on our journey, we travelled about nine miles W.N.W. over a Box flat, with stiff soil and melon-holes; after a few miles, it changed into an open silver-leaved Ironbark forest, with lighter soil. About six miles from our last camp, we came upon a fine creek (with Casuarinas and palm-trees), flowing from the mountains on a north-easterly course; and, about three miles further, to the W.N.W., we came to another creek, and numerous palm-trees growing near it. Following up the latter, we found a fine water-hole surrounded by reeds, and which is probably fed by a spring. The forest was well grassed; and a small Acacia, about fifteen or twenty feet high, with light green bipinnate leaves (from which exuded an amber-coloured eatable gum), formed groves and thickets within it. A Capparis, a small stunted tree, was in fruit: this fruit is about one inch long and three-quarters of an inch broad, pear-shaped and smooth, with some irregular prominent lines. Capparis Mitchelii has a downy fruit, and is common in the scrubs. A small trailing Capparis, also with oblong eatable fruit, was first observed on a hill near Ruined Castle Creek, in lat. 25 degrees 10 minutes: we met with it frequently afterwards. We were encamped in the shade of a fine Erythrina; and the Corypha-palm, Tristania, the flooded-gum, the silver-leaved Ironbark, Tripetelus, and a species of Croton, grew around us. A species of Hypochaeris and of Sonchus, were greedily eaten by our horses; the large Xeranthemum grew on the slopes, among high tufts of kangaroo grass. A species of Borage (Trichodesma zeylanica), with fine blue flowers, was first seen here; and the native raspberry, and Ficus muntia, were in fruit. In the afternoon, I went with Brown up the range, following the bed of our creek; and, having ascended a spur of sandstone, with gullies on each side, we came to a large basaltic mountain, clothed with fine open timber, and a great number of arborescent Zamias.

Dec. 10.--Accompanied by Charley, I went in search of a passage over the range. We ascended several hills in order to obtain general views, and found that the level country, over which we had travelled during the last two days, was of less extent than I had anticipated. To the north-east by east, ranges rise with the characteristic outlines of the basalt and phonolite,--in peaks and long stretched flat-topped hills, with undulations openly timbered extending at their base. One valley descended to the north-north-east; another to the northward. The principal range has a direction from south-west to north-east; it is flat on the top, is well grassed and openly timbered; but, to the northward, it becomes scrubby, and also changes its geological character. After having crossed the range--without any great difficulty, with the exception of some steep places--we came on gullies going down to the north-west; and, from the rocky head of one of them, the whole country to the west and northwest burst upon us. There was a fine valley, a flat country, plains, isolated long-stretched hills, and distant ranges; the highest points of the latter bearing 77 degrees E. and 76 degrees W.; and, as I hoped to reach them by Christmas time, I called them "Christmas Ranges." Not being able to discover a good slope on which our bullocks could travel, I descended at once into the gully, and followed it in all its windings; knowing well from experience that it is easier to find a passage up a mountain range than down it. The gully had all the characters of those of the Boyd; the same sandstone rock, the same abruptness, and the same vegetation; excepting, perhaps, a new Grevillea, with pinnatifid leaves and yellowish-white woolly flowers, which we found here. There was no water, except in some small holes full of gum leaves, which had rendered it unfit for use. After proceeding with great difficulty about three miles, we found that the gullies opened into a broad flat valley; in which fields of fat-hen, the Croton shrub, the native Tobacco, Erythrina, fine specimens of flooded-gum, Tristania, and the Moreton Bay ash, were growing in great abundance. Farther down, however, the Bricklow scrub covered the whole valley; the water-course disappeared almost entirely; and we were completely disappointed in our hopes of finding a fine country. Small plains opened on both sides of the valley, surrounded by Bricklow scrub, and with patches of Bricklow scattered over them, in which the Bottle-tree frequently made its portly appearance. A large flight of Wonga Wonga pigeons were feeding on the seeds of various species of Acacia; we shot two of them. No water was to be found in an extent of fifteen miles. The noisy call of the laughing Jackass (Dacclo gigantea) made me frequently ride back and examine more minutely those spots marked by a darker foliage; but the presence of this bird is no certain indication of water, though he likes the neighbourhood of shady creeks. I could not help thinking that a considerable creek must come from the north-west side of Mount Nicholson; and, seeing an isolated range to the south-west, I rode towards it, sure of finding water near it, if there was any to be found. We approached the range just before sunset, much tired, with two Wonga-Wongas and three iguanas at our saddles. I had just informed my Blackfellow, that I wished to encamp, even without water, when some old broken sheets of bark, remains of the frail habitations of the natives, caught my eye; a dry water-hole, though surrounded with green grass and sedges, showed that they had formerly encamped there, with water. This water-hole was found to be one of a chain of ponds extending along the edge of the scrub which covered the hill; and, on following it farther down, we came to a fine pool of water, which enabled us to encamp comfortably. Next morning, after having enjoyed an iguana, and finding several other ponds well supplied with water, we returned. In crossing several of the scrub plains before mentioned, it was agreeable to observe that the dense vegetation which covered them was not the miserable Burr and the wiry Vervain, but Senecios

45

and Sonchus (Sowthistle), which our horses greedily snatched as they waded through them. The soil is of a dark colour, very rich, but mild; and the rock below is basaltic. Kangaroos were feeding on the plains along the scrub; and Charley fired unsuccessfully at a fine "old man." I saw one emu, and Charley a drove of ten more. The country was remarkably rich in various kinds of game; and I was very sorry that we were not better sportsmen, to avail ourselves of so favourable a circumstance. We found a passage for our bullocks at the west side of the valley along which we had come down; the ascent was steep, but practicable. We followed the spur up to the principal range, where we found some difficulty in heading some steep gullies, which come up to the highest crest of the mountains. After some tiresome riding, I was fortunate enough to hit the head of the creek on which our party was encamped; and, following it down--over loose rocks, large boulders, and occasional steep falls--accompanied by my excellent little horse, which willingly followed wherever I led, I came into a more open country; and the report of a gun gave me the pleasing assurance that our camp was at no great distance. My Blackfellow quitted me on the range, as he had done before, on several similar occasions; and it was too evident that I could not rely upon him in times of difficulty and danger. Within the scrub on the range, we found five or six huts, lately constructed, of the natives; they come here probably to find honey, and to catch rock-wallabies, which are very numerous in the sandstone gullies. In the gully which I descended, a shrub with dark-green leaves was tolerably frequent; its red berries, containing one or two seeds, were about the size of a cherry, and very good eating when ripe. The new Grevillea, before mentioned, was also found here growing on a sandy soil; and a species of Clematis tied the shrubs into an almost impenetrable maze. The arborescent Zamia was as frequent here as on the slopes and flat tops of the basaltic mountains; it grows from six to ten feet high, and even higher, and is about a foot in diameter; and often, its dark scaly trunk, borne to the ground by the winds, raises its fine head like a reclining man.

There was a thunder-storm to the south-east and east on the 10th December. These thunder-storms are generally very local, belonging to distant valleys and ranges. Much rain had fallen at the foot of the range, but we had very little of it. Several of my companions suffered by eating too much of the cabbage-palm. The Blackfellows will doubtless wonder why so many noble trees had been felled here. One of our kangaroo-dogs followed a kangaroo, and did not return; a severe loss, as we have only one left out of five, and this one is young and diseased. Our little terrier keeps very well.

Dec. 12--After a clear night, the morning was misty, with a wall of clouds to the westward; at nine o'clock it cleared up, and loose cumuli passed over from the east; at eleven o'clock all clouds had disappeared, and a cool breeze set in from the northward. Charley did not succeed in bringing in the horses and cattle sufficiently early for starting on the long and difficult passage over the range. Our meat was all consumed; but we wished to reserve our bullocks for Christmas, which was, in every one of us, so intimately associated with recollections of happy days and merriment, that I was determined to make the coming season as merry as our circumstances permitted. This decision being final, every one cheerfully submitted to a small allowance, and did his best to procure game. Our latitude was 24 degrees 43 minutes.

Dec. 13.--We travelled along the spur at the west and south-west side of Erythrina creek, at which we had been encamped; and, after having headed the whole system of its gullies--keeping to the right along the main range for about three miles, we came to the spur on which I and Charley had ascended on our return, and which had a general direction to the north-west. When we arrived at the foot of the range, our cattle and horses were so jaded, and the water-hole still so far off, that I encamped here, more especially as the feed was young and rich, and as I had hopes of obtaining water by digging into the sand which filled the upper part of the valley. In this, however, I did not succeed; for, upon digging about three feet deep, I came on a layer of stiff clay very hard and dry. Fortunately, however, a thunder-storm came on towards the evening, which supplied our cattle as well as ourselves with water. This was the only time we encamped without a certainty of water, during our journey from Jimba to the head of the gulf, which occupied ten months. The whole night was showery, the wind and clouds coming from all directions.

Dec. 14.--We reached the water-holes I had discovered three days previous. Our cattle were very thirsty, notwithstanding the late rain, and they rushed into the water as soon as they got sight of it.

The hills, at the foot of which we are encamped, are composed of whinstone (basalt). Pebbles of conglomerate, of flint, and of quartz deeply coloured with iron, are, however, very frequent on the slopes. It is remarkable that that part of the range which is composed of basalt, is a fine open forest, whereas the basaltic hills of the large valley are covered with dense scrub. The Myal was frequent; and the fruit of the small lemon-tree was ripe.

I followed the watercourse which connects the water-holes on which we encamped, and met every where with Bricklow scrub. Mr. Gilbert ascended the hills, and stated that the whole valley to the westward appeared like an immense sea of scrub.

A thunder-storm was forming to the north-west, but was probably deflected by the ranges.

Dec. 15.--Last night we had two thunder-storms; one rose in the west, and

47

turned to the northward, following the Christmas Ranges; the other rose in the south, and turned to the east, probably attracted by Expedition Range. Still following the watercourse, we entered, after about four miles travelling, into the scrub. The watercourse was soon lost in the level ground, and water-holes appeared every where; the general direction of the waters seemed to be to the north-west. Four miles farther we came to a piece of open forest at the foot of a hill, which was covered with ironstone-pebbles. Here we encamped without water; but, having passed good water-holes not four miles distant, I sent Mr. Calvert and Brown to fetch some, whilst I and Charley went forward to examine the country. On my way to some ranges which I had seen to the eastward, I fell in with a dry watercourse, and, following it down for about half a mile from the camp, discovered a well-filled water-hole. The watercourse was found to join a creek with a deep and very wide bed, but dry. Muscle-shells strewed in every direction, and other appearances, indicated that, during the wet season, the whole country must be very swampy. The course of the creek was to the N. N. W., and it is joined by watercourses from the right and left; all now quite dry. After having followed the creek for about twelve miles, until sunset, without coming to the end of the scrub through which it trended, we were compelled to retrace our steps; in attempting which my companion, Charley, lost the track, but my good little horse, Jim Crow, guided us to the camp, which we reached about eleven o'clock. Mr. Calvert and Brown had not yet returned; although the report of their guns had been heard several times. The night was extremely cold, notwithstanding we were encamped under the shelter of trees: and it was therefore evident that we were at a considerable elevation above the level of the sea. The Box-tree of Jimba-flats, the Bricklow--in short, the whole vegetation of the scrubby country, west of Darling Downs, were still around us; and the Moreton Bay ash (a species of Eucalyptus)--which I had met with, throughout the Moreton Bay district, from the sea coast of the Nynga Nyngas to Darling Downs--was here also very plentiful.

Dec. 16.--Our cattle and our horses, with the exception of those we had used the night before, had strayed in search of water; but Charley found them on the sow-thistle plains, beyond our last camp. Messrs. Calvert, Murphy, and Brown, came in early this morning; they had lost their way in the dark, in consequence of remaining too long at the water-hole. They informed me that they had passed the night on an open piece of forest ground along a creek. This intelligence induced me to examine the locality: I therefore went with Brown, and found the creek, with a deep sandy, but dry bed, full of reeds; its direction being from south by west to north by east. I followed it up about eight miles, when the scrub receded from its left bank, and a fine open extensive flat stretched to the westward. I looked into the Casuarina thickets which occasionally fringed its bank, in search of water; but found none. I was frequently on the point of returning, but, induced by the presence of reeds, continued the search, until the scrub again approached the right side of the creek; and, in one of those chains of ponds which almost invariably exist at the outside of these scrubs, a small pool of water was found. This gave me fresh confidence, and I was eagerly examining the creek, when Brown exclaimed, "Plenty of water, sir! plenty of water!" and a magnificent lagoon, surrounded by a rich belt of reeds, lay before us. The natives must have been at this spot some time before, and have burned the grass; as the earth was now covered with a delicate verdure. The country appeared flat, and was so openly timbered with fine flooded gum-trees, that we could see for a considerable distance; a circumstance very favourable to us, in case of the natives proving hostile. It would appear that this place was frequently resorted to by the natives: the bark had been recently stripped in various places; the huts were in good repair, with heaps of muscle-shells and some kangaroo-bones about them. We returned to the camp with the joyous news; for I had been greatly perplexed as to the direction I ought to take. Charley returned very late with the strayed cattle, and reported that he had seen the smoke of the Blackfellow's fires all along the western ranges. This was welcome intelligence; for we knew that their presence indicated the existence of a good country. Yesterday in coming through the scrub, we had collected a large quantity of ripe native lemons, of which, it being Sunday, we intended to make a tart; but, as my companions were absent, the treat was deferred until their return, which was on Monday morning, when we made them into a dish very like gooseberry-fool; they had a very pleasant acid taste, and were very refreshing. They are of a light yellow colour, nearly round, and about half an inch in diameter; the volatile oil of the rind was not at all disagreeable.

The chains of water-holes within the scrub are covered with a stiff star-grass, having a great number of spikes rising from the top of the stem; and several sedges crowd around the moister spots. A stiff, wiry, leafless polygonaceous plant grows in the shallow depressions of the surface of the ground, which are significantly termed by the squatters "Melon-holes", and abound in the open Box-tree flats. A small shrubby Stenochilus with very green linear lanceolate leaves and red tubulous flowers, is frequent amongst the Bricklow.

The pools and lagoons contain Unios, Paludinas, and the lanceolate and oval Limnaeas. Fine dry weather has set in; the northerly breeze is still very regular; but the mornings, from eight to eleven, are very hot. A few mosquitoes have made their appearance, probably in consequence of the late rains. Charley killed a Diamond snake, larger than any he had ever seen before; but he only brought in the fat, of which there was a remarkable quantity. The Iguanas (Hydrosaurus, Gray) have a slight bluish tinge about the head and neck; but in the distribution of their colours, generally resemble H. Gouldii.

49

Mr. Gilbert found a land crab in the moist ground under a log of wood; and Mr. Calvert brought me a species of helix of a yellowish green colour.

Dec. 18.--It was with very great difficulty that we collected our horses and cattle; but we could not find one of our pack bullocks, which had concealed himself in the scrub, and, from the unfavourable situation of our camp, we were obliged to abandon it. Old bullocks, when tired, care very little about company, and even like to retire to any solitary spot, where there is good feed and water. Having nearly reached the end of our stage, we were overtaken by a thunder-storm from the south; which was followed by another from the west with very heavy rain. This was the first heavy rain to which we had been exposed, whilst on the day's march; for thunder-storms did not generally rise till after two o'clock; at which time we were usually secured in our tents.

The fine lagoons--which I called "Brown's Lagoons" after their discoverer-- and the good feed about them, induced me to stop for the purpose of killing the fat bullock which Mr. Isaacs had given us, and of drying it like the charqui of the South Americans; instead of waiting till Christmas, as we originally intended; especially as we were ignorant of the character of the country before us. Accordingly, on the 18th at five o'clock in the morning, it was slaughtered and cut into thin slices; which, before night, were nearly dried by the powerful heat of an almost vertical sun. We enjoyed ourselves very much on this occasion, and feasted luxuriously on fried liver at breakfast, on stuffed heart for luncheon, and on a fine steak and the kidneys for supper. Those who may have lived for so long a time as we had upon a reduced fare, will readily understand with what epicurean delight these meals were discussed.

Dec. 19.--We completed our job, by melting down the fat, with which our saddles, bridles, and all our leather gear, were well greased. In the afternoon Mr. Calvert and Charley, who had been sent after the bullock we had left behind, returned with him. They had found him quietly chewing the cud, in a Bricklow grove near a small pool of water.

Dec. 20.--Whilst employed in arranging our packs, Murphy and Charley went out to examine the surrounding country. On their return they informed me that they had met with a native camp, the inhabitants of which were probably out hunting, for they had left all their things behind.

Capparis Mitchelii was found in blossom. The cockatoo parrakeet of the Gwyder River, (Nymphicus Novae Hollandiae, GOULD.), the common white cockatoo, and the Moreton Bay Rosella parrot, were very numerous. We also observed the superb warbler, Malurus cyaneus of Sydney; and the shepherd's companion, or fan-tailed fly-catcher (Rhipidura); both were frequent. Several rare species of finches were shot: and a species of the genus Pomatorhinus, a Swan River bird, was seen by Mr. Gilbert. The latitude of this encampment was found to be 24 degrees 44 minutes 55 seconds.

Dec. 21.--As our meat was not entirely dry, I thought it advisable to remain another day at this place, which was usefully occupied by packing the fat into bags made of the hide of the animal. Besides the plants above-mentioned, a beautiful blue Nymphaea was found growing in the lagoon; and around it, among the reeds and high cyperaceous plants, a small labiate, a Gomphrena, the native Chamomile, and a Bellis were growing.

The days continue very hot. At 5 P.M. we had a thunder-storm from the southward: but little rain fell. It cleared up at seven o'clock; very heavy dew in the morning.

Dec. 22.--We travelled to-day about five miles in a north-north-west direction, and encamped at the creek where Charley and his companion had seen the huts of the natives, which we found deserted. Our route lay through a flat country, timbered with true box, (small Acacias forming the underwood), along a fine lagoon on which were a number of ducks; farther on, the Bastard box prevailed, with silver-leaved Ironbark, and patches of Bricklow scrub, of Vitex and of the native lemon. A small tree (a species of Acacia) was also seen about thirty or forty feet high, with slightly drooping branches, and lanceolate deep green phyllodia about one inch.

I reconnoitred with Charley, and found that the creek soon became enveloped by scrub: to the west and south-west rose ranges of a moderate elevation, parallel to which we travelled; plains frequently interspersed with scrub, which became more dense as it approached the foot of the ranges. From these appearances I determined upon sending my party back to Brown's Lagoons, to secure water; whilst I should examine the country in advance, in order to ascertain the extent of the scrub, in which we were entangled.

Dec. 23--During the night we had a tremendous thunder-storm from the southward with much rain, which did not cease till after midnight, and was succeeded by a hurricane from the east. We witnessed a remarkable meteor, of a fine bluish colour, stretching from E.N.E. to W.S.W. almost parallel to the thunder-clouds. The moon, a day from its full, to the eastward, probably produced this phenomenon.

The bower of the bowerbird (Chlamydera maculata, GOULD) was seen in the scrub; it is made of dry grass, and its approaches at either end were thickly strewn with snail shells and flint pebbles, which had been collected by the bird with great industry, but for what purpose we could not determine. Among the shells we found a Helix of a brownish colour and of an oval form, approaching that of Bulimus.

Whilst my companions returned to Brown's Lagoons, Mr. Calvert and Brown remained with me to examine the country. The creek which I followed down, almost entirely disappeared; but, five miles farther on, its channel was again observed, as deep as before, and was joined by several water-courses from the Christmas Ranges. The principal channel of the creek was lined with a species of Melaleuca, with slightly foliacious bark. Several species of sedges, and nutritious grasses, grew round the holes in which the water was constant. At about fifteen miles from the camp, the creek was joined by that which I had followed for some distance on the 15th December, and, about three miles farther down, it receives another considerable tributary; and, at their junction, it is a fine sheet of water. Here the country begins to open, with large Box-flats extending on both sides. Two small creeks come in from the scrubby hills to the eastward, but, at a short distance beyond their junction, almost the whole channel disappears. Soon after, we came to another creek, to the left of the first; but it disappeared in the same manner as the other. We came upon several lagoons, and found some very fine grass: the scrub reappeared on the rising ground about six miles north from the large sheet of water. A little farther on, we came to ridges of basaltic formation, openly timbered with silver-leaved Ironbark, and richly covered with young grasses and herbs, identical with those of the Darling Downs. Water holes with fine water were found at the foot of the hills. Mimosa terminalis was frequent; numerous flights of partridge pigeons (Geophaps scripta) were also seen.

Dec. 24.--We returned towards the camp, but, through some inattention, kept too much to the eastward, and passed through a country of an extremely diversified character, and very different in appearance from that we had just left. Here we passed an extensive Myal forest, the finest I had seen, covering the hilly and undulating country, interspersed with groves of the native lemon tree; a few of which were still sufficiently in fruit to afford us some refreshment. Occasionally we met with long stretches of small dead trees, probably killed by bush fires, alternating with Bricklow thickets: and then again crossed small plains and patches of open forest ground, which much relieved the tediousness of the ride through thick scrubs, which we had frequently to penetrate with both hands occupied in protecting the face from the branches. We also crossed chains of water-holes surrounded by a coarse stargrass; these now changed into creeks with deep and irregular beds, lined with Melaleucas, and now again dwindled into shallow channels, scarcely to be recognised amidst the surrounding scrub. A week before, these holes were hopelessly dry; but a recent thunder-storm had filled them; and had also made the ground soft and heavy, and had called into life thousands of small frogs, which, by an incessant croaking, testified their satisfaction at the agreeable change.

Dec. 25.--We returned to Brown's Lagoons, and entered our camp just as our companions were sitting down to their Christmas dinner of suet pudding and stewed cockatoos. The day was cloudy and sultry; we had had a heavy thunder-storm on Christmas eve.

Dec. 26.--During the night, scud passed from the east; in the morning we had some heavy showers without wind; it cleared up at ten o'clock, and we took advantage of four hours fair weather to travel on. We again passed the huts of the natives, and encamped about seven miles farther down the creek. We were, however, scarcely housed, when heavy showers of rain began to fall, and rendered the soil, which was a stiff loam, heavy and boggy.

Dec. 27.--Though we had hobbled our horses with straps and stirrup leathers, they had strayed, during the night, to the more open country, where they separated from each other in search of food; and it was not until after three hours search that Charley found the greater part of them. We had, however, watched the bullocks during the night, and were therefore enabled to proceed; which we did as far as the fine sheet of water before mentioned, when Charley again went in search of the missing horses, with which he returned after some time.

The showers continued until about 10 o'clock last night; at 3 A. M. the sky became clear, and continued so through the morning, except an occasional cloud from the eastward.

Mr. Calvert found a Bauhinia in blossom; which was not only different from the Bauhinia found afterwards at Comet River, but also from that of the Mitchell. Mr. Gilbert found a new species of sleeping lizard, with four lighter stripes on the dark brown ground along the back, and with dark spots on the sides. Mr. Roper shot some ducks, and I found a species of Ancylus; besides the species of Limnaea and Paludina, which we had previously met with.

Dec. 28.--We travelled over the Box-tree flat, until we reached the open basaltic ridges mentioned on the 23rd December, and kept along their base. The creek, which had disappeared on the flat, here again formed a large deep channel, lined with Melaleucas. Hollows existed along the hills, and water-holes ran in lines parallel to the creek; all now quite dry; a scrubby forest land alternated with open flats and Bricklow thickets. Water was very scarce; and having encamped my party, I started immediately to reconnoitre the country. I followed the creek to the northward, and found it lined by scrub; but the belt along its west side was narrow, and beyond it, a fine open undulating country was observed extending far to the south-west and west, in which direction the loom of distant ranges was seen. These plains, which had some patches of open forest land, were, at the request of my companion, Mr. Calvert, named "Albinia Downs." To the north-west, the mountain with the hummock lay close before us, throwing out subordinate spurs to the westward. In riding to the most northerly end of it, I fell in with a small water-course, which led me to a large creek coming from the south-west and west-south-west, with fine Casuarinas fringing its banks and forming a dark tortuous line amongst the light green foliage of the trees on the neighbouring flats. About six miles lower down, it was joined by the scrub creek on which we were encamped.

The sandy bed of the creek was entirely dry, and we must have encamped without water after a long and fatiguing ride, had not a heavy thunder-shower supplied us; we caught the rain in our pannikins as it dropt from our extended blankets.

The thunder-storm had passed, and the sun had set, when Brown, my blackfellow, suddenly threw back the blanket under which we sat, and pointed out to me a fine comet in a small clear spot of the western sky. I afterwards learned that this comet had been observed as early as the 1st December; but our constant travelling in level forest land had prevented us from seeing it before. The creek received the appropriate name of "Comet Creek."

Dec. 29.--Following the creek down, we found water in chains of ponds, and watercourses coming from a belt of scrub occupying the ground between the creek and the mountains. Fine, though narrow, but well-grassed flats extended along Comet Creek. We observed growing on the creek, the dwarf Koorajong (Grewia), a small rough-leaved fig tree, a species of Tribulus, and the native Portulaca. The latter afforded us an excellent salad; but was much more acid than I had found it in other parts of the country, where I had occasionally tasted it. The native melon of the Darling Downs and of the Gwyder, grew here also. Of animals, we saw several kangaroos, emus, native companions, and wallabies.

During our return to the camp, a hot wind blew from the south-west across Albinia Downs: the great extent of which sufficiently accounted for the high temperature. The only thermometer I had was unfortunately broken shortly after we started; this loss was severely felt by me throughout the journey, as we had no means of ascertaining the exact temperature. I made the latitude of our camp at Scrub Creek to be 24 degrees 25 minutes 42 seconds.

Dec. 30.--We travelled about seven miles to the north-east, crossed Comet Creek, and encamped at some water-holes, in a small creek coming out of the scrub below the range.

Our sportsmen gave chase to ten emus and a kangaroo on Albinia Downs: but the rottenness of the ground prevented their capture: rather tantalizing to hungry stomachs! I examined the basaltic rock on several spots, and found that it contained numerous crystals of Peridot. The sand in the bed of the river contains very minute particles of igneous rock. The slopes of the range of Comet Creek are composed of rich black soil, in some places without trees, in others openly timbered. Stones of a light coloured rock, with crystals of augite, pebbles of sandstone, of conglomerate, and of quartz, are scattered over the ground, or imbedded in the loamy beds of the water-courses. The belt of scrub at the foot of the slopes runs out in narrow strips towards the river, and these are separated by box-tree thickets, and open box-tree flats. A pea-plant, with ternate leaves, and fine yellow blossoms, was found near our camp: Portulaca was very abundant. The bronze-winged pigeon lived here on the red fruit of Rhagodia, and the black berries of a species of Jasmine; and seems also to pick occasionally the seed vessel of a Ruellia, which is very frequent on all the flats of Comet Creek.

During the night, a thunder-storm passed to the southward, but did not reach us; at 10 o'clock we observed very vivid lightning to the westward: the wind was from the north and north-east.

Dec. 31.--We travelled along the banks of the creek towards the north-east, but scarcely accomplished six miles, in consequence of its tortuous course. The water-hole which I had found when reconnoitring, was dried up, and we were glad to find a shallow pool, of which our thirsty cattle took immediate possession. The sand in the bed of the creek looked moist, but no water was found, after digging to a depth of five feet. The immediate neighbourhood of the creek was in some places open, in others covered with a shrubby Acacia, with long glaucous, and rather fleshy phyllodia. On both sides of the high banks are deep hollows, and chains of ponds, surrounded with reeds; but now quite dry, and covered with the dead shells of Limnaea, Paludina, and Unio.

Mr. Roper found an Agama, with light grey on the back, and a yellow belly. A small Chlamy-dophorus, (Jew lizard of the Hunter) was also seen, and is probably identical with the animal inhabiting the banks of that river. Brown accompanied me to reconnoitre the country; and we had scarcely travelled two miles along the creek, when my attention was attracted by the remains of a hut, consisting of a ridge pole, and two forked stakes, about six feet high, both having been cut with a sharp iron tomahawk. Neither of us doubted that this was the work of a white man, probably a runaway from the settlement at Moreton Bay. A few miles farther we came to an anabranch of the creek, which turned considerably to the westward. I followed it, and found a shallow watercourse that came out of the scrub, which I also examined in search of water. It led me to another deep channel within the scrub, which looked unusually green, and contained some very large water-holes; but there was no water in them. Turning round one of its bends, we saw a column of thick smoke rising from its left bank, near a fine pool of water. It was evident that a camp of natives was before us; we rode cautiously up to the water, near which we saw their numerous tracks, and then stopped to look around, but without dismounting. We were, however, very soon discovered by one of them, who, after staring at us for a moment, uttered a cry, resembling the word "whitefellow," "whitefellow," and ran off, followed by the whole party. We then rode up to the camp, and found their dinner ready, consisting of two eggs of the brush turkey, roasted opossums, bandicoots, and iguanas. In their "dillis," (small baskets) were several roots or tubers of an oblong form, about an inch in length, and half an inch broad, of a sweet taste, and of an agreeable flavour, even when uncooked; there were also balls of pipe-clay to ornament their persons for corroborris. Good opossum cloaks, kangaroo nets, and dillis neatly worked of koorajong bark, were strewed about; there were also some spears, made of the Bricklow Acacia: all were forgotten in the suddenness of their retreat. I could not resist the temptation of tasting one of the eggs, which was excellent; but, as they seemed to have trusted to our generosity, I left every thing in its place, and departed. Brown thought that one of them looked like a half-caste, and, as they had called us, as far as we understood, "whitefellows," I felt confirmed in my supposition, either that a white man was with them, or had lived among them very recently. I returned to the creek, in order to find another water-hole with water; but did not succeed, and had to encamp without it. During the night we heard the noise of a frog, "brrr, brrr;" probably a new species, for we had never heard that croak before. It seemed, however, to frighten Brown, who, like all blackfellows, is very timid after night-fall. Yesterday we met with a new leguminous shrub. It belongs to the section Cassia, and has a long pinnate leaf, the leaflets an inch long, and half an inch broad. Its pods were about a foot long, half an inch broad; and every seed was surrounded by a fleshy spongy tissue, which, when dry, gave to the pod a slightly articulate appearance. The seeds, when young, had an agreeable taste, and the tissue, when dry, was pleasantly acidulous, and was eaten by some of my companions without any ill effect, whilst others, with myself, were severely purged. To day I found the same plant in form of a tree, about thirty feet high, with a short stem, and long spreading shady branches.

CHAPTER IV

SWARMS OF COCKATOOS
ALLOWANCE OF FLOUR FURTHER REDUCED
NATIVE FAMILY
THE MACKENZIE
COAL
NATIVES SPEAKING A DIFFERENT IDIOM
MOUNT STEWART
BROWN AND MYSELF MISS THE WAY BACK TO THE CAMP
FIND OUR PARTY AGAIN, ON THE FOURTH DAY
NEUMAN'S CREEK
ROPER'S PEAK
CALVERT'S PEAK
GILBERT'S DOME
GREAT WANT OF WATER.

Jan. 1, 1845.--After a ride of about four miles down the creek, we came to a deep hole of good water, that had been filled by the late thunder-storms, the traces of which, however, had disappeared every where else. I found a red Passion flower, with three-lobed leaves, the lobes rounded: it was twining round the trunk of a gum tree, and rooted in a light sandy alluvial soil. A new species of Bauhinia, with large white blossoms, growing in small groves, or scattered in the scrub, particularly near the creeks, was conspicuous for its elegance, and was the greatest ornament of this part of the country. It is a tree about twenty-five feet high, with long drooping branches; the foliage is of a rich green colour, and affords a fine shade. A climbing Capparis, with broad lanceolate leaves, had also large white showy blossoms; and a fine specimen of this plant was seen growing in the fork of an old box tree, about twelve or fifteen feet from the ground; it was in fruit, but unfortunately was not yet ripe. There was also another species of the same genus, with yellow blossoms, in other respects very similar in appearance to the first. The white cedar was still abundant. When I returned to the camp, I found my companions busily engaged in straining the mud, which had remained in the water-hole after our horses and cattle had drunk and rolled in it. Messrs. Gilbert and Calvert had discovered a few quarts of water in the hollow stump of a tree; and Mr. Roper and Charley had driven the horses and cattle to another water-hole, about two miles off. Our latitude was 24 degrees 16 minutes 9 seconds.

Jan. 2.--I moved my camp to the water-hole, near which I had met with the natives, and halted at the outside of a Bauhinia grove. On visiting the spot where the blacks were encamped, it appeared that they had returned and carried away all their things, probably well contented that we had not taken more than the turkey's egg. The mosquitoes were a little troublesome after sunset and in the early part of the night; but, after that time, it was too cold for them. The flies were a much greater nuisance; at times absolutely intolerable, from the pertinacity with which they clung to the corners of our eyes, to the lips, to the ears, and even to the sores on our fingers. The wind was generally from the eastward during the morning, with cumuli; but these disappeared in the afternoon.

Brown found a crab, (a species of Gecarcinus?) the carapace about an inch and a quarter long, and one and a half broad, the left claws much larger than the right, the antepenultimate joint having a strong tooth on the upper side; it is found in moist places and in the lagoons, and, when these are dried up, it retires under logs and large stones.

Mr. Gilbert saw a large grey wallabi, and a small one which he thought was new. Another species of Agama was found, differing from the former by its general grey colour, with black spots on the back.

Jan. 3.--The night was clear; a fine easterly wind prevailed during the morning, with cumuli, which disappeared towards noon, when the sky became cloudless. Thunder-storms generally follow a very sultry calm morning. We travelled about ten miles in a N.N.E. direction, and came to the farthest water-hole I had seen when out reconnoitring. We passed in our journey through a very scrubby country, opening occasionally into fine flats thinly timbered with true box, which was at that time in blossom. I noticed a small tree (Santalum oblongatum, R. Br.), very remarkable for having its branches sometimes slightly drooping, and at other times erect, with membranous glaucous elliptical leaves, from an inch to an inch and a half long, and three-quarters broad, with very indistinct nerves, and producing a small purple fruit, of very agreeable taste. I had seen this tree formerly at the Gwyder, and in the rosewood scrubs about Moreton Bay, and I also found it far up to the northward, in the moderately open Vitex and Bricklow scrubs.

Several small lizards (Tiliqua), probably only varieties of the same species, amused us with the quickness of their motions when hunting for insects on the sunny slopes near the water-holes, and on the bark of the fallen trees; some were striped, others spotted, and there were some of a simple brownish iridescent colour. Our latitude was 24 degrees 6 minutes 36 seconds.

Jan. 4.--Brown accompanied me on my usual errand, to find, if possible, a larger supply of water, on which we might fall back, if the creek did not soon change its character. The scrub came close to the banks of the creek, but was occasionally interrupted by basaltic ridges with open forest, stretching to the westward. These ridges were on all sides surrounded with scrub, which did not flourish where the basaltic formation prevailed. Broad but shallow channels, deepening from time to time into large water-holes, follow in a parallel direction the many windings of the creek, with which they have occasionally a small communication. They seem to be the receptacles of the water falling within the scrub during the rainy season: their banks are sometimes very high and broken, and the bed is of a stiff clay, like that of the scrub, and is scattered over with pebbles of quartz and conglomerate. Whilst these Melaleuca channels keep at a distance varying from one to three miles from the creek, winding between the slight elevations of a generally flat country--long shallow hollows and a series of lagoons exist near the creek, from which they are separated by a berg, and are bounded on the other side by a slight rise of the ground. The hollows are generally without trees, but are covered with a stiff stargrass; and they frequently spread out into melon flats, covered with true Box. It is difficult to travel along the creek, especially with pack bullocks, as the scrub frequently comes close up to its banks; but the hollows, during the dry season, are like roads. In the channels within the scrub I found a large supply of water, in holes surrounded by sedges and a broad-leaved Polygonum, amongst which grew a species of Abutilon; the neighbouring dry channel was one beautiful carpet of verdure. In the scrub I found a plant belonging to the Amaryllideae (Calostemma luteum?) with a cluster of fine yellow blossoms. Flights of ducks were on the water, and scores of little birds were fluttering through the grasses and sedges, or hopping over the moist mud in pursuit of worms and insects. The water-holes were about six miles from our camp. I continued my ride about four miles farther along the creek, where I found the scrub had retired, and was replaced by an open silver-leaved Ironbark forest, in which the rich green feed relieved our eyes from the monotonous grey of the scrub, and quickened the steps of our horses. Here also basaltic ridges approached the creek, and even entered into its bed; among them were several fine water-holes. In our return to the camp we found abundance of water in the lagoons near the river, corresponding to the water-holes within the scrub. This local occurrence of water depends either upon thunder-storms favouring some tracts more than others, or upon the country here being rather more hilly, which allows the rainwater to collect in deep holes at the foot of the slopes.

Jan. 5.--We moved down to the water-holes of the basaltic ridges, being about nine miles in a N.N.W. direction from our last camp.

At three o'clock a.m. clouds formed very rapidly over the whole sky--which had been clear during the previous part of the night--and threatened us with wet. In the morning some few drops fell, with slight casterly winds; it cleared up, however, about nine o'clock a.m. with a northerly breeze.

Marsilea grows everywhere on the flats; and a fine little pea plant with a solitary red blossom, was found amongst the basaltic rocks round the water-hole. We observed, growing along the creek, another species of Portulaca, with linear fleshy leaves, erect stem, and small yellow flowers; and a half-shrubby Malvaccous plant, with small clustered yellow blossoms: the latter is common at the outside of scrubs in the Moreton Bay district. We also remarked, within the scrub, a small tree, with bright-green foliage, and three-winged capsules slightly united at the base; and another small tree, with deep-green coloured leaves, and two-winged capsules united in all their length; the last is nearly allied to Dodonaea.

I never before saw nor heard so many cockatoos as I did at Comet Creek. Swarms of them preceded us for one or two miles, from tree to tree, making the air ring with their incessant screams, and then returning in long flights to their favourite haunts, from which we had disturbed them. We saw four kangaroos; and shot some bronze-winged pigeons; in the crop of one I found a small Helix with a long spire,--a form I do not remember ever having seen before in the colony. A considerable number of small brown snakes were living in the water-hole; they were generally seen in the shallow water with their heads above the surface, but, at our approach, dived into the deepest part of the hole. Our daily allowance of flour was now reduced to three pounds. Our provisions disappear rapidly, and the wear and tear of our clothes and harness is very great; but, as our wants increase, our desires become more easily satisfied. The green hide furnishes ample means to preserve our shoes, by covering them with mocassins, and with materials for repairing the harness. The latitude of this camp was 23 degrees 59 minutes 6 seconds.

Jan. 6.--Leaving my companions at the camp well provided with both grass and water, I followed the creek, with Brown, in expectation of a long ride, as Messrs. Gilbert and Roper had been forward about nine miles in search of water, but without finding any. We very soon left the open country, and entered the vilest scrub we had ever before encountered. The parallel lines of lagoons disappeared, and the banks of the creek became very broken by gullies, so that the stiff soil of the neighbouring scrub, not being intercepted by lagoons, is washed by heavy rains into the bed of the creek, which was no longer sandy, but inclined to the formation of water-holes, the clay rendering it impervious to water. The Casuarina, which likes a light sandy soil, disappeared at the same time, and was succeeded by the narrow-leaved Melaleuca. The flooded-gum, however, kept its place, and frequently attained to a great size. About twelve miles from the camp, a small water-hole appeared in the bed of the creek. This was the first we had met with while travelling along its banks a distance of seventy miles; but, in proceeding about four miles farther, we passed a succession of fine water-holes well supplied with water; and others were found in the adjoining creeks. Afterwards, however, the water suddenly disappeared again; and for eight miles farther its bed was entirely dry, although fine grass was growing in it. We had every prospect of passing the night without water, as the sun was sinking fast; but we fortunately reached a small hole before dark, containing a little water, which we had to share with our horses, with a small brown snake, and with a large flight of bronze-winged pigeons; the latter, surprised at our presence, first alighted on the neighbouring trees to observe us, and then hurried down to take their evening draught.

Jan. 7.--I travelled farther down the river, and again came, after a ride of three miles, into a well-watered country, but still occupied by scrub; in which the Capparis, with its large white sweet-scented blossoms, was very frequent; but its sepals, petals, and stamens dropped off at the slightest touch. Its fruit was like a small apple covered with warts, and its pungent seeds were imbedded in a yellow pulp, not at all disagreeable to eat. At last the scrub ceased, and, over an open rise on the right side of Comet Creek, a range of blue mountains was discovered by my companion, promising a continuation of good country. At this time a fine water-hole was at hand, and invited us to stop and make our luncheon on dried beef and a pot of tea. Whilst I was preparing the tea, Brown went to shoot pigeons; and, whilst thus employed, he was surprised by the cooee of a Blackfellow; and, on looking round, he saw one on the opposite bank of the creek making signs to him, as if to ask in what direction we were going. Brown pointed down the creek; the black then gave him to understand that he was going upward to join his wife. We started about half-an-hour afterwards, and met with him, about two miles up the creek, with his wife, his daughter, and his son. He was a fine old man, but he, as well as his family, were excessively frightened; they left all their things at the fire, as if offering them to us, but readily accepted two pigeons, which had been shot by Brown. We asked them for water (yarrai) which, according to what we could understand from their signs, was plentiful lower down the creek. In returning homewards we cut off considerable angles of the creek, and passed through a much finer and more open country. On its left bank we passed a scrub creek containing magnificent lagoons. At my arrival in the camp, I was informed that natives had been close at hand, although none had showed themselves.

Jan. 8.--I moved my camp about eight miles to the northward, and halted at a fine water-hole in a scrub creek joining Comet Creek. A pretty little diver was amusing himself on the water. The country is very rich in game. Kangaroos and wallabies are very frequent; several brush turkeys were seen, and the partridge and bronze-winged pigeons are very plentiful. Our latitude was 23 degrees 51 minutes.

Jan. 9.--In travelling down to the water-hole, where we had met the Blackfellow and his family, we kept a little too much to the westward, in hope of finding a more open country; instead, however, of an improvement, we encountered sandy hills covered with a dense low scrub and cypress-pine. The latter almost invariably grows on the slight sandstone elevations in a scrubby country. After surmounting many difficulties, we came upon a broad scrub creek, in the dry bed of which we travelled down to Comet Creek, which we followed, and at last reached our intended camping place. Our cattle and luggage had suffered severely, and we devoted the next day to sundry repairs. The weather was very hot: the night clear. Our latitude was 23 degrees 41 minutes 14 seconds.

Jan. 10.--To prevent unnecessary loss of time by my reconnoitring excursions, and to render them less fatiguing to myself, I arranged that both the blacks should go with me, in order that I might send one back from the first favourable camping place, to bring the party on, whilst I continued to explore the country with the other. Under this arrangement, therefore, I went forward, and, following the creek, it was found to sweep to the eastward, round a high plain of rich black soil, and covered with luxuriant vegetation. This plain is basaltic, but, in the valley of the creek, sandstone crops out below it. The slopes from the plain to the creek are steep, and torn by deep gullies, which made travelling very fatiguing. As the creek again turned to the west and north-west, the water-holes increased both in size and number, although the flats within the valley were limited and intersected by watercourses. I sent Charley back when we were about seven miles N.W. by N. from our camp, and proceeded with Brown down the creek, which, at about four miles farther, to my inexpressible delight, joined a river coming from the west and north-west, and flowing to the east and north-east. It was not, however, running, but formed a chain of small lakes, from two to three and even eight miles in length, and frequently from fifty to one hundred yards broad, offering to our view the finest succession of large sheets of water we had seen since leaving the Brisbane. Its course continued through a very deep and winding valley, bounded by high but generally level land. The gullies going down to the river were generally covered with a belt of thick scrub, as was also the high land nearest to it; but, farther off, the country appeared to be more open, plains alternating with open forest land, but yet, in places, much occupied by tracts of almost impervious scrub of various extent. We met frequent traces of the natives, who had recently gone down the river, having previously burned the grass, leaving very little for our horses and cattle. At 8 o'clock P.M. a fine strong northerly breeze came up the river, flowing along its broad open valley, and which I supposed to be the sea breeze. This supposition was somewhat confirmed by a similar breeze occurring at the same time on the following evening.

The plains are basaltic, and occasionally covered with pebbles of white and iron-coloured quartz and conglomerate, and are in the vicinity of slight elevations, which are probably composed of sandstone and conglomerate, and usually covered with low scrub and cypress-pine. Sandstone crops out in the gullies of the valley, in horizontal strata, some of which are hard and good for building, others like the blue clay beds of Newcastle, with the impressions of fern-leaves identical with those of that formation. At the junction of Comet Creek and the river, I found water-worn fragments of good coal, and large trunks of trees changed into ironstone. I called this river the "Mackenzie," in honour of Sir Evan Mackenzie, Bart., as a small acknowledgment of my gratitude for the very great assistance which he rendered me in the preparations for my expedition. Farther down the river, the country became better watered, even at a distance from the river; some small creeks, winding down between scrubby sandstone hills, were full of water, and a chain of fine lagoons was crossed, covered with splendid blue Nymphaeas. Large coveys of partridge-pigeons rose from the burnt grass as we passed along, and ducks and pelicans were numerous on the stretches of water in the bed of the river. Heaps of fresh-water muscles lined the water-holes, which were teeming with fish, apparently of considerable size, as their splashing startled me several times during the night, and made me believe, for the moment, that a large tribe of natives were bathing.

A very stiff high grass became very general along the river. On the plains there were fields of native carrots, now dry; also of vervain and burr. The long-podded cassia was plentiful, and its young seeds tasted well, but considerably affected the bowels.

Cumuli passed from the north-east during the morning: the afternoon was clear, and the night bright.

When I returned to the camp on the 11th January, my companions told me, that upon their journey across the high plains they had observed a high range to the north-west.

Jan. 12.--I removed my camp down Comet Creek, and followed the Mackenzie for a few miles, as far as it was easy travelling along its bank. Comet Creek joins the Mackenzie in a very acute angle; the direction of the latter being east, and the course of the former, in its lower part, north-west. Our anglers caught several fine fishes and an eel, in the water-holes of the Mackenzie. The former belonged to the Siluridae, and had four fleshy appendages on the lower lip, and two on the upper; dorsal fin 1 spine 6 rays, and an adipose fin, pectoral 1 spine 8 rays; ventral 6 rays; anal 17 rays; caudal 17-18 rays; velvety teeth in the upper and lower jaws, and in the palatal bones. Head flat, belly broad; back of a greenish silver-colour; belly silvery white; length of the body 15-20 inches. It made a singular noise when taken out of the water.

We found here Unios of a fine pink and purple colour inside the valves, and a new species of Cyclas with longitudinal ribs. Small black ants, and little flies with wings crossing each other, annoy us very much, the one creeping all over our bodies and biting us severely, and the other falling into our soup and tea, and covering our meat; but the strong night-breeze protects us from the mosquitoes. A pretty lizard (Tiliqua) of small size, with yellowish spots on a brown ground, was caught, and seemed to be plentiful here about. The Acacia, with very long linear drooping leaves, that had been observed at the Dawson, re-appeared both on Comet Creek and the banks of the Mackenzie. Our latitude was 23 degrees 33 minutes 38 seconds.

Jan. 13.--We travelled about nine miles E.N.E. over the high land, and through open forest land, and several plains skirted on both sides by scrub. I observed a new species of Flindersia, a small tree about thirty feet high, with thin foliage and very regular branches, forming a spire. The latitude was 23 degrees 29 minutes.

Jan. 14.--After travelling about three miles in a north-easterly direction along the banks of the river--having, at about a mile from our camp, crossed a good-sized creek on its left bank--the river took a sudden bend to the westward, and a large creek coming from the northward, joined it almost at a right angle to its course. As we proceeded, we came suddenly upon two black women hurrying out of the water, but who, on reaching a distance in which they thought themselves safe, remained gazing at us as we slowly and peaceably passed by. In the bed of the river, which was here broad and sandy, a bean was gathered, bearing racemes of pink blossoms, and spreading its long slender stem over the ground, or twining it round shrubs and trees: its pods were from three to five inches long, and about half an inch broad, containing from four to six seeds, very similar to the horse-bean. This plant was afterwards found growing in the sandy beds, or along the bergs of almost all the broad rivers, and was always a welcome sight; for the seeds, after roasting and pounding them, afforded us a very agreeable substitute for coffee.

We passed some very high cliffs, which showed a fine geological section of horizontal layers of sandstone and coal-slate. There were also some layers of very good coal, but the greater part of those visible were of a slaty character. Nodules of Ironstone were very frequent in the sandstone.

64

After having fixed upon a place to pitch the tent, and after some refreshment, I started with my two black companions upon a reconnoitring excursion along the course of the river, which made several large bends, though its general direction was to the north-east. We passed over some very fine flats of Bastard-box, silver-leaved Ironbark, and white gum, with a few scattered Acacia-trees, remarkable for their drooping foliage, and mentioned under the date 22nd December. Farther on, we came again to scrub, which uniformly covered the edge of the high land towards the river. Here, within the scrub, on the side towards the open country we found many deserted camps of the natives, which, from their position, seemed to have been used for shelter from the weather, or as hiding-places from enemies: several places had evidently been used for corroborris, and also for fighting.

On a White-gum, which has long lanceolate green leaves, I found a species of Loranthus, with leaves resembling those of the silver-leaved Ironbark (Eucalyptus pulverulentus). Having reached a point down the river, in about lat. 23 degrees 18 minutes, from which some low ranges to the N.W. became visible, I returned to the camp. At the point where it turned, a dyke of basalt traverses the river. The country still maintained its favourable character, and the river contained fine sheets of water similar to those already described, on one of which a pelican floated undisturbed by our presence. Large heaps of muscle-shells, which have given food to successive generations of the natives, cover the steep sloping banks of the river, and indicate that this part of the country is very populous. The tracks of the natives were well beaten, and the fire-places in their camps numerous. The whole country had been on fire; smouldering logs, scattered in every direction, were often rekindled by the usual night breeze, and made us think that the Blackfellows were collecting in numbers around us,--and more particularly on the opposite side of the river; added to which, the incessant splashing of numerous large fishes greatly contributed to augment our fears. As a matter of precaution, therefore, we tied our horses near our sleeping-place, and gathered the grass which grew along the edge of the water for them to eat; and it was not till daylight that our alarm vanished.

Jan. 15.--Having now ascertained, beyond a doubt, that the Mackenzie flowed to the north-east, I returned to the camp, resolved upon leaving it and renewing my course to the west-north-west and north-west; but, as it was extremely doubtful whether we should find water in travelling across the country without a leading watercourse, and as we had failed in procuring a sufficient quantity of game, I determined to take this favourable opportunity of killing a bullock before leaving the river.

Jan. 16.--On returning, we found our party encamped about four miles lower down the river than where I had left them. I then removed them to a more convenient spot about two miles still lower down (lat. 23 degrees 21 minutes 30 seconds). Just at the moment we were preparing to shoot the bullock, we heard the cooee of a native, and in a short time two men were seen approaching and apparently desirous of having a parley. Accordingly, I went up to them; the elder, a well made man, had his left front tooth out, whilst the younger had all his teeth perfect; he was of a muscular and powerful figure, but, like the generality of Australian aborigines, had rather slender bones; he had a splendid pair of moustachios, but his beard was thin. They spoke a language entirely different from that of the natives of Darling Downs, but "yarrai" still meant water. Charley, who conversed with them for some time, told me that they had informed him, as well as he could understand, that the Mackenzie flowed to the north-east. Brown found an empty seed-vessel of the Nelumbium, in their camp. At sunset we killed our bullock, and during the 17th and 18th occupied ourselves in cutting up the meat, drying it in the sun, frying the fat, preparing the hide, and greasing our harness. Charley, in riding after the horses, came to some fine lagoons, which were surrounded by a deep green belt of Nelumbiums. This plant grows, with a simple tap root, in the deep soft mud, bearing one large peltate leaf on a leaf stalk, about eight feet high, and from twelve to eighteen inches in diameter, the flower-stalk being of the same length or even longer, crowned with a pink flower resembling that of a Nymphaea, but much larger: its seed-vessel is a large cone, with perpendicular holes in its cellular tissue, containing seeds, about three quarters of an inch in length. We found the following shells in the river, viz.; two species of Melania, a Paludina, the lanceolate Limnaea, a cone-shaped Physa (?), a Cyclas with longitudinal ribs, and the Unio before described. Murphy shot an Ostioglossum, a Malacopterygious fish, about three feet long, with very large scales, each scale having a pink spot. We afterwards found this fish in the waters flowing into the Gulf of Carpentaria; both on its eastern and western sides: and, according to the natives of Port Essington, to whom I showed the dried specimen, it is also found in the permanent water-holes of the Cobourg peninsula.

Jan. 18.--Leaving my party to complete the process of drying and packing the charqui, I started with my two black companions to examine the country to the north-west. After passing the gullies in the immediate neighbourhood of the river, we came to sandstone ridges covered with an almost impenetrable scrub; chiefly composed of stiff and prickly shrubs, many of them dead, with dry branches filling the intervals. As no grass grew on the poor soil, the bush-fires--those scavengers of the forest--are unable to enter and consume the dead wood, which formed the principal obstacle to our progress. Difficult, however, as it was to penetrate such thickets with pack-bullocks, I had no choice left, and therefore proceeded in the same direction. In a short time, we reached an open Bricklow scrub containing many dry water-holes, which, farther on, united into a watercourse. We passed a creek flowing to the eastward to join the Mackenzie, and continued our route through patches of Bricklow scrub, alternating with Bastard-box forest, and open Vitex scrub, in which the Moreton Bay ash was very plentiful. About eight miles from our camp, we came upon an open forest of narrow-leaved Ironbark (E. resinifera) and Bastard-box, covering gentle slopes, from which shallow well-grassed hollows descended to the westward. Coming again on scrub, and following it down in a westerly direction, we came to a dry creek; and found water in holes along the scrub. Considering this a favourable place for the camp, I sent Charley back, to guide my party through the scrub; whilst I proceeded with Brown to examine the creek upwards, to the north-west. After a ride of about five miles, during which several fine lagoons were seen, we reached a prominent hill of sandstone formation, surrounded by a most beautiful, open, silver-leaved Ironbark forest, changing occasionally into plains without a tree. I ascended the hill, and obtained a very extensive view from its summit. A range of peaks bore N. 57 degrees W.; another range, with undulating outline, was seen to the south-east; and another less prominent range bore N. 45 degrees W. The hill is in latitude 23 degrees 10 minutes, and bears the name of Mount Stewart, in compliment to Mr. Stewart, veterinary surgeon of Sydney, to whom I am indebted for great assistance and most valuable advice.

Towards the north-east, the country appeared to be very level, with only one low ridge, apparently at a great distance. To the south, and also to the west, some long-stretched flat-topped hills were visible, several extending as far as the eye could reach. I continued my ride in the direction of the range of peaks to the north-west, over an undulating country of varied character, now extending in fine downs and plains, now covered with belts of thick Bricklow scrub, with occasional ridges of open silver-leaved Ironbark forest. Among the latter was a rather stunted gum-tree, with a black scaly butt; it was very frequent, and greatly resembled the Moreton Bay ash. The numerous watercourses which I crossed, were all dry; and, when the approach of night compelled us to select a camping place, which we did in a small grove of Bricklow, we should have been without water, had not a thunder-storm with light showers of rain, enabled us to collect about a quart of it to make some tea. The next morning we continued our examination, passing over a country of scrub, plain, and forest land; and made our breakfast, and watered our horses, at a small pool of water that was collected in a hole of a little creek, after the last night's thunder-storm. About four miles from this spot, we again found permanent water, near the scrub; and, at three miles farther on, crossed a fine creek, with a reedy bed, along which lightly timbered flats extended; and, about six miles to the W. N. W., we found another creek, separated from the former by openly timbered ridges, and occasional patches of scrub. The flats along this creek and its tributaries were covered with the most luxuriant grass; but are without permanent water, although at present supplied by the late thunder-storms. Brown gave chase to an emu with several young ones, but did not succeed in capturing any of them.

We now commenced our return to the camp, and, being impatient to get on, put our horses into a canter; the consequence of which was that we lost our way, and were ignorant as to which side we had left the tracks. Thinking, however, that Mount Stewart would guide us, when we should come in sight of it, I kept a south-easterly course, which soon brought us into a thick Bricklow scrub. In passing the large flats of the last creek, which was here full of fine reedy water-holes, we observed a native; and Brown cooeed to him, and by a sign requested him to wait for us: but he was so frightened, by the sudden appearance of two men cantering towards him, that he took to his heels, and soon disappeared in the neighbouring scrub. We rode the whole day through a Bricklow thicket, which, in only three or four places, was interrupted by narrow strips of open country, along creeks on which fine flooded-gums were growing. The density of the scrub, which covered an almost entirely level country, prevented our seeing farther than a few yards before us, so that we passed our landmark, and, when night approached, and the country became more open, we found ourselves in a part of the country totally unknown to us. At the outside of the scrub, however, we were cheered by the sight of some large lagoons, on whose muddy banks there were numerous tracts of emus and kangaroos. In a recently deserted camp of the Aborigines, we found an eatable root, like the large tubers of Dahlia, which we greedily devoured, our appetite being wonderfully quickened by long abstinence and exercise. Brown fortunately shot two pigeons; and, whilst we were discussing our welcome repast, an emu, probably on its way to drink, approached the lagoon, but halted when it got sight of us, then walked slowly about, scrutinizing us with suspicious looks, and, when Brown attempted to get near it, trotted off to a short distance, and stopped again, and continued to play this tantalizing trick until we were tired; when, mounting our horses, we proceeded on our way. Supposing, from the direction of the waters, that we had left our former tracks to the left, I turned to the north-east to recover them; but it soon became very dark, and a tremendous thunder-storm came down upon us. We were then on a high box-tree ridge, in view of a thick scrub; we hobbled our horses, and covered ourselves with our blankets; but the storm was so violent, that we were thoroughly drenched. As no water-holes were near us, we caught the water that ran from our blankets; and, as we were unable to rekindle our fire, which had been extinguished by the rain, we stretched our blankets over some sticks to form a tent, and notwithstanding our wet and hungry condition, our heads sank wearily on the saddles--our usual bush pillow--and we slept soundly till morning dawned. We now succeeded in making a fire, so that we had a pot of tea and a pigeon between us. After this scanty breakfast, we continued our course to the north-east. Brown thought himself lost, got disheartened, grumbled and became exceedingly annoying to me; but I could not help feeling for him, as he complained of severe pain in his legs. We now entered extensive Ironbark flats, which probably belong to the valley of the Mackenzie. Giving our position every consideration, I determined upon returning to the mountains at which we had turned, and took a north-west course. The country was again most wretched, and at night we almost dropped from our saddles with fatigue. Another pigeon was divided between us, but our tea was gone. Oppressed by hunger, I swallowed the bones and the feet of the pigeon, to allay the cravings of my stomach. A sleeping lizard with a blunt tail and knobby scales, fell into our hands, and was of course roasted and greedily eaten. Brown now complained of increased pain in his feet, and lost all courage. "We are lost, we are lost," was all he could say. All my words and assurances, all my telling him that we might be starved for a day or two, but that we should most certainly find our party again, could not do more than appease his anxiety for a few moments. The next morning, the 21st, we proceeded, but kept a little more to the westward, and crossed a fine openly timbered country; but all the creeks went either to the east or to the north. At last, after a ride of about four miles, Brown recognized the place where we had breakfasted on the 19th, when all his gloom and anxiety disappeared at once. I then returned on my south-east course, and arrived at the camp about one o'clock in the afternoon; my long absence having caused the greatest anxiety amongst my companions. I shall have to mention several other instances of the wonderful quickness and accuracy with which Brown as well as Charley were able to recognize localities which they had previously seen. The impressions on their retina seem to be naturally more intense than on that of the European; and their recollections are remarkably exact, even to the most minute details. Trees peculiarly formed or grouped, broken branches, slight elevations of the ground--in fact, a hundred things, which we should remark only when paying great attention to a place--seem to form a kind of Daguerreotype impression on their minds, every part of which is readily recollected.

I rejoined my party at the creek which comes from Mount Stewart. The natives had approached Mr. Gilbert when out shooting, with a singular, but apparently friendly, noise: "Ach! Ach! Ach!" They had heard the cooce of my blackfellow Charley, and thought Mr. Gilbert wanted them; but, as he was alone, he thought it prudent to retire to the camp.

The thunder-storm, which we experienced on the night of the 19th, had completely changed the aspect of the country round Mount Stewart. All the melon-holes of the scrub, all the ponds along the creeks, all the water-holes in the beds of the creeks, were full of water; the creek at which we encamped, was running; the grass looked fresh and green; the ground, previously rotten, was now boggy, and rendered travelling rather difficult; but we were always at home, for we found water and grass everywhere.

The days from the 17th to the 23rd were exceedingly hot, but, during the early morning and the evening, the air was delightfully cool. Light casterly and northerly winds stirred during the day. Cumuli passed from the same quarters; and generally gathered during the afternoon, and became very heavy. The thunder-storms veered round from the west by the north to the eastward. The nights of the 21st, 22nd, and 23rd were bright and cold, with heavy dew. On the morning of the 23rd we had misty, loose, confluent clouds, travelling slowly from the north-east, with some drops of rain. I was now convinced that the rainy season had set in near the sea coast; for the clouds which came from that direction, had evidently been charged with rain; but, in passing over a large tract of dry country, they were exhausted of their moisture, and the north-easterly winds were too weak to carry them quickly so far inland.

The whole country I had travelled over, is composed of sandstone, with probably occasional outbreaks of igneous rocks, as indicated by the rich black soil. The plains and creeks abound in fossil wood, changed into iron-ore and silica. The soil is generally good, but some of the sandy flats are rotten: and the ridges are covered with pebbles.

The trees, with the exception of the flooded-gum, are of stunted habit; and scrub is here developed ad infinitum. A Grevillea (G. ceratophylla R.Br.?) with pinnatifid leaves, a small tree from fifteen to twenty feet high, and about four inches in diameter; a Melaleuca about the same size, with stiff lanceolate leaves, about two inches long and half an inch broad, and slightly foliaceous bark; and an Acacia with glaucous bipinnate leaves, of the section of the brush Acacias of Moreton Bay--grew on the sandy soil along the ridges; and a handsome Convolvulus with pink flowers adorned the rich plain south-east of Mount Stewart. I examined the wood of all the arborescent Proteaceae which I met with, and observed in all of them, with the exception of Persoonia, the great development of the medullary rays, as it exists in several species of Casuarina.

On the 23rd, 24th, and 25th January, the party moved over the country which I had reconnoitred, to a place about twenty-five miles north-west from Mount Stewart's Creek, and about thirty-four miles from the Mackenzie. In the vicinities of several of the camps, Charley found many nests of the native bee, full of the sweetest and most aromatic honey we had ever tasted. The wild Marjoram, which grows abundantly here, and imparts its fragrance even to the air, seemed to be the principal source from which the bee obtained its honey. We collected a considerable quantity of the marjoram, and added it to our tea, with the double intention, of improving its flavour, and of saving our stock; we also used it frequently as a condiment in our soup.

To the westward of our camp of the 25th January, was a large hill, which I called "West Hill;" and, to the north and north-east, several ridges confined the large valley of our creek and its tributaries. From a sandstone peak to the north-east, which I descended with Mr. Roper, I again saw the range of peaks which I had first observed from Mount Stewart in a W.N.W. direction; and the country to the north and north-east was evidently very mountainous: the valleys descending in a northerly direction. We rode along the ridges on a W.N.W. and west course, and came into the valley of another creek, which we crossed; and, passing several other ridges, which appear to be connected with West Hill, descended to a fine creek, in which we found a reedy water-hole of considerable size. The character of all these creeks is the same. Extensive flats of rotten ground, but beautifully clothed with tufts of grass, openly timbered with Moreton Bay ash and flooded-gum, ascend into gentle grassy slopes of silver-leaved Ironbark and bloodwood, and then rise into sandstone ridges with Acacia thickets and shrubby plants peculiar to the sandstone formation. An Acacia with very large falcate, glaucous phyllodia, and the Euphorbiaceous Severn-tree, were very plentiful; and Crinum grew in thousands on the sandy flats. After a very hot day, the night was bright and dewy: a light breeze was felt at 8 o'clock, which cooled the air.

Jan. 26.--I removed my camp to the reedy water-hole of yesterday, about five miles in the direction of west or west by north from our last encampment. Here I planted the last peach-stones, with which Mr. Newman, the present superintendent of the Botanic Garden in Hobart Town, had kindly provided me. It is, however, to be feared that the fires, which annually over-run the whole country, and particularly here, where the grass is rich and deep even to the water's edge, will not allow them to grow. To the creek on which we were encamped I gave the name of "Newman's Creek," in honour of Mr. Newman. It flows in a south-east and southerly course, and unites probably with West Hill Creek, on which we were encamped the day before, and with the large creek which we crossed on the 25th; both of which probably belong to the system of the Mackenzie. Mr. Calvert and Charley accompanied me in an excursion to the W.N.W., but, having crossed some ridges and coming to scrub, we took a direction to the northward. Fine Bastard-box flats and Ironbark slopes occupy the upper part of Newman's Creek. On the ridges, we observed Persoonia with long falcate leaves; the grass-tree (Xanthorrhaea); the rusty gum, and the Melaleuca of Mount Stewart. Having ascended the sandstone ridge at the head of Newman's Creek, we found ourselves on a table land out of which rose the peaks for which we were steering, and from which we were separated by fine downs, plains, and a lightly timbered country, with belts of narrow-leaved Ironbark growing on a sandy soil. On one of the plains quartzite cropped out; and silex and fossil wood lay scattered over the rich black soil: the latter broke readily, like asbestos, into the finest filaments, much resembling the fossil wood of Van Diemen's Land. It is difficult to describe the impressions which the range of noble peaks, rising suddenly out of a comparatively level country, made upon us. We had travelled so much in a monotonous forest land, with only now and then a glimpse of distant ranges through the occasional clearings in the dismal scrub, that any change was cheering. Here an entirely open country--covered with grass, and apparently unbounded to the westward; now ascending, first, in fine ranges, and forming a succession of almost isolated, gigantic, conical, and dome-topped mountains, which seemed to rest with a flat unbroken base on the plain below--was spread before our delighted eyes. The sudden alteration of the scene, therefore, inspired us with feelings that I cannot attempt to describe. Proceeding onwards we passed some water-holes; but, farther on, the water failed, except here and there in a few pools, in the creeks coming from the range, that had been filled by the last thunder-showers. These pools were generally lined with patches of a narrow-leaved tea tree; and were full of basaltic pebbles.

The breeze set in full and strong, as usual, at a quarter past eight o'clock; the night was bright and cool, and the following morning inexpressibly beautiful.

We enjoyed a dish of cockatoos for supper: the place abounds with them.

Jan. 27.--Charley went back to bring forward our party, whilst I proceeded with Mr. Calvert to reconnoitre the plains under the peaks, feeling confident of finding water at their foot. We passed over plains and lightly-timbered basaltic ridges, between which shallow creeks came down from the range, but we only found water in one or two holes. The plains in the neighbourhood of our intended camp were richly grassed; and a species of Hypoxis and the native Borage (Trichodesma zeylanica, R. Br.) adorned them with their bright yellow and blue blossoms. Farther on, however, the grass had been burnt, and was not yet recovered. As the day advanced, and the black soil became heated by the almost vertical sun, the heat from above and from below became almost insupportable.

Three peaks of this range were particularly striking; two of them seemed to be connected by a lower ridge, in a direction from S.E. to N.W. The south-eastern I called "Roper's Peak," after my companion, who afterwards ascended it with Murphy and Brown, and the north-western, "Scott's Peak," after Helenus Scott, Esq., of Glendon, Hunter's River, who had kindly assisted me in my expedition. In a W. by S. direction from these, and distant four or five miles, is another peak, to which I gave the name of "Macarthur's

Peak," after Mr. William Macarthur, of Cambden. All these peaks are composed of Domite; and Roper's and Scott's Peaks are surrounded by a sandstone formation, covered with a dense low scrub.

I passed between Roper's Peak and Macarthur's Peak, to the northward, and came in sight of another very remarkable cone, which I afterwards called Calvert's Peak, after my fellow-traveller, in consequence of his having suffered severely in its neighbourhood, as I shall soon have to mention.

I traced a creek at the east side of Macarthur's Peak to its head, and went down another on its west side to a large plain, which seemed to be limited to the westward by openly-timbered ridges. As we advanced into the plain, a most remarkable and interesting view of a great number of peaks and domes opened to the N.N.W. and N.W. There seemed no end of apparently isolated conical mountains, which, as they resemble very much the chain of extinct volcanos in Auvergne, might easily be mistaken for such; but, after changing the aspect a little, they assumed the appearance of immense tents, with very short ridge-poles. To the most remarkable of them, which had the appearance of an immense cupola, I gave the name of Gilbert's Dome, after my companion. Far to the N.N.W. a blue peak was seen rising behind a long range of mountains, and from the latter a valley seemed to descend to the W.N.W. A round hill, of a reddish colour, to the south or south-west of Macarthur's Peak, was called Mount Lowe, after R. Lowe, Esq. of Sydney. The general direction of these mountains seems to be from N. 60 degrees W. to S. 60 degrees E., and, if we compare them with the line of the coast in the neighbourhood of Broadsound and Shoalwater bay, bearing due east, it will be found that they are parallel to its direction. All the creeks which we examined, and which fell to the south-west, were entirely dry. On the ridges which bounded the plain to the westward, I met with Acacia pendula; and I may here remark that this appears to be the most northern limit of its habitat. Here also, in an old camp of the natives, we found a heap of muscle-shells, which were probably taken from some very deep and shady holes in the creek, but which were now without the slightest indication of moisture. Water failing us on the western slopes, I crossed to the east side, under the idea and hope that the north and north-east sides of the range, from being more exposed to the sea winds, would be better provided with water; and, passing to the left of Calvert's Peak, over low basaltic ridges, I came to a creek with a shallow bed, winding between basaltic ridges to the north-east. These ridges were lightly timbered, and covered with an abundance of dry grass: dark-green patches of scrub raised our hopes from time to time, and quickened our pace; but in vain, for no water was to be found. Fatigued and exhausted by thirst, both rider and horse wished for an early halt. We stopped, therefore, and hobbled our horses; and, when I had spread my saddle, my head sank between its flaps,

73

and I slept soundly until the cool night-air, and the brilliant moonlight, awoke me. I found my poor companion, Mr. Calvert, suffering severely from thirst, more so indeed than I did; but I was unfortunately labouring under a most painful diarrhoea, which of itself exhausted my strength. In the morning, to add to our distress, our horses were not to be found, and Mr. Calvert had a walk of four hours to get them: the poor brutes had rambled away in search of water, but found none. The scream of a cockatoo made me wish to continue our ride down the creek; but my companion was so completely exhausted that I resolved upon returning to the camp, but by a different route, passing to the east side of Scott's and Roper's Peaks. We found sandstone ridges to the very foot of the peaks. Although we passed many localities where water might have been expected, and travelled where three different rocks, domite, sandstone, and basalt, came in contact, and where springs are so frequently found, yet not a drop of water could we find. In travelling over the hot plains our horses began to fail us; neither whip nor spur could accelerate their snail-like pace; they seemed to expect that every little shade of the scattered trees would prove a halting-place; and it was not without the greatest difficulty that we could induce them to pass on. It was indeed distressingly hot: with open mouths we tried to catch occasional puffs of a cooler air; our lips and tongue got parched, our voice became hoarse, and our speech unintelligible. Both of us, but particularly my poor companion, were in the most deplorable state. In order to ease my horse, I tried to walk; but, after a few paces. I found it impossible; I was too much exhausted. At this distressing moment, however, we crossed the tracks of horses and bullocks, and then we knew we were near the camp, the sight of which, a short time afterwards, was most welcome to us.

Jan. 29.--Finding that one of the water-holes of the camp had dried up, and that the other was very muddy, we returned to larger water-holes two miles to the south-east. After having done this, I sent Mr. Gilbert and Charley down the creek, to ascertain its course, and to see whether it would be practicable to skirt the highland of peak range to the westward.

Last night thunder-storms were gathering to the south-west, but they did not come up to us. The night breeze is very strong and regular, and sets in invariably between a quarter and half-past eight o'clock; last night it was quite a gale, which I considered to be the indication of a change in the weather, and of rain.

John Murphy brought the flower of a yellow Hibiscus from Roper's Peak: it is certainly a new species.

Jan. 30.--Last night clouds gathered into a thunder-storm to the south-west, but it passed by with very little rain: heavy clouds hung round us, in every direction, but it seemed as if even their passage over the parched plains exhausted their moisture. In the east and south-east a heavy thunder cloud, with incessant lightning, was seen, but so distant that we could not hear the thunder. In the morning, loose clouds spread over the whole sky: this was the first cloudy day we had experienced for the last three weeks. Nature looks quite refreshed; the grass is so green, and the modest blue Ruellia so plentiful; whole fields of Crinum are in full blossom; and the Ironbark and flooded-gum with a denser and richer foliage than usual, afford us a most agreeable shade. I wish I could sufficiently describe the loveliness of the morning just before and after sunrise: the air so clear, so transparent; the sky slightly tinged with roseate hues, all nature so fresh, so calm, so cool. If water were plentiful, the downs of Peak Range would be inferior to no country in the world. Mr. Calvert collected a great number of Limnaea in the water-holes: its shell is more compact than those we have before seen, and has a slight yellow line, marking probably the opening at a younger age. Several insects of the genera Mantis and Truxalis were taken, but did not appear different from those we had previously collected.

Jan. 31.--We had a thunder-storm from the west, and thunder clouds in all quarters; but, as usual, very little rain. Mr. Gilbert returned from his exploratory ride, and stated that the plains extended far to the westward, and that they rose in that direction, forming a succession of terraces; and that another fine range of peaks, even more imposing than those of our Peak Range, reared their heads to the westward of the plains, converging towards the latter [Note at end of para.]; that all the creeks went down to the south and south-west; but that he found no water, except one fine lagoon about fifteen miles to the south-west, which was covered with ducks. He had observed the sign of an anchor, or broad-arrow, cut into a tree with a stone tomahawk, and which he supposed had been done, either by a shipwrecked sailor, or by a runaway convict from Moreton Bay, when it was a penal settlement: the neighbouring trees were variously marked by Blackfellows.

[Note. Captain P. P. King, who surveyed this part of the coast, informs me that the coast hills as seen from the sea, are generally of peaked form, particularly the remarkable elevation of Mount Funnel, at the back of Broad Sound--which is apparently not connected with the neighbouring ranges--and also that of Double Mount, which is visible from a distance of 60 miles. The Cumberland Islands also, which front the coast in the same vicinity, are of peaked shape, and one, Mount Dryander, on the west side of Whitsunday Passage, is a very high peak. In the Appendix to Captain King's Voyage, Dr. Fitton describes the islands, from the specimens which were submitted for his inspection, to be of primitive formation; and notices the following rocks: Compact felspar of a flesh-red hue, enclosing a few small crystals of reddish felspar and of quartz; Coane porphyritic conglomerate of a reddish hue; Serpentine; Slaty clay--which forms the general character of the Percy Islands. Repulse Island produced a compact felspar--a compound of quartz, mica, and felspar, having the appearance of decomposed granite. (King's Voyage, Appendix, p. 607.) Captain King also describes this portion of the coast to be more than usually fertile in appearance; and Captain Blackwood, of Her Majesty's Ship Fly, saw much of this part, and corroborates Captain King's opinion as to its fertility. It is hereabouts that the Araucaria Cunninghamiana grows in such abundance.]

Being too weak to travel, I sent Mr. Roper and Brown to the northward and to the north-east, to examine the country.

By my lunar observations, I made our longitude 148 degrees 19 minutes; our latitude was 22 degrees 57 minutes; so that our distance from Keppel Bay was 175 miles, and from Broad Sound 100. The Mackenzie probably disembogues into Keppel Bay, and if so, it will form the inlet to a fine country; for I suppose that all the creeks going down to the south and south-west, either fall into the Mackenzie itself, or join one of its tributaries.

Mr. Gilbert found the skull of a large kangaroo, the nasal cavity of which appeared unusually spacious. He brought home a new Malurus, and a Rallus: he also shot another species of Rallus on the water-hole near our encampment; he also brought in a true Caprimulgus.

On Mr. Roper's return, he informed me that he had met with a creek at the other side of the hills to the east of us; that the hills were covered with dense scrub, teeming with wallabis; and that the creek went to the north-east, several other creeks joining it; that, lower down, it was lined with Casuarinas, and that about seven miles from the hills, he found fine water-holes.

CHAPTER V

DIFFERENCE OF SOIL AS TO MOISTURE
PHILLIPS'S MOUNTAIN
ALLOWANCE OF FLOUR REDUCED AGAIN
HUGHS'S CREEK
TOMBSTONE CREEK
CHARLEY AND BROWN BECOME UNRULY
THE ISAACS
NATIVE WOMEN
COXEN'S PEAK AND RANGE
GEOLOGICAL CHARACTER
CHARLEY REBELS AGAIN AND LEAVES
BROWN FOLLOWS HIM
BOTH RETURN PENITENT
VARIATIONS OF THE WEATHER
SKULL OF NATIVE
FRIENDLY NATIVES VISIT THE CAMP.

Feb. 2.--Being much recovered, I took both Blackfellows with me, and again passed the defile east of Roper's and Scott's Peaks, and followed the watercourse rising from it to the northward. About two or three miles lower down, we found water in deep rocky basins in the bed of the creek. The rock was sandstone, fissured from south-west to north-east.

In passing the foot of the peaks, we found a species of Grewia (Dwarf Roorajong) covered with ripe fruit; the fruit is dry, but the stringy tissue which covers the seed, contains a slightly sweet and acidulous substance of a very agreeable taste. The fig-tree with a rough leaf, had plenty of fruit, but not yet ripe. Erythrina was both in blossom and in seed.

Sending Brown back to conduct our party to the water-holes we had found, and leaving the creek, which turned to the eastward, I continued my ride to the northward. I passed some gentle well-grassed slopes of narrow-leaved Ironbark and spotted gum; and also several basaltic ridges, which head out into small plains gently sloping to the east and north-east. They are formed of a rich black soil, and generally a shallow creek meanders through them: sandstone ridges formed their boundary lower down, where, at their foot, water-holes generally existed, either with a constant supply of water, or readily filled by thunder-showers. The basaltic ridges, as well as the plains, were covered with a fine crop of dry grass; but the sandstone ridges were frequently scrubby. The difference between the sandstone country and the basaltic plains and ridges, is very striking in respect to the quantity of water they contain: in the latter, rain is immediately absorbed by the cracked porous soil, which requires an immense quantity of moisture before it allows any drainage; whereas the sandstone forms steeper slopes, and does not absorb the rain so quickly, so that the water runs down the slopes, and collects in holes at the foot of the hills parallel to the creeks. Scrubs are frequent round the low rises of sandstone; and, where the country is level, and the soil loamy, the hollows are often filled with water by the thunder-storms. The moist character of this description of country is probably the cause of the vegetation being more dense than it is in the rich black soil of the plains; in which latter, the seeds of the grasses and herbs lie dormant, until the first rain falls, when they instantly germinate and cover the plain with their rapid and luxuriant growth, as if by enchantment; but which, from its nature, is incapable of maintaining the growth of scrubs and trees.

Feb. 3.--The dew was heavy through the night; and, in the morning, loose rainy clouds gathered from the east and north-east, which, however, disappeared about eleven o'clock. Charley went back to the camp, to bring it on, and I continued to reconnoitre to the north-west. After passing a sandstone ridge, I came to a creek, which went to the north-west, and which was supplied with water by the late thunder-showers. It was bounded on both sides by sandstone ridges, whose summits were covered with scrub and Acacia thickets; and by grassy slopes and flats bearing narrow-leaved Ironbark and Bastard-box. This would be a most beautiful country, if it contained a constant supply of water.

I observed on the ridges an Acacia, a small tree, from thirty to forty feet high, and from six to nine inches in diameter, and easily distinguished by its peculiar rough frizzled bark, similar to that of the Casuarina found at the ranges of the Robinson. It has a dark sweet-scented heartwood, like that of the Bricklow and the Myal and other Acacias, which I had previously met with. The creek turned to the north and north-east, into a plain, and joined a larger creek which came in from the right at about south-west. Near their junction, a very conspicuous peak was observed, with several small water-holes with water at its foot. I then returned to the spot to which Charley had been ordered to conduct the camp; but, as the party had not arrived, I feared that some accident might have happened, and therefore rode towards the water-holes from which Brown had gone back to the camp. I found the detention caused by the absence of the horses, which had strayed to the other side of the range.

Feb. 6.--Charley rode my horse after the missing ones, and returned with them about one o'clock to the camp; and then we proceeded about six miles due north, in the direction of a fine mountain of imposing character-- which I called "Phillips's Mountain," after one of my companions--and encamped in sight of Calvert's and Scott's Peaks, the former of which bore S. 22 degrees W., and the latter S. 7 degrees E. Our latitude was 22 degrees 43 minutes.

Acacia farnesiana grew in low shrubs along the plains, stretching its flexible branches over the ground; Mimosa terminalis (the sensitive plant) was very plentiful, and more erect than usual; a species of Verbena, with grey pubescent leaf and stem, was also abundant. The night breeze had been exceedingly strong during the last four days. At the camp of the 4th of February my companions shot twenty-one pigeons (Geophaps scripta), and five cockatoos; a welcome addition to our scanty meals. For a considerable time previous, I had reduced our allowance of flour to three pounds; but now, considering that we were still so far to the eastward, it was, by general consent of my companions, again reduced to a pound and a-half per diem for the six, of which a damper mixed up with fat was made every day, as soon as we reached our encampment.

Feb. 6.--I brought my camp forward about six miles farther to the north-by-east, to the water-holes I had found at the foot of the sandstone ridges; and, after having settled my camp, I went with my two Blackfellows in search of more water. About a mile and a-half north from the camp we came to an isolated peak, which I ascended, and from its summit enjoyed the finest view of the Peak Range I had yet seen. I attempted to sketch it in its whole extent, and gave to its most remarkable peaks separate names. A long flat-topped mountain I called "Lord's Table Range," after E. Lord, Esq., of Moreton Bay; and a sharp needle-like rock, which bore west-by-north, received the name of "Fletcher's Awl," after Mr. John Fletcher, whose kind contribution towards my expedition had not a little cheered me in my undertaking. Towards the east and north-east, a flat country extended, in which the smoke of several fires of the natives was seen, and, in the distance, several blue ranges were distinguished. To the northward, the country was very mountainous, and in the north-west, at a short distance, Phillips's Mountain reared its head. Many shallow valleys, at present of an earth-brown colour, led down from the range. A large creek--which probably collects all the waters that we had passed on the east side of the range, and which I descended during my ride of the 3rd February--flows down a very conspicuous valley to the eastward. I named this creek after--Stephens, Esq., of Darling Downs; and the peak on which I stood after--Campbell, Esq., of the same district. Both these gentlemen had shown the greatest hospitality to me and to my party during our stay at the Downs, before starting on the expedition. The rock of Campbell's Peak is domitic; at the top it is of a bluish colour and very hard, and contains very visible, though minute, crystals of felspar.

In a hollow between the two rocky protuberances on the west side of the hill, a noble fig-tree spread its rich dark-green shady foliage; and on the steep slopes Erythrina was frequent. I could not help contrasting the character of this place with the moist creeks and mountain brushes of the Bunya Bunya country near Moreton Bay, where I had been accustomed to observe the same plant. Proceeding to the N.N.E. we passed several creeks or watercourses, some fine open Ironbark slopes, and a sandstone range; and, following down a watercourse, came to a creek which seemed to originate in Phillips's Mountain. This creek contained water; it flowed to the south-east and east, and very probably joined Stephens's Creek. A rather stunted rusty gum grew plentifully on the sandstone ridges; pebbles of concretionary limestone were found in the creek, probably carried down from the basalt of Phillips's Mountain; and a deposit of concretionary limestone was observed in the banks of a creek, whilst passing one of the black plains, on this side of the range. A profusion of Calcedony, and fine specimens of Agate, were observed in many places, along the basaltic ridges. My black companions loaded themselves with the pretty agates, which they had never seen before, and which they evidently considered to be very valuable; but, after a little time, the weight became inconvenient, and they kept only a few, to strike fire with.

Feb. 7.--Having sent Brown back to guide our party to this creek, which is about six miles N. N. E. from yesterday's camping place, in latitude 22 degrees 32 minutes 27 seconds; I continued my ride with Charley to the north-west. We ascended a high sandstone range, and travelled for some miles along its flat summit. The country was very broken, but openly timbered, and occasionally of a most beautiful character; but frequently interrupted by patches of miserable scrub. Having in our progress brought Mount Phillips to bear south-west and south, we entered a fine open Bastard-box country, with slight undulations, and which seemed to extend to Peak Range. On the sandstone range I found Balfouria saligna R. Br., a shrub or small tree, with long linear-lanceolate leaves, and rather drooping branches, covered with very fragrant yellow blossoms; its seed-vessels varied from three to six inches in length, were terete, tapering to a point, and filled with silky seeds. The same little tree was subsequently observed, growing round the head of the gulf of Carpentaria, and also at Arnheim's Land. Another shrub (Gardenia?), with opposite, oval, rather rough leaves, and large white or light yellow blossoms, like those of the Jasmine in shape and fragrance, had been observed once before, but was very common between this latitude and Port Essington; at which place a species of Guettarda, resembling it very much, but with larger flowers, grows along the beach.

The last two days the mornings were clear; during the afternoon of each day cirrhi formed, which settling down, became confluent, and united into a dark cloud which promised rain, but dispersed towards evening; and the sun set in a cloudless horizon: in the morning, a northerly breeze is generally stirring, which renders that part of the day more agreeable for travelling.

Feb. 8.--I returned last night to the creek, from which I had sent Brown back, and found my companions encamped on a very fine water-hole. This morning we travelled to the water-holes I had seen about seven miles in advance to the north-west, and about five or six miles due north from Phillips's Mountain. After our mid-day meal, I set out again with the two Blackfellows, not only with a view to find water for the next stage, but to endeavour to make the table land again, and thence to pursue a more westerly course.

A great number of sandstone ranges, several of them very steep, and of considerable elevation, stretch parallel to each other from west to east, forming spurs from a higher mountain range to the westward, which is probably connected with Peak Range. It is composed of basalt, and partly covered with dense scrub, and in other parts openly timbered; where the scrub prevailed, the soil was shallow and rocky, but the soil of the open forest was deeper, and of the character of that of the plains. The deep gullies were all without water, but occasionally filled with patches of rich brush. Many creeks went down between the sandstone ranges: and they were generally bounded on both sides by fine well-grassed, narrow-leaved Ironbark slopes, and sweet herbage, on which numerous emus and kangaroos were feeding. In one of the glens among the ridges I observed a new gum-tree, with a leaf like that of the trembling poplar of Europe, and of a bright green colour, which rendered the appearance of the country exceedingly cheerful. It is a middle-sized tree, of irregular growth, with white bark; but the wood, not being free grained, was unfit for splitting. Lower down, water was found, without exception, in all the creeks, and was most abundant at the edge of the level country to the eastward, where the ridges disappear, by more or less gradual slopes. Travelling across these sandstone ranges, with their thick vegetation, and deep gullies and valleys, was exceedingly difficult. The bullocks upset their loads frequently in clambering up and down the rocky slopes, and our progress was consequently very slow. This induced me to give up the westerly course, and to look for a better-travelling country to the eastward; supposing, at the same time, that water would be found more abundant, as we approached the sea-coast.

I, therefore, returned to the camp, and on the 10th February, I travelled about six miles N. N. E., over several ranges and creeks, and came to a creek well supplied with water. On the following day, the 11th February, I travelled down this creek, and reached a flat country of great extent, lightly timbered with

Ironbark, Bastard-box, and Poplar-gum; but the water disappeared in the sandy bed of the creek, which had assumed a very winding course, and we had to encamp on a shallow pool left on the rocks, which, for a short distance, formed again the bed of the creek. Our latitude was 22 degrees 23 minutes, about thirteen miles E. N. E. from our camp of the 8th February.

Feb. 12.--We continued travelling along the creek, and halted at very fine water-holes, within some Bricklow scrub, which here made its appearance again. The stage did not exceed six miles east; but I did not venture to proceed farther until I had examined the country in advance, which did not look very promising. I named this creek "Hughs's Creek," after--Hughs, Esq., of Darling Downs.

The grass-tree grew very abundantly on the rocky sandstone ranges; and the Grevillea (G. ceratophylla, R. Br.?) with pinnatifid leaves, was not less common: on the upper part of Hughs's Creek, we first met with the drooping tea-tree (Melaleuca Leucodendron?), which we found afterwards at every creek and river; it was generally the companion of water, and its drooping foliage afforded an agreeable shade, and was also very ornamental. The slopes towards the flat country were sandy and rotten; but there were some fine hollows, with rich green grass, which very probably formed lagoons during the wet season. The whole country was very similar to that of Zamia Creek: it had the same extensive flats, the same geological features, the same vegetation, the same direction of the creek to the east and north-east. Just before the creek left the hills, it was joined by another; and, at their junction, sandstone cropped out, which was divided by regular fissures into very large rectangular blocks. These fissures had been widened by the action of water, which made them resemble a range of large tombstones, the singular appearance of which induced me to call this, which joins Hughs's Creek, "Tombstone Creek." This formation was very remarkable, and occupied a very considerable space. The strata of the sandstone dip towards the east and north-east off Peak Range; but, in other localities, I observed a dip towards the range.

A circumstance now occurred, which, as it seemed to augur badly for the welfare of our expedition, gave me much concern and anxiety. My two blacks, the companions of my reconnoitring excursions, began to show evident signs of discontent, and to evince a spirit of disobedience which, if not checked, might prove fatal to our safety. During my recent reconnoitre, they both left me in a most intricate country, and took the provisions with them. They had become impatient from having been without water at night; and, in the morning, whilst I was following the ranges, they took the opportunity of diverging from the track, and descended into the gullies; so that I was reluctantly compelled to return to the camp. My companions were highly

82

alarmed at the behaviour of the sable gentlemen, believing that they had concerted a plan to decamp, and leave us to our fate. I knew, however, the cowardly disposition of the Australian native too well; and felt quite sure that they would return after they had procured honey and opossums, in search of which they had deserted me. To impress their minds, therefore, with the conviction that we were independent of their services, the party started the next day as usual, and, on reaching a beautiful valley, three emus were seen on a green sunny slope, strutting about with their stately gait: Mr. Roper immediately laid the dog on, and gave chase. After a short time, the horse returned without its rider and saddle, and caused us a momentary alarm lest some accident had happened to our companion: shortly afterwards, however, we were made glad, by seeing him walking towards us, with a young emu thrown over his shoulder. He had leaped from his horse upon nearing the emus, had shot one in the head, and had taken a young one from the dog, which immediately pursued the third, an old one; but his horse escaped, which compelled him to return on foot, with the smallest of the birds. Messrs. Gilbert and Calvert went in search of the dog, and were fortunate enough to find him with the emu which he had killed. We were rejoiced at our success, and lost no time in preparing a repast of fried emu; and, whilst we were thus employed, the two Blackfellows, having filled their bellies and had their sulk out, made their appearance, both considerably alarmed as to the consequences of their ill-behaviour. Charley brought about a pint of honey as a peace-offering; and both were unusually obliging and attentive to my companions. At this time, I was suffering much pain from a severe kick from one of the bullocks, and felt unequal to inflict any punishment, and therefore allowed the matter to pass with an admonition only. But events subsequently proved that I was wrong, and that a decided and severe punishment would have saved me great trouble. I was, however, glad to find that their conduct met with the general indignation of my companions.

The Blackfellows told us, that they had caught a ring-tailed opossum, and had seen a black kangaroo with a white point at the end of the tail. Brown brought the fruit of a tree, which, according to his account, had the simple pinnate-leaf of the red cedar (Credela) with a dark purple-coloured fruit half an inch long, and one inch in diameter, with a thin astringent pericarp: the stony seed-vessel consisted of many carpels, which, if I remember rightly, were monosperme. It belongs probably to an Ebenaceous tree.

The wood-duck (Bernicla jubata) abounded on the larger water-holes which we passed; and the swamp-pheasant (Centropus Phasianus, GOULD) was heard several times among the trees surrounding the grassy hollows.

The smoke of extensive bush-fires was observed under Lord's Table Range, and along the western and south-western ranges. As we approached the place of our encampment of the 12th February, some Blackfellows were bathing in the water-hole, but fled as soon as we made our appearance.

The night of the 8th February was cloudy, with a little rain, which continued to the morning of the 9th, but cleared up at noon, and the weather became very hot. During the afternoon, thunder-storms passed to the north and north-west, and also to the east and east-south-east. On the 10th, thunder-storms again surrounded us on all sides, and from one, which broke over us in the night, a heavy shower fell. The night of the 11th was exceedingly cold; and the night breeze was observed to be less regular than formerly.

We were here very much troubled with a small black ant; infesting our provisions during the day and running over our persons, and biting us severely at night. A large yellow hornet with two black bands over the abdomen, was seen, humming about the water-holes. A crow was shot and roasted, and found to be exceedingly tender, which we considered to be a great discovery; and lost no opportunity of shooting as many as we could, in order to lessen the consumption of our dried meat. We again enjoyed some fine messes of Portulaca.

Feb. 12.--I went, accompanied by Mr. Roper and Charley, in a due north direction to reconnoitre the country. The flat continued for about eight miles, and then changed into slight undulations. Considerable tracts were covered with the Poplar-gum; and broad belts of Bricklow descended from the hills towards the east. In the scrub; Fusanus was observed in fruit, and the Stenochilus and the white Vitex in blossom; from the latter the native bee extracts a most delicious honey. A small tree, with stiff alternate leaves scarcely an inch long, was covered with red fruit of the form of an acorn, and about half an inch long, having a sweet pericarp with two compressed grain-like seeds, which had the horny albumen of the coffee, and were exceedingly bitter. The pigeons, crows, and cockatoos, fed upon them, we also ate a great number of them; but the edible portion of each seed was very small. It is a remarkable fact that trees, which we had found in full blossom or in fruit in October and November, were again observed to be in blossom and fruit in February.

We had to encamp at night without water; and although the clouds gathered in the afternoon of a very hot day, yet no thunder-storm came to our relief. The night breeze, which was in all probability the sea-breeze, set in about ten minutes to six.

Feb. 13.--The morning was very cloudy. I continued my course to the northward, and, coming to a watercourse, followed it down in the hopes of finding water: it led us to the broad deep channel of a river, but now entirely dry. The bed was very sandy, with reeds and an abundance of small

84

Casuarinas. Large flooded-gums and Casuarinas grew at intervals along its banks, and fine openly timbered flats extended on both sides towards belts of scrub. The river came from the north and north-west, skirting some fine ranges, which were about three miles from its left bank. As the river promised to be one of some importance I called it the "Isaacs," in acknowledgment of the kind support we received from F. Isaacs, Esq. of Darling Downs.

When we were approaching the river, the well-known sound of a tomahawk was heard, and, guided by the noise, we soon came in sight of three black women, two of whom were busily occupied in digging for roots, whilst the other, perched on the top of a high flooded-gum tree, was chopping out either an opossum or a bees' nest. They no sooner perceived us than they began to scream most dreadfully, swinging their sticks, and beating the trees, as if we were wild beasts, which they wished to frighten away. We made every possible sign of peace, but in vain: the two root-diggers immediately ran off, and the lady in the tree refused to descend. When I asked for water, in the language of the natives of the country we had left--"Yarrai" "yarrai," she pointed down the river, and answered "yarrai ya;" and we found afterwards that her information was correct. Upon reaching the tree we found an infant swaddled in layers of tea-tree bark, lying on the ground; and three or four large yams. A great number of natives, men, boys, and children, who had been attracted by the screams of their companions, now came running towards us; but on our putting our horses into a sharp canter, and riding towards them, they retired into the scrub. The yams proved to be the tubers of a vine with blue berries; both tubers and berries had the same pungent taste, but the former contained a watery juice, which was most welcome to our parched mouths. A similar tuber was found near Mount Stewart on the 18th January. We then proceeded down the river; but not succeeding in our search for water, returned to our camp, which was about fifteen miles distant. As soon as I arrived, I sent Mr. Gilbert and Brown down Hughs's Creek, to examine the country near its junction.

Very thick clouds came from the westward, from which a few drops of rain fell: thunder-storms were forming to the north-east and also to the west, but none reached us: the night was very cloudy and warm: the scud flying from the north-east.

Feb. 14.--After sunrise the weather cleared up again. All hands were now employed in shooting crows; which, with some cockatoos, and a small scrub wallabi, gave us several good messes.

Mr. Gilbert and Brown had, on their excursion, found a rushy lagoon on the left bank of the Isaacs, at a short half-mile from its junction with Hughs's Creek. Here they encamped; and, about 10 o'clock at night, the loud voices of

Blackfellows travelling down the river were heard; these also encamped at some small water-holes, not very distant from Mr. Gilbert, of whose presence they were not aware. Mr. Gilbert kept the horses tied up in case of any hostility; but was not molested. The blacks continued their loud conversations during the greater part of the night; and Mr. Gilbert departed very early in the morning without being seen by them. He continued to follow the river further down, and found that four large creeks joined it from the northward. Another creek also joined it from the southward; as subsequently observed by Mr. Roper. Beyond these creeks, several lagoons or swamps were seen covered with ducks, and several other aquatic birds, and, amongst them, the straw-coloured Ibis.

Feb. 15.--We travelled down to the above-mentioned lagoon, which was about ten miles east by north from our camp; its latitude, was by calculation, about 22 degrees 20 or 21; for several circumstances had prevented me from taking observations. As the river turned to the eastward, I determined to trace it up to its head; and set out with Mr. Gilbert and Brown to examine the country around the range which I had observed some days before and named "Coxen's Peak and Range," in honour of Mr. Coxen of Darling Downs. We passed the night at a small pool, but were not successful in discovering water in any of the numerous watercourses and creeks, which come down from Coxen's Range, or out of the belt of scrub which intervened between the range and the river. A loose variegated clayey sandstone, with many irregular holes; cropped out in the beds of the creek. Coxen's Peak and Range were found to be composed of horizontal strata of excellent sandstone, rising by steep terraces, on the western side, but sloping gently down to the east; its summit is covered with scrub, but its eastern slope with groves of grass-trees. The view from the top of Coxen's Peak was very extensive: towards the south-west and west, Peak Range was seen extending from Scott's and Roper's Peaks to Fletcher's Awl; and, beyond the last, other mountains were seen, several of which had flat tops. Mount Phillips seemed about thirty or forty miles distant; and a very indistinct blue hill was seen to the W.N.W. To the northward, ranges rose beyond ranges, and to the eastward, the country seemed to be flat, to a great extent, and bounded by distant mountains. To the southward, the eye wandered over an unbroken line of horizon, with the exception of one blue distant elevation: this immense flat was one uninterrupted mass of forest without the slightest break. Narrow bands of scrub approached the river from the westward, and separated tracts of fine open forest country, amongst which patches of the Poplar-gum forest were readily distinguished by the brightness of their verdure. A river seemed to come from the south-west; the Isaacs came from the north-west, and was joined by a large creek from the northward. There was no smoke, no sign of water, no sign of the neighbourhood of the sea coast;--but all was one immense sea of forest and scrub.

The great outlines of the geology of this interesting country were seen at one glance. Along the eastern edge of a basaltic table land, rose a series of domitic cones, stretching from south-east to north-west, parallel to the coast. The whole extent of country between the range and the coast, seemed to be of sandstone, either horizontally stratified, or dipping off the range; with the exception of some local disturbances, where basalt had broken through it. Those isolated ranges, such as Coxen's Range--the abruptness of which seemed to indicate igneous origin--were entirely of sandstone. The various Porphyries, and Diorites, and Granitic, and Sienitic rocks, which characterize large districts along the eastern coast of Australia, were missing; not a pebble, except of sandstone, was found in the numerous creeks and watercourses. Pieces of silicified wood were frequent in the bed of the Isaacs.

The nature of the soil was easily distinguished by its vegetation: the Bastard box, and Poplar gum grew on a stiff clay; the narrow-leaved Ironbark, the Bloodwood, and the Moreton Bay ash on a lighter sandy soil, which was frequently rotten and undermined with numerous holes of the funnel ant. Noble trees of the flooded-gum grew along the banks of the creeks, and around the hollows, depending rather upon moisture, than upon the nature of the soil. Fine Casuarinas were occasionally met with along the creeks; and the forest oak (Casuarina torulosa), together with rusty-gum, were frequent on the sandy ridges.

One should have expected that the prevailing winds during the day, would have been from the south-east, corresponding to the south-east trade winds; but, throughout the whole journey from Moreton Bay to the Isaacs, I experienced, with but few exceptions, during the day, a cooling breeze from the north and north-east. The thunder-storms came principally from the south-west, west, and north-west; but generally showed an inclination to veer round to the northward.

From Coxen's Range I returned to the river, and soon reached the place where I had met the Black-fellows. In passing out of the belt of scrub into the openly timbered grassy flat of the river, Brown descried a kangaroo sitting in the shade of a large Bastard-box tree; it seemed to be so oppressed by the heat of the noonday sun as to take little notice of us, so that Brown was enabled to approach sufficiently near to shoot it. It proved to be a fine doe, with a young one; we cooked the latter for our dinner, and I sent Brown to the camp with the dam, where my companions most joyfully received him; for all our dried meat was by this time consumed, and all they had for supper and breakfast, were a straw-coloured ibis, a duck, and a crow. As Mr. Gilbert and myself were following the course of the river, we saw numerous tracks of

Blackfellows, of native dogs, of emus, and kangaroos, in its sandy bed; and, when within a short distance of the place where I had seen the black women, loud cries of cockatoos attracted our notice; and, on going in their direction, we came to a water-hole in the bed of the river, at its junction with a large oak tree creek coming from the northward. This water-hole is in latitude 22 degrees 11 minutes; the natives had fenced it round with branches to prevent the sand from filling it up, and had dug small wells near it, evidently to obtain a purer and cooler water, by filtration through the sand. Pigeons (Geophapsscripta, GOULD.) had formed a beaten track to its edge; and, the next morning, whilst enjoying our breakfast under the shade of a gigantic flooded-gum tree, we were highly amused to see a flight of fifty or more partridge pigeons tripping along the sandy bed of the river, and descending to the water's edge, and returning after quenching their thirst, quite unconscious of the dangerous proximity of hungry ornithophagi. The cockatoos, however, observed us, and seemed to dispute our occupation of their waters, by hovering above the tops of the highest trees, and making the air resound with their screams; whilst numerous crows, attracted by a neighbouring bush fire, watched us more familiarly, and the dollar bird passed with its arrow-like flight from shade to shade.

We continued our ride six miles higher up the river, without finding any water, with the exception of some wells made by the natives, and which were generally observed where watercourses or creeks joined the river. In these places, moisture was generally indicated by a dense patch of green reeds. The bush fire, which was raging along the left bank of the river on which we were encamped for the night, fanned by the sea breeze, which set in a little after six o'clock, approached very near to our tent, but died away with the breeze; and the temperature cooled down, although no dew was falling. The fire, which was smouldering here and there along the steep banks of the river, was quickened up again by the morning breeze.

We observed a great number of very large dead shells of Limnaea and Paludina, in the dry water-holes and melon-holes along the scrub; some of them not even bleached; but every thing seemed to indicate this to be a more than usually dry season.

In the morning we returned to the camp. As I had not discovered a more convenient spot for killing another bullock, I decided upon stopping at the rushy lagoon, until we had provided ourselves with a fresh stock of dried beef. Accordingly, on the 17th February, we killed Mr. Gilbert's bullock, which turned out a fine heavy beast, and gave us a large supply of fat meat and suet. We had formerly been under the erroneous impression that fat meat would not dry and keep; and, consequently, had carefully separated the fat from the meat. Some chance pieces, however, had shown us, that it not only dried and kept well, but that it was much finer than the lean meat. We therefore cut up the fat in slices, like the lean; and it was found not only to remain sweet, but to improve with age. The only inconvenience we had experienced in this process, was a longer detention; and we had to remain four days, (to the 21st February) before the provision was fit for packing. On the 19th, immediately after breakfast, whilst we were busily employed in greasing our saddles and straps--a very necessary operation on a journey like ours, where every thing is exposed to the dust, and a scorching sun--Charley left the camp, and did not return before the afternoon. He had frequently acted thus of late; and it was one of the standing complaints against him, that he was opossum and honey hunting, whilst we were kept waiting for our horses and cattle. As I was determined not to suffer this, after his late misbehaviour, I reprimanded him, and told him that I would not allow him any food, should he again be guilty of such conduct. Upon this, he burst out into the most violent and abusive language, and threatened "to stop my jaw," as he expressed himself. Finding it, therefore, necessary to exercise my authority, I approached him to show him out of the camp, when the fellow gave me a violent blow on the face, which severely injured me, displacing two of my lower teeth; upon which my companions interfered, and manifested a determination to support me, in case he should refuse to quit us; which I compelled him to do. When he was going away, Brown told him, in a very consoling manner, that he would come by and bye and sleep with him. I was, however, determined that no one within the camp should have any communication with him; and therefore told Brown, that he had either to stop with me entirely, or with Charley. He answered that he could not quarrel with him; that he would sleep with him, but return every morning; and, when I replied that, in such a case, he should never return, he said that he would stop altogether with Charley, and walked off. If I had punished these fellows for their late misconduct, I should have had no occasion for doing so now: but full of their own importance, they interpreted my forbearance, by fancying that I could not proceed without them.

Previous to this occurrence, Charley had, during my absence from the camp, had an interview with the natives, who made him several presents, among which were two fine calabashes which they had cleaned and used for carrying water; the larger one was pear-shaped, about a foot in length, and nine inches in diameter in the broadest part, and held about three pints. The natives patted his head, and hair, and clothing; but they retired immediately, when he afterwards returned to them, accompanied by Mr. Calvert on horseback.

We started, on the 21st February, from our killing camp, and travelled a long stage; the day was very hot, and the heat of the rotten ground was intense. Our little terrier, which had so well borne former fatigues, died; and our remaining kangaroo-dog was only saved by Mr. Calvert's carrying him on his horse. It was a day well calculated to impress on the Blackfellows the difference between riding and walking, between finding a meal ready after a fatiguing journey, and looking out for food for themselves. Hearing Brown's cooee as we were travelling along, Mr. Roper stopped behind until Brown came up to him, and expressed his desire to rejoin my party, as he had had quite enough of his banishment and bush life; and, before sunset, he arrived quite exhausted at our camping-place, and begged me to pardon him, which I did, under the former condition, that he was to have no farther communication with Charley, to which he most willingly assented.

Feb. 22.--On a ride with Mr. Gilbert up the river, we observed several large reedy holes in its bed, in which the Blackfellows had dug wells; they were still moist, and swarms of hornets were buzzing about them. About eight miles north-west from the junction of North Creek with the river, a large flight of cockatoos again invited us to some good water-holes extending along a scrubby rise. Large Bastard-box flats lie between North Creek and the river. About four miles from the camp, the country rises to the left of the river, and ranges and isolated hills are visible, which are probably surrounded by plains. Wherever I had an opportunity of examining the rocks, I found sandstone; flint pebbles and fossil-wood are in the scrub and on the melon-hole flats.

At night, on my return, I had to pass Charley's camp, which was about a hundred yards from ours. He called after me, and, when I stopped, he came up to me, and began to plead his cause and beg my pardon; he excused his sulkiness and his bad behaviour by his temperament and some misunderstanding; and tried to look most miserable and wretched, in order to excite my compassion. My companions had seen him sitting alone under his tree, during almost the whole day, beating his bommerangs which he had received from the natives. I pitied him, and, after some consultation with my companions, allowed him to rejoin us; but upon the condition that he should give up his tomahawk, to which he most joyfully consented, and promised for the future to do every thing I should require. His spirit was evidently broken, and I should probably never have had to complain of him again, had no other agent acted upon him.

Feb. 23.--I moved on to the water-holes, which I had found the day before, and encamped in the shade of a Fusanus. The latitude was observed to be 22 degrees 6 minutes 53 seconds.

Feb. 24.--Mr. Gilbert and Brown accompanied me this morning upon an excursion. At about a mile and a-half from the camp, a large creek, apparently from the southward, joined the river, and water was found in a scrub creek four miles from the camp, also in wells made by the natives in the bed of the river; and, at about eight miles from the camp, we came upon some fine water-holes along the scrub. Here the birds were very numerous and various; large flights of the blue-mountain and crimson-winged parrots were seen; Mr. Gilbert observed the female of the Regent-bird, and several other interesting birds, which made him regret to leave this spot so favourable to his pursuit. He returned, however, to bring forward our camp to the place, whilst I continued my ride, accompanied by Brown. Several creeks joined the river, but water was nowhere to be found. The high grass was old and dry, or else so entirely burnt as not to leave the slightest sign of vegetation. For several miles the whole forest was singed by a fire which had swept through it; and the whole country looked hopelessly wretched. Brown had taken the precaution to fill Charley's large calabash with water, so that we were enabled to make a refreshing cup of tea in the most scorching heat of the day. Towards sunset we heard, to our great joy, the noisy jabbering of natives, which promised the neighbourhood of water. I dismounted and cooeed; they answered; but when they saw me, they took such of their things as they could and crossed to the opposite side of the river in great hurry and confusion. When Brown, who had stopped behind, came up to me, I took the calabash and put it to my mouth, and asked for "yarrai, yarrai." They answered, but their intended information was lost to me; and they were unwilling to approach us. Their camp was in the bed of the river amongst some small Casuarinas. Their numerous tracks, however, soon led me to two wells, surrounded by high reeds, where we quenched our thirst. My horse was very much frightened by the great number of hornets buzzing about the water. After filling our calabash, we returned to the camp of the natives, and examined the things which they had left behind; we found a shield, four calabashes, of which I took two, leaving in their place a bright penny, for payment; there were also, a small water-tight basket containing acacia-gum; some unravelled fibrous bark, used for straining honey; a fire-stick, neatly tied up in tea-tree bark; a kangaroo net; and two tomahawks, one of stone, and a smaller one of iron, made apparently of the head of a hammer: a proof that they had had some communication with the sea-coast. The natives had disappeared. The thunder was pealing above us, and a rush of wind surprised us before we were half-a-mile from the camp, and we had barely time to throw our blanket over some sticks and creep under it, when the rain came down in torrents. The storm came from the west; another was visible in the east; and lightning seemed to be everywhere. When the rain ceased, we contrived to make a fire and boil a pot of tea, and warmed up a mess of gelatine-soup. At eight o'clock the moon rose, and, as the weather had cleared, I decided upon returning to the camp, in order to hasten over this dreary country while the rain-water lasted. The frogs were most lustily croaking in the water-holes which I had passed, a few hours before, perfectly dry and never were their hoarse voices more pleasing to me. But the thunder-storm had been so very partial, that scarcely a drop had fallen at a distance of three miles. This is another instance of the singularly partial distribution of water, which I had before noticed at Comet Creek. We arrived at the camp about one o'clock a.m.; and, in the morning of the 25th February, I led my party to the water-holes, which a kind Providence seemed to have filled for the purpose of helping us over that thirsty and dreary land. Our bullocks suffered severely from the heat; our fat-meat melted; our fat-bags poured out their contents; and every thing seemed to dissolve under the influence of a powerful sun.

The weather in this region may be thus described: at sunrise some clouds collect in the east, but clear off during the first hours of the morning, with northerly, north-easterly, and easterly breezes; between ten and three o'clock the most scorching heat prevails, interrupted only by occasional puffs of cool air; about two o'clock P.M. heavy clouds form in all directions, increase in volume, unite in dark masses in the east and west, and, about five o'clock in the afternoon, the thunder-storm bursts; the gust of wind is very violent, and the rain sometimes slight, and at other times tremendous, but of short duration; and at nine o'clock the whole sky is clear again.

In the hollows along the Isaacs, we found a new species of grass from six to eight feet high, forming large tufts, in appearance like the oat-grass (Anthistiria) of the Liverpool Plains and Darling Downs; it has very long brown twisted beards, but is easily distinguished from Anthistiria by its simple ear; its young stem is very sweet, and much relished both by horses and cattle.

Feb. 26.--I set out reconnoitring with Mr. Gilbert and Charley. We found that the effects of the thunder-storm of the 24th extended very little to the north and north-west, having passed over from west to east. From time to time we crossed low ridges covered with scrub, and cut through by deep gullies, stretching towards the river, which became narrower and very tortuous in its course; its line of flooded-gum trees, however, became more dense. Within the reedy bed of the river, not quite five miles from the camp, we found wells of the natives, not a foot deep, but amply supplied with water, and, at four miles farther, we came to a water-hole, in a small creek, which had been supplied by the late rains; we also passed several fine scrub creeks, but they were dry. About ten miles from the wells another deep scrub creek was found, on the right hand of the river, full of water. Its bed was overgrown with reeds, and full of pebbles of concretions of limestone, and curious trunks of fossil trees, and on its banks a loose sandstone cropped out. Here we found the skull of a native, the first time that we had seen the remains of a human body during our journey. Near the scrub, and probably in old camping places of the natives, we frequently saw the bones of kangaroos and emus. I mention this fact in reference to the observations of American travellers, who very rarely met with bones in the wilderness; and to remark, that the climate of Australia is so very dry as to prevent decomposition, and that rapacious animals are few in number--the native dog probably finding a sufficiency of living food.

On the 25th there were thunder-storms, but they did not reach us. The night was cloudy, and we had some few drops of rain in the morning of the 26th, but the weather cleared up about ten o'clock; cumuli formed in the afternoon, and towards night thunder-storms were observed both in the east and west. I found a shrubby prickly Goodenia, about four or five feet high, growing on the borders of the scrub.

Feb. 27.--Mr. Gilbert, whom I had sent back from the wells of the natives to bring on the camp, had been prevented from doing so, and I had consequently to return the whole distance. The interruption was caused by our bullocks having gone back several miles, probably in search of better water, for we found them generally very nice in this particular.

The natives had, in my absence, visited my companions, and behaved very quietly, making them presents of emu feathers, bommerangs, and waddies. Mr. Phillips gave them a medal of the coronation of her Majesty Queen Victoria, which they seemed to prize very highly. They were fine, stout, well made people, and most of them young; but a few old women, with white circles painted on their faces, kept in the back ground. They were much struck with the white skins of my companions, and repeatedly patted them in admiration. Their replies to inquiries respecting water were not understood; but they seemed very anxious to induce us to go down the river.

We started at noon to Skull Creek, which, in a straight line, was fourteen miles distant, in a north by east direction. Loose cumuli floated in the hazy atmosphere during the whole forenoon, but rose in the afternoon, and occasionally sheltered us from the scorching sun. At four o'clock two thunder-storms formed as usual in the east and west, and, eventually rising above us, poured down a heavy shower of rain, which drenched us to the skin, and refreshed us and our horses and bullocks, which were panting with heat and thirst. Our stores were well covered with greasy tarpaulings, and took no harm.

Feb. 28.--Successive thunder-storms, with which this spot seemed more favoured than the country we had recently passed, had rendered the vegetation very luxuriant. The rotten sandy ground absorbed the rain rapidly, and the young grass looked very fresh. The scrub receded a little more from the river, and an open country extended along its banks. The scene was, therefore, most cheerful and welcome. Mr. Gilbert and Charley, who had made an excursion up the river in search of water, returned with the agreeable information that a beautiful country was before us: they had also seen a camp of natives, but without having had any intercourse with them.

93

Feb. 29.--It was cloudy in the morning, and became more so during the day, with easterly and north-easterly winds. As soon as our capricious horses were found, which had wandered more than eight miles through a dense Bricklow scrub, in search of food and water, we started and travelled about ten miles in a north-east direction, leaving the windings of the river to the left. The character of the country continued the same; the same Ironbark forest, with here and there some remarkably pretty spots; and the same Bastard-box flats, with belts of scrub, approaching the river. At about nine miles from Skull Creek, which I supposed to be in latitude 21 degrees 42 minutes, the Isaacs breaks through a long range of sandstone hills; beyond which the country opens into plains with detached patches of scrub, and downs, with "devil-devil" land and its peculiar vegetation, and into very open forest. The river divides into two branches, one coming from the eastward, and the other from the northward. It rained hard during our journey, and, by the time we reached the water-hole which Mr. Gilbert had found, we were wet to the skin.

In consequence of the additional fatigues of the day, I allowed some pieces of fat to be fried with our meat. Scarcely a fortnight ago, some of my companions had looked with disgust on the fat of our stews, and had jerked it contemptuously out of their plates; now, however, every one of us thought the addition of fat a peculiar favour, and no one hesitated to drink the liquid fat, after having finished his meat. This relish continued to increase as our bullocks became poorer; and we became as eager to examine the condition of a slaughtered beast, as the natives, whose practice in that respect we had formerly ridiculed.

As I had made a set of lunar observations at Skull camp, which I wished to calculate, I sent Mr. Roper up the north branch of the Isaacs to look for water; and, on his return, he imparted the agreeable intelligence, that he had found fine holes of water at about nine or ten miles distant, and that the country was still more open, and abounded with game, particularly emus.

CHAPTER VI

HEADS OF THE ISAACS
THE SUTTOR
FLINT-ROCK
INDICATIONS OF WATER
DINNER OF THE NATIVES APPROPRIATED BY US
EASTER SUNDAY
ALARM OF AN OLD WOMAN
NATIVES SPEAKING A LANGUAGE ENTIRELY UNKNOWN TO
CHARLEY AND BROWN
A BARTER WITH THEM
MOUNT M'CONNEL.

I was detained at this place from the 1st to the 4th March, from a severe attack of lumbago, which I had brought on by incautiously and, perhaps, unnecessarily exposing myself to the weather, in my botanical and other pursuits. On the 4th March. I had sufficiently recovered to mount my horse and accompany my party to Roper's water-holes. Basalt cropped out on the plains; the slight ridges of "devil-devil" land are covered with quartz pebbles, and the hills and bed of the river, are of sandstone formation.

A yellow, and a pink Hibiscus, were frequent along the river.

My calculations gave the longitude of 148 degrees 56 minutes for Skull Creek; my bearings however make it more to the westward; its latitude was supposed to be 21 degrees 42 minutes: the cloudy nights prevented my taking any observation.

March 5.--I sent Mr. Gilbert and Charley up the river, which, according to Mr. Roper's account, came through a narrow mountain gully, the passage of which was very much obstructed by tea-trees. They passed the mountain gorge, and, in about eight miles north, came to the heads of the Isaacs, and to those of another system of waters, which collected in a creek that flowed considerably to the westward. The range through which the Isaacs passes is composed of sandstone, and strikes from north-west to south-east. In its rocky caves, wallabies, with long smooth tails, had been seen by Brown; they were quite new to him, and, as he expressed himself, "looked more like monkeys than like wallabies." Mr. Gilbert and Charley came on two flocks of emus, and killed two young ones; and Charley and John Murphy hunted down another;

Charley fell, however, with his horse, and broke a double-barrelled gun, which was a very serious loss to us, and the more so, as he had had the misfortune to break a single-barrelled one before this.

The weather continued showery; loose scud passed over from the east and south-east, with occasional breaks of hot sunshine. The Corypha palm is frequent under the range; the Ebenaceous tree, with compound pinnate leaves and unequilateral leaflets, is of a middle size, about thirty feet high, with a shady and rather spreading crown.

We have travelled about seventy miles along the Isaacs. If we consider the extent of its Bastard-box and narrow-leaved Ironbark flats, and the silver-leaved Ironbark ridges on its left bank, and the fine open country between the two ranges through which it breaks, we shall not probably find a country better adapted for pastoral pursuits. There was a great want of surface water at the season we passed through it; and which we afterwards found was a remarkably dry one all over the colony: the wells of the natives, however, and the luxuriant growth of reeds in many parts of the river, showed that even shallow wells would give a large supply to the squatter in cases of necessity; and those chains of large water-holes which we frequently met along and within the scrubs, when once filled, will retain their water for a long time. The extent of the neighbouring scrubs will, however, always form a serious drawback to the squatter, as it will be the lurking place and a refuge of the hostile natives, and a hiding place for the cattle, which would always retire to it in the heat of the day, or in the morning and evening, at which time the flies are most troublesome.

March 7.--I moved my camp through the mountain gorge, the passage of which was rather difficult, in consequence of large boulders of sandstone, and of thickets of narrow-leaved tea-trees growing in the bed of the river. To the northward, it opens into fine gentle Ironbark slopes and ridges, which form the heads of the Isaacs. They seem to be the favourite haunts of emus; for three broods of them were seen, of ten, thirteen, and even sixteen birds. About four miles from the gorge, we came to the heads of another creek, which I called "Suttor Creek" after --Suttor, Esq., who had made me a present of four bullocks when I started on this expedition; four or five miles farther down we found it well supplied with fine water-holes. Here, however, patches of scrub again appeared. The ridges were covered with iron-coloured quartz pebbles, which rendered our bullocks footsore. The marjoram was abundant, particularly near the scrubs, and filled the air with a most exquisite odour. A mountain range was seen to the right; and, where the ranges of the head of the Isaacs abruptly terminated, detached hills and ridges formed the south-western and southern barrier of the waters of Suttor Creek.

March 8.--As we followed the creek about nine miles farther down, it became broader, and the Casuarinas were more frequent. Its bed was sandy, occasionally filled with reeds, and contained numerous water-holes, particularly where the sandstone rock formed more retentive basins.

During the last two days we had drizzling rain, which cleared up a little about noon and at night. The weather was delightfully cool; the wind was very strong from the eastward. I sent Mr. Roper forward to look for water, of which he found a sufficient supply. He stated that the country to the westward opened into fine plains, of a rich black soil; but it was very dry. The bluff terminations of the left range bore E. by S., and that on the right E.N.E.

March 9.--We moved to the water-holes found yesterday by Mr. Roper. On our way we crossed a large scrub creek, coming from the northward and joining Suttor Creek, which turned to the westward, and even W. by S. and W.S.W.

Mr. Gilbert and Charley made an excursion to the westward, in which direction Mr. Roper had seen a distant range, at the foot of which I expected to find a large watercourse. Wind continued from the east and south-east; about the middle of last night we had some rain.

A slender snake, about five feet long, of a greyish brown on the back, and of a bright yellow on the belly, was seen nimbly climbing a tree. The head was so much crushed in killing it that I could not examine its teeth.

Mr. Roper and John Murphy succeeded in shooting eight cockatoos, which gave us an excellent soup. I found in their stomachs a fruit resembling grains of rice, which was slightly sweet, and would doubtless afford an excellent dish, if obtained in sufficient quantity and boiled.

March 10.--We had slight drizzling showers towards sunset; the night very cloudy till about ten a.m., when it cleared up. The variety of grasses is very great; the most remarkable and succulent were two species of Anthistiria, the grass of the Isaacs, and a new one with articulate ears and rounded glumes. A pink Convolvulus, with showy blossoms, is very common. Portulaca, with terete leaves, grows sparingly on the mild rich soil.

Were a superficial observer suddenly transported from one of the reedy ponds of Europe to this water-hole in Suttor Creek, he would not be able to detect the change of his locality, except by the presence of Casuarinas and the white trunks of the majestic flooded-gum. Reeds, similar to those of Europe, and Polygonums almost identical as to species, surround the water, the surface of which is covered with the broad leaves of Villarsia, exactly resembling those of Nymphaea alba, and with several species of Potomogeton. Small grey birds, like the warblers of the reeds, flit from stem to stem; hosts of brilliant gyrinus play on the water; notonectes and beetles, resembling the hydrophili, live within it--now rising to respire, now swiftly diving. Limnaea, similar to those of Europe, creep along the surface of the water; small Planorbis live on the water-plants, to which also adhere Ancylus; and Paludina, Cyclas, and Unio, furrow its muddy bottom. The spell, however, must not be broken by the noisy call of a laughing jackass (Dacelo gigantea); the screams of the white cockatoo; or by the hollow sound of the thirsty emu. The latitude of this spot was 21 degrees 23 minutes S.

I examined the country northward for about five miles, crossing some small undulating or hilly downs of a rich black soil, where the Phonolith frequently cropped out. There were occasional tracts of "devil-devil" land, and patches of scrub, which, at no great distance, united into one mass of Bricklow. Tracing a little creek to its head, I crossed ridges with open forest. Mr. Gilbert and Charley returned, after having found, as I anticipated, a considerable watercourse at the foot of the westerly range. Suttor Creek was afterwards found to join this watercourse, and, as it was its principal tributary, the name was continued to the main stream.

March 12.--In travelling to Mr. Gilbert's discovery, we crossed large plains, and, at the end of six miles, entered into thick scrub, which continued with little interruption until we reached the dry channel of the Suttor. This scrub, like those already mentioned, varies in density and in its composition; the Bricklow acacia predominates; but, in more open parts, tufts of Bauhinia covered with white blossoms, and patches of the bright green Fusanus and silvery Bricklow, formed a very pleasing picture. The bed of the Suttor was rather shallow, sandy, and irregular, with occasional patches of reeds; its left bank was covered with scrub; but well grassed flats, with Bastard-box and Ironbark, were on its right. We encamped near a fine reedy water-hole, nearly half a mile long, in lat. 21 degrees 21 minutes 36 seconds. We had travelled about fifteen miles west by north from our last camp. Throughout the day the weather was cloudy and rainy, which rendered the tedious passage through the scrub more bearable.

March 13.--We proceeded six or seven miles down the river, in a S.S.W. course. The flats continued on its right side, but rose at a short distance into low ridges, covered either with scrub or with a very stunted silver-leaved Ironbark. On one of the flats we met with a brood of young emus, and killed three of them. The morning was bright; cumuli gathered about noon, and the afternoon was cloudy. The wind was from the eastward. The Suttor is joined, in lat. 21 degrees 25 minutes, by a large creek from the N.W. From the ridges on the left bank of the creek I obtained an extensive view. The bluff termination of the ranges on the head of the Isaacs bore N. 55 degrees E. Many high ranges were seen towards the north and north-east. Towards the south the horizon was broken only by some very distant isolated mountains. Peak Range was not visible. A group of three mountains appeared towards the north-west; one of them had a flat top. The whole country to the westward was formed of low ridges, among which the Suttor seemed to shape its winding course. The hills on which we stood, as well as the banks of the creek, were composed of flint-rock. Pebbles and blocks of Pegmatite covered the bed of the creek. This rock also cropped out along the river. This was the first time since leaving Moreton Bay that we met with primitive rocks, and I invite the attention of geologists to the close connection of the flint rock with granitic rocks; which I had many opportunities of observing in almost every part of the northern and western falls of the table land of New England.

A Melaleuca with very small decussate leaves, a tree about twenty-five feet high, was growing on the scrubby ridges. Flooded-gums of most majestic size, and Casuarinas, grew along the river; in which there were many large reedy water-holes. The season must be more than usually dry, some of the largest holes containing only shallow pools, which were crowded with small fishes, seemingly gasping for rain. A Ruellia, with large white and blue flowers, adorned the grassy flats along the Suttor. The latitude of this spot was 21 degrees 26 minutes 36 seconds.

March 14.--We removed down the river about eight miles S. S. W. to good water-holes, which had been seen by my companions the day before. Here the scrub approached the river, leaving only a narrow belt of open forest, which was occasionally interrupted by low ridges of stunted silver-leaved Ironbark. Pegmatite and Porphyry (with a very few small crystals of felspar) and Gneiss? were observed in situ. On our way we passed a fine lagoon. A dry but not hot wind blew from the S. S. W.; the night and morning were bright; cumuli with sharp margins hung about after eleven o'clock.

A pelican was seen flying down the river, and two native companions and an ibis were at the water-holes. Crows, cockatoos, and ducks were frequent. From the remains of mussels about these water-holes, the natives have enjoyed many recent meals.

I sent Mr. Roper and Charley down the river, who informed me, on their return late at night, that they had found water at different distances; the farthest they reached was distant about seventeen miles, in a water-hole near the scrub; but the bed of the river was dry. As they rode, one on the right and the other on the left side of the river, a Blackfellow hailed Charley and approached him, but when he saw Mr. Roper--who crossed over upon being called--he immediately climbed a tree, and his gin, who was far advanced in pregnancy, ascended another. As Mr. Roper moved round the base of the tree, in order to look the Blackfellow in the face, and to speak with him, the latter studiously avoided looking at Mr. Roper, by shifting round and round the trunk like an iguana. At last, however, he answered to the inquiry for water, by pointing to the W. N. W. The woman also kept her face averted from the white man. Proceeding farther down the river they saw natives encamped at a water-hole, who, as soon as they became aware of the approach of the two horsemen, withdrew with the greatest haste into the scrub; the men driving the shrieking women and children before them. Upon Mr. Roper galloping after them, one athletic fellow turned round and threatened to throw his bommerang, at this sign of hostility Mr. Roper prudently retired. Kangaroo and other nets made of some plant and not of bark, koolimans, bommerangs, waddies, and a fine opossum cloak were found at the camp, but were left untouched by our companions.

March 15.--Our party moved to the water-holes, where Mr. Roper had seen the natives; the latter had removed their property, and were not afterwards heard or seen by any of us. The general course of the river was about south-west, and is joined by several scrub creeks; its bed is broad and shallow, with numerous channels, separated by bergues; and the river itself is split into several anabranches. The scrub is generally an open Vitex; a fine drooping tea-tree lines the banks of the river; Casuarina disappears; the flooded-gum is frequent, but of smaller size. The Mackenzie-bean and several other papilionaceous plants, with some new grasses, grow in it. The most interesting plant, however, is a species of Datura, from one to two feet high, which genus has not previously been observed in Australia. I also found species of Heliotropium of a most fragrant odour.

Sandstone cropped out in several places, and red quartz pebbles were very abundant in some parts of the river; the sands of its bed are so triturated that no one would ever surmise the existence of granitic rocks, at sixteen or twenty miles higher up. The whole country was flat; no hill was visible, but, towards the end of our day's journey, we crossed a few slight undulations.

During the night of the 14th, southerly winds were followed by a gale from the eastward, with scud and drizzling rain. The morning of the 15th was cloudy with a little rain; wind southerly. Early in the night, a strong east-wind with drizzling long rain set in, but cleared up at midnight. The morning of the 16th was cloudy, with a southerly wind. Our lat. was 21 degrees 39 minutes 58 seconds.

March 17.--Mr. Gilbert and Brown went forward in search of water, supposing that they would find it at a convenient distance, but were unsuccessful, and, as they had taken neither guns nor provisions, they were obliged to return. Keeping, however, a little more to the left, on their return, they came to two fine water-holes at the foot of some ironstone ridges, where they passed the night, and reached the camp the following day, having had nothing to eat for twenty-four hours. The camp was then moved to these water-holes, about nine miles off, in a due west course. Fine water-holes were passed at a short half-mile from our camp; and, after crossing the northern anabranch of the river, we again found water.

The detection of isolated water-holes in a wooded country, where there is nothing visible to indicate its presence, is quite a matter of chance. We have often unconsciously passed well-filled water-holes, at less than a hundred yards distant, whilst we were suffering severely from thirst. Our horses and bullocks never showed that instinctive faculty of detecting water, so often mentioned by other travellers; and I remember instances, in which the bullocks have remained the whole night, not fifty yards from water-holes, without finding them; and, indeed, whenever we came to small water-holes, we had to drive the cattle down to them, or they would have strayed off to find water elsewhere. On several occasions I followed their tracks, and observed they were influenced entirely by their sight when in search of it; at times attracted by a distant patch of deeper verdure, at others following down a hollow or a watercourse, but I do not recollect a single instance where they found water for themselves. The horses, however, were naturally more restless and impatient, and, when we approached a creek or a watercourse after a long journey, would descend into the bed and follow it for long distances to find water; giving great trouble to those who had to bring them back to the line of march. Whenever they saw me halt at the place where I intended to encamp, they not only quickened their pace, but often galloped towards me, well knowing that I had found water, and that they were to be relieved of their loads. In looking for water, my search was first made in the neighbourhood of hills, ridges, and ranges, which from their extent and elevation were most likely to lead me to it, either in beds of creeks, or rivers, or in water-holes, parallel to them. In an open country, there are many indications which a practised eye will readily seize: a cluster of trees of a greener foliage, hollows with luxuriant grass, eagles circling in the air, crows, cockatoos, pigeons (especially before sunset), and the call of Grallina Australis and flocks of little finches, would always attract our attention. The margins of scrubs were generally provided with chains of holes. But a flat country, openly timbered, without any break of the surface or of the forest, was by no means encouraging; and I have frequently travelled more than twenty-five miles in a straight line without obtaining my object, In coming on creeks, it required some experience in the country, to know whether to travel up or down the bed: some being well provided with water immediately at the foot of the range, and others being entirely dry at their upper part, but forming large puddled holes, lower down, in a flat country. From daily experience, we acquired a sort of instinctive feeling as to the course we should adopt, and were seldom wrong in our decisions.

The ridges, near the water-holes on which we were encamped, are composed of an igneous rock containing much iron, with which the water was impregnated to such a degree, that our tea turned quite black and inky. The natives were very numerous in these parts, and their tracks were everywhere visible. They had even followed the tracks of Mr. Gilbert's and Brown's horses of the preceding day.

The night was bright; the day cloudy, and the wind easterly. I went with Charley, in the afternoon of the 17th, to examine the extent of the scrubby country, of which Mr. Gilbert had given us so poor an account. The channel of the river became narrow and deep, with steep banks, as it enters the scrub, and there the flooded gums entirely disappeared. The scrub is about eight miles long, and from two to three miles broad, and is tolerably open. The Bricklow is here a real tree, but of stunted growth, with regularly fissured bark, like that of the Ironbark (Eucalyptus resinifera). It has long broad falcate phyllodia, whilst another species of the same size has an irregular scaly bark, with small phyllodia, but of a greyer colour than those of the common Bricklow. Both species grow promiscuously together. Where the river left the scrub, it entered into a wild water-worn box flat, and cut up into several irregular channels, lined by a dense thicket of narrow-leaved Melaleucas of stunted growth and irregular shapes. The Box-tree itself is here a different species, the bark has deeper fissures, and the young wood is very yellow. I shall distinguish it by the name of "Water-box," as it grows exclusively near creeks, or on the neighbouring flats. I first observed it at the Mackenzie; its bark strips freely, but the stem is too short and irregular to be of any use.

In passing a low hill, at the foot of which the box-flat commenced, we came on a very distinct path of the natives, which led us to a deep water-hole, covered with luxuriant grass; containing but a small quantity of water. Farther on we came to a second hole better supplied, and to a third; and at last Charley cried out, "Look there, Sir! what big water!" and a long broad sheet of water stretched in sweeps through a dense Bauhinia and Bricklow scrub, which covered its steep banks. It is a singular character of this remarkable country, that extremes so often meet; the most miserable scrub, with the open plain and fine forest land; and the most paralysing dryness, with the finest supply of water.

Swarms of ducks covered the margin of the lake; pelicans, beyond the reach of shot, floated on its bosom; land-turties plunged into its waters; and shags started from dead trees lying half immersed, as we trod the well-beaten path of the natives along its banks. The inhabitants of this part of the country, doubtless, visit this spot frequently, judging from the numerous heaps of

102

muscle-shells. This fine piece of water, probably in the main channel of the Suttor, is three miles long, and is surrounded with one mass of scrub, which opens a little at its north-western extremity.

March 10.--I continued my ride, ten or twelve miles down the river; the scrub continued, but the immediate neighbourhood became a little more open; several trees were observed, that had been recently cut by the natives in search of honey or opossums. Emus were very numerous; sometimes a solitary bird, and at others two, three, four, and up to thirteen together, were seen trotting off in long file, and now and then stopping to stare at us. We caught a bandicoot with two young ones, which gave us an excellent luncheon. When we left the lake, Charley thought he could distinguish a plain to the northward; and, riding in that direction, I was agreeably surprised to find that the scrub did not extend more than a mile and a-half from the river; and that, beyond it, plains and open forest extended far to the northward; and fine ridges with most excellent feed, to the southward. The traveller who is merely following the course of a river, is unable to form a correct idea of the country farther off, unless hills are near, from which he may obtain extensive views. At the water-worn banks of the Mackenzie, I little expected that we were in the vicinity of a country like that of Peak Range; and I am consequently inclined to believe that much more available land exists along the banks of the Suttor, where its valley is covered with scrub, than we know anything about.

March 19.--The camp was removed to the lake of the Suttor, about twelve miles and a-half N. 80 degrees W. We chased a flock of emus, but without success; four of my companions went duck-shooting, but got very few; the others angled, but nothing would bite.

The day was cloudy; some drizzling rain fell in the morning; the night was clear. Lat. 21 degrees 37 minutes 31 minutes.

During my absence, my companions found a quantity of implements and ornaments of the natives, in the neighbourhood of our last camp.

On the plains I found two new species of Sida; and, on the tea-trees, a new form of Loranthus, with flowers in threes on a broad leafy bract, scarcely distinguishable from the real leaves.

March 20.--We travelled down to the water-holes, at which I had turned back. Sandstone rock cropped out on several spots, and pieces of broken quartz were strewed over the ground. All the water-holes along the low ridges and within the bed of the river, were full of water; and the district seemed to be one of those which, from their peculiar conformation of surface, are more frequently favoured by thunder-storms. Native companions flew down the river, and flights of ducks held their course in the same direction. With the

103

hope of finding a good supply of water lower down, we continued our journey on the 21st March. The creek frequently divided into channels, forming large islands of a mile and a mile and a-half in length, covered with scrub, and over which freshes had swept. All at once, the water disappeared; the deepest holes were dry; the Melaleucas were not to be found; the flooded-gums became very rare, and the rich green grass was replaced by a scanty wiry grass. The whole river seemed to divide into chains of dry water-holes, scarcely connected by hollows. Two miles farther we came to a fine large water-hole, surrounded by Polygonums and young water-grass, and, at two miles farther, to another, and in about the same distance to a third. Recent camps of the natives were on each of them, and a beaten path led from one to the other. One of these holes was crossed by a weir made of sticks for catching fish. Bones of large fish, turtle shells, and heaps of muscles, were strewed round the fire places.

The whole day was bright and very hot; the wind in the afternoon from E.S.E. The latitude of our last camp was 21 degrees 31 minutes 16 seconds, being about eighteen miles W.N.W. from the lake.

Mr. Roper and Brown rode about seven miles down the river, and found that it again formed a large regular bed well supplied with water; and that the country was of a more open character. They came suddenly upon two women cooking mussels, who ran off, leaving their dinners to their unwelcome visitors, who quickly dispatched the agreeable repast; farther on they saw four men, who were too shy to approach. Charley also, whilst bringing in the horses on the morning of the 22nd, passed a numerous camp, who quietly rose and gazed at him, but did not utter a single word.

I travelled with my party to the water-holes found by Mr. Roper; on approaching them, we crossed an extensive box-flat, near that part of the river where it is split into collateral chains of holes. Talc-schiste cropped out at the latter part of the journey; its strata were perpendicular, and their direction from north-west to south-east; its character was the same as that of Moreton Bay and New England; numerous veins of quartz intersected the rock.

The water-holes were surrounded by high Polygonums; blue Nymphaeas were observed in several of them; and ducks were very numerous.

The forenoon was cloudless and hot; cirrhous clouds formed in the afternoon; with a breeze from the E.S.E. Our lat. was 21 degrees 25 minutes.

Mr. Gilbert and Charley, when on a reconnoitring ride, met another party of natives; among them two gins were so horror-struck at the unwonted sight, that they immediately fled into the scrub; the men commenced talking to them, but occasionally interrupted their speeches by spitting and uttering a noise like pooh! pooh! apparently expressive of their disgust.

March 23.--The party moved on about ten miles to the north-east, and encamped at the junction of a large creek which comes from the S.S.E. Its character is similar to that of the Suttor; and I should not be surprised if it should prove to be the northern anabranch of that creek, and which we crossed on the 17th of March, the day before we arrived at the lake.

The country opens into lightly-timbered ridges, which are composed of a hard rock, the sharp pieces of which covered the ground, and made our animals foot-sore. It seems to me to be a clayey sandstone (Psammite) penetrated by silica. A coarse-grained sandstone and quartzite cropped out in that part of the river situated between the two camps. The melon-holes of the box-flats were frequently over-grown with the polygonaceous plant, mentioned at a former occasion; and the small scrub plains were covered with a grey chenopodiaceous plant from three to four feet high. The stiff-leaved Cymbidium was still very common, and two or three plants of it were frequently observed on the same tree; its stem is eatable, but glutinous and insipid.

The morning of Easter Sunday was very clear and hot; the wind from E.N.E. As soon as we had celebrated the day with a luncheon of fat damper and sweetened tea, I rode with Charley about seven or eight miles down the river, and found abundance of water, not only in the bed of the river, but in lines of lagoons parallel to it. Charley shot several ducks, which were very numerous upon the water. Whilst riding along the bank of the river, we saw an old woman before us, walking slowly and thoughtfully through the forest, supporting her slender and apparently exhausted frame with one of those long sticks which the women use for digging roots; a child was running before her. Fearing she would be much alarmed if we came too suddenly upon her,-- as neither our voices in conversation, nor the footfall of our horses, attracted her attention,--I cooeed gently; after repeating the call two or three times, she turned her head; in sudden fright she lifted her arms, and began to beat the air, as if to take wing,--then seizing the child, and shrieking most pitifully, she rapidly crossed the creek, and escaped to the opposite ridges. What could she think; but that we were some of those imaginary beings, with legends of which the wise men of her people frighten the children into obedience, and whose strange forms and stranger doings are the favourite topics of conversation amongst the natives at night when seated round their fires?

I observed a fine sienite on several spots; it is of a whitish colour, and contains hornblende and mica in almost equal quantities; granite was also seen, and both rocks probably belong to each other, the presence of hornblende being local. A very hard pudding-stone crops out about nine miles down the river. From the ridges, hills were seen to the N.N.E. and to the westward. Vitex scrub is met with in patches of small extent. A white crane, and the whistling duck, were seen. Black ducks and teal were most common, and Charley shot eight of them. On the banks of the more or less dry water-holes grows an annual leguminous plant, which shoots up into a simple stem, often to the height of twelve feet; its neck and root are covered with a spongy tissue; its leaves are pinnate, a foot or more in length, with small leaflets; it bears mottled yellow flowers, in axillary racemes; and long rough, articulate pods, containing small, bright, olive-green seeds. I first saw this plant at Limestone, near Moreton Bay, and afterwards at the water-holes of Comet River. It was extremely abundant in the bed of the Burdekin, and was last seen on the west side of the gulf of Carpentaria; I could, however, easily distinguish three species of this plant. [They belong probably to the two genera, Aeschynomene and Sesbania.]

Last evening, clouds gathered in the west, but cleared off after sunset; the night again cloudy, the forenoon equally so; in the afternoon the clouds were dissipated by a north-east wind.

March 24.--We travelled about nine miles N. 60 degrees W. along the river; a small creek joined from the westward. At night we had a heavy thunder-storm from the S.W.

March 25.--Weather very hot; clouds formed during the afternoon. We continued our journey along the river to lat. 21 degrees 3 minutes; the river winds considerably. We passed several hills at the latter part of the stage. I ascended one of them, on the right bank of the river, and obtained an extensive view of the country, which has a very uniform character. There were ridges and low ranges to the westward, one of which stretched from N. by W. far to the westward. The hill on which I stood was composed of limestone rock; it was flat-topped, with steep slopes at each end.

In lat. about 21 degrees 6 minutes, we crossed a large creek, densely lined with dropping tea trees, coming from the westward. It was here we first met with Careya arborea (Roxb.), a small tree from fifteen to twenty feet high, with elliptical leaves of soft texture, four inches long, and two in breadth; its fruit was about two inches long, contained many seeds, and resembled that of the Guava. Its leaves, however, had neither the vernation nor the pellucid dots of Myrtaceous trees. At the junction of the creek, a great number of small Corypha palms were growing, and my companions observed the dead stems of some very high ones, whose tops had been cut off by the natives, probably to obtain the young shoot. We passed hills of baked sandstone, before reaching the creek, and afterwards crossed a fine sandy flat, with poplar-gum. The river has a broad bed, at times dividing into several channels, lined with stately Melaleucas and flooded-gum, and again uniting into one deep channel, with long reaches of water surrounded by Polygonums, and overgrown with blue Nymphaeas, Damasoniums, and Utricularias, and inhabited by large flights of ducks. Rock occasionally enters into the bed of the river. The collateral lines of water-holes are rarely interrupted, and the ridges appear to be open on both sides of the river.

March 26.--We travelled along the river to lat. 20 degrees 53 minutes 42 seconds. Its course is almost due north. Yesterday, being out duck shooting, we came suddenly upon a camp of natives, who were not a little frightened by the report of our guns: they followed our tracks, however, with wailing cries, and afterwards all of them sat down on the rocky banks of the river, when we returned to our camp. To-day we passed the place of their encampment with our whole train, and it was remarkable that they neither heard nor saw us until we were close to them, though we had seen them from a great distance. All the young ones ran away. Dismounting from my horse, I walked up to an old man who had remained, and who was soon after rejoined by another man. We had a long unintelligible conversation, for neither Brown nor Charley could make out a single word of their language. They were much surprised by the different appearance of Charley's black skin and my own. Phillips wished to exchange his jacket for one of their opossum cloaks, so I desired him to put it on the ground, and then taking the cloak and placing it near the jacket, I pointed to Phillips, and, taking both articles up, handed the cloak to Phillips and the jacket to our old friend, who perfectly understood my meaning. After some time he expressed a wish to have the cloak back, and to keep the jacket, with which we had dressed him; but I gave him to understand that he might have his cloak, provided he returned the jacket; which arrangement satisfied him. A basket (dilli), which I examined, was made of a species of grass which, according to Charley, is found only on the sea coast.

We saw a Tabiroo (Mycteria) and a rifle bird. The morning was cloudy, but very hot. Numerous heavy cumuli formed during the afternoon.

March 27.--We travelled to lat. 20 degrees 47 minutes 34 seconds. The country along the river is undulating and hilly, and openly timbered. The rock is of sandstone, and the ground is covered with quartz pebbles. In lat. about 20 degrees 49 minutes, the Suttor is joined by a river as large as itself, coming from the S.W. by W., and which changes the course of the Suttor to the N.E. Just before the junction, the large bed of the Suttor contracts into one deep channel, filled in its whole extent by a fine sheet of water, on which Charley shot a pelican. I mention this singular contraction, because a similar peculiarity was observed to occur at almost every junction of considerable channels, as that of the Suttor and Burdekin, and of the Lynd and the Mitchell. I named the river, which here joins the Suttor, after Mr. Cape, the obliging commander of the Shamrock steamer. The bed of the united rivers is very broad, with several channels separated by high sandy bergues. The country back from the river is formed by flats alternating with undulations, and is lightly timbered with silver-leaved Ironbark, rusty gum, Moreton Bay ash, and water box. The trees are generally stunted, and unfit for building; but the drooping tea trees and the flooded-gum will supply sufficient timber for such a purpose.

At our camp, at the bed of the river, granite crops out, and the sands sparkle with leaflets of gold-coloured mica. The morning was clear and hot; the afternoon cloudy; a thunder-storm to the north-east. We have observed nothing of the sea-breeze of the Mackenzie and of Peak Range, along the Suttor; but a light breeze generally sets in about nine o'clock P.M.

Charley met with a flock of twenty emus, and hunted down one of them.

March 28.--We travelled down the river to latitude 20 degrees 41 minutes 35 seconds. The country was improving, beautifully grassed, openly timbered, flat, or ridgy, or hilly; the ridges were covered with pebbles, the hills rocky. The rocks were baked sandstone, decomposed granite, and a dark, very hard conglomerate: the latter cropped out in the bed of the river where we encamped. Pebbles of felspathic porphyry were found in the river's bed. At some old camping places of the natives, we found the seed-vessels of Pandanus, a plant which I had never seen far from the sea coast; and also the empty shells of the seeds of a Cycas. Mr. Calvert, John Murphy, and Brown, whom I had sent to collect marjoram, told me, at their return, that they had seen whole groves of Pandanus trees; and brought home the seed-vessel of a new Proteaceous tree. I went to examine the locality, and found, on a sandy and rather rotten soil, the Pandanus abundant, growing from sixteen to twenty feet high, either with a simple stem and crown, or with a few branches at the top. The Proteaceous tree was small, from twelve to fifteen feet high, of stunted and irregular habit, with dark, fissured bark, and large medullary rays in its red wood: its leaves were of a silvery colour, about two inches and a half long, and three-quarters broad; its seed-vessels woody and orbicular, like the single seed-vessels of the Banksia conchifera; the seeds were surrounded by a broad transparent membrane. This tree, which I afterwards found every where in the neighbourhood of the gulf of Carpentaria, was in blossom from the middle of May to that of June. The poplar-gum, the bloodwood, the melaleuca of Mt. Stewart, the Moreton Bay ash, the little Severn tree, and a second species of the same genus with smooth leaves, were growing on the same soil. The grasses were very various, particularly in the hollows: and the fine bearded grass of the Isaacs grew from nine to twelve feet in height. Charley brought me a branch of a Cassia with a thyrse of showy yellow blossoms, which he said he had plucked from a shrub about fifteen feet high.

We encamped about two miles from the foot of a mountain bearing about N.E. from us; I called it Mount McConnel, after Fred. McConnel, Esq., who had most kindly contributed to my expedition. The Suttor winds round its western base, and, at four or five miles beyond it, in a northerly direction, and in latitude 20 degrees 37 minutes 13 seconds joins a river, the bed of which, at the junction, is fully a mile broad. Narrow and uninterrupted belts of small trees were growing within the bed of the latter, and separated broad masses of sand, through which a stream ten yards broad and from two to three feet deep, was meandering; but which at times swells into large sheets of water, occasionally occupying the whole width of the river. Charley reported that he had seen some black swans, and large flights of ducks and pelicans. This was the most northern point at which the black swan was observed on our expedition.

CHAPTER VII

THE BURDEKIN
TRANSITION FROM THE DEPOSITORY TO THE PRIMITIVE
ROCKS
THACKER'S RANGE
WILD FIGS
GEOLOGICAL REMARKS
THE CLARKE
THE PERRY.

As this place afforded every convenience for killing and curing another bullock, we remained here for that purpose from the 29th March to the 2nd of April. The weather was favourable for our operations, and I took two sets of lunar observations, the first of which gave me longitude 146 degrees 1 minutes, and the second, 145 degrees 58 minutes. The mornings were generally either cloudless, or with small cumuli, which increased as the day advanced, but disappeared at sunset; the wind was, as far as I could judge, northerly, north-easterly, and easterly.

April 2.--The Suttor was reported by Charley to be joined by so many gullies and small creeks, running into it from the high lands, which would render travelling along its banks extremely difficult, that I passed to the east side of Mount McConnel, and reached by that route the junction of the Suttor with the newly discovered river, which I called the Burdekin, in acknowledgment of the liberal assistance which I received from Mrs. Burdekin of Sidney, in the outfit of my expedition. The course of this river is to the east by south; and I thought that it would most probably enter the sea in the neighbourhood of Cape Upstart. Flood marks, from fifteen to eighteen feet above the banks, showed that an immense body of water occasionally sweeps down its wide channel.

I did not ascend Mount McConnel, but it seemed to be composed of a species of domite. On the subordinate hills I observed sienite. The bed of the river furnished quite a collection of primitive rocks: there were pebbles of quartz, white, red, and grey; of granite; of sienite; of felspathic porphyry, hornblende, and quartz-porphyry; and of slate-rock.

The morning was cloudless. In the afternoon, heavy cumuli, which dissolved towards sunset; a strong wind from the north and north by east.

A very conspicuous hill, bearing E.N.E. from the junction of the rivers, received the name of Mount Graham, after R. Graham, Esq., who had most liberally contributed to my expedition.

Mr. Gilbert found a large calabash attached to its dry vine, which had been carried down by the waters. Several other very interesting cucurbitaceous fruits, and large reeds, were observed among the rubbish which had accumulated round the trees during the flood.

April 3.--We travelled up the Burdekin, in a north-north-west direction, to latitude 20 degrees 31 minutes 20 seconds. The country was hilly and mountainous; the soil was stony; and the banks of the river were intersected by deep gullies and creeks. The forest vegetation was the same as that on the lower Suttor. Among the patches of brush which are particularly found at the junction of the larger creeks with the river, we observed a large fig-tree, from fifty to sixty feet high, with a rich shady foliage; and covered with bunches of fruit. The figs were of the size of a small apple, of an agreeable flavour when ripe, but were full of small flies and ants. These trees were numerous, and their situation was readily detected by the paths of the natives leading to them: a proof that the fruit forms one of their favourite articles of food. The drooping tea trees, which had increased both in number and size, grew in company with an arborescent Calistemon, along the water's edge; and a species of Eucalyptus, somewhat resembling Angophora intermedia, was discovered at this spot: it occurs frequently to the northward, and is common round the gulf of Carpentaria. The small Acacia tree of Expedition Range was frequently seen in the forest, and was covered with an amber-coloured gum, that was eatable, but tasteless: Hakea lorea (R. Br.), and Grevillea ceratophylla (R. Br.); the Ebenaceous tree, and that with guava-like fruit (lareya), were all numerous. The bed of the river was covered with the leguminous annual I noticed at the Suttor; it grew here so high and thick that

110

my companions were unable to see me, though riding only a few yards from them.

Rock frequently crops out in the bed of the river, and in the neighbouring hills. Several hills at the right bank were formed by a kind of thermantide of a whitish grey, or red colour, and which might be scratched easily with a penknife. Other conical hills or short ranges, with irregular rugged crests, were composed of granite of many varieties, red and white, fine grained without hornblende, or containing the latter substance, and changing into sienite; and, at one place, it seemed as if it had broken through Psammite. I observed quartzite in several localities, and a hard pudding-stone extending for a considerable distance. We were, no doubt, on the transition from the depository to the primitive rocks; and a detailed examination of this interesting part of the country would be very instructive to the geologist, as to the relative age and position of the rocks.

A small fish, with yellow and dark longitudinal lines, and probably belonging to the Cyprinidae, was caught. Wind prevailed from the northward: the forenoon was cloudless; heavy cumuli in the afternoon.

We travelled at first on the right side of the river; but its banks became so mountainous and steep, and the gullies so deep, that we were compelled to cross it at a place where it was very deep, and where our horses and cattle had to swim. Many of our things got wet, and we were delayed by stopping to dry them.

April 4.--We moved our camp to latitude 20 degrees 24 minutes 12 seconds, a distance of about nine miles N.W. by N. We passed several granitic peaks and ranges; one of which I ascended, and enjoyed an extensive view. The character of the country changed very little: open narrow-leaved Ironbark forest on a granitic sand, full of brilliant leaflets of mica. Some deep creeks came from the eastward. To the west and north-west nothing was to be seen but ridges; but high imposing ranges rise to the north and north-east. At one spot, large masses of calcareous spar were scattered over the ground; they were probably derived from a vein in the granite.

Three black ducks, (Anas Novae Hollandiae) were shot. Tracks of native dogs were numerous; and a bitch came fearlessly down to the river, at a short distance from our camp. Our kangaroo dog ran at her, and both fell into the water, which enabled the bitch to escape.

April 5.--We re-crossed the river, which was not very deep, and travelled about nine miles N. 75 degrees W. The river flows parallel to a high mountain range, at about three or four miles from its left bank. I named this after Mr. Robey, another friendly contributor to my outfit. A large creek very probably carries

111

the waters from this range to the Burdekin, in latitude 20 degrees 23 minutes. The country was very ridgy and hilly; and we found it exceedingly difficult to proceed along the river. We observed the poplar-gum again in the open forest, and a fine drooping loranthus growing on it. Pandanus was also very frequent, in clusters from three to eight trees. The clustered fig-tree gave us an ample supply of fruit, which, however, was not perfectly mellow.

Veins of calcareous spar and of quartz were again observed. I ascended a lofty hill, situated about a mile and a half to the west of our encampment, and found it composed of felspathic porphyry, with a greyish paste containing small crystals of felspar; but, in the bed of the river, the same rock was of a greenish colour, and contained a great number of pebbles of various rocks, giving it the aspect of a conglomerate; but recognisable by its crystals of felspar, and from its being connected with the rock of the hill. From the top of the hill, which is wooded with a silver-leaved Ironbark, I saw a very mountainous country to the N.N.W. and northward, formed into detached ranges and isolated peaks, some of which were apparently very high; but to the north-west and west no ranges were visible.

A thunder-storm threatened on the 4th, but we had only some light showers: the morning of the 5th was very hot, and the afternoon rainy. Wind from north and north-east. Nights clear.

April 6.--We travelled about ten miles N. 35 degrees W. over a ridgy, openly timbered, stony and sandy country, and crossed several sandy creeks, in which a species of Melaleuca, and another of Tristania were growing. No part of the country that we had yet seen, resembled the northern parts of New England so much as this. The rock was almost exclusively granitic isolated blocks; detached heaps, and low ridges composed of it were frequently met with in the open forest. We passed two small hillocks of milkwhite quartz; fragments of this rock, as well as of calcareous spar, were often observed scattered over the ground. The river here made a large bend to the northward, still keeping parallel to Robey's Range, or a spur of it; and, when it again turned to the westward, another fine high range was visible to the north by east and north-east of it; which I named "Porter's Range," in acknowledgment of the kindness of another of the contributors to my expedition. Its latitude is about 20 degrees 14 minutes.

April 7.--Travelled about ten miles N. 70 degrees W. The country became more level, more open, and better grassed; the gullies were farther apart, and headed generally in fine hollows. Two large creeks joined the river from the westward; and a still larger one came from the northward, and which probably carries off the water from the country round a fine peak, and a long razorback mountain which we saw in that direction. North-west of Porter's

Range, and between it and the razorback, were two small peaks. The timber is of the same kind, but larger. The poplar-gum was more frequent, and we always found patches of fine grass near it; even when all the surrounding Ironbark bark forest was burnt. The large clustered fig-trees were not numerous along the river; we perhaps passed from three to five in the course of a day's journey; though young ones, without fruit, were often seen.

Heavy clouds gathered during the afternoon of the 6th, and it rained throughout the night; the wind was from N. and N.E. In the morning of the 7th some drops of rain fell, but the weather cleared up during the day; wind easterly. The moon changed this day, and we experienced a heavy thunderstorm during the afternoon.

April 8.--We travelled about nine miles N. 70 degrees W., to latitude 20 degrees 9 minutes 11 seconds. The river made a bend to the southward, and then, at a sharp angle, turned again to the north-west. At this angle a large creek joined it from the south; another instance of creeks joining larger channels, coming in a direction almost opposite to their course. Two other creeks joined the Burdekin during this stage; one from the south-west, and another from the north. The grass was particularly rich at these junctions. The river became considerably narrower, but still had a fine stream. Thunderstorms had probably fallen higher up its course, causing a fresh; for its waters, hitherto clear, had become turbid. Narrow patches of brush were occasionally met with along its banks, and I noticed several brush trees, common in other parts of the country. Besides the clustered fig, and another species with rough leaves and small downy purple fruit, there were a species of Celtis; the Melia Azederach (White Cedar); a species of Phyllanthus, (a shrub from six to ten feet high); an Asclepiadaceous climber, with long terete twin capsules; and several Cucurbitaceae, one with oblong fruit about an inch long, another with a round fruit half an inch in diameter, red and white, resembling a gooseberry; a third was of an oblong form, two inches and a half long and one broad; and a fourth was of the size and form of an orange, and of a beautiful scarlet colour: the two last had an excessively bitter taste. The night and morning were cloudy, with a southerly wind, but it cleared up at eleven o'clock. Cumuli in the afternoon, with wind from the south-east.

From our camp we saw a range of hills, bearing between N. 5 degrees W. and N. 10 degrees W.; they were about three miles distant. I called them "Thacker's Range," in acknowledgment of the support I received from--Thacker, Esq., of Sidney.

April 9.--We travelled about nine miles W. by N., and made our latitude 20 degrees 8 minutes 26 seconds. The western end of Thacker's Range bore N.E. Two large creeks joined the river from the south and south-west. The country was openly timbered; the Moreton Bay ash grew along the bergue of the river, where a species of Grewia seemed its inseparable companion. The flooded-gum occupied the hollows and slopes of the river banks, which were covered with a high stiff grass to the water's edge, and the stream was fringed with a thicket of drooping tea trees, which were comparatively small, and much bent by the force of floods, the probable frequency of which may account for the reduced size of the tree. The ridges were covered with rusty Gum and narrow-leaved Ironbark. An Erythrina and the Acacia of Expedition Range were plentiful. The grass was rich and of various species. The granite rock still prevailed. A felspathic rock cropped out near the second creek, where I met with a dark rock, composed of felspar and horneblende (Diorite.) Our camp was pitched at the foot of a series of small conical hills, composed of porphyry. A larger range to the southward of it was also porphyritic, very hard, as if penetrated by quartz, and containing small crystals of flesh-coloured felspar. Sienite cropped out on the flats between these two ranges. I commanded a most extensive view from the higher range. High and singularly crenelated ranges were seen to the south-west; detached peaks and hills to the westward; short ranges and peaks to the north; and considerable ranges between north and north-east. A river was observed to join the Burdekin from the ranges to the south-west.

Numerous kangaroos were seen bounding over the rocky slopes to the grassy glens below. A stunted silver-leaved Ironbark covered the hills.

April 10.--The night was very cold, particularly towards morning, and the dew heavy; the morning was calm; a breeze from the south-east set in at nine o'clock a.m.; cumuli formed about eleven o'clock, and became very heavy during the afternoon.

The country over which we travelled about eight miles N. by W., was one of the finest we had seen. It was very open, with some plains, slightly undulating or rising into ridges, beautifully grassed and with sound ground. We crossed the river I had seen the preceding day from the hill, and found it running. Two large creeks, one from the right and the other from the left, also joined the Burdekin. I observed Pegmatite of a white colour, and hornblende Porphyry and Diorite. A shrubby Clerodendron and an arborescent Bursaria, covered with white blossoms, adorned the forest. The latitude was 20 degrees 0 minutes 36 seconds.

April 11.--We continued our journey up the river, in a W.N.W. direction, for about ten miles. The first part of our journey lay through a most beautiful country. The hollows along the river were covered with a dense sward of various grasses, and the forest was open as far as the eye could reach. Farther on, however, we occasionally met with patches of Vitex scrub, and crossed some stony ridges. A small river joined from the north-east, at about a mile and a half from the last camp, and also two large creeks from the south-west. I ascended the hills opposite our camp, and looked over an immense and apparently flat country, out of which small peaks and short ranges rose. The hills on which I stood were composed of Pegmatite, with patches of white Mica in large leaflets. During the journey we found granite changing into gneiss, diorite, and quartz rock.

On the rocky crest of the hill, I gathered the pretty red and black seeds of a leguminous climbing shrub (Abrus precatorius). Phonolithic or basaltic pebbles made me suppose that we were near to a change of country. Our latitude was 19 degrees 58 minutes 11 seconds.

April 12.--We had scarcely travelled a mile and a half, when we had to cross a large creek, which increased in size higher up. Box-tree flats and open Vitex scrub extended along its banks, and the latter, according to Mr. Roper's account, changed into dense Bricklow scrub. At the junction of the creek and the river, we came on a dyke of basalt, the flat summit of which was so rough that we were compelled to travel along the flats of the creek, which for a long distance ran parallel to the Burdekin. The soil on the basalt was so shallow that it sustained only a scanty vegetation of grass and some few scattered narrow-leaved Ironbark trees. We crossed this dyke, however, and at about three miles descended from it into a fine narrow-leaved Ironbark flat, extending along the river, in which another large creek from the south-west joined the Burdekin. The flat was bounded by hills of limestone, cropping out in large blocks, with visible stratification, but without fossils. Having passed the third creek in the course of this day's journey, we encamped on the commencement of another basaltic dyke. The bed of the creek was full of blocks of Sienite, of hornblende Porphyry, of greenish Pegmatite, and of cellular Basalt. The river here formed a large sheet of water; large masses of a white Sienite protruded out of it, opposite the junction of the creek. The opposite bank exhibited a very perfect and instructive geological section of variously bent and lifted strata of limestone, which was afterwards found to contain innumerable fossils, particularly corals and a few bivalve shells. The Rev. W. B. Clarke, of Paramatta, kindly undertook to examine the fossils brought from this locality. One he determined to be an undescribed species of Cyathophyllum, and has done me the honour to give my name to it [Refer Note 1 at end of chapter]. The others belonged principally to the following genera, viz., Asterias, Caryophyllea, and Madrepora. The right bank of the river rose into steep cliffs of basalt, under which the clustered fig tree, with its dense foliage, formed a fine shady bower. The basaltic dyke was about a mile and a half broad, and I followed it about five miles up the river. Its summit was flat, rough, and rocky; at the distance of four miles from our camp it

115

receded a little from the river, and there limestone was observed, crowded with fossils like that on the opposite side of the river. Two miles farther, the bed of the river was formed by a felspathic rock, with beautiful dendrites. A small island, with a chain of lagoons on one side, and with the river on the other, was also composed of this rock, in contact with, and covered by, basalt in several places. There were small falls and rapids in several parts of the river. A beaten foot-path of the natives, and many fire-places, showed that this part of it was much frequented by them. Wallabies were very numerous between the cliffs of the felspathic rock; and the fine fig trees along the banks of the river were covered with ripe fruit. The river made a wide sweep round the left side of a large limestone hill, whilst a chain of deep basaltic water-holes continued on its right. The basalt ceased to the westward of the limestone hill, and was succeeded by considerable flats of Ironbark, Moreton Bay ash, and Bloodwood. The Capparis still exhibited a few showy flowers. I examined the country thus far on the 12th April, after the camp had been formed; on returning, I took with me a large supply of ripe figs, of which we partook freely, and which caused several of us to suffer severely from indigestion, though we had frequently eaten small quantities of them without inconvenience.

April 13.--We avoided the field of basalt by moving up the creek we last crossed, about four miles, and by crossing over to the flats of the river where the basalt terminated. These flats, however, were again interrupted by a basaltic dyke, over which we were compelled to travel, as the steep banks of the river were on one side, and black bare rocks, forming sometimes regular walls with a dense scrub between them, prevented us from turning to the other. After descending from the basalt, we crossed a good-sized creek from the south-west, and travelled over a fine open country to lat. 19 degrees 49 minutes 41 seconds.

Two hills were close to the left side of the Burdekin, which, at their base, were joined by a large running creek from the N.N.W. From the limestone hill of yesterday, no other hill was visible to the westward, though ranges and isolated hills lay to the north and north-east, and a high blue mountain to the south-west.

Some days ago I found, for the first time, Spathodea alternifolia (R. Br.), which we continued to meet with throughout the remainder of our journey. I saw but one flower of it, but its falcate seed-vessels, often more than a foot long, were very numerous. Pandanus spiralis was frequent. The box (Eucalyptus), on the flats along the creek, the soil of which is probably formed of the detritus of basaltic rock, had a lanceolate glossy leaf, uniting the character of the box with glossy orbicular leaves growing generally on the whinstone soil of the northern parts of the colony, and of the box with long

116

lanceolate leaves which prefers stiff flats on the tributary creeks of the Hunter. A Bottle-tree with a Platanus leaf (Sterculia?) grew in the scrub on the field of basalt, and was in full blossom. A pretty species of Commelyna, on the flats, a cucurbitaceous plant with quinquepalmate leaves and large white blossoms, grew along the river, the approaches of which were rendered almost inaccessible by a stiff high grass. Charley brought me the long flower-stalk of Xanthorrhaea from some ridges, which were, doubtless, composed of sandstone.

Two kangaroos were seen; they were of middle size, and of a yellowish grey colour, and seemed to live principally about the basaltic ridges.

The cooee of natives had been heard only once during our journey along the banks of the Burdekin; and the traces of their former presence had not been very frequently observed. Large lagoons full of fish or mussels form a greater attraction to the natives than a stream too shallow for large fish, and, from its shifting sands, incapable of forming large permanent holes. Wherever we met with scrub with a good supply of water, we were sure of finding numerous tracks of the natives, as game is so much more abundant where a dense vegetation affords shelter from its enemies.

April 14.--Last night, at seven o'clock, a strong breeze set in from the northward, and continued for about an hour, when it became perfectly calm. If this was the same breeze which we had observed at the Mackenzie at eight o'clock, and which set in earlier and earlier, as we travelled along the Isaacs and Suttor (though it was less regular in these places) until we felt it at about six o'clock, we were now most evidently receding from the eastern coast.

We travelled in a N. 60 degrees W. direction to lat. 19 degrees 45 minutes 36 seconds. A basaltic ridge, similar to those we had passed, extended in an almost straight line from south-east to north-west; it was covered with a scanty vegetation, with a few small narrow-leaved Ironbark trees and Erythrinas; the river now approached it, now left it in wide sweeps enclosing fine narrow-leaved Ironbark flats. To the south-west side of this ridge or dyke, the soil is basaltic, with box-trees and open Vitex scrub. The sharp conical hills of the white ant, constructed of red clay, were very numerous. A very perfect bower of the bower-bird was seen in a patch of scrub trees.

In a gully, a loose violet coloured sandstone cropped out, over which the basalt had most evidently spread. Farther on, the ridge enlarged and formed small hillocks, with bare rock cropping out at their tops;--a form of surface peculiar to the basaltic or whinstone country of this colony.

Charley shot the sheldrake of Port Essington, (Tadorna Rajah). The singular hissing or grinding note of the bower bird was heard all along the river; the fruit of the fig trees growing near, which seemed to supply it with its principal food during this part of the year.

April 15.--One of our bullocks had gone back on our tracks, and thereby prevented our starting so early as usual. We travelled in a N. 40 degrees W. direction to latitude 19 degrees 41 minutes 25 seconds. The basaltic country continued, and apparently extended a great distance from the river. The flats along the latter were less extensive. Sandstone cropped out in deep gullies, and in the bed of the river; it was naturally soft and coarse, but where it rose into hillocks near basalt, it changed into a fine baked sandstone, resembling quartzite, which, when in contact with the igneous rock, looked like burnt bricks. Near our camp, a dyke or wall of the aspect of a flinty red conglomerate, crossed the river from south-west to north-east. I believe that this rock belongs to the porphyries of Glendon, and of the upper Gloucester. We continued to feel the breeze, or rather a puff of wind, between 7 and 8 o'clock at night; it was often very strong and cold, and prevented the mosquitoes from molesting us.

April 16.--We proceeded north by west to latitude 19 degrees 32 minutes, and crossed several gullies coming from the basaltic ridges: these, however, receded far from the river, and large box and Ironbark flats took their place for about three miles, when the ridges re-appeared. Between four and five miles from the bar of red rock above mentioned, a fine large creek joined the Burdekin from the westward. The box and Ironbark forest was interrupted by slight rises of limestone full of corals; and by a higher hill of baked sandstone, at the foot of which a limestone hill was covered with a patch of Vitex scrub. The strata of the limestone seemed to dip to the southward.

The opposite banks of the river were ridgy, but openly timbered, and this fine country, with its well grassed flats, and its open ridges, seemed to extend very far on both sides. Messrs. Gilbert and Roper went to the top of the hill, and saw ranges trending from west to north, with that crenelated outline which I had before seen and mentioned: they distinguished a large valley, and the smoke of several fires of the natives along the range. A large lagoon was at the western foot of the hill on which they were. A large creek was seen, by Brown, to join the Burdekin from the north-east, at a short mile from our encampment. A baked sandstone and pudding-stone of a white colour projected into the river at the place, which not only exhibited the transition from one rock into the other, but it showed the action of igneous rocks on both, and gave a clue to the nature of the red rock I described yesterday. In the thicket which covered the rock, I observed Pomaderris of Moreton Bay. In decreasing our latitude, both Mr. Gilbert and myself were inclined to think that, whenever a bird or a plant disappeared, it was owing to that circumstance. In this, however, we were frequently mistaken: trees and herbaceous plants disappeared with the change of soil, and the decrease of moisture, and the birds kept to a certain vegetation: and, as soon as we came to similar localities, familiar forms of plants and birds re-appeared. Almost all the scrub-trees of the Condamine and Kent's Lagoon were still to be seen at the Burdekin; and the isolated waters near grassy flats were visited by swarms of little finches, which Mr. Gilbert had observed at Port Essington, and which, in all probability, belonged to the whole extent of country between that place and the region of the tropics. This slight change of vegetation, and particularly of the inland Flora, from south to north, is no doubt connected with the uniformity of the soil and climate: and the immense difference which exists between the eastern and western coast, has led men of science and of observation, not without good reason, to infer that this continent was originally divided into two large islands, or into an archipelago, which have been united by their progressive, and, perhaps, still continued, elevation. As an exception, however, to this remark, a very sudden change of the Flora was observed, when we entered into the basin of the gulf of Carpentaria, after leaving the eastern waters, although the Flora of the north-west coast and Port Essington, was little different from that of the gulf.

April 17.--We travelled about nine miles N. 40 degrees W. On our way we passed a hill of baked sandstone, and several gullies. About five miles from our last camp, a large creek joined the river; beyond that creek, the country was, without exception, open, and rather of a more undulating character; the flats were somewhat rotten: the river became narrower, but was still running strong; and numerous ducks sported on its shady pools.

April 18.--Last night we had a very cold north-easterly wind, and, during the day, some few drops of drizzling rain. We travelled about N. by W. to latitude 19 degrees 18 minutes 16 seconds. After passing some gullies, we came into a more broken and hilly country; the river formed here a large anabranch. The Ironbark trees, which timbered the extensive flat along the river, became much finer; but the soil was rotten: the poplar-gum grew on the stiff soil of the hollows. About six miles from our last camp, we came to ranges of high hills of a conical form, and with rounded tops, striking from west to east, and then entered a narrow valley, bounded on each side by rocky hills. Mr. Roper observed a rugged country to the northward, and a fine high range to the south-east. The whole country from the large flat to our camp, was composed of felspathic porphyry, containing crystals of felspar, and accidentally of quartz, in a paste varying in colour and hardness. In the bed of the river, I still found pebbles of pegmatite, granite, quartz, and basalt; indicating that a country of varied character was before us.

The stream wound its way from one side of the broad sandy bed to the other; and those parts where it flowed, were generally very steep, and covered with a

119

dense vegetation, whilst, on the opposite side, the banks sloped gently into the broad sands. Among the shrubs and grasses, a downy Abutelon was easily distinguished by its large bright yellow blossoms.

My Blackfellows procured several messes of ducks; and Brown brought me a piece of indurated clay with impressions of water-plants.

April 19.--Continuing our journey in a north-west direction, we passed over some very rocky hills, composed of indurated clay, and thin strata of sandstone, and pudding-stone. By moving along the foot of a range of high hills, we avoided all those deep gullies which intersected the banks of the river, and travelled with ease through a flat, well grassed Ironbark forest. The hills were covered, as usual, with stunted silver-leaved Ironbark. A large creek came from the range, and entered the river. A good section on its right bank exposed to view the strata of indurated clay and sandstone; and I was induced to believe that coal might be found below them. As we were passing over the flat between the creek and the river, we saw a native busily occupied in burning the grass, and eagerly watching its progress: the operation attracted several crows, ready to seize the insects and lizards which might be driven from their hiding places by the fire. Mr. Calvert, Brown, and Charley, rode nearly up to the man before he was aware of their approach; when he took to his heels, and fled in the greatest consternation.

Upon reaching the river, at about eight miles from our last camp, we found that it was joined by another river of almost the same size as the Burdekin: it had a stream, and came from the northward, whilst the course of the Burdekin at this place was from the west to east. From the junction a long range trended to the north-east, and moderate ranges bounded the valley of the river from the northward; another range extended along the left side of the Burdekin above the junction; and basaltic ridges, which had broken through the sandstone, approached on its right. The cucurbitaceous plant with palmate leaves, bore a fruit of the size of a large orange, of a fine scarlet colour when ripe; its rind is exceedingly bitter, but the seeds are eaten by birds. Mr. Phillips found a flesh-coloured drupaceous oblong fruit, about half an inch long, with a very glutinous pericarp, containing a slightly compressed rough stone: in taste it resembled the fruit of Loranthus, and the birds, particularly the coekatoos, appeared very fond of it. We all ate a great quantity of them, without the slightest injury. It grew on a small tree, and had a persistent calyx.

April 20.--We travelled in a N. 80 degrees W. course to latitude 19 degrees 9 minutes 88 seconds. Rocky ranges frequently approached the river, and deep and intricate gullies descended from them to the latter. Our progress was consequently very difficult, and we were compelled to ascend a very high hill to avoid its slopes towards the river, which were too steep for us to cross. As a recompense, however, for the difficulty of the ascent, I had the pleasure of finding some very interesting plants on its summit; particularly a small Acacia with verticillate leaves, which Dr. Binoe, the surgeon of H. M. S. Beagle, had found on the north-west coast; and two other Acacias equally new to me, and which were afterwards found to extend to the heads of the South Alligator River. From this hill we had a magnificent view of the country before us: it was enclosed on all sides by high mountain ranges, of which one in particular overtopped the rest. Porphyry was observed on several spots; indurated clay frequently; and, on the top of the hill below which we encamped, I found quartz porphyry, and at the foot a psammite? which I had met several times associated with talc-schiste.

April 21.--We continued our journey in a S. 50 degrees W. course to latitude 19 degrees 13 minutes. The country became still more mountainous; we passed, notwithstanding, many large well grassed flats, on which the timber grew to a greater size than we had observed it at the lower part of the river. The poplar-gum was very frequent in the hollow, and low stiff flats extended parallel to the river. The prevailing rock was talc-schiste, alternating with layers of psammite. On the hills and in the creeks, I frequently observed conglomerate, with many pieces of quartz.

The drooping Hakea of Kent's Lagoon (Hakea lorea, R. Br.; Grevillea lorea, R. Br. Prodr. Nov. Holl. I. p. 380) was in blossom; and on the rocky slopes I found a new species of Hakea, having linear lanceolate leaves with axillary fascicules of small brownish flowers: it was an arborescent shrub, from three to six feet high; and is nearly allied to H. arborescens (R. Br. Prodr. p. 386).

A high imposing range was visible to the northward.

April 22.--We travelled about nine miles west, making our latitude 19 degrees 12 minutes. Ranges ran parallel to the river at different distances: we left a very fine one to the south-west and south, from which the large creek we passed about two miles from our last camp, probably descends. Three miles farther, a river as large or even larger than the Burdekin, joins the latter from the westward and south-west-- the Burdekin coming down from the north-west. I was doubtful which of the two rivers I ought to follow; but finding, after a close examination, that the north-west branch was running, whilst the south-west one contained only large, long, but unconnected reaches of water, I determined upon following the north-west branch. I called the south-west branch the "Clarke," in compliment to the Rev. W. B. Clarke of Paramatta, who has been, and is still, most arduously labouring to elucidate the meteorology and the geology of this part of the world. About three miles above the junction, a creek of considerable size joined the Burdekin from the northward. Wherever the ridges approached the banks of the river, gullies which were scrubby at their heads, became numerous. After having encamped, I rode over to the "Clarke," to examine the intervening country. The flat along the Burdekin was about two miles and a half broad, and was skirted by silver-leaved Ironbark ridges. In approaching the Clarke, we came to a low basaltic range, which bounded its fine broad openly timbered valley to the northward. The bed of the river was formed by talc-schiste, in strata, the strike of which was from north by west to south by east, standing almost perpendicular, with a slight dip to the eastward. The stream was perpendicular on the line of striking. The pebbles in its bed were mostly basaltic, baked sandstone, conglomerate, quartz, sienite, and porphyry. I had observed the valley of this river from a high hill near our last camp, and had distinguished many headlands, which I now think were the bluff terminations of lateral basaltic ranges. The valley was bounded on its southern side by a long low range.

The blue mountain parrot was very frequent near our camp.

I have mentioned a small round eatable tuber, which I found in the basket of a native gin on the 2nd January. I here found it to be the large end of the tap root of a Potamogeton, or a plant nearly allied to that genus; I found it with another interesting water-plant, with foliated spikes of blue flowers, in a small water-hole near our last camp.

April 23.--We travelled about north-west to latitude 19 degrees 4 minutes 41 seconds, over a succession of fine flats; one or two of which were almost exclusively timbered with poplar-gum, which always indicated a sound stiff soil. These flats were separated by shallow gullies, and some Casuarina creeks, which come probably from the dividing ridges of the two rivers. Ridges and ranges were seen on both sides, at different distances. The Casuarina became more frequent along the banks of the river. It was rather remarkable that the Moreton Bay ash, which is so abundant along the Burdekin, was altogether wanting at the Clarke. Several lagoons were observed at the foot of the ridges; and near them we saw two flocks of the harlequin pigeon (Peristera histrionica). Talc-schiste cropped out in one of the deep creeks. Whilst travelling on the Burdekin, with the exception of some ducks and a few kangaroos, we had seen but very little game; but yesterday, when riding to the Clarke, two flocks of kangaroos passed me: a proof that the country is not so destitute of game as I had thought. The waters are inhabited by four varieties of fish; one was probably a Gristes, about eight inches long, and from one and a half to two inches broad, of a lanceolate shape, with bright yellow spots all over the body; a second smaller than Gristes, with dark stripes; a third about a foot long, and three inches broad, belonging to the Percidae; and a fourth, a small fish, which seemed to be allied to the Cyprinidae. Larger fish exist, probably, in the deep rocky basins of water which we occasionally passed; but we never succeeded in catching any; nor did we hear any of the splashing, which was so incessant during the night at the Mackenzie. The shell and bones of the turtle indicated its presence in the shady ponds fringed by drooping tea trees. Large holes in the banks immediately above the water, were probably inhabited by water rats or lizards. A common carpet snake was killed. Whenever we passed through open Vitex scrub, with its stiff loamy soil, we were sure of meeting a great number of the conical constructions of the white ant: they were from one to three feet high, very narrow, and tapering to a sharp point.

April 24.--To-day we travelled along the river over an open country, intersected by some gullies; the course of the river was, for about four miles, from north to south, and, at that distance from our camp, was joined by a river coming from the northward, which I now take the liberty of naming the "Perry," after Captain Perry, Deputy Surveyor-General, who has most kindly mapped my route from the rough plans sketched during the journey. The Burdekin here comes from the westward, and made a large bend round several mountains, composed of quartz porphyry, with a sub-crystalline felspathic paste. The latitude was 19 degrees 1 minutes (Unclear:)18.

April 25.--We travelled almost due west, about nine miles along the river, our latitude being 19 degrees 1 minutes 3 seconds. Our route lay through a fine well grassed country; the grass being very dense: at a distance from the river, I observed box flats, and poplar-gum flats; the latter are probably swampy during the rainy season. A good sized creek joined the Burdekin; a range of high hills extended along its left side, and its right became equally hilly as we approached our camping place. After establishing our camp, and making the necessary preparations, we killed one of our little steers, and found it in excellent condition. The graziers will judge by this simple fact, how well the country is adapted for pastoral pursuits; particularly when it is remembered that we were continually on the march, and had frequently to pass over very rocky ranges, which made our cattle footsore; and that the season was not the most favourable for the grass, which, although plentiful, was very dry. The steer gave us 120 lbs. of dried beef.

In this place I observed and calculated three sets of lunar observations; one gave longitude 144 degrees 4 minutes, and the other longitude 144 degrees 14 minutes. As usual, we greased our harness, although not without considerable discussion, as to whether it would not be more advisable to eat the fat than to apply it to the leather; we also repaired our packs and pack-saddles, and put every thing in travelling order.

On the 29th April we started from our killing camp, and travelled about seven miles N. 70 degrees W.; making our latitude 18 degrees 59 minutes. The ranges

123

now approached the banks of the river, and retarded our progress very much.

April 30.--In consequence of Charley's statement, that the banks of the river in advance were so steep and rocky that it would be impossible for us to pass, I left the river side, and crossed over the ranges, and had a very heavy stage for my bullocks; which I regretted the more, as Mr. Calvert and Brown, who returned to our last camp for a sword, had found the route by the river quite practicable. The ranges were composed of a Psammite, which was frequently baked, probably by neighbouring out-bursts of igneous rock. Several familiar forms of plants were discovered; also a new Eucalyptus, with a glaucous suborbicular subcordate leaf, and the bark of the rusty gum: a stunted or middle-sized tree, which grew in great abundance on the ranges. We passed a fine large but dry Casuarina creek, coming from the westward, with a broad sandy bed. A large tree, with dark green broad lanceolate stinging leaves, grew on its banks; it resembled the nettle tree, but belonged to neither of the two species growing in the bushes of the east coast.

Our last day's travelling had not advanced us more than five miles in a straight line, and we had not made any northing, our latitude being again 18 degrees 59 minutes; but we had left the mountains behind us, and had travelled, during the latter part of the stage, over well grassed, openly timbered flats. The ranges on the left side of the river extended several miles farther, but gradually sunk into a level country.

[Note 1: The following description of the fossiliferous limestone of the Burdekin, was communicated to me by the Rev. W. B. Clarke, F.G.S.

This rock consists of a semi-crystalline, greyish-brown marble, very like some varieties of Wenlock limestone.

The most conspicuous fossil is a coral, which appears to belong to the family of Cyathophyllidae. The genus is perhaps new; but this the want of specimens with which to compare it, does not allow me the means of verifying. It may, however, be classed provisionally as Cyathophyllum, to which in many respects it bears a great resemblance; and although it is somewhat contrary to the present rules of classification to assign a specific name from a person, yet, in order to do honour to my friend on account of his skill, diligence, and zeal as a naturalist, as well as a traveller, and as this is the first fossil coral brought away by the first explorer of the region in which its habitat is found, I venture to name it C. Leichhardti.

The description may be given as follows:

Cells concavely cylindrical, not dichotomous (thus distinguished from Caryophyllia), grouped but separate, laterally if at all proliferous.

124

Corallum beautifully stellular, formed by 30-35 slightly spirally-curving or regular radiating lamellae, which meet in a central point or overlap on a latitudinal axial line, and are divided by rectangular or outwardly convex and upwardly oblique dissepiments, which become, occasionally, indistinct or obsolete near the centre, thus not assuming the usual characteristic of Cyathophyllum, but rather one of Strombodes.

Surface longitudinally striated, the cellular structure being hidden in calcareous spar; the striae formed by the coalescing lamellae, which, at the extremities, seem to be occasionally denticulated, owing to the matrix interrupting their passage to the edge. This resembles what takes place in some Astraeidae.

The interior has more the features of Acervularia than Cyathophyllum; but there are patches of broken transverse septa in the rock which exhibit the features of the latter.

Associated with this is a branching coral, a fragment of which, in a small angle of one of the surfaces of the stone, exhibits the characters of Favosites. There are also traces of casts of Spirifers, one of which is near to S. Pisum of the Wenlock rocks. (Silur. Syst. pl. xiii. f. 9).

The description here given is deduced from the natural appearances under the lens, and not from artificial or regular sections. But the specimen admits of a partial substitute for this; for the surface is worn down and roughly polished, as is the case with all the exposed surfaces of ancient limestones in Australia; the result probably of the acidulous properties of rain water, or of the atmosphere, which, in a tropical climate, where violent showers alternate with great drought, is capable of producing various sensible changes in rocks in a long series of ages. Many rocks of limestone in New South Wales, even harder than the Burdekin marble, are actually grooved in short parallel furrows, over wide surfaces, and along their sides, by some similar agency.]

CHAPTER VIII

BROWN AND CHARLEY QUARREL
NIGHT WATCH
ROUTINE OF OUR DAILY LIFE, AND HABITS OF THE MEMBERS
OF THE PARTY
MOUNT LANG
STREAMS OF LAVA
A HORSE BREAKS HIS LEG, IS KILLED AND EATEN
NATIVE TRIBE
MR. ROPER'S ACCIDENT
WHITSUNDAY
BIG ANT HILL CREEK
DEPRIVED OF WATER FOR FIFTY HOURS
FRIENDLY NATIVES
SEPARATION CREEK
THE LYND
PSYCHOLOGICAL EFFECTS OF A SOJOURN IN THE WILDERNESS
NATIVE CAMP
SALT EXHAUSTED.

May 1.--We travelled west by north, to latitude 18 degrees 55 minutes 41 seconds, over almost a dead flat, which was only interrupted by a fine Casuarina creek, with a broad sandy bed, coming from the south-south-west. The soil was stiff, and the forest in which the Box tree prevailed, was very open. A species of Acacia, with narrow blunt phyllodia, about an inch long, with spinous stipules; Hakea lorea, and the Grevillea mimosoides (R. Br.), with very long linear leaves, were frequent. Towards the end of the journey, slight ridges, composed of flint rock, rose on our left; and the country became more undulating. Mr. Roper saw extensive ranges about fifteen miles distant; shortly before entering the camp, we passed a singularly broken country, in which the waters rushing down from a slightly inclined table land, had hollowed out large broad gullies in a sandy loam and iron ochre, which was full of quartz pebbles. The heavier masses had resisted the action of the waters, and remained like little peaks and islands, when the softer materials around them had been washed away. We met with grass lately burnt, and some still burning, which indicated the presence of natives. It was generally very warm during the hours of travelling, between eight and twelve o'clock, but the bracing air of the nights and mornings strengthened us for the day's labour; the weather altogether was lovely, and it was a pleasure to travel along such a fine stream of water. Easterly and north-easterly breezes still prevailed, though I expected that the direction of the winds would change as we passed the centre of York Peninsula.

Our two black companions, who until now had been like brothers-- entertaining each other by the relation of their adventures, to a late hour of the night; singing, chatting, laughing, and almost crying together; making common cause against me; Brown even following Charley into his banishment--quarrelled yesterday, about a mere trifle, so violently that it will be some time before they become friends again. When Mr. Calvert and Brown returned yesterday to the camp, they remarked that they had not seen the waterfall, of which Charley had spoken whilst at our last camp; upon which Charley insinuated that they had not seen it, because they had galloped their horses past it. This accusation of galloping their horses irritated Brown, who was very fond and proud of his horse; and a serious quarrel of a rather ridiculous character ensued. Keeping myself entirely neutral, I soon found that I derived the greatest advantage from their animosity to each other, as each tried to outdo the other in readiness to serve me. To-day, Charley, who was usually the last to rise in the morning, roused even me, and brought the horses before our breakfast was ready. Brown's fondness for spinning a yarn will soon, however, induce him to put an end to this feud with his companion and countryman. In the early part of our journey, one or other of our party kept a regular night-watch, as well to guard us from any night attack of the natives, as to look after our bullocks; but, latterly, this prudential measure, or rather its regularity, has been much neglected. Mr. Roper's watch was handed from one to another in alphabetical rotation at given intervals, but no one thought of actually watching; it was, in fact, considered to be a mere matter of form. I did not check this, because there was nothing apparently to apprehend from the natives, who always evinced terror in meeting us; and all our communications with them have been accidental and never sought by them. On that point, therefore, I was not apprehensive; and, as to the bullocks, they were now accustomed to feed at large, and we seldom had any difficulty in recovering them in the morning. I shall here particularise the routine of one of our days, which will serve as an example of all the rest. I usually rise when I hear the merry laugh of the laughing-jackass (Dacelo gigantea), which, from its regularity, has not been unaptly named the settlers' clock; a loud cooee then roused my companions,--Brown to make tea, Mr. Calvert to season the stew with salt and marjoram, and myself and the others to wash, and to prepare our breakfast, which, for the party, consists of two pounds and a-half of meat, stewed over night; and to each a quart pot of tea. Mr. Calvert then gives to each his portion, and, by the time this important

127

duty is performed, Charley generally arrives with the horses, which are then prepared for their day's duty. After breakfast, Charley goes with John Murphy to fetch the bullocks, which are generally brought in a little after seven o'clock a.m. The work of loading follows, but this requires very little time now, our stock being much reduced; and, at about a quarter to eight o'clock, we move on, and continue travelling four hours, and, if possible, select a spot for our camp. The Burdekin, which has befriended us so much by its direct course and constant stream, already for more than two degrees of latitude and two of longitude, has not always furnished us with the most convenient camps for procuring water. The banks generally formed steep slopes descending into a line of hollows parallel to the river, and thickly covered with a high stiff grass; and then another steep bank covered with a thicket of drooping tea-trees, rose at the water's edge; and, if the descent into the bed of the river was more easy, the stream frequently was at the opposite side, and we had to walk several hundred yards over a broad sheet of loose sand, which filled our mocassins, when going to wash. At present, the river is narrower, and I have chosen my camp twice on its dry sandy bed, under the shade of Casuarinas and Melaleucas, the stream being there comparatively easy of access, and not ten yards off. Many unpleasant remarks had been made by my companions at my choice of camping places; but, although I suffered as much inconvenience as they did, I bore it cheerfully, feeling thankful to Providence for the pure stream of water with which we were supplied every night. I had naturally a great antipathy against comfort-hunting and gourmandizing, particularly on an expedition like ours; on which we started with the full expectation of suffering much privation, but which an Almighty Protector had not only allowed us to escape hitherto, but had even supplied us frequently with an abundance--in proof of which we all got stronger and improved in health, although the continued riding had rather weakened our legs. This antipathy I expressed, often perhaps too harshly, which caused discontent; but, on these occasions, my patience was sorely tried. I may, however, complete the picture of the day: as soon as the camp is pitched, and the horses and bullocks unloaded, we have all our alloted duties; to make the fire falls to my share; Brown's duty is to fetch water for tea; and Mr. Calvert weighs out a pound and a-half of flour for a fat cake, which is enjoyed more than any other meal; the large teapot being empty, Mr. Calvert weighs out two and a-half pounds of dry meat to be stewed for our late dinner; and, during the afternoon, every one follows his own pursuits, such as washing and mending clothes, repairing saddles, pack-saddles, and packs; my occupation is to write my log, and lay down my route, or make an excursion in the vicinity of the camp to botanize, etc. or ride out reconnoitring. My companions also write down their remarks, and wander about gathering seeds, or looking for curious pebbles. Mr. Gilbert takes his gun to shoot birds. A loud cooee again unites us towards sunset round our table cloth; and, whilst enjoying our meals, the subject of the day's journey, the past, the present, and the future, by turns engage our attention, or furnish matter for conversation and remark, according to the respective humour of the parties. Many circumstances have conspired to make me strangely taciturn, and I am now scarcely pleased even with the chatting humour of my youngest companion, whose spirits, instead of flagging, have become more buoyant and lively than ever. I consider it, however, my invariable duty to give every information I can, whenever my companions inquire or show a desire to learn, and I am happy to find that they are desirous of making themselves familiar with the objects of nature by which they are surrounded, and of understanding their mutual relations. Mr. Roper is of a more silent disposition; Mr. Calvert likes to speak, and has a good stock of "small talk," with which he often enlivens our dinners; he is in that respect an excellent companion, being full of jokes and stories, which, though old and sometimes quaint, are always pure, and serve the more to exhilarate the party. Mr. Gilbert has travelled much, and consequently has a rich store of impressions de voyage: his conversation is generally very pleasing and instructive, in describing the character of countries he has seen, and the manners and customs of the people he has known. He is well informed in Australian Ornithology. As night approaches, we retire to our beds. The two Blackfellows and myself spread out each our own under the canopy of heaven, whilst Messrs. Roper, Calvert, Gilbert, Murphy, and Phillips, have their tents. Mr. Calvert entertains Roper with his conversation; John amuses Gilbert; Brown tunes up his corroborri songs, in which Charley, until their late quarrel, generally joined. Brown sings well, and his melodious plaintive voice lulls me to sleep, when otherwise I am not disposed. Mr. Phillips is rather singular in his habits; he erects his tent generally at a distance from the rest, under a shady tree, or in a green bower of shrubs, where he makes himself as comfortable as the place will allow, by spreading branches and grass under his couch, and covering his tent with them, to keep it shady and cool, and even planting lilies in blossom (Crinum) before his tent, to enjoy their sight during the short time of our stay. As the night advances, the Blackfellows' songs die away; the chatting tongue of Murphy ceases, after having lulled Mr. Gilbert to sleep; and at last even Mr. Calvert is silent, as Roper's short answers became few and far between. The neighing of the tethered horse, the distant tinkling of the bell, or the occasional cry of night birds, alone interrupt the silence of our camp. The fire, which was bright as long as the corroborri songster kept it stirred, gradually gets dull, and smoulders slowly under the large pot in which our meat is simmering; and the bright constellations of heaven pass unheeded over the heads of the dreaming wanderers of the wilderness, until the summons of the laughing jackass recalls them to the business of the coming day.

129

May 2.--We travelled in a N.W. direction to lat. 18 degrees 50 minutes 11 seconds; at first over the box flats, alternating with an undulating open country. About three miles before making our camp, we passed several small plains at the foot of what appeared to be basaltic ridges, and came to the dry channel of a river, with reeds and occasional water-holes, and lined with fine flooded-gum trees and Casuarinas, but without the dropping tea trees and the Moreton Bay ash, the latter of which seemed to be the prerogative of the Burdekin. At its left side a basaltic ridge rose, covered with thick scrub, and at its base extended a small plain, with black soil strewed with quartz pebbles. The river came, as well as I could judge, from the W.N.W. Mr. Roper and Brown caught a kangaroo, but they had a dangerous ride after it, and the poor brute, when hard pressed, showed fight, and endeavoured to lay hold of Mr. Roper.

In one of the creeks I observed pegmatite; pebbles of talc-schiste and of white quartz covered the bed of the river.

May 3.--We had to travel for a considerable distance in the bed of the river, for the hills approached close to its banks, and numerous deep gullies intercepted their slopes. When, however, the ridges receded, we passed several fine sound flats. The forest was open everywhere, and the grass was good, though old. After travelling about five miles, we saw a hill to the north-east, and, when we came almost abreast of it, the river turned to the eastward, and a wild field of broken basaltic lava rendered it impossible for us to follow its banks. The black rough masses of rock were covered with thick scrub, in which I observed numerous bottle trees with the platanus leaf. Keeping to the westward of the scrub, I followed a creek which farther on divided in a chain of ponds, into which the waters of the field of basalt, as well as of the basaltic ridges to the westward of it, collected. These ridges were perfectly level at their summits, and were connected with a table land which extended far to the west. At their foot sienite, quartz rock, and leptinite, were observed. After turning round the field of lava to the eastward, we entered into a large flat, with patches of narrow-leaved tea tree, with reedy swamps and fine flooded-gum trees, and made our camp at a strong running brook, without trees, but densely surrounded with reeds, ferns, and pothos. This stream formed the outlet of some fine lagoons, which extended along the steep slopes of the basaltic table land. I crossed the creek and its flat to the opposite hills. The flat was one level sheet or floor of basalt, here and there covered with a very shallow soil, but sometimes bare, though clothed with a fair supply of grass and with scattered flooded-gum trees. At the foot of the eastern hills, however, deep holes existed in a water-course, with black blocks of basalt heaped over each other, on which the fig tree with its dark green foliage formed a shady bower, most delightful during the heat of the day. The hills were composed of a lamellar granite, approaching the stratified appearance of gneiss, but the leaflets of mica, instead of forming continuous layers, were scattered. The east side of the narrow watercourse was of primitive rock, the west side basaltic. Having passed over the hills, I made the river at their east side. Its banks were open for access as far as the primitive rock extended, but another field of lava commenced higher up, and rendered any progress with our cattle impossible.

A native low shrubby Mulberry was found in this scrub, the fruit of which was good to eat, but of very small size.

From the top of the hills I enjoyed a most beautiful view of the valley of the river, with its large lagoons covered with Nymphaeas and Damasoniums. On one of the lagoons, Charley shot a Parra gallinacea, a bird which Mr. Gilbert had observed only at Port Essington. A well beaten path of the natives showed that they were numerous in this part of the country: we saw many of their camping places during the stage; and the fires of their camps were numerous; we saw a party of them, but they were too frightened to allow us to approach. Our latitude was 18 degrees 44 minutes 48 seconds. Our course was about N.N.W.

May 4.--We ascended the basaltic ridges, and reaching the table land, found it perfectly level, openly timbered, well grassed, but occasionally stony, by which our poor foot-sore bullocks suffered severely. About five miles north-west by west from our camp, we discovered an extensive valley with large lagoons and lakes, and a most luxuriant vegetation, bounded by blue distant ranges, and forming the most picturesque landscape we had yet met with. A chain of lagoons connected by a reedy brook followed the outlines of the table land, along the foot of its steep slopes. We descended by a tolerably gentle slope into the valley, and encamped near the reedy brook, which must be the same as that on which, lower down, our last camp was formed. Water, grass, hills, mountains, plains, forest land; all the elements of a fine pasturing country, were here united.

During one of the last stages, we discovered a leguminous tree, with the dark fissured bark of the Ironbark, but with large bipinnate leaves, the leaflets oblong, an inch in length; the pods broad and thin, and two or three inches long: this tree is common all over the northern part of the continent, and was found growing abundantly around Victoria, the principal settlement of Port Essington.

Mr. Roper and Brown, upon an excursion after ducks, which were very numerous on the lagoons, met with Blackfellows, who were willing to accost Brown, but could not bear the sudden sight of a white face. In trying to cross the valley, my course was intercepted every way by deep reedy and sedgy lagoons, which rendered my progress impossible. I saw, however, that this valley was also floored with a sheet of lava hollowed out into numerous deep basins, in which the water collected and formed the lagoons.

May 5.--I went with Charley to reconnoitre the upper part of the reedy brook, with a view to find a passage over the table land to the westward; at the same time I sent Mr. Roper and Brown to trace the river through the lagoons, and to examine whether there was any connection between them. I followed the base of the basaltic table land, along which the brook came down, and, after a two miles' ride on its banks, through oak trees, low fern trees, and several bush trees, found that it came down a valley deeply cut into the table land. The floor of the valley was of basaltic rock, and its steep slopes were covered with boulders of the same formation. The water ran in two distinct beds through the fissures, hollows, and caves of the rock. As our horses could not travel over the sharp edges of the rock without injuring their feet, we ascended the table land, and rode to the northward about four miles, and then came on plains, in which we distinguished a meandering band of green verdure, which proved to be the same brook we had left, or one of its head waters. We followed it through a series of plains, from one of which a blue mountain was visible to the north-west. I called it "Mount Lang," after Dr. Lang, the distinguished historiographer of New South Wales. Smoke was seen to the westward. At the right side of the brook, a stream of lava bounded the plains, and was, as usual, covered with dense scrub. Box, with occasional patches of narrow-leaved tea trees, grew along the plains. The forest was very open, and principally consisted of narrow-leaved Ironbark; the grass in the forest and on the plains, was of the best description. Finer stations for the squatter cannot exist.

May 6.--Following the brook about four miles farther, I came to its source at a gentle slope of basalt. Plains stretched along both sides of its course, and even beyond it. Luxuriant reeds, Plothos, and several deep green trees, crowded round its head. Kangaroos, which abounded particularly along the scrub, had formed numerous paths through the high grass to the water's edge. I now directed my course to the W.N.W., but soon found myself checked by a dyke or wall of basaltic lava, composed of boulders and tabular blocks heaped over each other in wild confusion, and covered by scrub; it stretched from N.W. to S.E. I travelled round its edge to the southward, after having made a vain attempt to cross it. The outlines of the stream ran out in low heads into the flat table land, and there we met occasionally with springs and chains of water-holes which united lower down into a water-course, which, after following alternately the outline of the scrub, and turning into the stream of lava, became lost among its loose rocks. The lava was very cellular; the basalt of the table land solid. The whole appearance of this interesting locality showed that the stream of lava was of much more recent date than the rock of the table land, and that the latter was probably formed under water, whilst the cellular scorified lava was poured out into the open air. The stream of lava enlarged so much, and descended into so broad a valley, that I considered it to be the head of the Burdekin. I walked across it, in order to ascertain the presence of water, but found nothing but deep dry hollows surrounded with drooping tea trees, and the black basaltic rocks covered with wild bottle-tree scrub. It joined the valley of lagoons very much like the valley of the reedy brook, and seemed to unite with the latter, and to expand all over the large basin. Numerous headlands protruded from the table land into the valley of lagoons, between the stream of lava and reedy brook. Many of them were composed of quartzite and pegmatite [Graphic granite, composed of quartz and laminated felspar.--ED.], the detritus of which formed sandy slopes very different from the black and loamy soil of the table land and its plains. Several isolated hills and short ridges rise out of the basaltic floor of the valley of lagoons; they are composed of a different rock; and if it may be allowed me to judge by the colour and by analogy, I should say that they were pegmatite and quartzite. It would, therefore, appear that the valley of lagoons is connected with three streams of lava; one following down the river to the southward, a second coming down the valley of Reedy Brook from W.N.W., and the third coming from the N.W. The course of the Burdekin has no connection with this valley, but runs apparently along its eastern side, and divides the primitive rocks from the streams of lava; for I had not observed any lava on its left bank.

In returning to our camp, we saw a great number of women and children, who ran away upon seeing us, screaming loudly, which attracted some young men to the spot, who were much bolder and approached us. I dismounted and walked up within five yards of them, when I stopped short from a mutual disinclination for too close quarters, as they were armed with spears and waddies. They made signs for me to take off my hat, and to give them something; but, having nothing with me, I made a sign that I would make them a present upon returning to the camp. They appeared to be in no way unfriendly, and directed us how to avoid the water. When I reached the camp, I found that the Blackfellows had been there already, and had been rather urgent to enter it, probably in consequence of the small number of my companions then present, who, however, managed to keep them in good humour by replying to their inquiries respecting our nature and intentions; among which one of the most singular was, whether the bullocks were not our gins. This occurred last night; in the morning they returned again in great numbers, and climbed the trees on the other side of the brook to observe what was doing within the camp. It now became necessary to show them our superiority; which we attempted to do by shooting at a kite, numbers of which were perched on the neighbouring trees; our shots, however, unfortunately missed, and the natives answered the discharge of the gun with a shout of laughter. At this time, however, Mr. Roper, Charley, and myself returned from our excursion, when they became quiet. I threw a tin canister over to them, and they returned me a shower of roasted Nymphaea fruit. It seems that the seed-vessels of Nymphaea and its rhizoma form the principal food of the natives; the seeds contain much starch and oil, and are extremely nourishing. I then gave them some pieces of dried meat, intimating by signs that it must be grilled; soon afterwards they retired. Mr. Roper came in with sad tidings; in riding up the steep bank of the river, his horse, unable to get a footing among the loose rocks, had fallen back and broken its thigh. I immediately resolved upon going to the place where the accident had happened, and proposed to my companions, that we should try to make the best of the meat, as the animal was young and healthy, and the supply would greatly assist in saving our bullocks to the end of our long journey; and they declared themselves willing at all events to give a fair trial to the horse-flesh. Our bullocks were foot-sore and required rest. We, therefore, shot the horse, skinned and quartered it the same night; and ate its liver and kidneys, which were quite as good as those of a bullock.

May 7.--We cut the meat in slices, and dried it; and though there was some prejudice against it, it would have been very difficult to have detected any difference between it and beef; particularly if the animals had been in the same condition.

May 8.--As I found it necessary to follow the right bank of the river, in order to get out of this intricate country, I sent Mr. Gilbert and Charley to trace the river through the valley of lagoons. Having accomplished their object, they informed me that the river had no connexion with the lagoons of the large valley, but that several very large ones were even on its left bank; and that all tree vegetation disappeared from its banks where it passed through a part of the valley of lagoons.

May 9.--As my bullocks were still extremely foot-sore, it was necessary that we should travel only by short stages until they recovered; consequently, the day's journey did not exceed five miles in a N.N.E. direction; and, with the exception of some ridges, upon excellent travelling ground, along the left bank of the river. The latter formed, as I have already stated, the line of separation, first, between basalt and granite, and afterwards between basalt and a quartzose rock (probably baked Psammite). The country was beautifully open and well grassed; the river forming a simple channel, without trees, well filled with water and flowing between chains of lakes and lagoons on either side; one of which was covered with flocks of ducks and pelicans, resembling islands of white lilies.

Beyond the almost treeless flats round the lagoons, Casuarinas and Callistemon re-appeared along the river.

We saw some Blackfellows in the distance, who immediately withdrew as we approached them; but the tribe, which we had met at Reedy Brook, came to the other side of the river, and had much to say; we did not, however, take any notice of them, until we had unloaded our bullocks and finished our luncheon, when I went down to them, and gave them a horn of one of our slaughtered bullocks. Roper had saved the mane of his horse, and threw it over to them, but it seemed to frighten them very much. We inquired by signs as to the course of the river, and we understood by their answers, that it came a long way from the northward. At Reedy Brook the natives had given my companions to understand that the brook had its source not very far off to the W.N.W., by pointing at their heads, then at the brook, and then in the direction mentioned. I was therefore inclined to trust to their information about the river's source. They threw some yam-roots over to us, the plant of which we were not able to ascertain: and after that they retired.

May 10.--This morning they came again, and, when our bullocks were loaded and we were about to start, I went down to them and took a sort of leave. We had scarcely proceeded half a mile, when we missed the tinkling of our bell, and found that Charley had forgotten to put it on the horse's neck, and had left it behind. Mr. Calvert and Brown, therefore, returned to look for it, and, upon reaching the place where the camp had been made, saw the natives examining and beating every part of it; at the approach of the horsemen, however, they retired to the other side of the river; but when they turned their horses' heads, after having found the bell, the natives followed them, and threw three spears after them--whether it was out of mere wantonness, or with hostile intentions, I do not know, though I was inclined to believe the first. It was, nevertheless, a warning to us not to repose too much confidence in them. Mr. Roper met to-day with a severe accident, which nearly cost him his life. It was a very common practice to make our horses stop by catching them by the tails; as he tried to do this with his horse, which was not yet accustomed to him, the animal struck out at him, and kicked him with both feet on the chest. Roper happily recovered after some faintness, but complained for several days afterwards of external pain. We travelled this day about four miles and a half N.N.E. along the river side, following a well-beaten path of the natives.

The river was again confined in its own valley, with quartzose rocks (Psammite) on one side, and the falls of the basaltic table land on the other. Basalt was, however, observed here about on several spots at the left bank, and quartz porphyry composed the ridges near our last encampment. The river divided here into a great number of anabranches, but all confined in the same valley, and united by intermediate channels. The bed of it had again become sandy, with small pebbles of pegmatite and quartz. Casuarinas were plentiful on its banks; the poplar-gum, and the Moreton Bay ash on the adjacent flats; Tristania, with pubescent leaves round some lagoons; narrow-leaved Ironbark, and poplar-gum grew on the hills; and rich grass every where.

The night was clear, but the morning foggy, and the dew very heavy. The wind was from the northward, and, as usual, very strong after sunset.

May 11.--We travelled four miles to the E.N.E. The anabranches of the river continued; the ranges of quartz porphyry approached several times close to the river. Oak trees and drooping Melaleucas grew abundantly in its bed, and along the banks. Higher up we crossed fine flats with lagoons and lakes covered as usual with Nymphaeas. We encamped in latitude 18 degrees 32 minutes 37 seconds, after passing a Casuarina creek, with high banks and a sandy bed. This creek separated the table land from a broken low range of hills, composed of a coarse-grained sandstone. The banks of the river here seemed to have been swept away; a broad sheet of sand, covered with fine drooping tea trees, was slightly furrowed by a narrow stream of water, which seemed for the greater part filtering through the sands; chains of water-holes at its left side, fringed with Casuarinas, appeared to be anabranches of the river, and to be connected with the main stream during the rainy season.

I have to mention that a species of Sciadophyllum, nearly allied to Sc. lucidum, (Don. iii. p. 390,) was found in the lava scrub of the valley of lagoons: it was a small tree with large digitate leaves, each of them composed of from eleven to thirteen oblong acuminate, glabrous leaflets, which were about five inches long; and it attracted the attention of my companions as much by its ornamental foliage as its numerous terminal racemes of bright scarlet coloured flowers.

After having celebrated Whit-Sunday with a double allowance of fat cake and sweetened tea, I started with Charley to reconnoitre the country to the westward. Our friendly stream not only turned to the north, but afterwards to north-east and east-north-east; and though I had not succeeded in leaving it from Reedy Brook--not having been able to cross the lava streams of the basaltic table land--I now concluded, from the nature of the pebbles, and sands of the creek which we had crossed last, that the basalts and lavas had ceased, and that a passage to the westward would be practicable.

I followed the Casuarina Creek up to its head, and called it "Big Ant-hill Creek," in consequence of numerous gigantic strangely buttressed structures of the white ant, which I had never seen of such a form, and of so large a size.

136

The general course of the creek was north-north-west: for the first ten miles it was without water, but its middle and upper course was well provided with fine reedy holes, the constant supply of water in which was indicated by Nymphaeas, and other aquatic plants. At its left side near the junction I observed, as before mentioned, a coarse grained sandstone, and, at less than a mile higher up, I found flint rock; and, wherever I examined afterwards, the rocks proved to be coarse grained granite and pegmatite, the decomposition of which formed a sandy soil on the slopes, and clayey flats along the creek. The latter, however, were very limited. The ant-hills were intimately connected with the rock, as the ants derived their materials for building from the minute particles of clay among the sand. The primitive rock was cut with deep gullies and ravines, and several tributary creeks joined Big Ant-hill Creek from the primitive side. The basaltic table land, which extended all along the right side of the creek, formed steep slopes into its valley, and were generally topped with loose basaltic boulders. The table land was highest near the creek, and its drainage was not towards the creek, but to the south-west, into the valley of lagoons. White quartz rock was observed in a few places on the right side of the creek, where the primitive rock seemed to encroach into the territory of the basalt; and felspathic porphyry formed probably a dyke in the pegmatite, but was most evidently broken by the basalt. Where the upper part of the creek formed a shallow watercourse, and turned altogether into the primitive formation, a plain came down from the west-north-west with a shallow watercourse, which continued the separation of the two formations; the right side of the plain being basaltic, the soil of the Box and Ironbark forest loamy, with sharp pieces of the rock; the left side being sandy, and covered with a very pleasing poplar gum forest, in which the grotesque ant-hills were exceedingly numerous. About two miles higher up the plain, separated into several distinct plains, the largest of which was from twelve to fifteen miles long, and from two to three miles broad, and came from Mount Lang; another plain came from an isolated razorback hill, and a third continued on the line of contact of the basaltic and primitive rocks. The upper parts of the small creeks, which come down in these plains, were full of water, and had their source generally between heaps of bare basaltic rocks, surrounded by rich grass, and a scanty scrub of Pittosporum, of the native mulberry, of the fig-tree, and of several vines, with Polypodiums, Osmundas, and Caladiums growing between them.

Several other hills and mountains rose on the table land, generally with open plains at their base. The greater part, however, was open forest, principally of narrow-leaved Ironbark and Box, and occasionally poplar-gum.

One locality was particularly striking: a great number of rocky basins within the basalt, and surrounded by its black blocks, formed evidently so many lagoons during the wet season, as sedges and Polygonums--always inhabitants of constantly moist places--grew abundantly in most of them. These basins were situated between low basaltic rises, along which narrow flats frequently extended. The flooded gum-trees were fine and numerous, and made me frequently believe that I was approaching a creek. I rode, however, over eighteen miles of country to the westward without observing the slightest watercourse. Long flats bounded by slight undulations extended some to the northward, and others to the westward; but their inclination was imperceptible. I passed some hills and plains; and ascending one of the hills, I obtained a fine view. To the west by south I saw other isolated mountains: the country to the westward was not broken by any elevation; a fine long range was visible to the north-west.

It was now 3 o'clock P.M., and my Blackfellows had left me, as usual; my horse was foot-sore, and neither the poor animal nor myself had tasted water for the last thirty-six hours. Under these circumstances, though I ardently desired to push on to the north-west ranges, I thought it prudent to return; and after a short rest to my horse, during which I chewed some dry pieces of beef, I rode on my way back until 9 o'clock, and then encamped. The coldness of the night reminded me too strongly of the pleasures of the fire and the heavy dew which had fallen, though a comfort to my horse, rendered it difficult to light one; by dint of patience, however, I succeeded, and then stretched myself, hungry and thirsty as I was, by the side of a large Ironbark log; whilst my horse, which I had hobbled and tethered, drooped his head over me, little inclined either to feed or move. I started early in the morning of the 14th, and passed between Mount Lang and Razorback Hill. At the foot of the latter I met a small creek, which I followed through a long series of plains until I came on my old track, not very far from Big Ant-hill Creek. At the sight of water, which we had been without full fifty hours, my horse and I rushed simultaneously into it, and we drank, and drank, and drank again, before I could induce myself to light a fire and make some tea, which was always found to be much more wholesome, and to allay thirst sooner than the water alone.

Near the large water-hole at which I halted, was an old camping place of the natives, and the remnants of many a hut lay scattered round two large flooded gum trees. The smoke of the natives fires was seen in every direction. This part of the country is doubtless well supplied with water-holes: but as they are unconnected with a watercourse, the traveller, unless by accident, has little chance of finding them.

In returning along Ant-hill Creek, I passed a few native men sitting before their gunyas; they were not a hundred yards from me, yet they remained silent and motionless, like the black stumps of the trees around them, until the strange apparition passed by. At sunset, just as I was taking the saddle from my horse, I heard a cooee, and not considering it prudent to encamp in the vicinity of the natives, I began to tighten up the girths again; but, at the same time, answered the cooee, and soon after I saw Master Charley and his wearied horse descending from the opposite range. He had not had anything to eat since the morning of the preceding day, and was therefore exceedingly pleased to meet me. He had not been able to follow me, in consequence of the foot-soreness of his horse, but he had succeeded in finding a small spring at the foot of Mount Lang, near which the natives had often and recently encamped.

May 15.--We returned to our camp. The natives [These natives are probably the same as, or are connected with, the tribe that frequent Rockingham Bay, who have always been noticed for their friendly bearing in communications with ships visiting that place. Rockingham Bay is situated due east from the position of Dr. Leichhardt's party.--Note by Capt. King.] had visited my companions, and behaved very amicably towards them, making them not only presents of spears and wommalas, but supplying them with seed-vessels of Nymphaea, and its mealy roasted stems and tubers, which they were in the habit of pounding into a substance much resembling mashed potatoes. They took leave of my companions to go to the sea-coast, pointing to the east and east by south, whither they were going to fetch shells, particularly the nautilus, of which they make various ornaments.

May 16 and 17.--We moved our camp about twenty miles N.N.W. to latitude 18 degrees 16 minutes 37 seconds, to one of the head brooks of Big Ant-hill Creek. We travelled the whole distance over the basaltic table-laud without any impediment. The natives approached our camp, but retired without any communication.

I had not found any westerly waters on my ride of the 13th, but had seen a range to the north-west, and that was the goal of a new exploration. As we had been fortunate enough to find water at the contact of the primitive and basaltic formation, I wished to follow the same line of contact as long as it would not carry us much out of our course. We crossed, in a northerly direction, several granitic ranges which ran out into the table land, and were separated from each other by very large swamps, at the time mostly dry, and covered with a short withered swamp grass, but bearing the marks of frequent inundations. The bed of these swamps was perfectly level, and formed by an uninterrupted sheet of basalt. Chains of water-holes between the ranges, which I hoped would lead me to creeks, were lost in the level of these swamps; indeed, these granitic ranges were remarkably destitute of watercourses. The coarse elements of the decomposed rock, principally pegmatite, had formed uniform slopes, in which even heavy showers of rain

139

were readily absorbed; but rounded blocks of rock, sometimes curiously piled, protruded from the granitic sands. Pandanus spiralis fringed the scattered water-holes; and Grevillea chrysodendron, (R. Br.) formed a wreath, of pale silver-colour, round the swamps, but grew on sandy soil. White cranes, the ibis, geese, native companions, and plovers, were very numerous; and the large ant-hills scattered through the forest at the foot of the hills, looked like so many wigwams.

From one of the ranges I had another view of the north-west range, and we started for it, leaving the primitive country behind us. A cold, southerly wind set in on the morning of the 18th, which made Brown and myself shiver, and I most gladly availed myself of a flannel shirt, whilst Brown covered himself with his blanket. We rode about five hours over an undulating forest land, interrupted by one or two plains, and for the greater part exceedingly stony. We came at last to fresh burnt grass, and observed recent marks of the stone tomahawk of the natives; and, having passed a stony slope, with irregular low stony ridges, we saw an oak-tree creek before us, on the opposite side of which rose the granitic range for which we had directed our course. This creek also ran on the line of contact of primitive and basaltic rocks; the primitive side was cut by gullies and ravines, whilst the basalt formed a steep uninterrupted slope, though covered with boulders which had been carried down even into the sandy bed of the creek, where they were intermingled with those of granite and pegmatite. I called this creek "Separation Creek," in allusion to its geological relations: at the point where we met it, it turned to the north and north-west, which made me believe that it was a westerly water; but in this I was mistaken.

We had some slight showers of drizzling rain during the afternoon. The wind veered towards evening to the northward, and the night was clear.

We saw several kangaroos, and their tracks to the water showed that they were numerous. One of them, which we saw in the creek, was of a light grey colour, with rich fur and a white tail.

May 19.--We returned to the camp. A cold easterly wind continued during the day; low rainy clouds in the morning formed into heavy cumuli during the afternoon.

My geological observations lead me to the conclusion, that an immense valley between granitic ranges has here been filled by a more modern basaltic eruption, which (supposing that Mount Lang is basaltic in the centre of elevation) rose in peaks and isolated hills, but formed in general a level table land. The basalt has been again broken by still more recent fissures, through which streams of lava have risen and expanded over the neighbouring rock.

May 20.--We moved our camp about eighteen miles N.N.W., to Separation Creek, the latitude of which was 18 degrees 2 minutes 22 seconds.

John Murphy found Grevillea chrysodendron in blossom, the rich orange colour of which excited general admiration. The stringy-bark tree, and Tristania, were growing on the sandy soil, and the latter near watercourses. Several native bustards (Otis Novae Hollandiae, GOULD.) were shot, and I found their stomachs full of the seeds of Grewia, which abounded in the open patches of forest ground. In crossing a plain we observed, under the shade of a patch of narrow-leaved tea trees, four bowers of the bowerbird, close together, as if one habitation was not sufficient for the wanton bird to sport in; and on the dry swamps I mentioned above, small companies of native companions were walking around us at some distance, but rose with their sonorous cu-r-r-r-ring cry, whenever Brown tried to approach them. [The natives of Argyle call the cry of the native companion, Ku-ru-duc Ku-ru-duc; the natives of Port Essington call the bird Ororr.--NOTE BY CAPT. KING]

May 21.--I went with Brown to reconnoitre the course of the creek, and to ascertain whether it flowed to the westward. We soon found, however, that it turned to the north and north-east, and that it was still an eastern water. As far as I followed it down, it formed the separation between the primitive rocks and the basalt, but received several creeks from the westward. In riding along we heard the cooees of natives, and passed several large camping places near the large water-holes of the creek. A Blackfellow emerged suddenly from the creek, holding a Casuarina branch in his hand, and pointing to the westward. We made a sign that we were going down the creek, and that we had no intention of hurting him; the poor fellow, however, was so frightened that he groaned and crouched down in the grass. Wishing not to increase his alarm, we rode on. I followed up one of the largest tributary creeks coming from the westward towards its head; it was lined with Casuarinas and flooded-gum trees, like Separation Creek, and came from an entirely granitic country, ridges and ranges, with some high hills, bounding its valley on both sides; it soon divided, however, into branches, and as one turned too much to the north and the other to the south, I kept between them to the westward, and passed over a hilly, broken, granitic country. Large blocks of granite crested the summits of the hills, and their slopes were covered with Acacia thickets, and arborescent Hakeas and Grevilleas. A dwarf Acacia, with rhomboid downy phyllodia, an inch long, grew between the rocks. The natives were busy on the hills, cutting out opossums and honey. We heard their calls and the cries of their children. As we descended into another valley, the whole slope was on fire; we passed through it, however, with little difficulty. We crossed ridges after ridges, passed from one little creek and watercourse to another, all of which turned to the northward. At last, heartily tired, and almost despairing of attaining the object of our search, viz., a western water, we came into a valley which went down to the south-west; and, following it down, found that it joined a larger one which went to the westward. A broad creek, with the drooping tea tree and a sandy bed, gave us the promise of soon finding water; and, following the tracks of numerous kangaroos and native dogs, we came to a small pool. After passing over very rocky granitic hills, we came into a more open country; the banks of the creek became reedy, and water was more abundant, and at last a fine pool, surrounded by a rich belt of reeds, was before us. Brown was fortunate enough to shoot two ducks; and, as the sun was setting behind a neighbouring hill, we made our camp for the night.

May 22.--We returned to our companions, and by taking a W.N.W. course, we avoided all the ranges and gullies that we had crossed yesterday. At the westerly creek I found a rose-coloured Sterculia, with large campanulate blossoms and tomentose seed-vessels: the tree had lost all its foliage. I had met with this species on the rocky ranges of Moreton Bay (at Mount Brisbane), but there it was a low shrub, whereas in this place, and all round the gulf of Carpentaria, it formed a middle sized tree with spreading branches. A new Hakea, with long thin terete leaves (different from H. lorea) and Grevillea chrysodendron, grew along the creek. Grevillea ceratophylla (R. Br.) and another Grevillea, with a compound terminal thyrsus, and long lanceolate falcate leaves, grew on the slopes, in company with a Xylomelum, with smooth and smaller seed-vessels than those of X. pyriforme. The rocky ridges were occupied by the stringy-bark, fine Cypress-pine trees, the stunted silver-leaved Ironbark, a Eucalyptus, with very scanty foliage, orange-coloured blossoms, seed-vessels longitudinally ribbed, and as large as the egg of a fowl; its butt was covered with a lamellar bark, but the upper part and the branches were white and smooth; also by another Eucalyptus, with a scaly butt like the Moreton Bay ash, but with smooth upper trunk and cordate ovate leaves, which was also new to me; we called it the Apple-gum. We frequently met with the grass tree (Xanthorrhaea.)

May 23.--We moved our camp to the westerly creek I had found the day before, which with several others formed the heads of a river, flowing to the N.W. I called this river the "Lynd," after R. Lynd, Esq., a gentleman to whom I am under the greatest obligation, for his unmeasured liberality and kindness enabled me to devote my time exclusively to the pursuits of science and exploration.

The nights had been as usual very cold, and the dew very heavy. The prevailing breeze was from the east, veering towards evening to the north-east; during the morning a cold south-east wind. The rock was primitive, granite and pegmatite in several varities, with a few exceptions of anagenitic formation. Near the place of our first encampment on the Lynd, in lat. 17 degrees 58 minutes, I observed a sienite, to which the distribution of the hornblende in layers had given the stratified appearance of gneiss. Another rock was composed of felspar and large leaflets of white mica, or of quartz and white mica. The veins which traversed these rocks were all of quartz, which, within the pegmatite, enlarged into big masses and hills, particularly where basaltic rock was near. Mr. Gilbert and Charley went down the creek to find water and a practicable road, in case the country should prove mountainous and rocky. I had a view from a small peak near our camp; the country was full of ridges, but openly timbered, and I saw a low range to the northward, trending from east to west.

May 24.--It was the Queen's birth-day, and we celebrated it with what--as our only remaining luxury--we were accustomed to call a fat cake, made of four pounds of flour and some suet, which we had saved for the express purpose, and with a pot of sugared tea. We had for several months been without sugar, with the exception of about ten pounds, which was reserved for cases of illness and for festivals. So necessary does it appear to human nature to interrupt the monotony of life by marked days, on which we indulge in recollections of the past, or in meditations on the future, that we all enjoyed those days as much, and even more, than when surrounded with all the blessings of civilized society; although I am free to admit, that fat-cake and sugared tea in prospectu might induce us to watch with more eagerness for the approach of these days of feasting. There were, besides, several other facts interesting to the psychologist, which exhibited the influence of our solitary life, and the unity of our purpose, on our minds. During the early part of our journey, I had been carried back in my dreams to scenes of recent date, and into the society of men with whom I had lived shortly before starting on my expedition. As I proceeded on my journey, events of earlier date returned into my mind, with all the fantastic associations of a dream; and scenes of England, France, and Italy passed successively. Then came the recollections of my University life, of my parents and the members of my family; and, at last, the days of boyhood and of school--at one time as a boy afraid of the look of the master, and now with the independent feelings of the man, communicating to, and discussing with him the progress of my journey, the courses of the rivers I had found, and the possible advantages of my discoveries. At the latter part of the journey, I had, as it were, retraced the whole course of my life, and I was now, in my dreams, almost invariably in Sydney, canvassing for support, and imagining that, although I had left my camp, yet that I should return with new resources to carry us through the remainder of our journey. It was very remarkable, that all my companions were almost invariably anticipating the end of our journey, dreaming that they reached the sea-coast, and met with ships, or that they were in Port Essington

143

and enjoying the pleasures of civilized life; whilst I, on awaking, found my party and my interests on the place where I had left them in my dreams. During the leisure moments of the day, or at the commencement of night, when seated at my fire, all my thoughts seemed riveted to the progress and success of my journey, and to the new objects we had met with during the day. I had then to compel myself to think of absent friends and past times, and the thought that they supposed me dead or unsuccessful in my enterprize, brought me back immediately to my favourite object. Much, indeed the greater portion, of my journey had been occupied in long reconnoitring rides; and he who is thus occupied is in a continued state of excitement, now buoyant with hope, as he urges on his horse towards some distant range or blue mountain, or as he follows the favourable bend of a river; now all despairing and miserable, as he approaches the foot of the range without finding water from which he could start again with renewed strength, or as the river turns in an unfavourable direction, and slips out of his course. Evening approaches; the sun has sunk below the horizon for some time, but still he strains his eye through the gloom for the dark verdure of a creek, or strives to follow the arrow-like flight of a pigeon, the flapping of whose wings has filled him with a sudden hope, from which he relapses again into a still greater sadness; with a sickened heart he drops his head to a broken and interrupted rest, whilst his horse is standing hobbled at his side, unwilling from excessive thirst to feed on the dry grass. How often have I found myself in these different states of the brightest hope and the deepest misery, riding along, thirsty, almost lifeless and ready to drop from my saddle with fatigue; the poor horse tired like his rider, footsore, stumbling over every stone, running heedlessly against the trees, and wounding my knees! But suddenly, the note of Grallina Australis, the call of cockatoos, or the croaking of frogs, is heard, and hopes are bright again; water is certainly at hand; the spur is applied to the flank of the tired beast, which already partakes in his rider's anticipations, and quickens his pace--and a lagoon, a creek, or a river, is before him. The horse is soon unsaddled, hobbled, and well washed; a fire is made, the teapot is put to the fire, the meat is dressed, the enjoyment of the poor reconnoiterer is perfect, and a prayer of thankfulness to the Almighty God who protects the wanderer on his journey, bursts from his grateful lips.

May 25.--We travelled about eight miles down the Lynd. The country was very mountainous; granitic and pegmatite ranges bounded the valley on both sides.

May 26.--We continued our journey over the most mountainous and rocky country we had ever passed. The ranges formed the banks of the river itself, and even entered its bed, which gradually enlarged and was frequently formed by several channels fringed with large drooping tea trees. At the end of the stage, basalt was found to have broken through the granite.

144

May 27.--The river turned more to the northward, and, joined by many gullies, wound its way between wild and rocky, though low ranges. At a place where it left a range of rugged little peaks, basalt re-appeared at its banks, and extended for some distance, now filling flats with its rough and cellular blocks and pebbles, and again forming small hillocks of black bare rock. As soon, however, as the river had fairly left the basaltic formation, fine large flats of a light sandy soil succeeded on both sides; on which Pandanus spiralis grew in great abundance, and to a larger size than we had seen before. The bed of the river became very broad, and was covered with sands, shingle, and pebbles of the rocks of its upper course. I passed through a broad rocky gap of a range tending from east to west, and, at about two miles beyond and to the north-west of it, we encamped, in lat. 17 degrees 54 minutes 40 seconds.

In passing this gap, on a previous reconnoitring ride with Brown, I met with several natives with their wives and children, encamped at the north entrance of it. When they saw us, the men poised their spears, and shook their waddis to frighten us, but when, notwithstanding their menaces, we approached them, they left all their goods, and with their weapons only hurried up the rocks with wonderful agility. Three koolimans (vessels of stringy bark) were full of honey water, from one of which I took a hearty draught, and left a brass button for payment. Dillis, fish spears, a roasted bandicoot, a species of potatoe, wax, a bundle of tea-tree bark with dry shavings; several flints fastened with human hair to the ends of sticks, and which are used as knives to cut their skin and food; a spindle to make strings of opossum wool; and several other small utensils, were in their camp. One of my Blackfellows found a fine rock-crystal [Note at end of para.] in one of their bags, when we passed the place next day with our bullocks. The poor people had evidently not yet ventured to return. The natives we had formerly met, had generally watched our movements from a distance, and had returned to their camp as soon as we had fairly left it; but these seemed too much frightened; and I should not be surprised to find that the mountainous nature of their country had given them a greater share of superstition.

[Note: This shows how far the custom extends throughout the continent, of considering the rock-crystal as sacred; whether it be that it has been transmitted from tribe to tribe, or that the native was everywhere inclined to pick up a shining stone, and to consider it endowed with peculiar virtues. From the absence of brilliant ores, or precious stones, in the bags and dillis of the natives, I concluded, that neither precious stones nor brilliant metallic substances existed in the country where they lived. Those with whom we came in contact, generally admired our gold and silver chains and watches very much, but had nothing to show in return except broken shells from the sea-coast]

145

Among the new and interesting scrubs and trees which we met with at almost every step, I shall only mention a small Grevillea, from one to two feet in height, with pubescent pinnatifid leaves, and a simple or compound thyrsus of scarlet flowers; Cochlospermum gossypium, the native cotton tree of Port Essington, whose bright showy yellow blossoms and large capsules full of silky cotton, attracted our attention; its leaves are deciduous, and the trees were entirely leafless; a fine species of Calytrix on the rocks, and two of Loranthus on the drooping tea tree, the drooping foliage of which one of them imitated, whilst the other belonged to the group I mentioned as found at the Suttor, with its flowers inserted on a leafy bract.

Exocarpus latifolius is so different from E. cupressiformis, in its foliage and aspect, that I did not suspect their near relation, until I found blossom and fruit: the ripe kernel as well as its yellow succulent leaf-stalk have a very agreeable taste; a leguminous shrub, about five or six feet high, with purple blossoms gathered into terminal oblong heads; this would be an ornament to our gardens. Along the river we discovered a large tree, about forty or fifty feet in height, with rather singularly disposed horizontal branches and rich dark green foliage; its leaves were oblong acute, and frequently a foot long; its flowers formed dense heads, which grew into a fleshy body marked with the arcoles of every flower. It is either Sarcocephalus or Zuccarinia, or nearly allied to them. The tree has never been seen on easterly waters, but it was the invariable companion of all the larger freshwater rivers round the gulf. A fine species of Gomphrena was found in the sandy bed of the river. A species of Terminalia, a fine shady tree, with spreading branches and broad elliptical leaves, grew along the sandy creeks; and another smaller one with Samara fruit preferred the rocky slopes. Both of these, and a third species growing on the west side of the gulph, which I shall have to mention hereafter, supplied us with fine eatable gum, and a fourth species, with smooth leaves, had an eatable fruit of a purple colour.

The view I obtained from one of the hills near our yesterday's camp was very characteristic. The country was broken by low ranges of various extent, formed by exceedingly rocky hills and peaks, which lifted their rugged crests above the open forest that covered their slopes. Heaps of rocks with clusters of trees, particularly the smooth-leaved fig tree, the rose-coloured Sterculia, Exocarpus latifolius, were scattered over the slopes, or grew on the summits, to which they gave the resemblance of the lifted crest of an irritated cockatoo, particularly when huge fantastic blocks were striking out between the vegetation. As we travelled along, ranges of hills of this character appeared one after another; to which wallums and wallabies fled for security as we scared them from the river's side; the rose-breasted cockatoo (Cocatua Eos, GOULD.) visited the patches of fresh burnt grass, in large flocks;

146

bustards were numerous on the small flats between basaltic hillocks, where they fed on the ripe fruit of Grewia.

On the evening of the 27th May, we killed one of our bullocks, which had suffered more than any of the others by the journey, in consequence of his having carried our ammunition, which had decreased comparatively little, and the great weight of which had raised large lumps on his ribs, which had formed into ulcers. We were very disagreeably disappointed in not finding sufficient fat to fry the liver, which was our favourite dish; even the fat of the marrow had disappeared and had left a watery tissue, which, when grilled for some time, turned into a yellow substance, having the taste of the fried yolk of an egg. We dried our meat on the 28th, 29th, and 30th. I took a set of lunar sights, and calculated my longitude 143 degrees 30 minutes.

May 31.--We had scarcely left, our camp, when swarms of crows and kites (Milvus isiurus) took possession of it, after having given us a fair fight during the previous days, whilst we were drying the meat. Their boldness was indeed remarkable, and if the natives had as much, we should soon have had to quit our camp. Proceeding, we travelled over a broken and very stony country, with a stiff soil, but mixed with so much sand that even the Severn tree grew well. There was another small tree, the branches of which were thickly covered with bright green leaves; it had round inferior fruit, about half an inch in diameter, which was full of seeds: when ripe, it was slightly pulpy and acidulous, and reminded me of the taste of the coarse German rye bread. In consequence of this resemblance, we called this little tree the Bread tree of the Lynd. I ate handfulls of this fruit without the slightest inconvenience. A species of Pittosporum, and several Acacias, Pandanus, and the leguminous Ironbark, were scattered through an open forest of Ironbark and lanceolate box. I observed here a very ornamental little tree, with drooping branches and linear lanceolate drooping leaves three inches long; it very much resembled a species of Capparis that I had seen at the Isaacs. Its blossoms are very small, and the calyx and corolla have each five divisions; the stamens are opposite the petals; it bore a fruit like a small apple, with a hard outside, but pulpy and many seeded within, like Capparis; the calyx was attached to the base of the fruit.

The rock was still granitic, with small outbreaks of basalt; the leaflets of white mica were visible everywhere in the soil and in the large ant-hills, whose building materials were derived from the decomposed felspar. The bed of the river was frequently rocky, and very broad, with low banks and no water. The highest flood-marks we observed were from six to eight feet above the level of the bed; these marks were on the trunks of Casuarinas, Melaleucas, and flooded-gum, which grew along the channel. The country in general had a winterly appearance; and the grass round the camp was dry, but I observed

147

the fine grass of the Isaacs, and many varieties which grow on the Suttor and Burdekin, which will yield an excellent feed in the proper season; and, even at the present, neither our bullocks nor horses were starving.

The part of the country in which we were, possesses great interest in a meteorological point of view. In the centre of the York Peninsula, between the east coast and the gulf, and on the slopes to the latter, as might be expected, the northerly and easterly winds which set in so regularly after sunset, as well along the Burdekin as on the basaltic table land, failed, and were succeeded here by slight westerly and easterly breezes, without any great and decided movement in the atmosphere; and westerly winds, which had formerly been of rare occurrence, became more frequent and stronger. The days, from the stillness of the air, were very hot; but at night the dews were heavy, and it was very cold. Charley asserted that he had seen ice at our last camp.

The black cockatoo (Calyptorhynchus Banksii) has been much more frequently observed of late.

We used the last of our salt at the last camp; and what we should do without it, was a question of considerable interest. As I had never taken salt with me in my reconnoitring expeditions, and had never felt the want of it with dried beef, either grilled or raw, I recommended my companions to eat their meat in the same state; and, in fact, good dry beef, without any farther preparation, was much relished by all of us: for, when grilled, it became ashy and burnt, particularly when without fat; and, if stewed, although it yielded a good broth, it became tough and tasteless. The meat of the last bullock was very hard and juiceless, and something was to be done to soften it, and make it palatable: as we had no fat, we frequently steamed it with water, but this rendered it tough, without facilitating in the least the mastication; and its fibres, entering between our teeth, rendered them exceedingly tender, and caused us much pain. After a week's trial, and several experiments, we returned to our former practice of stewing it, and in a very short time relished it as much without salt, as we had formerly done with it.

148

CHAPTER IX

THE STARRY HEAVENS
SUBSTITUTE FOR COFFEE
SAWFISH
TWO-STORIED GUNYAS OF THE NATIVES
THE MITCHELL
MURPHY'S PONY POISONED
GREEN TREE-ANT
NEW BEVERAGE
CROCODILE
AUDACITY OF KITES
NATIVES NOT FRIENDLY
THE CAMP ATTACKED AT NIGHT BY THEM
MESSRS. ROPER AND CALVERT WOUNDED, AND MR. GILBERT KILLED.

June 1.--Mr. Gilbert and Charley made an excursion down the river last night, to look for water, but, as they did not return in the morning, and as water had been found, after they left, about four miles lower down, we started to meet them. Observing a swarm of white cranes circling in the air, and taking their flight down the river, I concluded that we should meet with a good supply of water lower down, and, therefore, passed the nearest water-hole; but, the country and the bed of the river being exceedingly rocky, our progress was very slow. After proceeding about eight miles, we came to the junction of a river from the south-west with the Lynd; and encamped at some small pools of water in latitude 17 degrees 45 minutes 40 seconds: having travelled, during the last two stages, in a west-north-west direction.

June 2.--When we left our camp this morning, Mr. Gilbert and Charley returned from their ride; they had come on our tracks last night, but, surrounded as they were by rocky hills and gullies, had been compelled to encamp. We travelled about seven miles and a half, and crossed three good sized creeks, joining the Lynd from the north east. The river divided several times into anabranches, flowing round, and insulating rocky hills and ridges. It was much better supplied with water, and contained several large reedy lagoons. An elegant Acacia, about thirty or thirty-five feet high, grew on its small flats: it had large drooping glaucous bipinnate leaves, long broad pods, and oval seeds, half black, and half bright red.

149

June 3.--We continued our journey down the river, about seven or eight miles. The first three miles were very tolerable, over limited box-flats near the river. As we approached the ranges again, the supply of water increased; and we passed one large poel, in particular, with many ducks and spoonbills on it. But the ranges approached the banks of the river on both sides, and formed either precipitous walls, or flats so exceedingly rocky, that it was out of the question to follow it. We, therefore, ascended the hills and mountains, and with our foot-sore cattle passed over beds of sharp shingles of porphyry. We crept like snails over these rocky hills, and through their gullies filled with boulders and shingles, until I found it necessary to halt, and allow my poor beasts to recover. During the afternoon, I examined the country in advance, and found that the mountains extended five miles farther, and were as rocky as those we had already passed. But, after that, they receded from the river, and the country became comparatively level. To this place I brought forward my party on the 4th June, and again descended into the valley of the river, and encamped near a fine pool of water in its sandy bed, in latitude 17 degrees 34 minutes 17 seconds. Here, last night, I met a family of natives who had just commenced their supper; but, seeing us, they ran away and left their things, without even making an attempt to frighten us. Upon examining their camp, I found their koolimans, (vessels to keep water) full of bee bread, of which I partook, leaving for payment some spare nose rings of our bullocks. In their dillies I found the fleshy roots of a bean, which grows in a sandy soil, and has solitary yellow blossoms; the tuber of a vine, which has palmate leaves; a bitter potato, probably belonging to a water-plant; a fine specimen of rock-crystal; and a large cymbium (a sea shell), besides other trifles common to almost all the natives we had seen. Their koolimans were very large, almost like small boats, and were made of the inner layer of the bark of the stringy-bark tree. There was no animal food in the camp.

The whole extent of the mountainous country passed in our two last stages, was of porphyry, with crystals of quartz and felspar in a grey paste; on both sides of it, the rock was granite and pegmatite; and, at the north-west side of the gorge, I observed talc-schist in the bed of the river.

The vegetation of the forest, and along the river, did not vary; but, on the mountains, the silver-leaved Ironbark prevailed.

The general course of the Lynd, from my last latitude to that of the 4th June, was north-west.

Sleeping in the open air at night, with a bright sky studded with its stars above us, we were naturally led to observe more closely the hourly changes of the heavens; and my companions became curious to know the names of those brilliant constellations, with which nightly observation had now, perhaps for the first time, made them familiar. We had reached a latitude which allowed us not only to see the brightest stars of the southern, but, also of the northern hemisphere, and I shall never forget the intense pleasure I experienced, and that evinced by my companions, when I first called them, about 4 o'clock in the morning, to see Ursa Major. The starry heaven is one of those great features of nature, which enter unconsciously into the composition of our souls. The absence of the stars gives us painful longings, the nature of which we frequently do not understand, but which we call home sickness:--and their sudden re-appearance touches us like magic, and fills us with delight. Every new moon also was hailed with an almost superstitious devotion, and my Blackfellows vied with each other to discover its thin crescent, and would be almost angry with me when I strained my duller eyes in vain to catch a glimpse of its faint light in the brilliant sky which succeeds the setting of the sun. The questions: where were we at the last new moon? how far have we travelled since? and where shall we be at the next?--were invariably discussed amongst us; calculations were made as to the time that would be required to bring us to the end of our journey, and there was no lack of advice offered as to what should, and ought to be done.

At several of our last camps the cry of the goat suckers, and the hooting of owls, were heard the whole night; and immediately after sunset, the chirping of several kinds of crickets was generally heard, the sound of which was frequently so metallic, as to be mistaken for the tinkling of our bell. At Separation Creek, we first met with the ring-tailed opossum; and, on the table land, often heard its somewhat wailing cry.

June 5.--We travelled, in a direct line, about nine miles west by north, down the river, although the distance along its banks was much greater; for it made a large bend at first to the northward, and afterwards, being turned by a fine conspicuous short range, to the westward. I named the Range after W. Kirchner, Esq., another of the supporters of my expedition. The river was here, in some places, fully half a mile broad, and formed channels covered with low shrubs, among which a myrtle was frequent. Between the ranges, the river became narrower: and, before it reached Kirchner's Range, a large creek joined it from the eastward; and another from the southward, after it had passed the range. The flats increased on both side of the river, and were openly timbered with box and narrow-leaved Ironbark. The rock near our yesterday's camp was talc-schist. Farther down sienite was observed, which contained so much hornblende as to change occasionally into hornblende rock, with scattered crystals of quartz. Granite and pegmatite were round some lagoons near the creek from the southward. The clustered fig tree of the Burdekin, became again more frequent; but Sarcocephalus was the characteristic tree of the river. The Acacia of Expedition Range and of the upper Lynd, grew to a comparatively large size in the open forest. We observed a cotton tree (Cochlospermum), covered with large yellow blossoms, though entirely leafless; and we could not help thinking how great an ornament this plant would be to the gardens of the colony.

As the water-holes became larger, water-fowl became more plentiful; and Brown succeeded in shooting several wood-ducks and a Malacorhyncus membranaceus. The bean of the Mackenzie was very abundant in the sandy bed of the river; we roasted and ate some of its fruit; it was, however, too heavy, and produced indigestion: Mr. Phillips pounded them, and they made an excellent substitute for coffee, which I preferred to our tea, which, at that time, was not very remarkable for its strength.

June 6.--We travelled about nine miles west by north to latitude 17 degrees 30 minutes 47 seconds. The first part of the stage was over an undulating country timbered with box and Ironbark; but the latter part was hilly and mountainous: the mountains were so rocky, where they entered the bed of the river, that we were obliged to leave its banks, and travel over a very difficult country.

On the small flats, the apple-gum grew with a few scattered Moreton Bay ash trees; on the bergues of the river we found the white cedar (Melia azedarach), Clerodendron; an asclepiadaceous shrub with large triangular seed-vessels; and, on the hills, the blood-wood and stringy-bark. The rock, as far as I examined it, was of porphyry of great hardness, and composing hills of an almost conical form.

June 7.--The same difficult country not only continued, but rather increased. Charley told me last night, on his return from a walk, that he had found sandstone. To-day we travelled over porphyries like those of the last stage: but, about four miles from the last camp, steep sandstone rocks with excavations appeared on our left, at some distance from the river, from which they were separated by porphyry; but, farther on, they approached the river on both sides, and formed steep slopes, which compelled us to travel along the bed of the river itself. Two large creeks joined the river from the southward, one of which was running, and also made the river run until the stream lost itself in the sandy bed. At the end of the stage, however, the stream re-appeared, and we were fairly on the fourth flowing river of the expedition: for the Condamine, although not constantly, was raised by rains, and showed the origin of its supply, by the muddy nature of its waters; the Dawson commenced running where we left it; and the Burdekin, with several of its tributaries, was running as far as we followed it. The waters of the Dawson, the Burdekin, and the Lynd, were very clear, and received their constant supply from springs.

152

We passed a camp of natives, who vere very much alarmed at the report of a gun, which Mr. Gilbert happened to fire when very near them; this he did in his anxiety to procure a pair of Geophaps plumifera, for his collection. These pretty little pigeons had been first observed by Brown in the course of our yesterday's stage, who shot two of them, but they were too much mutilated to make good specimens. We frequently saw them afterwards, but never more than two, four, or six together, running with great rapidity and with elevated crest over the ground, and preferring the shady rocks along the sandy bed of the river. I tried several methods to render the potatoes, which we had found in the camps of the natives, eatable; but neither roasting nor boiling destroyed their sickening bitterness. At last, I pounded and washed them, and procured their starch, which was entirely tasteless, but thickened rapidly in hot water, like arrow-root; and was very agreeable to eat, wanting only the addition of sugar to make it delicious; at least so we fancied.

June 8.--We travelled about nine miles west-north-west. The country was in general open, with soft ground on the more extensive flats; although sandstone ranges approached the river in many places. Four good-sized creeks entered the river from the southward. The sandstone, or psammite, was composed of large grains of quartz mixed with clay of a whitish red or yellow colour; it frequently formed steep cliffs and craggy rugged little peaks.

The stringy-bark grew to a fine size on the hills, and would yield, together with Ironbark and the drooping tea-tree, the necessary timber for building. A new species of Melaleuca and also of Boronia were found, when entering upon the sandstone formation.

The wind for the last few days has been westerly; cumuli forming during the day, dissolved towards sunset; the days were very hot, the nights mild and dry. It was evident that we had descended considerably into the basin of the gulf.

June 9.--We travelled about ten miles north-west. Box-tree flats, of more or less extent, were intercepted by abrupt barren craggy hills composed of sandstone, which seemed to rest on layers of argillaceous rock. The latter was generally observed at the foot of the hills and in the bed of the river; it had in most places been worn by the action of water. The stringy-bark became even numerous on the flats, in consequence of the more sandy nature of the soil: but the hills were scrubby, and Mr. Gilbert reported that he had even seen the Bricklow. The grass of the Isaacs grew from twelve to fifteen feet high, in the hollows near the river, which was, as usual, fringed with Sarcocephalus; a species of Terminalia; the drooping tea-tree; and with an Acacia which perfumed the air with the fragrant odours of its flowers. We gathered some blossoms of the drooping tea-tree, which were full of honey, and, when soaked, imparted a very agreeable sweetness to the water. We frequently observed great quantities of washed blossoms of this tree in the deserted camps of the natives; showing that they were as fond of the honey in the blossoms of the tea-tree, as the natives of the east coast are of that of the several species of Banksia.

June 10.--We travelled about five miles north-north-west to latitude 17 degrees 9 minutes 17 seconds. The flats, the rugged hills, and the river, maintained the same character. Creeks, probably of no great extent, joined the Lynd from the south side of all the hills we passed both yesterday and to-day.

The weather was very fine, although exceedingly hot during the day; but the nights were mild, and without dew. An easterly and south-easterly wind blew during the whole day, moderated a little at sunset, and again freshened up after it; but the latter part of the night, and for an hour and a half after sunrise, was calm. I was induced to think that this wind originated from the current of cold air flowing from the table-land of the Burdekin down to the gulf, as the easterly winds west of New England do, and as the westerly winds of Sydney during July and August, which are supposed to be equally connected with the table-land of New England and of Bathurst. The westerly winds occurring at the upper Lynd, do not militate against such a supposition, as they might well belong to an upper current coming from the sea.

Two new fishes were caught; both were very small; the one malacopterygious, and resembling the pike, would remain at times motionless at the bottom, or dart at its prey; the other belonged to the perches, and had an oblong compressed body, and three dark stripes perpendicular to its length; this would hover through the water, and nibble at the bait. Silurus and Gristes were also caught.

Brown rendered himself very useful to us in shooting ducks, which were very numerous on the water-holes; and he succeeded several times in killing six, eight, or ten, at oneshot; particularly the Leptotarsis, GOULD, (whistling duck) which habitually crowd close together on the water. Native companions were also numerous, but these birds and the black cockatoos were the most wary of any that we met. Whilst travelling with our bullocks through the high grass, we started daily a great number of wallabies; two of which were taken by Charley and John Murphy, assisted by our kangaroo dog. Brown, who had gone to the lower part of the long pool of water near our encampment, to get a shot at some sheldrakes (Tadorna Raja), returned in a great hurry, and told me that he had seen a very large and most curious fish dead, and at the water's edge. Messrs. Gilbert and Calvert went to fetch it, and I was greatly surprised to find it a sawfish (Pristis), which I thought lived exclusively in salt water. It was between three and four feet in length, and only recently, perhaps a few days, dead. It had very probably come up the river during a flood, for the water-hole in which the creature had been detained, had no connection with the tiny stream, which hardly resisted the absorbing power of the sands. Another question was, what could have been the cause of its death? as the water seemed well tenanted with small fish. We supposed that it had pursued its prey into shallow water, and had leaped on the dry land, in its efforts to regain the deep water. Charley also found and brought me the large scales of the fish of the Mackenzie, and the head-bones of a large guard-fish.

June 11.--We travelled about eight miles due north. The bed of the river was very broad; and an almost uninterrupted flat, timbered with box and apple-gum, extended along its banks. We were delighted with the most exquisite fragrance of several species of Acacia in blossom.

June 12.--We travelled about nine miles N.N.W. to lat. 16 degrees 55 minutes. The flats were again interrupted by sandstone ranges. One large creek, and several smaller ones joined the river.

June 13.--We accomplished nine miles to-day in a N.N.W. direction. The country was partly rocky; the rock was a coarse conglomerate of broken pieces of quartz, either white or coloured with oxide of iron; it greatly resembled the rock of the Wybong hills on the upper Hunter, and was equally worn and excavated. The flats were limited, and timbered with apple-gum, box, and blood-wood, where the sand was mixed with a greater share of clay; and with stringy-bark on the sandy rocky soil; also with flooded-gum, in the densely grassed hollows along the river. The Severn tree, the Acacia of Expedition Range, and the little bread tree, were frequent along the banks of the river. A species of Stravadium attracted our attention by its loose racemes of crimson coloured flowers, and of large three or four ribbed monospermous fruit; it was a small tree, with bright green foliage, and was the almost constant companion of the permanent water-holes. As its foliage and the manner of its growth resemble the mangrove, we called it the Mangrove Myrtle.

Brown shot fifteen ducks, mostly Leptotarsis Eytoni, GOULD.; and Charley a bustard (Otis Australasianus), which saved two messes of our meat.

The river was joined by a large creek from the south-west, and by several small ones; we passed a very fine lagoon, at scarcely three miles from our last camp.

June 14.--We travelled nine miles north by west, to lat. 16 degrees 38 minutes. The box-tree flats were very extensive, and scattered over with small groves of the Acacia of Expedition Range. The narrow-leaved Ironbark had disappeared with the primitive rocks; the moment sandstone commenced, stringy-bark took its place. We passed some lagoons, crossed a good sized

155

creek from the south-west, and saw a small lake in the distance. At the latter part of the stage the country became more undulating. The edges of the stiff shallows were densely covered with the sharp pointed structures of the white ants, about two or three feet high. They were quite as frequent at the upper part of the river, where I omitted to mention them. We saw a very interesting camping place of the natives, containing several two-storied gunyas, which were constructed in the following manner: four large forked sticks were rammed into the ground, supporting cross poles placed in their forks, over which bark was spread sufficiently strong and spacious for a man to lie upon; other sheets of stringy-bark were bent over the platform, and formed an arched roof, which would keep out any wet. At one side of these constructions, the remains of a large fire were observed, with many mussel-shells scattered about. All along the Lynd we had found the gunyas of the natives made of large sheets of stringy-bark, not however supported by forked poles, but bent, and both ends of the sheet stuck into the ground; Mr. Gilbert thought the two-storied gunyas were burial places; but we met with them so frequently afterwards, during our journey round the gulf, and it was frequently so evident that they had been recently inhabited, that no doubt remained of their being habitations of the living, and constructed to avoid sleeping on the ground during the wet season.

June 15.--We travelled about nine miles and a half down the river, over a country like that of yesterday, the tree vegetation was, however, more scanty, the forest still more open, the groves of Acacia larger. Brown returned with two sheldrakes (Tadorna Raja), four black ducks (Anas Novae Hollandiae), four teals (Querquedula castanea); and brought the good news that the Lynd joined a river coming from the south-east, with a rapid stream to the westward.

June 16.--We left the Lynd, along which we had journeyed from lat. 17 degrees 58 minutes to lat. 16 degrees 30 minutes, and travelled about twelve miles W.N.W., when we encamped at the west side of a very long lagoon Though I did not see the junction of the two rivers myself, Mr. Roper, Brown, and Charley, informed me, that the Lynd became very narrow, and its banks well confined, before joining the new river; which I took the liberty of naming after Sir Thomas Mitchell, the talented Surveyor-General of New South Wales; they also stated that the Lynd was well filled by a fine sheet of water. The bed of the Mitchell was very broad, sandy, and quite bare of vegetation; showing the more frequent recurrence of floods. A small stream meandered through the sheet of sand, and from time to time expanded into large water-holes: the river was also much more tortuous in its course than the Lynd, which for long distances generally kept the same course. The Mitchell came from the eastward, and took its course to the west-north-west. At the sudden bends of the river, the bergue was interrupted by gullies, and occasionally by deep creeks, which seemed, however, only to have a short course, and to be the outlets of the waters collecting on the flats and stiff plains at some distance from the river. The bergue was covered with fine bloodwood trees, stringy-bark and box. At a greater distance from the river, the trees became scanty and scattered, and, still farther, small plains extended, clothed but sparingly with a wiry grass. These plains were bounded by an open forest of the Acacia of Expedition Range. This little tree gave us a good supply of a light amber-coloured wholesome gum, which we sometimes ate in its natural state, or after it had been dissolved by boiling. Towards the end of the day's stage, we came to several very fine lagoons; one of which was several miles long, and apparently parallel to the river: it was exceedingly deep, and covered with the broad leaves of Villarsia and Nymphaea, and well stocked with numerous large fish, which betrayed their presence by an incessant splashing during the early part of the night. John Murphy caught the small striped perch of the Lynd; and another small perch-like fish, with a broad anal fin, which had already excited our admiration at the Lynd, by the beauty of its colours, and by the singularity of its movements. Charley saw the Silurus and the guardfish, and caught several of the broad-scaled fish of the Mackenzie; one of which, a most beautiful specimen, has been preserved and sent to Mr. Gould.

When we left our last camp at the Lynd, John Murphy's pony was missing. Charley went to look for it, and did not join us before we had arrived at our camp, after an unusually long and fatiguing stage. He brought us the melancholy news that he had found the poor beast on the sands of the Lynd, with its body blown up, and bleeding from the nostrils. It had either been bitten by a snake; or had eaten some noxious herb, which had fortunately been avoided by the other horses. Accidents of this kind were well calculated to impress us with the conviction of our dependence on Providence, which had hitherto been so kind and merciful.

As all our meat was consumed, I was compelled to stop, in order to kill one of our little steers. It proved to be very fat, and allowed us once more to indulge in our favourite dish of fried liver. Although we were most willing to celebrate the anniversary of the battle of Waterloo, and to revive our own ambitious feelings at the memory of the deeds of our illustrious heroes, we had nothing left but the saturated rags of our sugar bags; which, however, we had kept for the purpose, and which we now boiled up with our tea: our last flour was consumed three weeks ago; and the enjoyment of fat cake, therefore, was not to be thought of. Should any of my readers think these ideas and likings ridiculous and foolish, they may find plenty of analogous facts by entering the habitations of the poor, where I have not only witnessed, but enjoyed, similar treats of sugared tea and buttered bread.

In crossing one of the creeks we found a species of Acacia [Inga moniliformis, D. C. Prod. Vol. II. p. 440, where it is described as having been found at Timor.], with articulate pods and large brown seeds; it was a small tree with spreading branches, and a dark green shady foliage: it occurred afterwards on all the creeks and water-holes until we reached our destination.

It was at the lower part of the Lynd that we first saw the green-tree ant; which seemed to live in small societies in rude nests between the green leaves of shady trees. The passer by, when touching one of these nests, would be instantaneously covered with them, and would soon be aware of their presence by the painful bites they are able, and apparently most ready, to inflict.

June 19.--We travelled about eight miles N. 50 degrees W. lat. 16 degrees 22 minutes 16 seconds and again encamped at a very deep lagoon, covered near its edges with Villarsias, but without Nymphaeas. The soil of the flat round the lagoon, was very stiff and suitable for making bricks. The country along the Mitchell was an immense uninterrupted flat with a very clayey soil, on which the following plants were frequent: viz. Grevillea, Cerotaphylla, and Mimosoides, a Melaleuca with broad lanceolate leaves, Spathodea and a Balfouria, R. Br.

Whilst walking down by the lagoon, I found a great quantity of ripe Grewia seeds, and, on eating many of them, it struck me, that their slightly acidulous taste, if imparted to water, would make a very good drink; I therefore gathered as many as I could, and boiled them for about an hour; the beverage which they produced was at all events the best we had tasted on our expedition: and my companions were busy the whole afternoon in gathering and boiling the seeds.

Charley and Brown, who had gone to the river, returned at a late hour, when they told us that they had seen the tracks of a large animal on the sands of the river, which they judged to be about the size of a big dog, trailing a long tail like a snake. Charley said, that when Brown fired his gun, a deep noise like the bellowing of a bull was heard; which frightened both so much that they immediately decamped. This was the first time that we became aware of the existence of the crocodile in the waters of the gulf.

June 20.--We travelled about ten miles north-west, and avoided the gullies by keeping at a distance from the river. Plains covered with high dry grass alternated with an open forest; in which we observed Spathodea, Bauhinia, a Balfouria, groves of Cochlospermum gossypium, and several other trees, which I had seen in the scrubs of Comet River; among which was the

158

arborescent Cassia with long pods. A Bauhinia, different from the two species I had previously seen, was covered with red blossoms, which, where the tree abounded, gave quite a purple hue to the country. The stringy-bark, the bloodwood, the apple-gum, the box, and the flooded-gum, grew along the bergue of the river.

We passed some fine lagoons at the latter end of the stage. The banks of the river were so steep, that the access to its water was difficult; its stream, deep and apparently slow, occupied about half the bed, which was perhaps one hundred and eighty, or two hundred yards broad. The soil was very sandy, and three deep channels parallel to the river were overgrown with high stiff grass. A pretty yellow Ipomoea formed dense festoons between the trees that fringed the waters. The unripe seeds of Cochlospermum, when crushed, gave a fine yellow colour, shaded into an orange hue.

Large flocks of Peristera histrionica (the Harlequin pigeon) were lying on the patches of burnt grass on the plains, they feed on the brown seeds of a grass, which annoyed us very much by getting into our stockings, trowsers, and blankets. The rose-breasted cockatoo, Mr. Gilbert's Platycercus of Darling Downs, and the Betshiregah (Melopsittacus undulatus, GOULD.) were very numerous, and it is probable that the plains round the gulf are their principal home, whence they migrate to the southward. The white and black cockatoos were also very numerous.

John Murphy caught four perches, one of which weighed two pounds. The purple ant of the east coast has disappeared, and a similar one with brick-coloured head and thorax, but by no means so voracious, has taken its place.

The flooded-gum and the bloodwood were in blossom: this usually takes place, at Moreton Bay, in November and December. This different state of vegetation to the northward and southward, may perhaps account for the periodical migration of several kinds of birds.

June 21.--A shower of rain fell, but cleared up at midnight. We travelled nine miles north-west to lat. 16 degrees 9 minutes 41 seconds, over a country very much like that of the two preceding stages, and past several fine lagoons, richly adorned by the large showy flowers of a white Nymphaea, the seed-vessels of which some families of natives were busily gathering: after having blossomed on the surface of the water, the seed-vessel grows larger and heavier, and sinks slowly to the bottom, where it rots until its seeds become free, and are either eaten by fishes and waterfowl, or form new plants. The natives had consequently to dive for the ripe seed-vessels; and we observed them constantly disappearing and reappearing on the surface of the water. They did not see us until we were close to them, when they hurried out of the water, snatched up some weapons and ran off, leaving their harvest of

159

Nymphaea seeds behind. Brown had visited another lagoon, where he had seen an old man and two gins; the former endeavoured to frighten him by setting the grass on fire, but, when he saw that Brown still approached, he retired into the forest. We took a net full of seeds, and I left them a large piece of iron as payment. On returning to the camp, we boiled the seeds, after removing the capsule; but as some of the numerous partitions had remained, the water was rendered slightly bitter. This experiment having failed, the boiled seeds were then (Unclear:)tied with a little fat, which rendered them very palatable and remarkably satisfying. The best way of cooking them was that adopted by the natives, who roast the whole seed-vessel. I then made another trial to obtain the starch from the bitter potatoes, in which I succeeded; but the soup for eight people, made with the starch of sixteen potatoes, was rather thin.

We were encamped at a small creek, scarcely a mile from the river, from which John Murphy and Brown brought the leaves of the first palm trees we had seen on the waters of the gulf. They belonged to the genus Corypha; some of them were very thick and high.

The mornings and evenings were very beautiful, and are surpassed by no climate that I have ever lived in. It was delightful to watch the fading and changing tints of the western sky after sunset, and to contemplate, in the refreshing coolness of advancing night, the stars as they successively appeared, and entered on their nightly course. The state of our health showed how congenial the climate was to the human constitution; for, without the comforts which the civilized man thinks essentially necessary to life; without flour, without salt and miserably clothed, we were yet all in health; although at times suffering much from weakness and fatigue. At night we stretched ourselves on the ground, almost as naked as the natives, and though most of my companions still used their tents, it was amply proved afterwards that the want of this luxury was attended with no ill consequences.

We heard some subdued cooees, not very far from our camp, which I thought might originate from natives returning late from their excursions, and whose attention had been attracted by our fires. I discharged a gun to make them aware of our presence; after which we heard no more of them.

June 22.--We travelled about twelve miles N. W. 6 degrees W. to lat. 16 degrees 3 minutes 11 seconds, and encamped at a swamp or sedgy lagoon, without any apparent outlet; near which a great number of eagles, kites, and crows were feasting on the remains of a black Ibis. We passed a very long lagoon, and, in the latter part of our stage, the country had much improved, both in the increased extent of its forest land, and in the density and richness of its grass.

June. 23.--We travelled eight or nine miles in a W. N. W. direction to latitude 16 degrees 0 minutes 26 seconds, over many Bauhinia plains with the Bauhinias in full blossom. The stiff soil of these plains was here and there marked by very regular pentagonal, hexagonal, and heptagonal cracks, and, as these cracks retain the moisture of occasional rains better than the intervening space, they were fringed with young grass, which showed these mathematical figures very distinctly. We passed a great number of dry swamps or swampy water-holes; sometimes however containing a little water. They were surrounded by the Mangrove myrtle (Stravadium), which was mentioned as growing at the lower Lynd. The bottom of the dry swamps was covered with a couch grass, which, like all the other grasses, was partly withered.

Bustards were numerous, and the Harlequin pigeon was seen in large flocks. Wallabies abounded both in the high grass of the broken country near the river, and in the brush. Mr. Roper shot one, the hind quarters of which weighed 15 1/2 lbs.: it was of a light grey colour, and was like those we had seen at Separation Creek. Charley and Brown got seventeen ducks, on one of the sedgy lagoons.

I visited the bed of the river: its banks were covered with a rather open vine brush. Palm trees became numerous, and grew forty or fifty feet high, with a thick trunk swelling in the middle, and tapering upwards and downwards. Sarcocephalus, the clustered fig-tree, and the drooping tea-tree, were also present as usual. The bed of the river, an immense sheet of sand, was full a mile and a half broad, but the stream itself did not exceed thirty yards in width.

During the night we had again a few drops of rain.

June 24.--We continued our journey about nine miles west by north to latitude 15 degrees 59 minutes 30 seconds, over a rather broken country alternating with Bauhinia plains and a well-grassed forest. The banks of a large lagoon, on which several palm trees grew, were covered with heaps of mussel-shells. Swarms of sheldrakes were perching in the trees, and, as we approached, they rose with a loud noise, flying up and down the lagoon, and circling in the air around us. A chain of water-holes, fringed with Mangrove myrtle, changed, farther to the westward, into a creek, which had no connection with the river, but was probably one of the heads of the Nassau. We crossed it, and encamped on a water-hole covered with Nymphaeas, about a mile from the river, whose brushy banks would have prevented us from approaching it, had we wished to do so.

Though the easterly winds still prevailed, a slight north-west breeze was very distinctly felt, from about 11 o'clock a.m.

161

June 25.--We travelled about ten miles N.N.W. to latitude 15 degrees 51 minutes 26 seconds, but did not follow the river, which made large windings to the northward. It was very broad where Brown saw it last, and, by his account, the brush was almost entirely composed of palm trees. He saw a little boat with a fine Cymbium shell floating on the water. Our road led us over a well grassed forest land, and several creeks, which, although rising near the river, appeared to have no communication with it. Some plains of considerable size were between the river and our line of march; they were well grassed, but full of melon-holes, and rose slightly towards the river, forming a remarkable water-shed, perhaps, between the Nassau and the Mitchell. As we approached the river, we entered into a flat covered with stunted box, and intersected by numerous irregular water-courses. The box was succeeded by a Phyllanthus scrub, through which we pushed, and then came to a broad creek, filled with fine water, but not running, although high water-marks on the drooping tea-trees proved that it was occasionally flooded. We did not understand, nor could we ascertain, in what relation this singular country and the creek stood to the river, of which nothing was to be seen from the right bank of the creek.

The scrub, and the high grass along the creek, were swarming with white flanked wallabies, three of which Brown and Charley succeeded in shooting; and these, with a common grey kangaroo caught by Spring, and five ducks shot by Brown, provided our larder with a fine supply of game.

When I first came on the Lynd, I supposed that it flowed either independently to the head of the gulf, or that it was the tributary of a river which collected the waters of the York Peninsula, and carried them in a south-west or south-south-west course to the head of the gulf of Carpentaria. Such a course would have corresponded to that of the Burdekin at the eastern side, and the supposition was tolerably warranted by the peculiar conformation of the gulf. I expected, therefore, at every stage down the Lynd, at every bend to the westward, that it would keep that course. But, having passed the latitude of the head of the gulf, as well as those of the Van Diemen and the Staaten rivers, the Lynd still flowed to the north-west; and then, when it joined the Mitchell, I imagined that the new river would prove to be the Nassau; but, when it passed the latitude of that river, I conjectured that it would join the sea at the large embouchure in the old charts, in latitude 15 degrees 5 minutes--the "Water Plaets" of the Dutch navigators. To follow it farther, therefore, would have been merely to satisfy my curiosity, and an unpardonable waste of time. Besides, the number of my bullocks was decreasing, and prudence urged the necessity of proceeding, without any farther delay, towards the goal of my journey. I determined therefore to leave the Mitchell at this place, and to approach the sea-coast--so near at least, as not to risk an easy progress--and to pass round the bottom of the gulf.

June 26.--We travelled, accordingly, about seven miles almost due west, the latitude of our new camp being 15 degrees 52 minutes 38 seconds. On our way we passed some very fine long water-holes; some of which were surrounded with reeds, and others covered with the white species of Nymphaea; groves of Pandanus spiralis occupied their banks. Some fine plains, full of melon-holes, but well grassed, separated from each other by belts of forest-land, in which the Pandanus was also very frequent, were crossed during the day.

June 27.--We travelled eight miles W.S.W. over a succession of plains separated by belts of forest, consisting of bloodwood, box, apple-gum, and rusty-gum. Some plains were scattered over with Bauhinias. The holes along the plains are probably filled with water during the rainy season; dead shells of Paludina were extremely numerous, and we found even the shield of a turtle in one of them. At the end of the stage, we skirted some dense scrub, and encamped at one of the lagoons parallel to a dry creek, which must belong to the Nassau, as its latitude was 15 degrees 55 minutes 8 seconds. The lagoon was covered with small white Nymphaeas, Damasoniums, and yellow Utricularias; and on its banks were heaps of mussel-shells. The smoke of natives' fires were seen on the plains, in every direction; but we saw no natives. Brown approached very near to a flock of Harlequin pigeons, and shot twenty-two of them. A young grey kangaroo was also taken.

The kites were so bold that one of them snatched the skinned specimen of a new species of honey-sucker out of Mr. Gilbert's tin case; and, when we were eating our meals, they perched around us on the branches of overhanging trees, and pounced down even upon our plates, although held in our hands, to rob us of our dinners;--not quite so bad, perhaps, as the Harpies in the Aeneid, but sufficiently so to be a very great nuisance to us.

Yesterday and to-day we experienced a cold dry southerly wind, which lasted till about 11 o'clock A. M., when it veered to the south-west, but at night returned again, and rendered the air very cold, and dry, which was very evident from the total absence of dew. The forenoon was very clear; cumuli and cirrho-cumuli gathered during the afternoon. The sky of the sunset was beautifully coloured. After sunset, the clouds cleared off, but, as the night advanced, gradually collected again.

A circumstance occurred to-day which gave me much concern, as it showed that the natives of this part were not so amicably disposed towards us as those we had hitherto met:--whilst Charley and Brown were in search of game in the vicinity of our camp, they observed a native sneaking up to our bullocks, evidently with the intention of driving them towards a party of his black companions, who with poised spears were waiting to receive them. Upon detecting this manoeuvre, Charley and his companion hurried forward to prevent their being driven away, when the native gave the alarm, and all took to their heels, with the exception of a lame fellow, who endeavoured to persuade his friends to stand fight. Charley, however, fired his gun, which had the intended effect of frightening them; for they deserted their camp, which was three hundred yards from ours, in a great hurry, leaving, among other articles, a small net full of potatoes, which Charley afterwards picked up. The gins had previously retired; a proof that mischief was intended.

June 28.--We crossed the creek, near which we had encamped, and travelled about nine miles wost, over most beautifully varied country of plains, of forest land, and chains of lagoons. We crossed a large creek or river, which I believed to be the main branch of the Nassau. It was well supplied with water-holes, but there was no stream. Loose clayey sandstone cropped out in its bed, and also in the gullies which joined it. A small myrtle tree with smooth bark, and a leafless tree resembling the Casuarina, grew plentifully on its banks. We saw smoke rising-in every direction, which showed how thickly the country was inhabited. Near the lagoons we frequently noticed bare spots of a circular form, about twelve or fifteen feet in diameter, round each of which was a belt of ten, twelve, or more fire places, separated from each other by only a few feet. It seems that the natives usually sit within the circle of fires; but it is difficult to know whether it belonged to a family, or whether each fire had an independent proprietor. Along the Lynd and Mitchell, the natives made their fires generally in heaps of stones, which served as ovens for cooking their victuals. Bones of kangaroos and wallabies, and heaps of mussel-shells, were commonly seen in their camps; but fish bones were very rarely observed. It was very different, however, when we travelled round the head, and along the western side, of the gulf; for fish seemed there to form the principal food of the natives.

At the end of our stage, we came to a chain of shallow lagoons, which were slightly connected by a hollow. Many of them were dry; and fearing that, if we proceeded much farther, we should not find water, I encamped on one of them, containing a shallow pool; it was surrounded by a narrow belt of small tea trees, with stiff broad lanceolate leaves. As the water occupied only the lower part of this basin, I deposited our luggage in the upper part. Mr. Roper and Mr. Calvert made their tent within the belt of trees, with its opening towards the packs; whilst Mr. Gilbert and Murphy constructed theirs amongst the little trees, with its entrance from the camp. Mr. Phillips's was, as usual, far from the others, and at the opposite side of the water. Our fire place was made outside of the trees, on the banks. Brown had shot six Leptotarsis Eytoni, (whistling ducks) and four teals, which gave us a good dinner; during

164

which, the principal topic of conversation was our probable distance from the sea coast, as it was here that we first found broken sea shells, of the genus Cytherea. After dinner, Messrs. Roper and Calvert retired to their tent, and Mr. Gilbert, John, and Brown, were platting palm leaves to make a hat, and I stood musing near their fire place, looking at their work, and occasionally joining in their conversation. Mr. Gilbert was congratulating himself upon having succeeded in learning to plat; and, when he had nearly completed a yard, he retired with John to their tent. This was about 7 o'clock; and I stretched myself upon the ground as usual, at a little distance from the fire, and fell into a dose, from which I was suddenly roused by a loud noise, and a call for help from Calvert and Roper. Natives had suddenly attacked us. They had doubtless watched our movements during the afternoon, and marked the position of the different tents; and, as soon as it was dark, sneaked upon us, and threw a shower of spears at the tents of Calvert, Roper, and Gilbert, and a few at that of Phillips, and also one or two towards the fire. Charley and Brown called for caps, which I hastened to find, and, as soon as they were provided, they discharged their guns into the crowd of the natives, who instantly fled, leaving Roper and Calvert pierced with several spears, and severely beaten by their waddies. Several of these spears were barbed, and could not be extracted without difficulty. I had to force one through the arm of Roper, to break off the barb; and to cut another out of the groin of Mr. Calvert. John Murphy had succeeded in getting out of the tent, and concealing himself behind a tree, whence he fired at the natives, and severely wounded one of them, before Brown had discharged his gun. Not seeing Mr. Gilbert, I asked for him, when Charley told me that our unfortunate companion was no more! He had come out of his tent with his gun, shot, and powder, and handed them to him, when he instantly dropped down dead. Upon receiving this afflicting intelligence, I hastened to the spot, and found Charley's account too true. He was lying on the ground at a little distance from our fire, and, upon examining him, I soon found, to my sorrow, that every sign of life had disappeared. The body was, however, still warm, and I opened the veins of both arms, as well as the temporal artery, but in vain; the stream of life had stopped, and he was numbered with the dead.

As soon as we recovered from the panic into which we were thrown by this fatal event, every precaution was taken to prevent another surprise; we watched through the night, and extinguished our fires to conceal our individual position from the natives.

A strong wind blew from the southward, which made the night air distressingly cold; it seemed as if the wind blew through our bodies. Under all the circumstances that had happened, we passed an anxious night, in a state of most painful suspense as to the fate of our still surviving companions. Mr.

165

Roper had received two or three spear wounds in the scalp of his head; one spear had passed through his left arm, another into his cheek below the jugal bone, and penetrated the orbit, and injured the optic nerve, and another in his loins, besides a heavy blow on the shoulder. Mr. Calvert had received several severe blows from a waddi; one on the nose which had crushed the nasal bones; one on the elbow, and another on the back of his hand; besides which, a barbed spear had entered his groin; and another into his knee. As may be readily imagined, both suffered great pain, and were scarcely able to move. The spear that terminated poor Gilbert's existence, had entered the chest, between the clavicle and the neck; but made so small a wound, that, for some time, I was unable to detect it. From the direction of the wound, he had probably received the spear when stooping to leave his tent.

The dawning of the next morning, the 29th, was gladly welcomed, and I proceeded to examine and dress the wounds of my companions, more carefully than I had been able to do in the darkness of the night.

Very early in the morning we heard the cooees of the natives, who seemed wailing, as if one of their number was either killed or severely wounded: for we found stains of blood on their tracks. They disappeared, however, very soon, for, on reconnoitring about the place, I saw nothing of them. I interred the body of our ill-fated companion in the afternoon, and read the funeral service of the English Church over him. A large fire was afterwards made over the grave, to prevent the natives from detecting and disinterring the body. Our cattle and horses fortunately had not been molested.

The cold wind from the southward continued the whole day; at night it fell calm, and continued so until the morning of the 30th June, when a strong easterly wind set in, which afterwards veered round to the north and north-west.

Calvert and Roper recovered wonderfully, considering the severe injuries they had received; and the wounds, which I feared as being the most dangerous, promised with care and patience to do well. As it was hazardous to remain long at the place, for the natives might return in greater numbers, and repeat their attack, as well on ourselves as the cattle, I determined to proceed, or at least to try if my wounded companions could endure to be removed on horseback. In a case like this, where the lives of the whole party were concerned, it was out of the question to attend only to the individual feelings and wishes of the patients; I felt for their position to the fullest extent that it was possible for one to feel towards his fellow creatures so situated; but I had equal claims on my attention. I had to look exclusively to the state of their wounds, and to the consequences of the daily journey on their constitutions; to judge if we could proceed or ought to stop; and I had reason to expect, or at least was sanguine enough to hope, that although the temporary feelings of acute pain might make them discontented with my arrangements, sober reflection at the end of our journey would induce them to do me justice.

The constant attention which they required, and the increased work which fell to the share of our reduced number, had scarcely allowed me time to reflect upon the melancholy accident which had befallen us, and the ill-timed death of our unfortunate companion. All our energies were roused, we found ourselves in danger, and, as was absolutely necessary, we strained every nerve to extricate ourselves from it: but I was well aware, that the more coolly we went to work, the better we should succeed.

CHAPTER X

INDICATIONS OF THE NEIGHBOURHOOD OF THE SEA
NATIVES MUCH MORE NUMEROUS
THE SEA; THE GULF OF CARPENTARIA
THE STAATEN
A NATIVE INTRUDES INTO THE CAMP
THE VAN DIEMEN
THE GILBERT
SINGULAR NATIVE HUTS
CARON RIVER
FRIENDLY NATIVES
THE YAPPAR
MR. CALVERT RECOVERED
MODE OF ENCAMPMENT
SWARMS OF FLIES
ABUNDANCE OF SALT
NATIVES FRIENDLY, AND MORE INTELLIGENT.

July 1.--We left the camp where Mr. Gilbert was killed, and travelled in all about fourteen miles south-west, to lat. 16 degrees 6 minutes. We passed an extensive box-tree flat, and, at four miles, reached a chain of water-holes; but, during the next ten miles, we did not meet the slightest indication of water. Box-tree flats of various sizes were separated by long tracts of undulating country, covered with broad-leaved tea-trees, Grevillea ceratophylla, and G. mimosoides, and with the new species of Grevillea, with broad lanceolate leaves. We had to skirt several impassable thickets and scrubs of tea-tree, in one of which Pandanus abounded. At last, just as the sun was setting, and we were preparing to encamp in the open forest without water, we came to a creek with fine water-holes covered with Villarsias. Charley shot a native companion; a Fabirou was seen crossing our camp. My wounded companions got on uncommonly well, notwithstanding the long stage, and I now had all reason to hope, that their wounds would not form any impediment to the progress of our journey.

July 2.--We travelled ten miles south-west over a country exactly like that of yesterday; and encamped at a shallow water-hole in a creek, which headed in a tea-tree thicket, a grove of Pandanus being on its north side, and a small box-flat to the southward. Though the country was then very dry, it is very probably impassable during the rainy season. The tea-tree thickets seemed liable to a general inundation, and many shallow water-holes and melon-holes were scattered everywhere about the flats. The flats and elevations of the surface were studded with turreted ant-hills, either forming single sharp cones from three to five feet high, and scarcely a foot broad at their base, or united into a row, or several rows touching each other, and forming piles of most remarkable appearance. The directions of the rows seemed to be the same over large tracts of country, and to depend upon the direction of the prevailing winds. I found Verticordia, a good sized tree, and a Melaleuca with clustered orange blossoms and smooth bark, which I mentioned as growing on the supposed Nassau.

July 3.--We followed the tea-tree creek about four miles lower down, and encamped near some fine rocky water-holes, in which I discovered a yellow Villarsia, resembling in its leaves Villarsia inundata, R. Br.

Our day's journey was a short one in consequence of our having started so late. The delay was caused by Charley having captured an emu, a flock of which he met when fetching the horses. By holding branches before him, he was enabled to approach so close to them, that he shot one dead with a charge of dust shot. It was a welcome prize, and repaid us for the delay. To our wounded friends the delay itself was a welcome one.

The mussel-shells of these water-holes appeared to be narrower and comparatively longer than those we had previously seen. Pandanus was, as usual, very frequent; but a middle sized shady wide spreading tree, resembling the elm in the colour and form of its leaves, attracted our attention, and excited much interest. Its younger branches were rather drooping, its fruit was an oblong yellow plum, an inch long and half an inch in diameter, with a rather rough kernel. When ripe, the pericarp is very mealy and agreeable to eat, and would be wholesome, if it were not so extraordinarily astringent. We called this tree the "Nonda," from its resemblance to a tree so called by the natives in the Moreton Bay district. I found the fruit in the dilli of the natives on the 21st June, and afterwards most abundantly in the stomach of the emu. The tree was very common in the belt of forest along the creek.

The wind, during the last two days, was southerly, south-westerly, and westerly, freshening up during the afternoon. The forenoon was very hot: the night clear, and rather cool towards morning. I observed many shooting stars during the two last nights.

July 4.--We travelled seven miles in a south-west direction, to lat. 16 degrees 15 minutes 11 seconds, over an entirely flat country, covered with a very open forest of box, of bloodwood, and of the stiff-leaved Melaleuca, with the arborescent Grevillea already mentioned, and with a species of Terminalia with winged fruit. In the more sandy tracts of bloodwood forest, grew the Nonda, the Pandanus, and the apple-gum. The shallow creek was surrounded by a scrub of various myrtaceous trees, particularly Melaleucas. The creek afterwards divided into water-holes, fringed with Stravadium, which, however, lower down gave way to dense belts of Polygonum. The water was evidently slightly brackish; the first actual sign of the vicinity of the sea. A young emu was killed with the assistance of Spring; and a sheldrake was shot by Brown. Native companions were very numerous, and were heard after sunset, all round our camp. The stomach of the emu was full of a small plant resembling chickweed, which grew round the water-holes.

The smoke of the natives' fires was seen to the south and south-west.

July 5.--We travelled over full twenty miles of country, although the distance from camp to camp, in a straight line, did not exceed fourteen, in a south by west direction; the latitude of our new camp was 16 degrees 27 minutes 26 seconds. After passing several miles of tea-tree forest, intermixed with box, and alternating with belts of grassy forest land, with bloodwood and Nonda, we entered upon a series of plains increasing in size, and extending to the westward as far as the eye could reach, and separated from each other by narrow strips of forest; they were well-grassed, but the grasses were stiff. Tea-tree hollows extended along the outskirts of the plains. In one of them, we saw Salicornia for the first time, which led us to believe that the salt water was close at hand. Having crossed the plains, we came to broad sheets of sand, overgrown with low shrubby tea-trees, and a species of Hakea, which always grows in the vicinity of salt water. The sands were encrusted with salt, and here and there strewed with heaps of Cytherea shells. Beyond the sands, we saw a dense green line of mangrove trees extending along a salt water creek, which we headed, and in which Brown speared the first salt water mullet. We then came to a fine salt water river, whose banks were covered with an open well grassed forest; interrupted only by flat scrubby sandy creeks, into which the tide entered through narrow channels, and which are probably entirely inundated by the spring tides. Not finding any fresh water along the river I went up one of the creeks, and found fresh water-holes, not in its bed, but parallel to it, scarcely a mile from the river. When crossing the plains, the whole horizon appeared to be studded with smoke from the various fires of the natives; and when we approached the river, we noticed many well beaten footpaths of the natives, who are found generally in greater numbers and stronger tribes near the sea coast, where the supply of food is always more abundant and certain.

The first sight of the salt water of the gulf was hailed by all with feelings of indescribable pleasure, and by none more than by myself; although tinctured with regret at not having succeeded in bringing my whole party to the end of what I was sanguine enough to think the most difficult part of my journey. We had now discovered a line of communication by land between the eastern coast of Australia, and the gulf of Carpentaria: we had travelled along never failing, and, for the greater part, running waters: and over an excellent country, available, almost in its whole extent, for pastoral purposes. The length of time we had been in the wilderness, had evidently made the greater portion of my companions distrustful of my abilities to lead them through the journey; and, in their melancholy conversations, the desponding expression, "We shall never come to Port Essington," was too often overheard by me to be pleasant. My readers will, therefore, readily understand why Brown's joyous exclamation of "Salt Water!" was received by a loud hurrah from the whole party; and why all the pains, and fatigues, and privations we had endured, were, for the moment, forgotten, almost as completely as if we had arrived at the end of the journey.

July 6.--remained in camp the whole of this day, to rest the poor animals, which had been much fatigued by our last long stage. Charley shot a duck (Malacorhynchus membranaceus); and he, Brown, and John Murphy, went to the salt water to angle. My expectations, however, of catching fish in the salt water, and of drying them, were sadly disappointed. The whole amount of their day's work was, a small Silurus, one mullet, and some small guard-fish.

The weather continued fine, the forenoon usually very hot, but the air was cooled in the afternoon by a south-west breeze; the nights were clear and rather cold.

When I left Moreton Bay, I had taken a spare set of horse-shoes with me for every horse. They were shod at our leaving the Downs, but they soon lost their shoes; and, as our stages were short, and the ground soft, I did not think it necessary to shoe them again. In travelling along the Burdekin, however, and the upper Lynd, they became very foot-sore; but still there was a sufficient change of good country to allow them to recover; I had been frequently inclined to throw the spare shoes away, but they had as often been retained, under the impression that they might be useful, when we came to the gulf, to barter with the natives for food, particularly for fish. Finding, however, that the natives were hostile, and scarcely wishing to have any farther intercourse with them, I decided upon leaving the horse-shoes, and several other cumbersome articles behind; and they were consequently thrown, with two spare gun barrels, into the water-hole at which we were encamped. The natives will probably find them, when the holes dry up; and, if preserved, they will be a lasting testimonial of our visit.

July 7.--Charley told me that he had followed the river up to its termination. I consequently kept a little more to the left, in order to head it, and travelled two or three miles through a fine bloodwood and Nonda forest, the verdant appearance of which was much increased by the leguminous Ironbark, which grew here in great perfection. Two emus had just made their breakfast on some Nonda fruit when we started them, and Charley and Brown, assisted by Spring, succeeded in killing one of them.

We soon came to a salt-water river, with a broad sandy bed, perfectly free of vegetation, although its banks were fringed with drooping tea-trees. The tide being low, we were enabled to ford it. Whilst crossing it, a flock of black-winged pelicans stood gravely looking at us. The latitude of the ford, which was two miles and a half south from our last camp, would be 16 degrees 30 minutes, which corresponds with that of the Staaten, marked at the outline of the coast. A well grassed open forest extended along both sides of the river; and, at its left, large deep Nymphaea lagoons were parallel to it. South of the Staaten, we travelled over a forest country, similar to that of former stages, and which might be aptly distinguished by the name of Grevillea Forest; as Gr. mimosoides (R. Br.) is its characteristic feature; though a rather stunted stiff-leaved tea-tree was more numerous. Some slight rises were covered with thickets of the Acacia of Expedition Range. The last six or seven miles of our stage were over an immense box-flat. We passed many spots lately burnt by the natives, and saw the smoke of their fires in every direction. We encamped on a good sized creek, on which grew the articulate podded Acacia, the Mangrove Myrtle (Stravadium), and the drooping tea-tree. As soon as we had pitched our tents, we cut up the hind quarters of the emu into slices for drying; but we had to guard it by turns, whip in hand, from a host of square-tailed kites (Milvus isiurus).

John Murphy and Charley, whilst riding round the camp to ascertain if natives were in the neighbourhood, came on one of their camps occupied chiefly by women, and a few old men, who immediately ran off, but set the grass on fire as they went, to prevent the approach of the horsemen; and left behind them their waddies, spears, and a good supply of potatoes. At dusk, when Charley brought in the horses, two of which we tethered near the camp, the form of a native glided like a ghost into our camp, and walked directly up to the fire. John, who saw him first, called out, "a Blackfellow! look there! a Blackfellow!" and every gun was ready. But the stranger was unarmed, and evidently unconscious of his position; for, when he saw himself suddenly surrounded by the horses and ourselves, he nimbly climbed a tree to its very summit, where he stood between some dry branches like a strange phantom or a statue. We called to him, and made signs for him to descend, but he not only remained silent, but motionless, notwithstanding all the signs and noise we made. We then discharged a gun, but it had not the intended effect of inducing him to speak or stir. At last I desired Charley to ascend the neighbouring tree, to show him that we could easily get at him if necessary. This plan was more successful; for no sooner were Charley's intentions perceived, than our friend gave the most evident proof of his being neither deaf nor dumb, by calling out most lustily. He pooh'd, he birrrred, he spat, and cooeed; in fact, he did everything to make the silent forest re-echo with the wild sounds of his alarm; our horses, which were standing under the tree, became frightened, and those which were loose ran away. We were much afraid that his cooees would bring the whole tribe to his assistance, and every one eagerly proffered his advice. Charley wished to shoot him, "or," said he, "you will all be killed; I do not care for myself, but I care for your being killed and buried." Others wished to remove from the spot, and so give him an opportunity of escaping. I was, of course, horrified at the idea of shooting a poor fellow, whose only crime, if so it might be called, was in having mistaken our fire for that of his own tribe: so I went to our own fire, which was at a short distance, where he could see me distinctly, and then made signs for him to descend and go away. He then began to be a little more quiet, and to talk; but soon hallooed again, and threw sticks at myself, at my companions, and at the horses. We now retired about eight yards, to allow him to escape, which we had not done before, because I feared he might imagine we were afraid of his incantations, for he sang most lamentable corrobories, and cried like a child; frequently exclaiming, "Mareka! Mareka!!" This word is probably identical with Marega; the name given by the Malays to the natives of the north coast, which is also called by them "Marega." [Capt. King's Intertropical Survey of Australia, vol. I. p. 135.] After continuing his lamentations for some time, but of which we took no notice, they gradually ceased; and, in a few minutes, a slight rustling noise was heard, and he was gone: doubtless delighted at having escaped from the hands of the pale-faced anthropophagi.

July 8.--This morning the whole tribe, well armed, watched us from a distance; but they allowed us quietly to load our bullocks, and depart, without offering us the least annoyance. Their companion will, no doubt, leave a dreadful account of the adventures of last night to his black posterity.

We travelled about twelve miles south by west to latitude 16 degrees 47 minutes; at first over an almost uninterrupted box-flat, full of melon-holes, and with many small holes in the ground, which caused our horses and cattle to stumble at almost every step. The dry melon-holes were covered with dead

Paludinas, with shells of a large crab, and of the fresh water turtle. At about seven miles, we passed a strip of Blackwood forest, with many Nonda trees; and crossed a small creek. The latter part of the stage was again over a large box-flat, intersected by shallow grassy depressions, timbered with flooded-gum. We saw on the rising ground some open scrub, with scattered Bauhinias and Cochlospermums. Our encampment was at a creek on the south side of a slight rise, with Bauhinia trees, and near good water-holes. The creek, like all the others we had passed, flowed to the westward.

Near our camp we examined three holes, full six feet deep, and four feet in diameter, communicating with each other at their bottom. They were about three feet apart, and appeared to have been dug with sharp sticks. I have not the slightest idea for what purpose they were intended. They were most certainly not dug to obtain roots; and it seemed unlikely for wells; for the water, even in this unusually dry season, was very abundant.

The white ant-hills, which are built in rows, had, during this stage, a direction from north by west to south by east, and, as I have before mentioned a conjecture that the little builders would expose the narrowest side of their habitation to the weather side, the prevailing winds would be from the north.

July 9.--We travelled thirteen or fourteen miles south by west to latitude 17 degrees 0 minutes 13 seconds, at first crossing a box-flat, and after that a succession of greater or smaller plains, separated by a very open Grevillea forest. These plains were well grassed, or partly covered with a species of Euphorbia, which was eaten by our horses and cattle; and also with the long trailings of the native melon; the fruit of which tastes very tolerably, after the bitter skin has been removed; but when too ripe, the fruit is either insipid or nauseous. The bustard seems to feed almost exclusively on them, for the stomach of one, which Brown shot, was full of them.

The apple-gum, which we had missed for some time, again made its appearance, accompanied by another white gum, with long narrow leaves. As we approached the creek, at which we afterwards encamped, the vegetation became richer, and the melon-holes enlarged into dry water-holes, which were frequently shaded by the Acacia with articulate pods (Inga moniliformis). The two species of Terminalia, of the upper Lynd, were numerous; and a small green looking tree, which we found growing densely along the creek, had wood of a brown colour, which smelt like raspberry jam; and, upon burning it, the ashes produced a very strong lye, which I used in dressing the wounds of my companions. This tree was found in great abundance on all the rivers and creeks round the gulf, within the reach of salt water; and when crossing Arnheim Land, though less frequently.

Sandstone cropped out in the banks of the creek, and formed the reservoirs

173

in its bed.

Last night, and the night before, we experienced a very cold wind from the southward.

The laughing Jackass (Dacelo cervina, GOULD) of this part of the country, is of a different species from that of the eastern coast, is of a smaller size, and speaks a different language; but the noise is by no means so ridiculous as that of Dac. gigantea: he is heard before sunrise, and immediately after sunset, like his representative of the eastern coast. The latter was observed as far as the upper Lynd, where the new one made his appearance.

We crossed a bush fire, which had been lighted just before we came to the creek, but we did not see the incendiaries. In the morning of the 10th July, however, they had discovered our tracks, and followed them until they came in sight of the camp; but retired as soon as they saw us: and when they met Charley returning with the bullocks, they ran away. After half-an-hour's travelling towards the south-west, we came to the Van Diemen, which is marked in Arrowsmith's map in latitude 17 degrees. It was about seventy or eighty yards broad, with steep banks and a fine sandy bed, containing detached pools of water surrounded by Polygonum, and extremely boggy. My horse stuck in the mud, and it was with great difficulty that I extricated him.

As our meal bags were empty, and no sign of game appeared, I decided upon selecting a good open camping place, for the purpose of killing our last little steer. The country was a fine open grassy forest land, in which the apple-gum prevailed, and with many swampy grassy lagoons covered with white, blue, and pink Nymphaeas. The box tree grew in their immediate neighbourhood.

In the bed of the Van Diemen we saw some well constructed huts of the natives; they were made of branches arched over in the form of a bird-cage, and thatched with grass and the bark of the drooping tea-tree. The place where we encamped had been frequently used by the natives for the same purpose. Our attention was particularly attracted by a large heap of chaff, from which the natives appeared to have taken the seeds. This grass was, however, very different from the panicum, of the seeds of which the natives of the Gwyder River make a sort of bread; and which there forms the principal food of the little Betshiregah (Melopsittacus undulatus, GOULD).

The night was calm, clear, and cold.

The kites became most daring and impudent. Yesterday, I cleaned the fat gizzard of a bustard to grill it on the embers, and the idea of the fat dainty bit made my mouth water. But alas! whilst holding it in my hand, a kite pounced down and carried it off, pursued by a dozen of his comrades, eager to seize the booty.

174

We killed our little steer in the afternoon of the 10th, and the next day we cut the meat into slices, and hung it out on a kangaroo net: the wind was high, the sun warm, and our meat dried most perfectly. Whilst we were in the midst of our work, some natives made their appearance. I held out a branch as a sign of peace, when they ventured up to hold a parley, though evidently with great suspicion. They were rather small, and the tall ones were slim and lightly built. They examined Brown's hat, and expressed a great desire to keep it. In order to make them a present, I went to the tents to fetch some broken pieces of iron; and whilst I was away, Brown, wishing to surprise them, mounted his horse, and commenced trotting, which frightened them so much, that they ran away, and did not come again. One of them had a singular weapon, neatly made, and consisting of a long wooden handle, with a sharp piece of iron fixed in at the end, like a lancet. The iron most probably had been obtained from the Malays who annually visit the gulf for trepang. Some of their spears were barbed.

July 12.--The meat had dried so well, that I started this morning; having completed the operation of drying in rather more than a day. It was, of course, necessary to spread the meat out for several days, to prevent its becoming mildewed. This was done every day after arriving at our camping-place.

Our killing camp was about five miles south-west from the Van Diemen; and we travelled in the same direction about eight miles farther, through a most beautiful country, consisting of an open forest timbered with the box-tree, apple-gum, and white-gum; it was well grassed, and abundantly supplied with water. We crossed a small river with a course west by north; it had a broad sandy bed, numerous pools of water, and steep banks: the latter were covered with Sarcocephalus and drooping tea-trees. I called it the "Gilbert," after my unfortunate companion. Five miles farther, we came to a fine creek, at which we encamped. Its water-holes were surrounded by the Nelumbiums of the Mackenzie, and by a fine yellow Ipomoea, with larger flowers than that described as growing at the Mitchell. We gathered a considerable quantity of Nelumbium seeds, which were very palatable, and, when roasted and pounded, made a most excellent substitute for coffee.

July 13.--Our horses had enjoyed the green feed round the lagoons near our killing camp, so much, that they returned to it during the night, and caused a delay until noon, when we resumed our journey. The first part of the stage was over fine well-watered forest land. We crossed two creeks, with good water-holes, in one of which was a fishing weir. The country to the south of the last creek changed to a succession of plains of various sizes, extending mostly to the westward, and very open undulations scattered over with rather stunted trees of Grevillea mimosoides, G. ceratophylla, Terminalia, Bauhinia, and Balfouria? an apocynaceous tree. And again we passed over box and apple-gum flats, which, by their rich verdure, refreshed the eye tired with the uniform yellow colour of the dry grass, in which the whole country was clothed. We saw the bush fires of the natives every where around us; and many large tracts which had been recently burnt. The sun was getting very low, and my patients were very tired, and yet no water was to be seen. Cumuli, which had been gradually collecting from one o'clock in the afternoon, cast their shadows over the forest, and deceived the eye into the belief that the desired creek was before us. At last, however, to our infinite satisfaction, we entered into a scrub, formed of low stunted irregularly branched tea-trees, where we found a shallow water-course, which gradually enlarged into deep holes, which were dry, with the exception of one which contained just a sufficient supply of muddy water to form a stepping-stone for the next stage. Our latitude was 17 degrees 19 minutes 36 seconds.

July 14.--We travelled about eleven miles S.S.W. to latitude 17 degrees 28 minutes 11 seconds, over an immense box-flat, interrupted only by some plains and by two tea-tree creeks; the tea-trees were stunted and scrubby like those of our last stage. At the second creek we passed an old camping place of the natives, where we observed a hedge of dry branches, and, parallel to it, and probably to the leeward, was a row of fire places. It seemed that the natives sat and lay between the fires and the row of branches. There were, besides, three huts of the form of a bee-hive, closely thatched with straw and tea-tree bark. Their only opening was so small, that a man could scarcely creep through it; they were four or five feet high, and from eight to ten feet in diameter. [A hut of this description, but of smaller dimensions, is described by Capt. King, at the North Goulburn Island.--King's Voyage, vol. I. p. 72.] One of the huts was storied, like those I noticed on the banks of the Lynd. It would appear that the natives make use of these tents during the wet and cold season, but encamp in the open air in fine weather.

A brown wallabi and a bustard were shot, which enabled us to save some of our meat. We encamped at a fine long water-hole, in the bed of a scrubby creek.

July 15.--Mr. Roper's illness increased so much that he could not even move his legs, and we were obliged to carry him from one place to another; I therefore, stopt here two days, to allow him to recover a little.

July 17.--We travelled about ten miles south 55 degrees west over an almost uninterrupted box and Melaleuca flat, free from melon-holes and grassy swamps, but full of holes, into which our horses and bullocks sank at every step, which sadly incommoded our wounded companions.

About two miles and a half from our camp, we came to the Caron River

(Corners Inlet), which deserved rather the name of a large creek. Its sandy and occasionally rocky bed, was dry; but parallel lines of Nymphaea lagoons extended on both sides. The drooping tea-tree was, as usual, very beautiful. We skirted a tea-tree scrub, without a watercourse, about two miles and a half south of the "Caron," and passed some undulations, with Grevillea forest. To the south-west of these undulations, we came to a chain of lagoons; from which several white cranes and a flight of the black Ibis rose. Brown shot one of the latter, which, when picked and cleaned for cooking, weighed three pounds and a half; it was very fat, and proved to be excellent eating. Cytherea shells were again found, which showed that the salt water was not very far off.

Charley gave a characteristic description of this country, when he returned from a ride in search of game: "It is a miserable country! nothing to shoot at, nothing to look at, but box trees and anthills." The box-forest was, however, very open and the grass was good; and the squatter would probably form a very different opinion of its merits. When we were preparing to start in the morning some natives came to look at us; but they kept within the scrub, and at a respectable distance.

July 18.--We travelled south-west by west, over a succession of plains, and of undulating Grevillea forest, which changed into tea-tree thickets, and stunted tea-tree scrubs, on a sandy soil with Salicornia, Binoe's Trichinium, and several other salt plants. At about five miles from the camp, we came to salt-water inlets, densely surrounded by mangroves, and with sandy flats extending along their banks, encrusted with salt. Charley rode through the dry mangrove scrub, and came on a sandy beach with the broad Ocean before him. We had a long way to go to the east and S.S.E. to get out of the reach of the brackish water, and came at last to grassy swamps, with a good supply of fresh water. We encamped in lat. 17 degrees 41 minutes 52 seconds; about ten miles south by west from our last camp. Charley was remarkably lucky to-day, in catching an emu, and shooting six teals, a brown wallabi of the Mitchell, and a kangaroo with a broad nail at the end of its tail. Brown also shot a sheldrake and a Malacorhynchus membranaceus. During the time that we were travelling to the southward, we had a north-east wind during the forenoon, which in the afternoon veered round to the east and south. Such a change, in a locality like ours, was very remarkable; because, in the neighbourhood of the sea, it was natural to expect a sea breeze, instead of which, however, the breeze was off the land. The cause can only be attributed to a peculiar formation of the country south and south-east of the gulf.

July 19.--We travelled seven miles and a half due south, through a succession of stunted tea-tree thickets and tea-tree forests, in which the little bread-tree of the Lynd was common. We passed two creeks with rocky beds, the one with salt water, and the other fresh. The natives had been digging here, either for shells or roots. We came to a fine river with salt water about two hundred and fifty or three hundred yards broad, with low banks fringed with stunted mangroves. The well beaten foot-path and the numerous fire-places of the natives, proved how populous the country must be. In following a foot-path, we came to some large lagoons, but containing very little water; the natives had been digging in the dry parts, perhaps for the roots of Nymphaea. We encamped at one of them in lat. 17 degrees 49 minutes.

The country along the river was an open box-forest. Natives cooeed around us; and we saw a man and his gin, and farther on two others busily occupied in burning the grass. When Charley came to the lagoon he saw a black boy, who immediately retreated out of sight. Two straw-necked Ibises and seven ducks were shot. Mr. Roper had suffered much by the long rides of the last stages; but his health was improving, notwithstanding. The Nonda tree had disappeared north of the Van Diemen, and the emu here feeds on the fruit of the little Severn tree, which is so excessively bitter, as to impart its quality to the meat, and even to the gizzard and the very marrow.

As we approached the salt water, the various species of Eucalyptus, with the exception of the box, disappeared, and various species of tea-tree (Melaleuca) took their place; they grew even on the sands with incrustations of salt, and gave way only to the mangroves, which were bathed by the brine itself.

We now commenced collecting the gum of the broad-leaved Terminalia of the upper Lynd, and boiled it for Mr. Roper, who liked it very much.

We recognised one of the kites (Milvus isiurus), which had followed us from our last killing camp, down to the head of the gulf.

July 20.--This morning, the bullocks had strayed farther than usual, and, whilst we were waiting for them, some natives came to the rocks opposite our camp; and one of them beckoned me to come over to him. They had been observing our camp last night, for some time after the rising of the moon, and I had caused Brown to discharge his gun, in order to drive them away. They did not, however, trouble us then any farther, but encamped at a neighbouring lagoon; showing evidently that they expected no harm from us. When the bold fellow invited me to come over to him, I hesitated at first, as they might have disturbed us when loading our bullocks; but, as the animals did not appear, I took my reconnoitring bag with some iron nose rings, and made Brown follow me at some distance with the double barrelled gun, and went over to them. After much hesitation, four of them approached me. I made them presents, which gained their confidence, and they began to examine and admire my dress, my watch, etc. It was singular that the natives were always most struck with our hats. We made them understand where we came from and whither we were going, and it seemed that they understood us better than we could understand them. When the bullocks arrived, we returned to our camp, accompanied by the natives, who had lost all fear after the tokens of friendship they had received: and when we started, they joined our train and guided us on their foot-path (Yareka) along the salt water creek (Yappar.) They very much admired our horses and bullocks, and particularly our kangaroo dog. They expressed their admiration by a peculiar smacking or clacking with their tongue or lips. The fine river changed very soon into a salt water creek, coming from south by west. We passed some very beautiful rocky lagoons under the abrupt terminations of low sandstone hills, which were openly timbered at the top, but surrounded by thickets of the little Severn tree. The box-tree grew on the flats which separated the ridges from the creek, with the small bread-tree, the bloodwood and pandanus. As the Mangrove disappeared, the drooping tea-tree took its place. Several rocky bars crossed the "Yappar," which seemed to be the name by which the natives called it; but only one was broad enough to allow us to cross safely with our horses and bullocks. Here our black friends took their leave of us; they seemed very desirous of showing us their whole country, and of introducing us to their tribe, which was probably very numerous. After crossing the creek in lat. 17 degrees 54 minutes or 55 minutes, and longit. 140 degrees 45 minutes approx., we travelled due west, and came at once into an undulating hilly country. The hills were composed of iron-sandstone; their summits were generally very openly timbered with apple-gum and a new white-barked tree; but their bases were covered with thickets of the little Severn tree. The intervening flats bore either a box-tree with a short trunk branching off immediately above the ground; or a middle-sized tea-tree, with a lanceolate leaf, or thickets of stunted tea-tree. We travelled full thirteen miles without water, or any decided water-course. We passed several dry water-holes shaded by the broad-leaved Terminalia; and saw many Acacias twenty-five and thirty feet in height, with a slender trunk, and an elegant drooping foliage: it very much resembled the Acacia of Expedition Range; but the drooping habit and more distant leaflets of its bipinnate leaves, showed at once their difference. We had travelled five hours and a half, and Mr. Roper rode up to me several times, to complain of his inability to go any farther. I encouraged him, however, and at sunset, we reached a creek, but it was dry; and, although we travelled until dark along its winding course, and saw many deep holes on its flats, and although fresh burnings showed that the natives had been there, yet no water was to be found, and we were obliged to encamp without it. We, therefore, hobbled and tethered all the horses, and watched the bullocks. Charley followed the creek for some distance in search of water, but returned without finding any.

July 21.--When Charley was riding after our hobbled horses, he came, at about two miles N. E., from our camp, to another watercourse, with well filled rocky water-holes. When he brought this welcome intelligence, we immediately loaded our bullocks, and moved to these water-holes; on which it appeared some natives had encamped very lately. The country around was broken and scrubby; but in general it was well-grassed, with a sound soil. Our latitude was 17 degrees 52 minutes 53 seconds.

The wind, during the last two days, was from the southward in the forenoon, and from the westward in the afternoon. The nights were calm and clear, but very cold.

Mr. Calvert had happily recovered so much as to be able to resume his duties; and, notwithstanding the fatigues of the last long stage, Mr. Roper had slightly improved.

July 22.--Last night was beautifully clear and calm, until midnight, when a cold south wind set in, which made us all shiver with cold. I had not felt it so much since the night of Mr. Gilbert's death, nor since we left the upper Lynd and the table land of the Burdekin. The wind was equally strong in the morning from the south-east, and veered in the course of the day to the south and south-west.

We travelled about eight miles and a half W.N.W. to lat. 17 degrees 50 minutes 28 seconds, at first passing over a scrubby country, which changed into box flats when we approached the waterless creek, at which we encamped on the night of the 20th. To the westward of this creek, box flats alternated with tea-tree thickets; and opened at last into a large plain, which we crossed at its southern termination, where it was three miles broad; it appeared boundless to the northward. Plains of the same character had been dimly seen through the open forest to the northward, for some time before we came to the one we crossed. This was not covered with the stiff grass, nor the dry wind-grass of the plains north of the Staaten; but it bore a fine crop of tender grasses, which rendered them infinitely more valuable for the pasture of horses and cattle. At the west side of the plain, we found a chain of fine long lagoons, surrounded by Polygonum, and apparently well stocked with fish.

Charley and Brown caught an emu, with the assistance of the dog, which became every day more valuable to us.

Since Mr. Gilbert's death, the arrangements of our camp have been changed. I now select an entirely open space, sufficiently distant from any scrub or thicket, even if we have to go a considerable distance for water. Our pack-saddles are piled in two parallel lines close together, facing that side from which a covered attack of the natives might be expected. We sleep behind this kind of bulwark, which of itself would have been a sufficient barrier against the spears of the natives. Tired as we generally are, we retire early to our

180

couch; Charley usually takes the first watch, from half-past six to nine o'clock; Brown, Calvert, and Phillips follow in rotation; whilst I take that portion of the night most favourable for taking the altitude. John Murphy has his watch from five to six. We generally tethered three horses, and kept one bridled; and, with these arrangements, we slept as securely and soundly as ever; for I felt sure that we had nothing to fear, as long as our tinkling bell-horse, and perhaps a second horse, was moving near us. The natives considered our animals to be large dogs, and had frequently asked whether they would bite (which I affirmed, of course); so that they themselves furnished us with a protection, which otherwise I should not have thought of inventing.

July 23.--When Charley returned this morning with the horses, he told me, that a fine broad salt-water river was again before us. I kept, therefore, at once to the southward, and feared that I should have to go far in that direction before being able to ford it. After travelling about two miles, we came in sight of it. It was broad and deep, with low rocky banks. Salicornia grew along the small gullies into which the tide flowed; some struggling stunted mangroves were on the opposite side; and the plains along the right side of the river were occupied by a scanty vegetation, consisting of Phyllanthus shrubs, scattered box, and the raspberry-jam trees. We had travelled, however, more than a mile on its bank, when we came to a broad rocky barrier or dam extending across the river, over which a small stream of brackish water rippled, and, by means of this, we crossed without difficulty. I now steered again north-west by west, and passed at first some fine shady lagoons, and for the next six miles, over an immense plain, apparently unlimited to the north and north-east. At its west side we again found Polygonum lagoons, which were swarming with ducks, (particularly Malacorhynchus membranaceus), and teal (Querquedula). Box, raspberry-jam trees, and Acacia, (Inga moniliformis, D.C.) formed a shady grove round these lagoons, which continued towards the south-east. Their latitude was 17 degrees 49 minutes 35 seconds. Smoke was visible in every part of the horizon. Charley, Brown, and John, shot fourteen ducks, and increased this number towards evening to forty-six ducks, five recurvirostris, one small red-shank, and two spoon-bills: the latter were particularly fat, and, when ready for the spit, weighed better than three pounds; the black ducks weighed a pound and three-quarters. The Malacorhynchus was small, but in good condition, and the fat seemed to accumulate particularly in the skin of the neck.

The south wind, as usual, visited us again last night, and made it exceedingly cold. This intense cold is probably owing to the large plains, over which the wind passes. We were never so much troubled by swarms of flies, as during the last two days; it was impossible to get rid of them by any means.

July 24.--We travelled about six miles north-west to latitude 17 degrees 48

181

minutes, and crossed several plains separated by belts of open forest, and came to a fine salt-water river; the banks were steep but not high, and stunted mangroves grew on the water's edge: the raspberry-jam tree covered the approaches to the river. Salicornia and Binoe's Trichinium grew round the dry ponds, and along the small water-courses, into which the tide flowed. We found a good crossing place at a fishery of the natives; who--to judge by the number of their tracks through the soft mud, and by the two large camps on both sides of the river, which were covered with fish-bones--must be very numerous. We continued our journey for about a mile and a half from the river, and came to some grassy fresh-water lagoons, although the Salicornias at first made me think they were brackish.

Shortly after starting this morning, we saw a brood of thirteen emus, on the plain which we were about to cross. John, Charley, and the dog pursued them, and killed the old one; which, however, severely wounded poor Spring in the neck. When we came up to them with the train, the twelve young ones had returned in search of their mother; upon which Brown gave chase with Spring, and killed two. This was the greatest sport we ever had had on our journey. Upon making our camp, we cut part of their meat into slices, and dried it on green hide ropes; the bones, heads, and necks were stewed: formerly, we threw the heads, gizzards, and feet away, but necessity had taught us economy; and, upon trial, the feet of young emus was found to be as good and tender as cow-heel. I collected some salt on the dry salt ponds, and added it to our stew; but my companions scarcely cared for it, and almost preferred the soup without it. The addition, however, rendered the soup far more savoury, at least to my palate.

July 25.--We travelled N. 60 degrees W. and, at two miles, reached a salt-water creek, which we crossed at a fishing place of the natives. Soon afterwards we came on other shallow half dry salt-water creeks, the dry parts of which were covered with thick incrustations of salt, some of which we collected. Our bullocks were very seriously bogged in crossing one of them. After passing this intricate meshwork of boggy channels, we entered upon an immense plain, with patches of forest appearing here and there in the distance. It was well grassed, but its sandy patches were covered with Salicornia. This plant abounded particularly where the plain sloped into the system of salt-water creeks; the approaches of which were scattered over with the raspberry-jam tree. A west-north-west and west course led me constantly to salt water; and we saw a large expanse of it in the distance, which Charley, to whose superior sight all deference was paid, considered to be the sea. I passed some low stunted forest, in which a small tree was observed, with stiff pinnate leaves and a round fruit of the size of a small apple, with a rough stone, and a very nauseous rind, at least in its unripe state. To the westward of this belt of

182

forest, we crossed extensive marshes covered with tender, though dry grass, and surrounded by low Ironstone ridges, openly timbered with stunted silver-leaved Ironbark, several white gums, and Hakea lorea, R. Br. in full blossom. We had not seen the latter for a long time, although Grevillea mimosoides, with which it was generally associated, had been our constant companion.

Beyond the ridges, we came again on salt-water creeks, and saw sheets of sand, which looked like the sea from the distance. I turned to the south and even south-east; and, finding no water, we were compelled to encamp without it, after a very long and fatiguing stage. Whilst we were occupied in tethering and hobbling our horses, and eating our supper, Charley, whose watch it was, allowed the bullocks to stray in search of water, and the next morning he was so long absent whilst looking for them, that my exhausted companions became impatient; and I thought it advisable to send them back to our last camp with as many pack-horses as we could muster, myself remaining alone to guard the rest of our property. They found three of the bullocks on the plain, in the most wretched condition, and met Charley returning with four others, which had made an immense round along all the salt-water creeks. My companions, however, were fortunate enough to find a fresh water lagoon about three miles west of our last camp. John and Charley returned after moon-rise, with three pack-horses, and arrived at my camp at a quarter to seven in the morning. I had been in a state of the most anxious suspense about the fate of our bullocks, and was deeply thankful to the Almighty when I heard that they were all safe. I had suffered much from thirst, having been forty-eight hours without water, and which had been increased by a run of two miles after my horse, which attempted to follow the others; and also from a severe pain in the head, produced by the impatient brute's jumping with its hobbled forefeet on my forehead, as I was lying asleep with the bridle in my hand; but, after drinking three quarts of cold tea which John had brought with him, I soon recovered, and assisted to load our horses with the remainder of our luggage, when we returned to join our companions. The weather was very hot during the day, but a cool breeze moved over the plains, and the night, as usual, was very cold.

Yesterday morning, John and Brown rode down to a hollow to look for water, whilst we were waiting for the bullocks. At their return, they stated that they had come to two salt-water creeks, all full of salt, of which they brought several lumps. I started immediately with Mr. Calvert and Brown, and, sure enough! I found the broad bed of a creek one mass of the purest and whitest salt. Lumps of it had crystallized round stems of grasses which the wind had blown into the water. A little higher up the creek, a large pool of water was full of these lumps, and in less than ten minutes we collected more than sufficient to supply us for the rest of the journey. Ship loads of pure salt

183

could have been collected here in a very short time, requiring nothing but drying and housing, until it could be removed. Its appearance was quite new and wonderful to me, who had been so busily employed in scraping the incrustations full of mud from the dry beds of the creeks.

Yesterday, Brown shot a black-winged pelican; the pectoral muscles and the extremities of which proved good eating; but the inside and the fat were of a nauseously fishy taste. Charley shot a bustard, and John a black ibis. The smoke of the Black-fellows' fires was seen to the southward. The fresh grass of recent burnings extended over all the plains, and even near our waterle encampment, where its bright verdure made us believe that we approached a fresh water swamp.

July 27.--I stopped at this camp to allow our cattle to recover from their fatigue; intending afterwards to proceed up the river until I came into the zone of fresh water, which we had left, and then to continue my course to the west and north-west. During our stay in this place, Mr. Calvert found a piece of pack canvass, rolled round some utensils of the natives.

July 28.--We travelled about ten miles south by east; but were soon compelled by the salt-water creeks to leave the river, which seemed to come from south-south-east. We crossed several mangrove creeks, one of which contained a weir formed by many rows of dry sticks. These creeks were too boggy to be forded in any part where the tide reached, and we had to follow them up for several miles, until their beds divided into lagoons. Here the drooping tea-tree re-appeared, which I considered to indicate the presence of fresh water, at least for a part of the year. I found them, however, at times, on salt-water rivers, not on the level of the salt water, but high on the banks within the reach of the freshes during the rainy season. In turning again towards the river, we crossed a large plain, from which pillars of smoke were seen rising above the green belt of raspberry-jam trees which covered the approaches to the river. After passing some forest of Moreton Bay ash, bloodwood, clustered box, Acacia (Inga moniliformis), and a few Bauhinias, we came to another salt-water creek, with a sandy bed and deposits of fine salt. Very narrow flats extended along both sides of the creek, and rose by water-torn slopes into large treeless plains. The slopes were, as usual, covered with raspberry-jam trees. I saw smoke to the south-ward, and, on proceeding towards it, we came to a fine lagoon of fresh water in the bed of the creek.

July 29.--We travelled about five miles and a half south-south-east up the creek, and encamped in latitude 18 degrees 2 minutes. The character of the country was the same. When about two miles from our last camp, we came upon a tribe of natives fishing in a water-hole, near which a considerable quantity of large and small fish was heaped. The men made a tremendous noise, which frightened our bullocks, and hastened to the place where their gins were. The latter, among whom was a remarkably tall one, decamped at our approach. A fine shell of Dolium was in their camp, which we passed through. After we had passed by, the natives followed us; upon which I returned towards them, and hung a nose ring on the branch of a small tree. This sign of friendly disposition on my side, emboldened them to approach me and demand a parley. I, therefore, dismounted, and, accompanied by Charley, divided some empty tin canisters among them, with which they seemed highly satisfied. They were altogether fine men. Three or four old men with grey beards were amongst them; and they introduced a young handsome lad to me, with a net on his head and a quill through his nose, calling him "Yappar." He was probably a youth of the Yappar tribe who had been sent forward as a messenger to inform them of our having passed that country. Seeing my watch, they pointed to the sun; and appeared to be well acquainted with the use of my gun.

Further up the creek, we again saw some storied gunyas of the natives.

July 30.--We travelled about ten miles west by south, over an immense plain, with here and there a solitary tree, or a small patch of forest. It was full of melon-holes, and much resembled the plains of the Condamine. Salicornia and Binoe's Trichinium were wanting. At the west side of the plain, a green belt of forest stretched from north to south. Before we entered into it, and into the valley of the creek, along which it extended, we passed some open forest of stunted silver-leaved Ironbark. On the slopes of the plains we met, as usual, the raspberry-jam tree thickets, and on the flats and hollows along the creek, the clustered box; whilst, on the banks of the creek, grew the broad-leaved Terminalia and Acacia (Inga moniliformis). Following the creek up about half a mile, we found a fine rocky water-hole. The rock was a clayey Ironstone.

When entering upon the plain in the morning, we saw two emus on a patch of burnt grass. Brown and Charley gave chase to them; but Brown's horse stumbled and threw him, and unfortunately broke the stock of the double barrelled fowling piece, and bent the barrels. Spring took hold of the emu, which dragged him to the lagoon we had left, pursued by Charley on foot. The emu plunged into the water, and, having given Spring and Charley a good ducking, made its escape, notwithstanding its lacerated thigh. Three harlequin pigeons, and six rose-breasted cockatoos (Cocatua Eos, GOULD.), were shot on the plains.

The weather was delightful; a fine breeze from the east cooled the air.

July 31.--We made about ten miles due west, the latitude of our camp being 18 degrees 6 minutes 42 seconds. After passing some Ironstone ridges,

185

covered with stunted silver-leaved Ironbark, we entered upon a large plain, from which we saw some low ranges to the south, and smoke to the W. 20 degrees S. I followed this course about seven miles; but the smoke was still very distant, and, perceiving a belt of forest to the westward, I took that direction, passed the head of a small creek which went to the southward, crossed some box forest and Ironbark ridges, and came into an open country, with alternating plains and ridges, which, even at the present season, was very pretty, and must, when clothed in the garments of Spring, be very beautiful. The creek which we had met at the east side of the forest, had swept round the ridges, and was now again before us, pursuing a north-west course. A fine plain extended along it, on which I observed Acacia Farnesiana of Darling Downs, the grass of the Isaacs, and several grasses of the Suttor. The holes of the creek were shaded by large Terminalias, and by a white gum, with slightly drooping foliage of a pleasing green colour. We followed the creek down, and soon came again to Ironstone ridges.

I had sent Charley forward to look for water, and, when he joined us again, he told me that there was a water-hole, but that natives, for the greater part gins, were encamped on it. I could not help taking possession of it, as there were none besides, to our knowledge; and our bullocks and horses were fatigued by a long stage. I, therefore, rode up to it alone; the gins had decamped, but a little urchin remained, who was probably asleep when his mother went. He cried bitterly, as he made his way through the high grass, probably in search for his mother. Thinking it prudent to tie an iron ring to his neck, that his parents might see we were peaceably inclined, I caught the little fellow, who threw his stick at me, and defended himself most manfully when I laid hold of him. Having dismissed him with an angry slap on his fat little posteriors, he walked away crying, but keeping hold of the iron ring: his mother came down from the ridge to meet him, laughing loud, and cheering with jokes.

I observed ironstone pebbles, and large pieces of a fine grained flaggy sandstone on the first plains we crossed; the sandstone was excellent to sharpen our knives.

186

CHAPTER XI

SYSTEMATIC GRASS BURNINGS OF THE NATIVES
NATIVE CARVING
AUDACITY OF THE NATIVES OVERAWED
THE ALBERT, OR MAET SUYKER
NATIVE MODE OF MAKING SURE OF A DEAD EMU
BULLOCK BOGGED; OBLIGED TO KILL IT
NATIVE DEVICE FOR TAKING EMUS
BEAMES'S BROOK
THE NICHOLSON
RECONNOITRE BY NIGHT
SMITH'S CREEK
THE MARLOW.

August 1.--We travelled about seven miles west by north. Silver-leaved Ironbark ridges, of a dreary aspect, and covered with small shining brown iron pebbles, alternating with small plains and box-flats, extended generally to the northward. Some of the hills were open at their summits, timbered with apple-gum, and covered with white ant-hills; their bases were surrounded with thickets of the Severn tree. We encamped at a fine Nymphaea lagoon, in the rich shade of a white drooping gum tree. A large but dry creek was near us to the westward. The grass was excellent.

August 2.--We travelled twelve miles west-north-west, over a fine box-flat, crossed a good sized creek, about five miles from the camp, and, to the westward of it, passed over seven miles of Ironbark ridges. We descended from them into the valley of a creek fringed with the white-gum tree, and followed it down for about three miles before we found water. We encamped at a good water-hole, at the foot of the ridges, in latitude 18 degrees 0 minutes 42 seconds. Brown and Charley, who had gone two miles lower down, told me that they had found salt-water, and deposits of very fine salt. Many lagoons were on the flats, surrounded by Polygonums, and frequented by ducks, spoonbills, and various aquatic birds. They had shot, however, only one teal and a spoonbill. In travelling down the creek, we frequently started wallabies. Geophaps plumifera was very frequent on the Ironbark ridges. A cormorant with white breast and belly, and the rose cockatoo were shot; the former tasted as well as a duck. Brown collected a good quantity of the gum of Terminalia, and the seeds of the river bean, which made an excellent coffee.

187

The native bee was very abundant.

The natives seemed to have burned the grass systematically along every watercourse, and round every water-hole, in order to have them surrounded with young grass as soon as the rain sets in. These burnings were not connected with camping places, where the fire is liable to spread from the fire-places, and would clear the neighbouring ground. Long strips of lately burnt grass were frequently observed extending for many miles along the creeks. The banks of small isolated water-holes in the forest, were equally attended to, although water had not been in either for a considerable time. It is no doubt connected with a systematic management of their runs, to attract game to particular spots, in the same way that stockholders burn parts of theirs in proper seasons; at least those who are not influenced by the erroneous notion, that burning the grass injures the richness and density of the natural turf. The natives, however, frequently burn the high and stiff grass, particularly along shady creeks, with the intention of driving the concealed game out of it; and we have frequently seen them watching anxiously, even for lizards, when other game was wanting.

August 3.--We travelled, for the first two miles, N. 60 degrees W. over scrubby ironstone ridges, and then entered upon a fine plain, from which smoke was seen to the west and north-west. I chose the latter direction, and passed over ironstone ridges covered with stunted silver-leaved Ironbark; and a species of Terminalia, a small tree, with long spathulate glaucous leaves, slightly winged seed-vessels, and with an abundance of fine transparent eatable gum; of which John and Brown gathered a great quantity. Some of the ridges were openly timbered with a rather stunted white-gum tree, and were well grassed; but the grass was wiry and stiff. At the end of our stage, about sixteen miles distant from our last camp, we crossed some rusty-gum forest; and encamped at a fine water-hole in the bed of a rocky creek, shaded by the white drooping gum, which seemed to have taken the place of the flooded gum. Groves of Pandanus spiralis grew along the creek, which ran to the north by east. All the small watercourses we passed, inclined to the eastward. Charley found the shell of a Cytherea on an old camping-place of the natives, which indicated our approach to the salt water.

A native had carved a representation of the foot of an emu in the bark of a gum-tree; and he had performed it with all the exactness of a good observer. It was the first specimen of the fine arts we had witnessed in our journey.

August 4.--We travelled about ten miles west-north-west, over scrubby ridges, plains, and box-flats. In a patch of rusty-gum forest we found Acacia equisetifolia, and the dwarf Grevillea of the upper Lynd in blossom; the thyrsi of scarlet flowers of the latter were particularly beautiful. As we entered into the plains, Binoe's Trichinium and Salicornia re-appeared.

I steered towards the smoke of a Blackfellow's fire, which we saw rising on the plains; the fire was attended to by a gin. Charley went forward to examine a belt of trees visible in the distance; and John Murphy followed a hollow in the plain, and succeeded in finding a fine lagoon, about half a mile long, partly rocky and partly muddy, surrounded by Polygonums, and fields of Salicornia. A few gum trees, and raspberry-jam trees grew straggling around it; but no dry timber was to be found, and we had to make a fire with a broken down half dried raspberry-jam tree. Our meat bags were now empty, and it was necessary to kill another bullock, although the spot was by no means favourable for the purpose. Natives were around us, and we saw them climbing the neighbouring trees to observe our proceedings. When Charley joined us, he stated that a fine broad salt-water river was scarcely a quarter of a mile from the lagoon; that he had seen a tribe of natives fishing, who had been polite enough to make a sign that the water was not drinkable, when he stooped down to taste it, but that freshwater was to be found in the direction of the lagoon, at which we were encamped. No time was to be lost, and, as the afternoon had advanced, we commenced operations immediately. Though the bullock was young, and in excellent working condition, the incessant travelling round the gulf had taken nearly all the fat out of him, and there was scarcely enough left to fry his liver. At sunset, we saw the natives approaching our camp, with loud vociferations, swinging their spears, and poising and putting them into their wommalas. We immediately saddled and mounted two of our horses, and discharged a pistol. The latter stopped their noise at once; and some cowered down to the ground. John and Charley rode slowly towards them; at first they tried to face, and then to surround the horsemen; but John and Charley separated, and threatened to cut them off from the river. As soon as they saw their supposed danger, they ran to the river, plunged in, and crossed it. We were very watchful during the night, but were not disturbed. Next morning, natives passed at some distance, but showed no inclination to molest us.

August 5.--We cut our meat into slices, and, although we were reduced in number, we had become so expert, that we had finished a full sized bullock by half past eleven, A. M. The process occupied four of us about four hours and a half; John and Brown were employed in putting it out on the kangaroo net to dry. The strong sea breeze dried it beautifully; but it attracted much moisture again in the night, and was very moist when we packed it into the bags at starting.

The sea breeze set in on the 4th at 11 o'clock, became very strong during the afternoon, lessened at sunset, and died away about 9 o'clock, P. M. when it became thick and foggy. This was the case on the 5th, 6th, and 7th, and was

189

very regular.

August 6.--We left the large lagoon, which, as I was prevented from making an observation, I supposed to be in latitude 17 degrees 47 minutes v. 48 minutes, and followed the winding course of the river up to latitude 17 degrees 57 minutes. The river, I am inclined to think, is the Albert of Captain Stokes, and the Maet Suyker of the Dutch Navigators, and its general course is from south-south-west, to north-north-east. Plains, forest country, open scrub frequently broken by gullies, alternated with each other. Several large and deep basins parallel to the river, were dry. The rough-leaved fig tree, the white cedar, and a stiff-leaved Ipomoea with pink blossoms, grew on its sandy banks; and some low straggling mangroves at the water's edge. The day was far advanced, and I became very anxious about our moist meat; and feared that we should have to encamp without water. We saw burnt grass every where, and logs were even still burning; and fresh water could not be very far off, but yet we were unable to detect it. At last, I observed some trees, of a fresher appearance than usual, beyond a small rise; and, riding up to it, found a small water-hole surrounded by Polygonums: on examination, it was found to contain only a very small quantity of water, yet what remained was good. Charley, who returned afterwards, said that he had been before at this water-hole, and had found a tribe of natives encamped on it, one of whom lifted his spear against him, but his courage forsook him upon observing Charley still riding towards him, when he and the whole camp took to their heels, leaving a good supply of Convolvulus roots, and of Terminalia gum behind them. We found shells of Cymbium and Cytherea, an enormous waddie, which could have been wielded only by a powerful arm, nets and various instruments for fishing, in their deserted camp.

August 7.--I thought it advisable to stop here, and give our meat a fair drying. The natives were not seen again. Charley and John took a ride to procure some game, and came to a salt-water creek, which joined the river about three miles from our camp; the river flowed in a very winding course from the eastward. They found some good fresh water-holes, at the head of the salt-water.

August 8.--We travelled about seven miles E.S.E. over plains and Ironbark ridges. The approaches of the creek, broken by watercourses and gullies, were covered with thickets of raspberry-jam trees. The rock cropped out frequently in the creek, which was said to be very rocky lower down. The salt-water Hibiscus, a species of Paritium, Adr. Juss. (Hibiscus tiliaceus? Linn. D.C. Prodr. I. p. 454) grew round the water-holes. We found the same little tree at the salt-water rivers on the west coast of the gulf, and at Port Essington. I had formerly seen it at the sea coast of Moreton Bay; its bark is tough and fibrous, and the heart-wood is brown with a velvety lustre.

190

August 9.--When Charley returned with the horses, he told us, that, when he was sitting down to drink at a water-hole about three miles up the creek, ten emus came to the other side of the water; keeping himself quiet, he took a careful aim, and shot one dead; then mounting his horse immediately, he pursued the others, and approaching them very near, succeeded in shooting another. He broke the wings of both and concealed them under water. It is a singular custom of the natives, that of breaking the wings upon killing an emu; as the wings could only slightly assist the animal in making its escape, should it revive. But in conversation with Brown as to the possibility of one of the emus having escaped, he said very seriously: "Blackfellow knows better than white fellow; he never leaves the emu without breaking a wing. Blackfellows killed an emu once, and went off intending to call their friends to help them to eat, and when they came back, they looked about, looked about, but there was no emu; the emu was gone--therefore the Blackfellows always broke the wings of the emus they killed afterwards." This was, however, very probably one of Brown's yarns, made up for the occasion.

I sent Mr. Calvert and Charley to fetch the game, whilst we loaded the bullocks, and by the time they returned, we were ready to start. The emus were fine large birds, but not fat; this season seemed to be unfavourable for them. When we came out into the plain, we saw the smoke of the natives to the southward, and I steered for it, supposing that they were either near the river, or at all events not far from fresh water. After two miles travelling, we crossed another creek with fine Polygonum water-holes, and, emerging from it into a second plain, we saw a flock of emus in the distance. Chase was given to them, and with the assistance of Spring, one was caught. Loaded with three emus, we travelled over a succession of plains, separated by narrow belts of timber, mostly of-box, bloodwood, and tea-tree. The plains were broken by irregular melon-holes, which rendered our progress slow and fatiguing. We came to Ironbark ridges, and to the very spot where the natives had been burning the grass, but no watercourse, nor lagoon was seen. Brown rode farther to the southward, and observed the tracks of the natives in that direction, but found nothing but box-tree flats. I sent Charley forward to the westward, and followed slowly in the same direction; night overtook us, when we were crossing a large plain, but Charley had lighted a large fire, which guided us, and made us believe that he had found water. He was indeed at the steep banks of the river Albert, but it was still salt. We hobbled and tethered all the horses, and watched the bullocks. Fortunately we had provided ourselves with some water, which allowed half a pint to every man, so that we felt the inconvenience of a waterless camp less than formerly. Besides, we had fresh meat, which made a great difference in our desire for water. It was a beautiful night, and even the dew was wanting, which had been such a hindrance to drying our meat during the previous nights. During my watch, I

191

seated myself on one of the prominences of the steep banks, and watched the loud splashings of numerous large fish which momentarily disturbed the tranquillity of the mirror-like surface of the water. Brown had found a bar across the river, and, on examination it proved perfectly dry during low water, and allowed us to cross, after having brought our bullocks and horses down the steep banks, which, however, was not effected without great difficulty. We had most fortunately hit the very spot where such a crossing was possible. Brown saw a great number of fine fish in the river, which he called "Taylors." The natives had been here frequently: the grass had been recently burnt, and fish bones indicated this as one of their habitual camping places. We could not, however, discover where they quenched their thirst. I sent Charley forward in a north-west direction to look for water. When we came out into the plains which stretched along both sides of the river as far as the eye could reach, we saw smoke very near us on the right. I went towards it, until I found that it rose on the opposite side of the river we had just crossed; Brown, however, detected a pool of slightly brackish water in a deep creek at a short distance from its junction with the river. It was too boggy for our cattle to approach, but it allowed us to quench our own thirst. We now re-entered the plains, and followed the track of Charley, who soon returned with the pleasing intelligence that he had found some fine water-holes. These were in the bed of a creek, surrounded by a band of forest composed of box, raspberry-jam trees, and the broad-leaved Terminalia, the fruit of which was eaten by the black cockatoo. The slopes of the water-holes were steep and boggy, and one of our bullocks was so exhausted that he slipped on the steep banks, rolled into the water, and got so severely bogged, that we were compelled to kill him, after trying everything in our power to extricate him. On the 12th August we cut him up. The night, however, was very foggy with heavy dew, which prevented the meat from drying. The miserably exhausted state of the animal had rendered the meat very flabby and moist, and it not only dried badly, but was liable to taint and to get fly-blown.

August 13.--We had a fine sea-breeze from the northward, which dried the outside of the meat well enough, but not the inside, so that it became in many parts so putrid that I had to throw them away, although we saved a good deal by splitting the puffed pieces, and exposing the inside to the air.

The natives had surrounded the water-hole on which we encamped with a barricade or hedge of dry sticks, leaving only one opening to allow the emus to approach the water. Near this the natives probably kept themselves concealed and waited for the emus; which in these parts were remarkably numerous. On the 11th, John, Charley, and Brown, rode down three birds, and, on the 14th, they obtained four more, two of which were killed by John Murphy, who rode the fleetest horse and was the lightest weight. The possibility of riding emus down, clearly showed in what excellent condition our horses were. Even our bullocks although foot-weary upon arriving at the camp, recovered wonderfully, and played about like young steers in the grassy shady bed of the creek, lifting their tails, scratching the ground with their fore feet, and shaking their horns at us, as if to say, we'll have a run before you catch us.

The latitude of these water-holes was 18 degrees 4 minutes 27 seconds, and they were about nine miles from the crossing place of the river, which I calculated to be in longitude 139 degrees 20 minutes (appr.). The plains were covered with flocks of small white cockatoos, (Cocatua sanguinea, GOULD.) which Mr. Gilbert had mentioned as having been found in Port Essington: their cry was rather plaintive, and less unmelodious than the scream of the large cockatoo; nor were they so shy and wary, particularly when approaching the water.

August 15.--Our beasts were so heavily laden with the meat of two bullocks, that I found it rather difficult to carry the additional meat of the emus. We, however, divided every emu into four parts--the chest, the rump, and the two thighs--and suspended each of the latter to one of the four hooks of a packsaddle; the remaining parts were carried on our horses.

We travelled about eight miles north-north-west, over a succession of plains, interrupted by some watercourses, and a good sized creek. At the end of the day's stage, we found a small pool of water in a little creek which we had followed down. According to Charley's account, salt-water existed a mile lower down. Though our arrival at the camp was very late, we set immediately to work, and cut up the four emus, which I put on ropes and branches to dry. Fortunately, a cold dry south-east wind set in, which very much assisted us in the operation of drying. The sea breeze was strong, as usual, during the day; clouds gathered very suddenly about 11 o'clock, P. M. to the southward and south-east, and rose very quickly with a strong south-east wind; they passed as quickly as they came; when the wind ceased. Another mass of clouds formed, and rose quite as suddenly, and, having passed, the sky became quite clear, and a cold strong wind set in from the south-east, which lasted for the next two days, and rendered the nights of the 16th and 17th August cold, dry, and dewless.

We had forgotten to drive our bullocks to the water, which they had passed not five yards off, and in sight of which they had been unloaded; the poor brutes, however, had not the instinct to find it, and they strayed back. Charley started after them the same night, and went at once to our old camp, supposing that the bullocks had taken that direction; but they had not done so; they had wandered about seven miles from the camp, without having found water.

August 16.--We travelled about twelve miles west-north-west, first over plains, but afterwards, and for the greater part of the stage, over openly timbered well-grassed box-flats, which seemed to bound the plains to the southward; they were drained by no watercourse, but contained many melon holes. I changed my westerly course a little more to the northward, and again crossed a succession of plains, separated by hollows. These hollows were covered with thickets of small trees, principally raspberry-jam trees; and contained many dry water-holes, either in regular chains or scattered. They, no doubt, formed the heads of creeks; as we invariably came on decided watercourses whenever we followed hollows of this character down to the northward. After sunset, we came to a dry creek, and were compelled to encamp without water. We took care, however, to watch our bullocks, and hobble and tether our horses, which enabled us to start early in the morning of the 17th, when we followed the creek about seven miles north-east, and there found some very fine water-holes within its bed, in latitude 17 degrees 51 minutes, at which we encamped, to allow our cattle to recover; for they had had very little water during the two last days. Smoke was seen to the north-west, north, and north-east. Charley shot two more emus, and I felt the loss of our bullock very much, as it became difficult to carry the additional meat, which, however, was too valuable to be wasted or thrown away. Although we had followed the creek for seven miles, we did not find it joined by any of those hollows we had crossed the day before; and it would appear that the intervening plains extended far to the north-ward, and that the hollows and creeks converged only very gradually towards each other.

August 18.--Last night we were busily employed in cutting up and drying our two emus, in which operation we were favoured by a slight breeze from the south-east. As we had no fat nor emu oil to fry the meat with, I allowed a sufficient quantity of meat to be left on the bones, which made it worth while to grill them; and we enjoyed a most beautiful moonlight night over a well grilled emu bone with so much satisfaction, that a frequenter of the Restaurants of the Palais Royal would have been doubtful whether to pity or envy us.

We travelled to the north-west, because, whenever I kept a westerly course, I had almost always to follow creeks down to the northward to obtain water; and, notwithstanding a north-west course, had, on previous occasions, generally brought us to salt-water.

For the first three miles, we passed several plains, and crossed a creek in which we recognised a Casuarina, which tree we had not seen since we left the Mitchell. We then came to a river from thirty to forty yards broad, and apparently very deep; the water was very soft, but not brackish, although affected by the tide, which caused it to rise about two feet. A narrow belt of brush, with drooping tea-trees, the Corypha palm, the Pandanus, and Sarcocephalus, grew along the water's edge. The box, the broad-leaved Terminalia, and the Inga moniliformis (articulate podded Acacia), covered the gullies which came down from the plains, and the flats along the river. We proceeded four or five miles up the river, in a south-west direction, in order to find a crossing place. Large plains occupied both sides, on which numerous patches of grass had been lately burnt; which indicated the presence of natives. Fish were very plentiful, and Charley said he had seen a crocodile. The plains and banks of the river were well grassed, and adapted for cattle and horses. We encamped in latitude 17 degrees 57 minutes. [This cannot possibly be 17 degrees 57 minutes--it is about 17 degrees 52 minutes--(Note by Mr. Arrowsmith.)]

August 19.--The river was joined by a running creek from south-south-west, which we had to follow up about five miles, where it formed a very narrow channel between thickets of palm trees, drooping tea-trees, Sarcocephalus, and particularly Pandanus, which crowded round the tiny stream. We again travelled north-west, over several plains, separated by belts of timber, and, at the end of about five miles, came to a fine brook, whose pure limpid waters flowed rapidly in its deep but rather narrow channel, over a bed of rich green long-leaved water plants. Magnificent tea-trees, Casuarinas, and Terminalias, gave a refreshing shade, and Pandanus and Corypha palms added to the beauty of the spot.

The plains were well-grassed, but full of melon-holes. I observed on them a few small trees, belonging to the Sapindaceae, with pinnate and rather drooping leaves, with a light grey bark, exuding a good eatable gum.

I called the brook "Beames's Brook," in acknowledgment of the liberal support I received from Walter Beames, Esq. of Sydney.

We again enjoyed here the young shoots of the Corypha palm.

August 20.--We crossed Beames's brook without difficulty, and travelled about two miles north-west, over a plain, when we came to a river with a broad sandy bed and steep banks, overgrown with large drooping tea-trees. Its stream was five or six yards broad and very shallow. Parallel lines of deep lagoons covered with Nymphaeas and Villarsias were on its west side. The bergue between the river and the lagoons was covered with bloodwood and leguminous Ironbark; and fine box flats were beyond the lagoons.

I called this river the "Nicholson," after Dr. William Alleyne Nicholson, of Bristol, whose generous friendship had not only enabled me to devote my time to the study of the natural sciences, but to come out to Australia. The longitude of the Nicholson was 138 degrees 55 minutes (approx.)

After passing the box flats along the river, we entered into a country covered with thickets and scrub, rarely interrupted by small patches of open forest, and travelled about fourteen miles north-west from the river, when the setting sun compelled us to encamp, without having been able to find water. Just on entering the scrub, we saw four emus walking gravely through a thicket of the little Severn tree, picking its bitter fruit, and throwing occasionally a wondering but distrustful glance at our approaching train. Charley and Brown, accompanied by Spring, gave chase to them, and killed one, which was in most excellent condition. When we came to the camp, we secured the horses, and watched the bullocks, as was usual on such occasions, and fried and enjoyed our fresh meat as well as we could. To satisfy my companions I determined to reconnoitre the country in advance by moonlight; and allowed them to return to the lagoons of the Nicholson, should I not have returned by 10 o'clock next morning. Accordingly, I started with Charley when the moon was high enough to give me a fair view of the country, and followed the star Vega as it declined to the westward. As we advanced, the country improved and became more open. It was about midnight when Charley, in passing a patch of thick scrub, noticed a slight watercourse, which increased rapidly into large water-holes. These were dry, and covered with withered grass, but, on resuming our westerly course, we came in a very short time to a creek with a succession of rocky basins. It was unaccountable how these deep holes could have become so soon dry, as every one of them must have been full immediately after the rainy season. After following the creek for about two hours, Charley remarked that the cracked mud of one of the large water-holes was moist, and, on digging about a foot deep, a supply of water collected, abundantly sufficient for ourselves and for our horses. The channel divided several times, and Charley examined one branch, and I took the other. Thus separated from my companion, I caught the cheerful glance of a fire before me, and, as I approached, a great number of them became visible, belonging to a camp of the natives. Though I wished to ascertain whether they were encamped near a water-hole, or near wells, several of which we had observed higher up the creek, I thought it prudent, unarmed as I was, to wait for Charley. I cooeed, which disturbed the dogs of the camp; but the cold wind blew so strong from the east, that I feared Charley would either not hear my cooee, or I not his. The discharge of his gun, however, showed me where he was, and we were soon together again. We passed the camp; the fires sparkled most comfortably in the cold night. We examined the creek, but saw neither natives nor water. Two miles lower down, however, we came to fine water-holes with a good supply. We stopt here for an hour, to make a pot of tea, and to allow our horses to feed. We had followed the creek so far to the north-east and east, that we were, according to my calculation, about ten miles N.N.E. from our camp. Trusting in Charley's almost instinctive powers, I allowed him to take the lead, but he, being drowsy in consequence of a sleepless night, kept too much to the right, and missed our tracks. As the appointed time for my return had elapsed, and I was sure that my companions had gone back, I changed my course to go at once to the lagoons of the Nicholson; and came on the tracks of the returning party, which we followed to the lagoons, where my companions had already safely arrived. We had been on the saddle from 10 o'clock at night, to 6 o'clock in the afternoon of the next day, and, with the exception of one hour, had ridden the whole time through the most dreary and scrubby country, and were, of course, extremely fatigued. Most annoying, however, was the idea that all our fatigues had been to no purpose, except to show to my companions that I was right in my supposition, that a good day's journey parallel to the coast would invariably bring us to water.

August 22.--We travelled about eighteen miles N.N.W., to those water-holes we had found on our reconnoitring ride. Their latitude was 17 degrees 39 minutes. The country was so very scrubby and difficult, that we travelled from morning until long after sunset before we reached the place. The long journey had both tired and galled our bullocks and horses, and our packs had been torn into pieces by the scrub. This induced me to stay a day at this creek (which I called Moonlight Creek, as it had been found and explored during moonlight), to allow some rest both to my bullocks and myself, whom the long riding had much exhausted, and also to re-arrange our packs.

The composition of the scrub depended on the nature of the soil. The narrow-leaved tea-tree, in shrubs from five to seven feet high, and the broad-leaved tea-tree from twenty to twenty-five feet high, grew on a sandy loam, with many ant-hills between them; the little Severn tree and the glaucous Terminalia preferred the light sandy soil with small ironstone pebbles, on which the ant-hills were rare, or entirely wanting; the raspberry-jam tree crowded round water-holes, which were frequently rocky; and the bloodwood, the leguminous Iron-bark, the box, and apple-gum, formed patches of open forest.

We collected a great quantity of Terminalia gum, and prepared it in different ways to render it more palatable. The natives, whose tracks we saw everywhere in the scrub, with frequent marks where they had collected gum--seemed to roast it. It dissolved with difficulty in water: added to gelatine soup, it was a great improvement; a little ginger, which John had still kept, and a little salt, would improve it very much. But it acted as a good lenient purgative on all of us.

We found the days, when travelling in the scrub, excessively hot, for the surrounding vegetation prevented us from feeling the sea-breeze; very cold easterly and south-easterly winds prevailed during the night.

August 24.--Mr. Calvert and Brown, whom I had sent to reconnoitre the country, returned with the sad intelligence that they had found no water. They had crossed a great number of creeks of different sizes, with fine rocky water-holes, which seemed all to rise in scrubby ironstone hills, and had a course from S. W. to N. E. and E. N. E.; but towards their heads they were dry, and lower down they contained salt water. The two explorers had unfortunately forgotten their bag of provisions, and were consequently compelled to return before they could accomplish their object. As I anticipated a very long stage, and perhaps a camp without water, I had some wallabi skins softened and tied over our quart pots filled with water, which enabled us to carry about eight quarts with us.

August 25.--We accordingly started early, and travelled for several miles through a pretty open broad-leaved tea-tree forest, formed by small trees from twenty to thirty feet high. This changed, however, into dense scrub, which we could only avoid by keeping more to the westward, in which direction the tea-tree forest seemed to extend to a great distance. Here we passed several tea-tree swamps, dry at this time, level, like a table, and covered with small trees, and surrounded by a belt of fine box-trees and drooping water-gum trees. In order to come to a watercourse, I again crossed the thick scrub which covered the undulations of iron-stone to the northward, and came to a fine rocky creek, which Brown recognised as one of those he had seen, but which contained only salt water lower down. We consequently continued our journey to the north-west, through tea-tree forest, and over some very large tea-tree swamps, and came at last to a creek and to a small river, along which we travelled until darkness compelled us to encamp. It had fine water-holes, and was densely shaded with drooping tea-trees; but the holes were dry, with some few exceptions of small wells of the natives. The latitude of our camp was 17 degrees 25 minutes.

We had seen a great number of pigeons and white cockatoos, and we were sure that a greater supply of water was near, as many patches of burnt grass showed that the natives had been here very lately. Next morning, the 26th, when Charley returned with the horses, he told us that we had passed a fine lagoon, not a mile and a half off, at the left bank of the river, which the night had prevented us from seeing, and which the horses had found when returning on their tracks. We moved our camp to this lagoon, which was covered with Villarsia leaves, and contained a reddish water coloured by very minute floating bodies of that colour. The natives had surrounded it with dry sticks, leaving an opening on one side, for the purpose of taking emus, as

198

before described. These birds were very numerous, and lived exclusively on the fruit of the little Severn tree, which was excessively bitter and imparted its quality to the meat; Charley and Brown, assisted by the dog, killed one of them. A cockatoo was shot, which in form and colours resembled the large white cockatoo, but was rather smaller, and the feathers of the breast were tipped with red. We saw the bones of a Jew fish, and a broken shell of Cymbium, in an old camp of the natives near the lagoon.

The apple-gum, the box, and the Moreton Bay ash composed a very open well-grassed forest, between the lagoon and the river; the latter had an E. N. E. and almost easterly course. I called this river or large creek, "Smith's Creek," after Mr. Smith, a gentleman who had shown us the greatest kindness and attention when we were staying at Darling Downs.

Our journey round the head of the gulf had shown that the "Plains of Promise" of Capt. Stokes extended from Big Plain River to the Nicholson, and that they extended farthest to the southward, along two large salt water rivers in the apex of the gulf, the more westerly of which was no doubt the Albert of Capt. Stokes, and the Maet Suyker of the Dutch navigators. These plains were bounded to the southward by box-flats, and drained by numerous creeks, which in their lower course were tolerably supplied with water. The most interesting fact, and which had already been observed by Capt. Stokes, was the moderate temperature of this part of the country. If my readers compare my observations on the weather from lat. 15 degrees 55 minutes at the east coast, to lat. 17 degrees 39 minutes on the west coast of the gulf, they will be struck by the general complaint of "cold nights." If they compare the direction of the winds, they will find that at the east coast the southerly and south-south-westerly winds were very cold, and that they became southerly and south-easterly at the apex, and turned still more to the eastward, at the west coast. In comparing these directions of the wind, I was led to the conclusion, that the large plains were the origin and the cause of these winds.

The bracing nature of the winds and of the cold nights, had a very beneficial influence on our bodies; we were all well, with the exception of Mr. Roper, who still suffered from the wound in his loins, and from a distressing diarrhoea. I am not aware of the season in which Capt. Stokes explored this part of the country; but it must not be forgotten, that the same causes which would produce cold winds in the winter, might be the cause of hot winds in the summer.

August 27.--We travelled about seventeen miles N. N. W. to lat. 17 degrees 11 minutes 9 seconds, through an uninterrupted scrub and broad-leaved tea-tree forest. Half way we crossed a broad watercourse, with long tracks of burnt grass. The Pandanus and the bloodwood grew on its limited flats. At the end of our stage, we came to a rocky watercourse, which we followed down, and in which a native dog betrayed to us a deep pool of water, covered with Villarsia leaves, and surrounded by Polygonums. Many of the dry water-holes we had passed were surrounded by emu traps; the tracks of these birds were exceedingly numerous, A grove of Pandanus was near the water on the sandy banks of the creek.

August 28.--We travelled about eleven miles N. N. W. to lat. 17 degrees 2 minutes 12 seconds, through the bleakest scrubby country we had ever met: nothing but tea-tree scrub, and that not even cheered by the occasional appearance of a gum tree, or of the blood-wood. After ten miles, we came to a salt water creek, rocky, with detached pools of water and deposits of salt. Following it up, we came to a well beaten foot-path of the natives, which brought us in a short time to a good supply of drinkable, though very brackish water. The sandstone hills before us and to the northward, were covered with low shrubs and the broad-leaved tea-tree, with wiry and stiff grasses, and looked very unpropitious. The rock was composed of quartz pebbles of different colours, imbedded in a red clayey paste.

We have commenced to carry with us not only our quart pots, but also our two gallon pot full of water.

August 29.--We travelled to lat. 16 degrees 58 minutes 27 seconds long. 138 degrees 25 minutes; a distance of about eight miles N.N.W. and N.W. over a more open country, with occasional patches of thick scrub. We crossed several watercourses and creeks; and came to a small river which flowed to the N. by E. and which I called the "Marlow," after Capt. Marlow of the Royal Engineers, who had kindly assisted me in the outfit of my expedition. We went down the river about two or three miles, and came to a plentiful supply of water, which was indicated, a long time before we arrived at it, by the call of the red-breasted cockatoos, noticed a few days since; but which was probably only a variety of the common species.

A low shrubby Acacia with sigmoid phyllodia was frequent on the hills. A little fly-catcher (Givagone brevirostris?) charmed us with its pretty note at our last camps. Bronze-winged pigeons were very numerous, and I saw a pair of Geophaps plumifera rising from under a shady rock, as I was riding down a rocky creek. Two black ducks and three cockatoos were shot; the long reaches of water down the river were covered with water-fowl, and Charley and Brown were so desirous of procuring some messes of black ducks, that they did their best to persuade me to stop; but, being anxious to escape from this scrubby country, I did not yield to their solicitations.

The crops of the large cockatoos were filled with the young red shoots of the Haemodorum, which were almost as pungent as chillis, but more aromatic;

the plant abounded on the sandy soil. The small cockatoo of the plains, which we saw again in great numbers, seems to feed on a white root and on the honey of the whole seed-vessel, or the flower-bud, of the drooping tea-tree.

The first part of the night was clear, but it became foggy and cloudy after midnight. In the morning, the dew was dropping from the trees, but the grass and our things were not at all wet.

August 30.--We travelled about ten miles N. 60 degrees W. over a scrubby though a little more open country, full of enormous massive ant-hills, surpassing even those of Big Ant-Hill Creek, in height and circumference, and came, at the distance of eight miles from our camp, to a low scrub on sandy soil with shallow watercourses. Salicornia grew in abundance; and emu tracks were very frequent. Coming on a broad foot-path of the natives, I followed it to the south-west, and came to some fine fresh water-holes in the bed of a creek, surrounded by high drooping tea trees, which were in blossom and covered with swarms of white cockatoos. These water-holes were in lat. 16 degrees 55 degrees, and situated to the south-west of some low scrubby hills. We encamped in a grove of Pandanus. The natives had just left, and the tea-tree bark was still smoking from the fire which had spread from their camp.

Large flights of the small white cockatoo came to the water. The flying-fox visited the blossoms of the tea-tree at night, and made an incessant screeching noise. Charley shot one of them, which was very fat, particularly between the shoulders and on the rump, and proved to be most delicate eating.

August 31.--It rained the whole day; in consequence of which I gave my cattle a rest. The rain came from the westward, but continued with a southerly wind; it ceased with wind from the S.E. and E.S.E. Lightning was observed to the south-west. We erected our tents for the first time since Mr. Gilbert's death; using tarpaulings and blankets for the purpose. Our shots amused themselves by shooting Blue Mountainers for the pot; and a strange mess was made of cockatoo, Blue Mountainers, an eagle hawk, and dried emu. I served out our last gelatine for Sunday luncheon; it was as good as when we started: the heat had, however, frequently softened it, and made it stick to the bag and to the things with which it was covered.

The fire places of the natives were here arranged in a straight line, and sheltered from the cold wind by dry branches: they were circular, the circumference was slightly raised, and the centre depressed and filled with pebbles, which the natives heat to cook their victuals.

The bell which one of our horses carried, was unaccountably broken at our last camp; and it was quite a misery to hear its dull jarring sound, instead of the former cheerful tinkling. One of our horses had separated from the rest, and had gone so far up the creek, that Charley did not return with it until very late in the afternoon of the 1st September, which compelled us to stop at our camp.

CHAPTER XII

HEAPS OF OYSTER-SHELLS
FALSE ALARM OF A NATIVE IN THE CAMP
TURNER'S CREEK
WENTWORTH'S CREEK
JOURNALS LOST; FOUND AGAIN
THE VAN ALPHEN
IMPORTANCE OF TEA
CHOICE OF BULLOCKS FOR AN EXPEDITION
CHOICE OF A DOG
THE CALVERT
THE ABEL TASMAN
GLUCKING BIRD AGAIN
DISCOVER A MODE OF USING THE FRUIT OF THE PANDANUS
SEVEN EMU RIVER
CROCODILE
THE ROBINSON
SHOAL OF PORPOISES
NATIVE METHOD OF PREPARING THE FRUIT OF THE PANDANUS AND CYCAS FOR FOOD
MR. ROPER CONVALESCENT
WEAR AND TEAR OF CLOTHES
SUCCEED IN DRESSING THE SEEDS OF STERCULIA
THE MACARTHUR
FRIENDLY PARLEY WITH CIRCUMCISED NATIVES
STORE OF TEA EXHAUSTED
MEDICAL PROPERTY OF THE GREVILLEA DISCOVERED.

Sept. 2.--We travelled N.W. by W. and came, after passing some of the usual tea-tree scrub, to an undulating country, with scattered shrubs of the salt water tea-tree, which grew particularly on the sandy heads of salt water creeks. Salicornia was another sure indication of salt water; and, after about seven or eight miles, our course was intercepted by a broad salt-water creek. Its bed, however, was sandy, and the water shallow, which enabled us to cross it a little higher up, without difficulty. We turned again to the N.W. by W., steering for one of the numerous smokes of the natives' fires which were visible in every direction. We soon came, however, to broad sands with deep impressions of the tracks of emus, wallabies, and natives; and to sandy depressions sloping

202

towards narrow salt-water creeks densely fringed with Mangroves. A large river was no doubt before us. To get out of this difficult meshwork of salt-waters, I turned to the south-west, and continued in this direction until the sands, Mangrove creeks, and Salicornias, disappeared, and we were again fairly in the scrubs, which however we found more open, and frequently interspersed with bloodwood and Pandanus. I sent Charley and Brown in different directions to look for water, and a small pool with brackish ferruginous nasty water was found, which made a very miserable tea, and affected our bowels. In the Mangrove creeks we found Telescopium, Pleurotoma; and heaps of oyster-shells, for the first time on our journey. Arcas were frequent, but no Cytheras. The mussels (Unios) of the slightly brackish water were small, but plentiful.

It was on this stage that we first met with a leafless species of Bossiaea, from three to five feet high, with compressed stem, and branches of the habit of Bossiaea scolopendrium, with yellow blossoms, and smooth many-seeded pods little more than an inch long. This shrub was one of the principal components of all the scrubs we passed from this place to Limmen Bight, and was also found, though less frequently, towards the centre of Arnheim's Land.

The day was exceedingly hot, though cloudy; the wind from the east: the night cool, without wind.

When Brown and Charley rejoined us, the former appeared so much alarmed and agitated, that I thought they had met some natives, and had received some injury, although they said they had not. My imagination was working on the possibility of an attack of the natives, and I consequently laid myself down without taking my boots and trowsers off, to be ready at a moment's notice, and rose several times in the course of the night to see that the watches were strictly kept. In the morning watch, John Murphy roused me by saying that he saw a native: I felt certain now that an attack was about to be made upon us. I, therefore, immediately gave the alarm, and every one had his gun ready, when it was discovered that our own Brown was the man whom John had mistaken for a strange native. He had left his couch without being observed, and, when he returned, it was too dark to recognize him; he was, however, very near losing his life, or at least being shot at, for his wild yells "tis me! tis me!" which he uttered when he became aware of his dangerous position, were not understood, but only increased our belief that they were the war-cry of attacking natives.

The creek, on a water-hole of which we encamped in lat. 16 degrees 54 minutes 50 seconds, was doubtless one of the heads of the broad salt-water creek we crossed, and which I called "Turner's Creek," after Cowper Turner,

Esq. of Sydney:

Sept. 3.--We travelled about nine miles west by north, through an open tea-tree forest skirting the heads of those scrubby creeks which went down to the salt water, the dark mangrove line of which we had seen yesterday. But we crossed four good sized dry creeks, lined with drooping tea-trees and white-gum trees. Their banks and flats were covered with groves of Pandanus, whose stately crowns were adorned with red-fruited cones: the seed-vessels contained in their stringy texture a rich mellow pear-like substance, which however was hot, and made our lips and tongues very sore. We encamped on some water-holes, with excellent water, in a fifth creek, which lower down contained some fine reaches of brackish water covered with wild geese (Anseranas melanoleuca, GOULD.) and black ducks. As Charley was watching some geese, an emu walked up to him, which he shot; he succeeded besides in getting two geese, which were in most excellent condition, and weighed better than five pounds each.

A well beaten foot-path of the natives led up a broad salt-water creek, to the northward of the creek on which we were encamped, and which joined it lower down. Charley, when going after the horses, saw a camping place of the natives with spears and the usual utensils: but the inhabitants had either not yet returned from their hunting and fishing excursions, or had left it, frightened by the frequent discharge of our guns.

Sept. 4.--We travelled about eleven miles west by north. The first three miles and a half led us through scrub; we forded a salt-water creek about thirty yards broad, and then, for the next four miles, proceeded through a scrubby country, and came to a second salt-water creek as broad as the first, but containing only pools of water. The scrub now opened, and the last four miles lay through a fine box-flat, bounded by long hollows surrounded with drooping tea-trees and the white water-gum, the bright foliage of which formed a most agreeable contrast with the dull green of the scrubs and the box-trees. After crossing a small sandy creek, along which grew a few Sarcocephalus, we came to a large creek lined with drooping tea-trees and Sarcocephalus, and encamped on a fine pool of water, within its deep bed. I named this creek after W.C. Wentworth, Esq. M.C. who had kindly contributed to the outfit of my expedition.

At early dawn, a flight of wild geese filed in long line over our camp, the flapping of their wings was heavy, but short, and the note they emitted resembled that of the common goose, but was some-what shriller. In the box-flat we started a flock of emus, and Spring caught a fine male bird. It would have been highly amusing for a looker on to observe how remarkably eager we were to pluck the feathers from its rump, and cut the skin, to see how thick the fat was, and whether it was a rich yellow, or only flesh-coloured. We had, indeed, a most extraordinary desire for anything fat; and we soon found where to look for it. In the emu it accumulates all over the skin, but particularly on the rump, and between the shoulders, and round the sternal plate. To obtain the oil, we skinned those parts, and suspended them before a slow fire, and caught the oil in our frying pan; this was of a light yellowish colour, tasteless, and almost free from scent. Several times, when suffering from excessive fatigue, I rubbed it into the skin all over the body, and its slightly exciting properties proved very beneficial. It has always been considered by the white inhabitants of the bush, a good anti-rheumatic.

The sea breeze from the northward still continued during the day; the nights were clear and dewy, but ceased to be so cold.

I found a piece of granite and a fragment of fortification agate in the sandy bed of the creek.

Sept. 5.--We travelled about ten miles west by north, to lat. 16 degrees 48 minutes 22 seconds. Having passed a rather open forest of bloodwood, apple-gum, and leguminous Ironbark, with isolated patches of scrub, and some dry teat-ree swamps with heaps of calcined mussel-shells, we came to a thick stringy-bark forest, on a sandy soil, with a hard sandstone cropping out frequently. This opened into the flats of a sandy Pandanus creek, which we crossed; and, three miles farther, we came to another broad creek with salt water. Its bed was rocky, and we forded it easily. I followed one of its branches for several miles, and found, after passing its salt-water pools, a small pool of fresh water in its rocky sandy bed, near which I observed an old camping place of the natives. I was considerably in advance of my train, and the dog was with me. As I was examining the pool of water and the numerous tracks round it, an emu came walking along the shady bed of the creek; I immediately mounted my horse and pursued it with the dog, and caught it after a very short run; to prevent its wounding the dog, I dismounted to kill it, when my horse became frightened, broke loose, and ran away. I returned with the emu to the water, and when the train arrived, I sent Charley after the horse, whilst I walked about two miles further up the creek to find a better supply of water. Not succeeding, however, I returned and encamped at the small pool, which we enlarged with the spade, and obtained a sufficient supply of very good water. Charley returned with the horse, but my saddlebags, my journals and a calabash were lost. I was in great anxiety, and blamed myself severely for having committed such an act of imprudence. Charley went, however, a second time on foot, and succeeded in finding everything but the calabash, which was a great loss to our dog.

In the camping place of the natives, I found a large round stone of porphyry, upon which the natives were accustomed to break the seed-vessels of Pandanus. I could discover no indications of this rock in the creek, not even the smallest pebble; and I am consequently inclined to think that this stone was brought by the natives from a considerable distance to the south-west. But, from the broken pieces of granite of our last camp, it became evident that a rocky primitive country, like that of the upper Lynd, could not be very distant. Even the vegetation agreed well with that of the same locality; as the dwarf Grevillea, G. chrysodendrum, and the falcate Grevillea of the upper Lynd, were here again observed. The tea-trees along the banks of the creek, as far as the salt-water extended, were leafless and dead. This may be accounted for by a succession of dry years in which usual freshes have not taken place; and by the supposition that the drooping tea-tree cannot live on water entirely salt.

Sept. 6.--We travelled twelve miles north-west, through Pandanus and bloodwood forest, alternating with scrub, stringy-bark forest, and tea-tree thickets; and, in the latter part of the stage, through broad-leaved tea-tree forest. We encamped at a fine river, with a bed three hundred yards broad from bank to bank, but with a narrow channel of running water. This channel was fringed with the water Pandanus, which we first observed at Beames's Brook; the sandy bed was covered with drooping tea-trees and Grevillea chrysodendrum. Charley shot a bustard, the stomach of which was filled with seeds of Grewia, with small yellow seeds, and some beetles. On this stage, we again passed some of those remarkable dry tea-tree swamps--surrounded with heaps of very large mussel shells--evidently showing that they had been a long time under water, though they were now overgrown with small tea-trees, perhaps five or six years old; and which proved, like the drooping tea-trees on the banks of the creek, that the last few years had been exceedingly dry. I supposed the river to be the Van Alphen of the Dutch navigators, as its latitude, where I crossed it, was about 16 degrees 41 minutes, and its longitude I calculated to be 137 degrees 48 minutes.

Sept. 7.--We travelled about nine miles N. N. W. to latitude 16 degrees 35 minutes; the first part of the stage was scrubby, the latter part undulating with a fine open stringy-bark forest. The trees were tall, but rarely more than a foot in diameter. Here we met with hard baked sandstone, of a whitish grey colour. About seven miles from our camp, we saw a low blue range to the westward; and, soon after, passed a sandy Pandanus creek, with scrubby broken banks: this was joined by a second, and both together entered a broad tea-tree creek, coming from the south-west, in which we found a fine pool of water covered with white and yellow Villarsias and yellow Utricularias.

The rose-coloured Sterculia, and a smooth broad-leaved Terminalia, were observed on the sandy flats of the creek; and a small fan-leaved palm

(Livistona humilis, R. Br.), a small insignificant trunkless plant, growing between sandstone rocks, was here first observed. A taller species of this palm, as we subsequently found, formed large tracts of forest on the Cobourg Peninsula, and near the Alligator rivers.

As our tea bag was getting very low, and as I was afraid that we should have to go a long time without this most useful article, I thought it advisable to make a more saving arrangement. We had, consequently, a pot of good tea at luncheon, when we arrived at our camp tired and exhausted, and most in want of an exciting and refreshing beverage. The tea-leaves remaining in the pot, were saved and boiled up for supper, allowing a pint to each person. In the morning, we had our soup, and drank water ad libitum. Tea is unquestionably one of the most important provisions of such an expedition: sugar is of very little consequence, and I believe that one does even better without it. We have not felt the slightest inconvenience from the want of flour; and we were a long time without salt. The want of the latter, however, made us costive, and, when we began to use it again, almost every one of us had a slight attack of diarrhoea.

Our horses were still in excellent condition, and even improving; and our five bullocks also kept in good working order, although the oldest of them rather lagged behind. In choosing bullocks for such a journey, one should be particularly careful to choose young powerful beasts, about five or six years old, and not too heavy. All our old and heavy bullocks proved to be bad travellers; only one had borne the journey until now, and he was only preserved by great care and attention. During summer, the ground is so hot, and frequently so rotten, that even the feet of a dog sink deep. This heat, should there be a want of water during a long stage, and perhaps a run after game in addition, would inevitably kill a soft dog. It is, therefore, of the greatest importance to have a good traveller, with hard feet: a cross of the kangaroo dog with the bloodhound would be, perhaps, the best. He should be light, and satisfied with little food in case of scarcity; although the dried tripe of our bullocks gave ample and good food to one dog. It is necessary to carry water for them; and to a little calabash, which we obtained from the natives of the Isaacs, we have been frequently indebted for the life of Spring.

Sept. 8.--We travelled about ten miles north-west by west, to latitude 16 degrees (Unclear:)81 minutes. The first and last parts of the stage were scrubby, or covered with a dense underwood of several species of Acacia, Grevillea chrysodendrum and a species of Pultenaea with leafless compressed stem. The intervening part of our journey was through a stringy-bark forest, with sandy, and frequently rotten soil, on sandstone ridges or undulations. Some patches of stiffer soil were covered with box or with straggling apple-gum and bloodwood. In the scrub, I again observed Fusanus with pinnate

207

leaves. Several good sized dry sandy creeks were surrounded with Pandanus. We saw a low range in form of a horse-shoe, to the westward; and a higher one beyond it in the distance. We encamped at a small river, which had just ceased running, but contained in its bed two chains of small deep ponds full of perches, and shaded with Pandanus and drooping tea-trees, which grew to a large size all over the bed between the two ponds. I named this river the "Calvert," in acknowledgment of the good services of Mr. Calvert during our expedition, and which I feel much pleasure in recording. We saw two emus, and Brown killed one of them, with the assistance of the dog, which received a severe cut in the neck from the sharp claw of the bird.

The whole country round the gulf was well-grassed, particularly before we crossed the Nicholson; and on the plains and approaches to the rivers and creeks. The large water-holes were frequently surrounded with a dense turf of Fimbristylis (a small sedge), which our horses liked to feed upon. Some stiff grasses made their appearance when we approached the sea-coast, as well on the plains as in the forest. The well-known kangaroo grass (Anthisteria) forms still one of the principal components of the pasture. The scrubby country had a good supply of a tufty wind-grass; and, although the feed was dry during this part of the year, our horses and cattle did exceedingly well, as I have already mentioned. Both took an occasional bite of some Acacias, of Grevillea chrysodendrum, and of several other shrubs. Cattle driven over the country we have passed, by short stages, and during the proper season, would even fatten on the road.

When we approached the water-hole on which we were going to encamp, John observed a fine large Iguana in the water, which was so strikingly coloured that he thought it different from those we had previously seen.

Xyris, Philydrum, a species of Xerotes, and an aromatic spreading herb, grew in great abundance round the water. I found a great quantity of the latter in the stomach of the emu. A species of Crotolaria, two or three feet high, with simple woolly oblong or oblongo-lanceolate leaves, and with a beautiful green blossom of the form and size of that of Kennedya rubicunda, grew in the bed of the river. Great numbers of large bright yellow hornets, with some black marks across the abdomen, visited the water. Flies were exceedingly troublesome: but the mosquitoes annoyed us very rarely, and only where water was very abundant. The nights have been very dewy, but not cold. The wind in the morning from the south-east, veering round to the northward during the day.

Sept. 9.--We travelled north-west by north, and for several miles, through a scrubby stringy-bark forest, when we came to steep sandstone ridges, composed of a hard flaggy horizontally stratified rock. Higher ranges were seen to the W.N.W. and west; and I found myself fairly caught between rocky hills when I least expected them, but hoped to enter upon a country corresponding in its character with the low coast marked down in the map, in this latitude. I turned to the northward, and found a practicable path between the hills, and came, after crossing a small sandy creek to a fine salt-water river, as broad as any we had seen. High hills were at its left bank; and, as we followed it up in a direction S. 60 degrees W., the right became more broken, and the vegetation richer. A very conspicuous foot-path led us through heaps of cockle shells to a fishing station of the natives, where they seemed to have a permanent camp; the huts being erected in a substantial manner with poles, and thatched with grass and the leaves of Pandanus; there were extensive fire places containing heaps of pebbles; and an abundance of fish bones. The weir was, as usual, formed with dry sticks, across a shallow part of the river. A spring of fresh water was below the camp at the edge of high water. As the tide was high, and an abundant supply of fresh water was found in a creek which joined the river a few hundred yards from the fishery, we encamped on the creek, in lat. 16 degrees 28 minutes 57 seconds, lon. 137 degrees 23 minutes. I consider this river to be the "Abel Tasman" of the Dutch navigators: and that it is probably joined by the Calvert. Its flats were well-grassed, and very openly timbered with bloodwood, stringy-bark, leguminous Ironbark, then in blossom, and a large tree with white smooth bark, spreading branches, and pinnate leaves. The salt water Hibiscus (Paritium) and Acacia (Inga moniliformis), were also in blossom.

Charley, Brown, and John, went to spear some fish, but the tide was out, the water shallow, and the fish were gone. Charley saw here, for the first time, the Torres Straits pigeon (Carpophaga luctuosa, GOULD.)

The little creek, at which we were encamped, had formed its channel through sandstone rock; and its narrow bed, containing a ferruginous water supplied by springs, was crowded with high reeds, and shaded with various trees of a dense green foliage. Frogs croaked, and crickets chirped, the whole night; and the call of goat-suckers, and the hooting of owls, were heard in every direction; large fish were splashing in the water; wallabies were bleating as they came down to the creek, and saw our horses; and mosquitoes by their loud humming prevented our sleeping. This noise of animal life during the night formed an agreeable contrast to the dead silence which we had observed at almost all our camps around the gulf, with the exception of the one occupied on the 1st September, and of that at the Marlow, where the flying-fox was the merry reveller of night.

Sept. 10.--We were again too late for low tide, to cross at the fishery of the natives, and consequently travelled about two miles and a half higher up, passing in our way three other fisheries; where we crossed the river, the bed was very wide, and covered with shrubs, shingle, and blocks of sandstone; but its rapid stream of fresh water was only about fifteen or twenty yards broad, and three feet deep. At the left side of the river, we saw four or five fine Cycas palms, from eight to ten feet high, and the stem from six to nine inches in diameter. High rocky sandstone ridges extended on the same side, in a direction parallel to the river, and at the distance of two or three miles. They were covered with scrub, open box, and stringy-bark forest; and the wallabi and kangaroo tracks going down to the river, were very numerous. The appearance of the Cypress pine, which formed groups within the stringy-bark forest, and particularly on the rises and sandy slopes, was of a most striking character. A new species of Grevillea, and also of Calythrix, were found in blossom. Beyond the ridges, the stringy-bark forest was obstructed by the leguminous shrub with broad stem (Bossiaea). Several Pandanus creeks went down to the north-east; and the second contained a little water. After travelling about twelve miles to the north-west by north, we encamped at a fine creek with large pools of water, in lat. 16 degrees 21 minutes. During the night, we heard the well-known note of what we called the "Glucking bird," when we first met with it, in the Cypress pine country, at the early part of our expedition. Its re-appearance with the Cypress pine corroborated my supposition, that the bird lived on the seeds of that tree.

Sept. 11.--We travelled about twelve miles north by west, over a country in which scrub, stringy-bark forest, and Cypress pine thickets alternated. We passed some patches of broad-leaved tea-tree forest. The raspberry-jam tree became again more frequent. About a mile from the camp, we crossed a small creek with water; and at seven miles further, another, but it was dry; and, at the end of the stage we came to a fine sandy creek with large pools. Seeing that the natives had encamped here frequently, and some very lately, by the heaps of broken Pandanus fruit, I did not hesitate to pitch our tents; but, on examining the water, I was greatly disappointed in finding it so brackish that the horses and cattle would not drink it. I, therefore, started with Charley in search of better, and, in the upper part of the creek, we found some large water-holes just dried up: but, on digging, they yielded an ample supply of good water. On this little excursion, we were fortunate enough, by the aid of Spring, to kill two emus; but the poor dog again received some deep scratches.

The camps of the natives were, as usual, distinguished by heaps of shells of Cytherea, oysters, fresh-water mussels, and fish bones. The fresh-water mussel was small, and of a yellowish colour.

We had some few drops of rain at about half-past 11 o'clock, A. M,

Sept. 12.--The horses, though hobbled, had strayed so far in search of water, that we had to wait for them until 1 o'clock. We started, however, but, after travelling a short distance, finding the day far advanced, and our chance of finding water very doubtful, I determined to return to the water-hole which we had dug yesterday; about two miles and a half west by south. The flats of the creek were well-grassed; large drooping tea-trees with groves of Pandanus grew on the hollows near the creek, and tea-tree thickets farther off.

I frequently tasted the fine-looking fruit of the Pandanus, but was every time severely punished with sore lips and a blistered tongue; and the first time that I ate it, I was attacked by a violent diarrhoea. I could not make out how the natives neutralized the noxious properties of the fruit; which, from the large heaps in their camps, seemed to form no small portion of their food. The fruit appeared either to have been soaked, or roasted and broken, to obtain the kernels; for which purpose we invariably found large flat stones and pebbles to pound them with. I supposed that they washed out the sweet mealy matter contained between the stringy fibres, and that they drank the liquid, as they do with the honey; and that their large koolimans which we had occasionally seen, were used for the purpose. I, consequently, gathered some very ripe fruit, scraped the soft part with a knife, and washed it until all the sweet substance was out, and then boiled it; by which process it lost almost all its sharpness, had a very pleasant taste, and, taken in moderate quantities, did not affect the bowels. The fruit should be so ripe as to be ready to drop from the tree.

Sept. 13.--We travelled about ten miles N. 50 degrees W., through a succession of tea-tree and Cypress pine thickets of the worst description, interrupted by three creeks, the first dry, the second with pools of brackish water, and the third with chains of Nymphaea ponds within and parallel to its bed. We came at last to the steep banks of a salt-water creek densely covered with Cypress pine scrub, and followed it for several miles up to its head, when two kites betrayed to us a fine lagoon, surrounded with Polygonums and good pasture. The natives were either able to drink very brackish water, or they carried the necessary supply of fresh water to these Pandanus groves, at which they had evidently remained a long time to gather the fruit.

Sept. 14.--We travelled three or four miles north-west, through a tea-tree forest, when the country opened, and a broad salt-water river intercepted our course. It came from W.S.W., and went to E.N.E. We proceeded eight or ten miles along its banks before we came to fresh water. In its immediate neighbourhood, the country was beautifully grassed, and openly timbered with bloodwood, stringy-bark, the leguminous Ironbark, and the white-barked tree of the Abel Tasman. Over the short space of eight miles we saw at least one hundred emus, in flocks of three, five, ten, and even more, at a time: they had been attracted here by the young herbage. We killed seven of them, but they were not fat, and none seemed more than a year old. The extraordinary success induced me to call this river, the "Seven Emu River."

By following a track of the natives, I found a fine well in the bed of the river, under the banks; the water was almost perfectly fresh; and that of the river was only slightly brackish. A fishing weir crossed the stream, where it was about twenty yards broad, and from two to three feet deep. We were occupied to a late hour of the night in cutting up our emus. I had intended to stop the next day, but, as our camp in the bed of the river was surrounded by a thick underwood; as the dew was very heavy, the water brackish, and the young feed dangerous for our cattle, which had fed so long on dry grass, I thought it prudent to continue my journey. The longitude of this river, according to my daily distances, was 137 degrees 5 minutes.

Sept. 15.--We travelled about fifteen miles N. 25 degrees W., passing for the first eight miles over a very fine available country, but without meeting with water, or even with a watercourse. Beyond that, however, the country became more undulating, and we crossed, for about four miles, a most wretched sandstone scrub. Here we saw some natives, but they avoided us. The scrub opened upon fine box flats, with numerous shallow watercourses; farther on, they were interrupted by scrubby or thickly timbered elevations, on which we met with some Cycas palms from thirty to fifty feet high, thick at the butt, and tapering gradually towards the crown. At one of the shallow creeks, which suddenly became rocky, and probably formed falls and rapids in the wet season, we struck upon a well beaten foot-path of the natives, which led us through Cypress pine thickets, and over open lawns to a creek, whose right bank was covered with Cycas groves of the most strikingly picturesque appearance; and here I observed that the Cycas, although it generally has a simple stem, frequently grew with two or three arms. The foot-path went up the creek: lower down, I found broad, deep, but dry water-holes; and, still lower, Salicornia indicated the approach to the salt water. The foot-path conducted us from one Zamia grove to another, which alternated with fine forest composed principally of white-gum, the fresh green foliage of which was extremely pleasing to the eye. I observed some large wells, ten or twelve feet deep, and eight or ten in diameter, which the natives had dug near the Zamia groves, but they were without the slightest indication of moisture. I continued to follow the path for five miles, until I came to a broad-leaved tea-tree forest. The sun was then low, and my companions far behind: I, therefore, returned to ascertain the cause of their delay; and found that our old bullock had refused to carry his pack, and it had been put on a horse; but that, even then, the poor beast was scarcely able to crawl before us. His weakness had been occasioned by a diarrhoea brought on by the green feed and the brackish water at Seven Emu River; and I congratulated myself on not having remained there longer, as probably all my bullocks would have been equally affected. We encamped without water, hobbled our horses, and watched the bullocks, which were all very tired and little inclined to feed during the greater part of the night.

Our emu meat became tainted, in consequence of the heat and the long stage.

Sept. 16.--We continued our course N. 25 degrees W. and, at the end of two miles, came to another foot-path of the natives, which I requested Charley to follow. We passed through tea-tree forest, and a succession of Cycas groves, and came out into plains, and to the heads of sandy creeks with tea-tree shrubs and Salicornia. We were just turning to the westward, expecting to find a large salt-water river before us, when we heard Charley's gun, the signal of his having found water. He soon after joined us, and guided us on the foot-path, three miles south-west, to a large well, near a much frequented camping place of the natives, under the banks of a magnificent salt-water river. Its banks were covered with a close forest of Cycas palms. The well was formed by the natives, who had raised a wall of clay, by which they caught the fresh water which sparingly oozed out of a layer of clay very little above the mark of high water.

We unloaded our bullocks: but, having watered our horses, we found that the supply of the well was not even sufficient for them, and that it was filling very slowly. The poor bullocks had, therefore, to wait until the water could again collect. We had fairly to defend it against our horses, which eagerly pressed towards the water, or stood anxiously waiting on the steep slopes, like cats and dogs round a dog's meat cart, now and then uttering a neigh of discontent. When Charley first discovered the well, he saw a crocodile leaning its long head over the clay wall, enjoying a drink of fresh water.

The river or creek at which we encamped, and which I called "Cycas Creek," at two miles lower down, entered a still larger river coming from the westward, which I called the "Robinson," in acknowledgment of the liberal support which I received from J. P. Robinson, Esq., in the outfit of my expedition. Charley saw a shoal of porpoises in it when he went down the river to fetch the horses. Wishing to ascertain how far the salt water extended, and whether any fresh water lagoons were near us, I took Charley, and followed a foot-path of the natives which led up Cycas Creek, and passed a succession of Cycas groves, of tea-tree forest with bloodwood and white-gum, and some Cypress pine thickets. After seven miles, the salt water ceased, and a ledge of rock separated it from a fine pool of slightly brackish water, on which some natives were encamped, but they left the place directly we made our appearance. I crossed, and found on the left side a fine rocky lagoon, above the level of the water in the creek. After paying a visit to the deserted camp, we returned to our companions, made our dinner on tainted emu meat, reloaded our bullocks and horses, and travelled by moonlight up to the lagoon. About three miles before we reached it, we were obliged to leave our old bullock, as he refused to walk any farther: but Mr. Calvert and Brown brought him next morning to the camp.

As we passed the Cycas groves, some of the dry fruit was found and tasted by several of my companions, upon whom it acted like a strong emetic, resembling in this particular the fruit of Zamia spiralis, (R. Br.) of New South Wales. The natives, at this season, seemed to live principally on the seeds of Pandanus spiralis, (R. Br.) and Cycas; but both evidently required much preparation to destroy their deleterious properties. At the deserted camp of the natives, which I visited yesterday, I saw half a cone of the Pandanus covered up in hot ashes, large vessels (koolimans) filled with water in which roasted seed-vessels were soaking; seed-vessels which had been soaked, were roasting on the coals, and large quantities of them broken on stones, and deprived of their seeds. This seems to show that, in preparing the fruit, when ripe, for use, it is first baked in hot ashes, then soaked in water to obtain the sweet substance contained between its fibres, after which it is put on the coals and roasted to render it brittle when it is broken to obtain the kernels.

I also observed that seeds of Cycas were cut into very thin slices, about the size of a shilling, and these were spread out carefully on the ground to dry, after which, (as I saw in another camp a few days later) it seemed that the dry slices are put for several days in water, and, after a good soaking, are closely tied up in tea-tree bark to undergo a peculiar process of fermentation.

The Cycas disappeared where the fresh water commenced; and it seemed to be confined to the sandy soil near the salt water.

Sept. 17.--I stopped at Cycas Creek, to allow our old bullock to recover, as it was easier for us to drive him than to carry his meat, heavily laden as our other bullocks were.

The emu meat became so tainted that it affected our bowels, and I had consequently to reserve it for the dog. As the nutritious qualities of our meat decreased, I had increased the daily allowance from five pounds to seven; allowing two pounds and a half for breakfast, the same quantity for luncheon, and two pounds for dinner. Mr. Roper had slowly recovered, but sufficiently to mount his horse without assistance.

We were sadly distressed for want of clothing. The few shirts which we had taken with us, became so worn and threadbare, that the slightest tension would tear them. To find materials for mending the body, we had to cut off the sleeves, and, when these were used, pieces were taken from the lower part of the shirt to mend the upper. Our trowsers became equally patched: and the

214

want of soap prevented us from washing them clean. We had, however, saved our shoes so well, by wearing mocassins while travelling along the eastern coast, that every one was well provided, particularly after the death of Mr. Gilbert, whose stock of clothes I divided among my companions.

Sept. 18.--I went with Charley to reconnoitre the country between Cycas creek and the Robinson. A foot-path led us from one to the other, passing through a series of Cycas groves, box and tea-tree forest, and thickets of tea-tree and Cypress pine. The latter covered long tracts near the Robinson, and frequently attained a large size.

The river was about two hundred yards broad, with sleep banks intersected by deep gullies. Two tea-tree creeks, which entered it at the point where our examination stopped, contained fresh water in the upper part of their short courses. We crossed the river by a rocky bar, and, below it, was another, on which the natives had erected a rude wall of stone, for catching fish. The upper bar was not covered even by the tide; but, above it, the water although very bitter, was not salt. We found here the carcase of a crocodile; and the skull of another was found near our camp at Cycas Creek. After crossing the river, we followed down its left bank to the lower ford, in order to find some fresh water, and at last came to a small tea-tree gully with two pools of water, near which some natives were encamped; there were, however, only two very old men in the camp at the time, who, on seeing us, began to chaunt their incantations. We were too anxious to examine the water to stand upon ceremony, and, when they saw us approach, they retired across the river to their friends, who were probably occupied at no great distance in collecting the seeds of Pandanus and Cycas. In the camp, we observed Cycas seeds sliced and drying on the ground; and some Pandanus seeds soaking in large vessels; emu bones were lying in the ashes, and the feet of the emu were rolled up and concealed between the tea-tree bark of the hut. A small packet contained red ochre to colour their bodies, and larger packets contained soaked Cycas seeds, which seemed to be undergoing fermentation. They were of a mealy substance, and harmless; but had a musty taste and smell, resembling that of the common German cheese. There was also a very large stone tomahawk made of greenstone; and some fans of emu feathers.

In returning, we chased and shot an emu.

Sept. 19.--We moved our camp to the water-holes at the left bank of the Robinson, about six miles and a half west by north, from the head of the salt-water in Cycas Creek. The longitude of the Robinson is, according to my reckoning, 136 degrees 43 minutes. On our way we again met the natives, men, women, and children, who ran away screaming loudly. I visited their camp again, and found that they had been there to fetch the emu feet; but had left all the other things behind. I went with Brown to examine the country before us. The first three or four miles lay through an open well-grassed forest and over some small plains, on which we gave an unsuccessful chase to three emus. The Cycas disappeared as we receded from the river. We passed a small scrubby creek, and a long tract of stringy-bark forest, mixed with bloodwood and Pandanus, and patches of Cypress pine. Here we again observed the gum-tree with orange blossoms and large ribbed seed-vessels, which we found at the upper Lynd, and had called Melaleuca gum. Sterculia was frequent, and we collected a great quantity of its ripe seeds. We passed several dry swamps, surrounded with tea-tree thickets, and heaps of fresh water mussel shells. A rich iron-stone rock cropped out frequently; its surface had the appearance of having been netted.

In a tract of broad-leaved tea-tree forest, we came to a watercourse, which led us to a fine creek surrounded with Pandanus and drooping tea-trees, and containing a chain of deep water-holes in its bed. Its course was from west to east.

Sept. 20.--We removed our camp to the creek I had found last night, about nine miles north-west from the Robinson. On our way, we saw two flocks of emus, and Spring caught one of the birds. According to Charley, who is a native of Bathurst, the emus of this part of the country are much smaller than those of his country, which frequently yield from two to three gallons of oil; but very few of the gulf emus contained fat enough to fry their own liver; and their skin was as dry as that of the native dog. A similar difference has been observed in the bustard, which, at the gulf, rarely weighed more than three pounds and a half; whereas individuals of twenty and twenty-eight pounds weight have been shot to the southward.

I succeeded here in cooking the seeds of Sterculia, which had recently been gathered; first by separating them from their prickly husks, and roasting them slightly, and then pounding and boiling them for a short time. They produced not only a good beverage with an agreeable flavour, but ate well and appeared to be very nourishing. They contained a great quantity of oil.

Brown caught an Agama, of a light yellowish colour, about a foot long.

The nights had been generally cloudy, with the exception of the last, which was clear with heavy dew. The days were very hot before the setting in of the sea breeze, which now generally took place at half past eleven. But the refreshing breeze was little felt in the close stringy-bark forest, which, with the dust rising under our bullocks' feet, rendered the heat almost suffocating.

Sept. 21.--Our journey to-day was in a N. 50 degrees W. direction for about eleven miles, through stringy-bark forest, in which the Melaleuca and the

216

Cypress pine were either scattered, or formed small patches of forest. We then crossed a shallow sandy creek surrounded with thickets of Cypress pine; passed some broad-leaved tea-tree forest, and came to a fine open country timbered with tea-tree, and, farther on, with box and white gum. After fifteen miles, our course was intercepted by the largest salt-water river we had yet seen, and we turned at once to the W.S.W. in order to head it. Deep hollows surrounded by tea-trees, but quite dry, extended parallel to the river. We observed several islands in the river; and it was joined by some deep creeks filled with salt water at their lower parts, but dry higher up. The whole country was equally open and well grassed. The leguminous Ironbark, the white-barked tree of the Abel Tasman, the fig tree, and Sterculia in fruit, grew in the forest; and the white water-gum in the hollows, the drooping tea-tree at the level of the freshes, and a species of salt-water Casuarina below it.

I called this river the "Macarthur," in acknowledgment of the liberal support my expedition received from Messrs. James and William Macarthur of Cambden.

When we were passing through the stringy-bark forest, about four or five miles from the camp of the 20th, we heard the calls of some natives behind us, and I stopped our train to ascertain what they wanted: they were soon perceived running after us, and, when they were sufficiently near, I dismounted and advanced slowly to have a parley, and was met by an old man with three or four young fellows behind him. As soon as he saw that I intended to make him a present, he prepared one in return; and when I gave him some rings and buckles, he presented me with some of the ornaments he wore on his person. As our confidence in each other was thus established, some of my companions and several others of the natives came up, and we exchanged presents in a very amicable manner. They were all well made, good looking men; and one young man, whose body was coloured red, was even handsome, although his expression was somewhat wild and excited. All of them seemed to have been circumcised. Charley told me afterwards, that, at my first approach, some of them held their bommerangs ready to throw, but I do not think that it was more than a simple attitude of defence, in case I should have proved the aggressor. On my inquiring about water, they pointed in the direction which we were going, and seemed to say, "It is far, but it is large; Baco! Baco! Umara!" they frequently repeated with emphasis. John also told me that an old man had made signs of a large water, but not fit to drink, and was very anxious for us to change our course, Mr. Roper had understood the same. But, as long as we were ignorant what was before us, the pantomime and words of the natives enabled us to form but very vague and hopeless guesses. It was easy to understand them, when we knew the reality. These natives must have had some intercourse with white men, or Malays, for they knew the use of a knife, and valued it so highly, that one of them offered a gin for one. They appeared equally acquainted with the use of our fire-arms. No doubt they had seen the Malays, and probably some had accompanied them to the islands; as it is a common custom of the Malays to take natives home with them, that they may become friendly to them when fishing for trepang at this part of the gulf.

As the stage lengthened, our old bullock began to lag behind, and at last lay down incapable of walking any farther. In the hope of finding water, I continued my journey until the decline of day compelled me to encamp. We watched our bullocks as usual during the night, and I was distressed to find that another of them, a young but heavy beast, had suffered so much, that I feared he would soon have to be slaughtered, and the number of our pack bullocks be again reduced.

Sept. 22.--I sent Mr. Calvert and Charley back to fetch the bullock, whilst we continued our journey up the river. The country maintained the same character, being open and well-grassed. At the end of about seven miles, we came to a range of sandstone hills with horizontal strata, deeply fissured and worn by the waters and the atmosphere. A creek at the northern side of the range was dry; but, at its southern foot, there was another, which contained several small pools and two deep rocky basins with an ample supply of water. Here, therefore, we encamped to wait for our old bullock, which I now resolved to kill; being well aware that he would be a constant drawback to our progress. Wallabies were exceedingly numerous, and their tracks as broad as the foot-paths of the natives. Our lat. was 16 degrees 5 minutes 26 seconds; long. according to reckoning, 136 degrees 10 minutes.

Mr. Calvert and Charley had succeeded in driving our bullock to within about three miles of our camp, where he had again lain down. As soon as the moon rose, I went with Charley to bring him on; but when we came to the place where they had left him, he was gone. It was impossible even for Charley to track him in the uncertain moonlight; and, as the night was very cold and foggy along the flats and hollows of the river, we made a fire, to wait for daylight. By a most unfortunate accident, my hat caught fire, and was consumed in an instant; it was a great loss to me in such a climate, and under daily exposure to a most powerful sun. I had to make shift with a small bag made of strong canvass, the long end of which I turned over my face to shade it. When the sun rose, we resumed our search, and succeeded in finding the poor beast, after tracking him for six miles across the country; he had evidently rambled in search of water, and had generally been attracted by shady hollows, in which any one would have reasonably expected to find it. He had, however, been completely unsuccessful; the hollows appeared to have been dry for a very long time; he travelled tolerably well to our camp, where he was immediately killed, skinned, quartered, and cut up. His meat was not quite so flaccid and watery as that of our last bullock; but it was by no means good. He was an old, and a heavy beast, and the experience we had of him strongly corroborates my observations, that such beasts can neither bear the fatigues of a long journey, nor travel with a load, unless regularly well fed and watered.

On this occasion we made a grand discovery, of which we afterwards profited greatly. A portion of the skin of the bullock was dried, and a certain quantity was added to our soup at night; which we soon found to be not only a great improvement, but to be in itself much preferable to the tasteless meat of our knocked-up bullocks. The stomach was also made use of on this occasion, as our useful dog, Spring, was well provided with emu meat. We had our last pot of tea on the 22nd, and we were now fairly put on dry beef and water.

By a mere accident, we discovered a remarkable medicinal property of the glutinous secretion of the seed-vessels of a drooping Grevillea. John Murphy, having no pockets in his trowsers, put the seeds which he found during the stage into his bosom, close to the skin, where he had already deposited a great number of Sterculia, and was much inconvenienced by the starry prickles which surround the seeds. Afterwards, finding the drooping Grevillea in fruit, he gathered some capsules and placed them as before stated. Upon arriving at the camp, he felt great pain; and, on examining the place, he saw, to his greatest horror, that the whole of the skin of the epigastric region was coloured black, and raised into a great number of painful blisters. Upon his showing it to me, I thought that it was caused by the Sterculia prickles having irritated the skin, and rendered it more sensitive to the sharp properties of the exudation of the seed-vessels of Grevillea. Brown, however, merely touched the skin of his arm with the matter, when blisters immediately rose; showing clearly its properties. The discoloration of the skin was like the effects of nitrate of silver.

Sept. 24.--When Charley returned with the horses from a higher part of the river, he told us that he had seen so many wallabies and such numerous tracks of emus and crocodiles, that I sent John and Brown to procure some game. They returned with only a red wallabi (Halmaturus agilis) and a spoonbill. According to their account, the river enlarged into an immense sandy bed, like that of the Lynd, and was covered with trees and shrubs, very much resembling those of that river. Its course was from the westward; and in that direction large plains extended. They had seen three crocodiles, one of which lay in the shade of a Sarcocephalus tree. The bean of the Mackenzie grew plentifully along the river, and was covered with ripe seeds. In the morning of the 25th, I sent John and Brown to collect as many of them as they could, for coffee; whilst I and Charley went to reconnoitre the country for water. A

219

W.N.W. course brought us so much into sandstone ranges, gullies, and heads of creeks, that we turned to the northward, until we came again into the open box and tea-tree forest, mixed with bloodwood and gum. About four miles from the camp, we found water-holes supplied by springs, and which had just been left by the natives, who were busy in burning the grass along the ridges, and on the fine intervening flats. It was here that I again met with a species of Banksia, on the sandy flats immediately below the sandstone ranges, which was either a variety of B. integrifolia, or a species very nearly allied to it. We found it afterwards all over Arnheim's Land, especially on the table land and on the rocky heads of the South Alligator River, where it grew on sandy flats surrounding the rocks, and particularly round sandy swamps. The Cypress-pine and Pandanus were frequent, but Sterculia was rare. We remarked that the little finches generally anticipated us in the harvest of the ripe fruit of the latter. About eight miles from the springs, after crossing a great number of small dry sandy watercourses, we came to a fine creek with two large Nymphaea ponds.

On our return, we ran down an emu, the stomach of which was full of the fruit of the little Severn tree. The meat of the whole body was so exceedingly bitter, that I could scarcely eat it. Brown and John had returned with a good supply of beans, and of the large eatable roots of a Convolvolus growing on the plains. The former allowed us again a pot of coffee at luncheon for the next three weeks. This coffee had at first a relaxing effect, but we soon became accustomed to it, and enjoyed it even to the grounds themselves.

Sept. 26.--We removed our camp to the water-holes I had found the day before. We crossed the river at the head of the salt water, where the shallow stream of fresh water was about fifteen yards broad. Sandstone ridges were all round our last camp, and on the opposite side of the river, where it was joined by a deep Pandanus creek. John Murphy told me that he shot a fish at the crossing place, which had the first ray of the dorsal fin very much prolonged, like one of the fresh-water fishes of Darling Downs; they had been in such a hurry to roast it, that I had no chance of examining it.

The day was exceedingly hot, particularly from 7 to 11 o'clock, when the strong sea breeze set in from the north-east.

Sept. 27.--I went with Brown to reconnoitre the country to the north-west. About a mile from the camp, we crossed a fine creek with a chain of ponds and a tiny stream densely fringed with Pandanus. To the north-west of it, we rode through a succession of scrubby and open stringy-bark forest of tea-tree flats and thickets, and over long tracts of stringy-bark saplings which had been recently burned. The Melaleuca gum was very frequent in the stringy-bark forest: the Cypress-pine formed either small thickets or occurred scattered. Sterculia, which at the time was particularly valuable to us, was rare.

Red ironstone cropped out every where, and formed large shallow basins, surrounded by tea-tree thickets; like those swamps I have mentioned on several occasions. About eight miles from the camp, we crossed a good sized waterless creek, with drooping tea-trees, and groves of Pandanus; and about three miles farther, came to a large creek with some very long water-holes, which were all stocked with small fish. On our return, it became so dark that we missed our tracks; and, by keeping too much to the eastward, we came to a very wild rocky country, in which the large Pandanus creek, as well as that on which we were encamped, changed their character so much that we crossed without recognising them. We encamped out, and the next morning, the 28th, we changed our course to the southward, which brought us to a little hill we had passed two days before, and which Brown immediately recognised: thus affording another instance of the quickness of his eye, and of his wonderful memory for localities. We returned on our former bullock tracks to the camp; and having taken some breakfast, and loaded our bullocks, we immediately started for the water-holes, which were situated about eleven miles to the north-west, in lat. 15 degrees 47 minutes 23 seconds.

Sept. 29.--I reconnoitered with Charley in a north by west course, and travelled through a most wretched country. Cypress-pine thickets alternated with scrubby stringy-bark forest, acacia and tea-tree thickets, and with broad tea-tree forest. The Bossiaea with broad leafless stem, was one of the principal components of the scrub. About eight miles from our camp, we crossed a small creek with good water-holes; and at four miles and a half further, came to a river with several channels, separated by high and irregular bergues, with a sandy bed containing large pools of water surrounded with water Pandanus and drooping tea-trees. Acacia neurocarpa, and a species of Cassia, which we had observed since leaving Seven Emu River, grew on the sands. After giving our horses a short rest, during which we refreshed ourselves with a pot of Sterculia coffee, we returned towards our camp; but, wishing to find a more open road, kept more to the eastward, and came sooner than I expected to Sterculia Creek: which name I had given to the creek on which we were encamped, in reference to the groves of Sterculias of both species, rose-coloured as well as heterophylla, which grow on its banks. We followed it up for seven miles, when the setting sun, and our great fatigue, induced us to stop. The creek changed its character every quarter of a mile, forming now a broad sandy or pebbly bed, then a narrow channel between steep banks; and again several channels, either with fine water-holes, or almost entirely filled up and over-grown with a scanty vegetation. On the banks, thickets alternated with scrubs and open country, and, lower down, the country became very fine and open. Early in the morning of the 30th, we started again, and arrived at the camp after a long ride, both hungry and tired.

CHAPTER XIII

CAPE MARIA
OBLIGED TO LEAVE A PORTION OF OUR COLLECTION OF
NATURAL HISTORY
LIMMEN BIGHT RIVER
HABITS OF WATER BIRDS
NATIVE FISH TRAP
THE FOUR ARCHERS
THE WICKHAM
THE DOG DIES
IMMENSE NUMBER OF DUCKS AND GEESE
THE ROPER
THREE HORSES DROWNED
OBLIGED TO LEAVE A PORTION OF MY BOTANICAL
COLLECTION
MORE INTERCOURSE WITH FRIENLDY NATIVES, CIRCUMCISED
HODGSON'S CREEK
THE WILTON
ANOTHER HORSE DROWNED
ANXIETY ABOUT OUR CATTLE
AN ATTACK ON THE CAMP FRUSTRATED
BOILS
BASALT AGAIN
INJURIOUS EFFECTS OF THE SEEDS OF AN ACACIA.

Oct. 1.--The camp was moved forward to the river we had found on the 29th, about thirteen miles north by west from our camp at Sterculia Creek. About a mile from the river, we passed a large swampy lagoon, round which the natives had burned the grass. Several flocks of whistling ducks (Leptotarsis Eytoni, GOULD) and many black Ibises were here. We heard the call of the "Glucking bird" every night during the last fortnight, particularly from about 2 to 5 o'clock a.m. I called this river the "Red Kangaroo River;" for, in approaching it, we first saw the Red Forester of Port Essington (Osphanter antilopinus, GOULD). The longitude, according to my reckoning, was 136 degrees.

Oct. 2.--We travelled about eleven miles north by west, to lat. 15 degrees 25 minutes 18 seconds, over an undulating country, if possible even worse than that of the last two stages. Low sandy rises were covered with stringy-bark trees and saplings, and the depressions were either thickly beset with different species of Acacia, of Pultanaea, of the broad-stemmed Bossiaea, or formed shallow basins of red ironstone covered and surrounded with tea-tree scrub. On the higher elevations, the Cypress-pine thickets proved even worse than the scrub. We crossed only one sandy little creek, and came, at the end of the stage, to the head of a small Pandanus creek, which improved rapidly, and, a little way down, contained fine Nymphaea ponds. Charley went still farther down, and, in an old camp of the natives, found Cythereas and the head of a crocodile.

It was during this stage, and among the scrub and underwood of the sandy hills, that we first met with Grevillea pungens (R. Br.), a shrub from two to five feet high, with pale-green pinnatifid pungent leaves, and racemes of red flowers. Flagellaria indica, L. was very abundant near the creek; and our bullocks fed heartily upon it: particularly in this most wretched country, where the grass was scanty and hard.

Although the days were exceedingly hot, the air immediately before and after sunrise was most agreeable.

Oct. 3.--We travelled about six miles and a half north by west, over a country equally scrubby as that of the preceding stage. The saplings had been killed by a bush fire, and a hurricane, which must have swept over the country some years ago, had broken and uprooted the larger trees, which lay all to the west and north-west. Since then, saplings had sprung up, and, with the remains of the old trees, formed a most impervious scrubby thicket, through which we could move but very slowly. About a mile from our camp, we crossed a salt-water creek nine or ten yards broad. There was some vine brush, with plenty of Flagellarias, growing along its banks. A little farther, we crossed a freshwater creek, which was larger than the preceding. Both appeared to come from some conspicuous ranges, about six or eight miles to the westward. About five miles farther, we encamped on a sandy creek with fine pools of water.

Oct. 4.--We were obliged to remain here, as the horses, not finding sufficient food in the neighbourhood of the camp, had strayed so far through the scrub, that they were not found before 2 o'clock in the afternoon, when it was too late to proceed.

Oct. 5.--We continued our course north by west, through a similar wretched country, and, at the end of about six miles, came to some hills, on the north side of a broad sandy creek, from which we distinguished the white sands of the sea coast, and the white crest of breakers rolling towards the land. In the bed of the creek as well as on its banks, the back bones of cuttle-fish were numerous. Charley and John went down to the beach, and brought back several living salt-water shells. I proceeded up the creek in a south-west

223

direction, and came, at about three miles, to some pools of good water, with a tolerable supply of young feed. The range we had seen yesterday, was still about eight or ten miles distant, tending from S.S.E. to N.N.W.; it was steep and naked, and was composed of a white rock which proved to be a baked sandstone, nearly resembling quartzite in its homogeneous texture.

Oct. 6.--One of our bullocks had become so weak that he was unable to carry his load; it was, therefore, put on one of our spare horses, which were still in excellent condition. I steered for one of the detached mountains at the northern end of the range, and travelled about twelve miles north-west, before we came to its foot. We had, however, to leave our bullock on the way, as the difficult nature of the country and diarrhoea together had completely exhausted him. Scrub and dense underwood continued over a rather undulating country to the foot of the range, which was itself covered with open forest. We passed through a gap between the last two hills of the range, and Charley and Brown, whom I had sent forward in different directions, and who had both been on the highest hill, stated that they had distinctly seen an island in the sea; which could be no other than that marked Cape Maria in Arrowsmith's map. They had also seen a large river to the northward, coming from the west; and clearly distinguished large sandy plains extending along it as far as the eye could reach. At the west side of the range, we soon came to a small salt-water creek with small sandy and sometimes boggy Salicornia plains, surrounded with the scrubby salt-water tea-tree, which possessed an odour very much resembling that of a Blackfellow. We proceeded about six miles to the southward, when the country became more open, with an abundance of fine young feed for our horses and cattle. The water was slightly brackish, and, strange enough, it became more so the higher we went up the creek.

Whilst we were at our last camp, Charley met a long file of native women returning, with their dillies and baskets full of shell fish, to the range; near which, very probably, fresh water existed. We saw their numerous tracks, and a footpath leading to the river; and heard their cooees round our present camp, which may have interfered with one of their camping places. Our lat. was 15 degrees 14 minutes.

Oct. 7.--John and Charley went back to fetch the bullock, and, in the mean time, I occupied myself in examining our packs, in order to dispense with such things as were least necessary; for, with an additional weight of 130 pounds of dried meat and hide, our pack bullocks were overloaded, and it was now imperative upon me to travel as lightly as possible. Thus I parted with my paper for drying plants, with my specimens of wood, with a small collection of rocks, made by Mr. Gilbert, and with all the duplicates of our zoological specimens. Necessity alone, which compelled me to take this step, reconciled me to the loss.

Our bullock came in during the afternoon, and was immediately killed, skinned, and quartered.

Oct. 8.--We cut the meat into slices, and put them out to dry.

Oct. 9.--I went with Brown to examine the country along the river, which I called "Limmen Bight River;" from its disemboguing into Limmen Bight. Charley had been at the upper part of the creek on which we were encamped, and found it running and fresh; which made me believe, that those pools of very brackish water we had previously seen, belonged to a different watercourse. I rode with Brown to the westward, over a succession of ironstone ridges covered with stringy-bark scrub. These ridges formed steep headlands into the broad flat valley of the river. Along the valley, bare sandy and boggy plains alternated with tea-tree thickets and mangrove swamps, in one of which our horses got deeply bogged. After five miles we came on a large piece of salt water, which, according to Brown, was a tributary creek of the river. It flowed between low banks fringed with tea-trees. We followed a foot-path of the natives, who seemed very numerous, which led towards another range west by south; and crossed several tea-tree creeks, Pandanus groves, and swamps full of a high blady grass. We observed some springs, with but little water however, though densely surrounded with ferns (Osmunda). After about seven miles, we were stopped by a fern swamp full of fine box-trees, with a thick jungle of high stiff grasses and ferns (Blechnum). A small running creek formed its outlet, and contained a chain of deep ponds covered with Nymphaeas, and surrounded with Typha (bull-rush), the youngest part of the leaves of which is very tolerable eating. Large swarms of ducks (Leptotarsis Eytoni, GOULD), rose with their peculiar whistling noise, at our approach.

Oct. 10.--I moved my camp to the chain of lagoons, which we found yesterday; and our horses and cattle enjoyed the fine feed. The largest hill of the range to the westward, bore south-west from our camp. A species of Hibiscus with large pink flowers, but small insignificant leaves, and another small malvaceous shrub with white flowers grew round the camp.

Oct. 11.--Last night we saw long flights of geese (Anseranas melanoleuca, GOULD) and swarms of ducks, passing our camp from west to east; which made us very naturally suppose that large lagoons of fresh water existed at the head of the fern swamp, of which our little Typha brook formed the outlet. Brown and Charley were very desirous of getting some of these geese, and concocted a plan either to induce me to follow the brook up, or to stop me altogether. Not knowing their intentions, I sent Brown after the cattle, and Charley to find a crossing place. They met, however, at those supposed lagoons, and amused themselves in shooting geese, and (after having probably

225

enjoyed an off-hand dinner of roasted goose) they returned at 2 o'clock, complaining of course, that the cattle had strayed very far. Though I had been very much annoyed by waiting so long, I was pleased in finding that they had shot four geese. In order, however, to show my sable companions that their secret manoeuvres only tended to increase their own labour, I ordered the bullocks to be loaded immediately they arrived, and proceeded to get out of this intricate country as soon as possible. We travelled west by north, over a tolerable open country, leaving the salt-water plains to the right, and crossed several well beaten foot-paths, and a sort of play ground on which the natives seem to have danced and crawled about, as it bore the impressions of both hands and feet. After four miles, we came to a broad salt-water creek, the high banks of which were covered with numerous heaps of Cytherea shells, which had lived in the mud of the creek. We followed it up about a mile, when it ended in a hollow coming from the range. After passing this, our course was intercepted by another large creek, which compelled us to go to the south and even to south-east along the western side of the range which we had seen from Typha brook. We followed it up about two miles, and found some ponds of slightly brackish water, in which, however, Nymphaea grew, and several small freshwater fish lived; and near them the track of a crocodile was observed by Charley. Open country alternated with thick Acacia underwood along this creek, and its grass was still coarse and blady. Many gullies came down from the range; which was composed of baked sandstone, with not very distinct stratification, and irregularly broken blocks. At a lagoon which we passed in the commencement of the stage, Brown shot three more geese; thus disclosing to us the haunts of those numerous flights we had seen. We roasted four of our geese for dinner, and they formed by far the most delicious dish our expedition had offered: the others were stewed for the next breakfast; and they were equally good: though a whole night's stewing might have robbed them of a little of their rich flavour.

We had frequently observed the flight of waterfowl, at the commencement of night, and a little before dawn. At Cycas Creek, Spoonbills, Ibises, and Whistling ducks came at night fall to the fresh water, and left it in the morning. The geese flew past at night from an open lagoon to the westward, to more confined ponds at the head of the fern swamp to the eastward. It would appear that they prefer a sheltered situation for the night, and large open sheets of water by day.

The nights were usually dewy, in consequence of the moist sea breeze, which blew almost the whole day from east and E. N. E., and set in frequently as early as 9 or 10 o'clock. The morning, from about 7 o'clock till the sea breeze set in, was exceedingly hot; but, before sunrise, it was most delightful; the myriads of flies which crowded round us during the day, and the mosquitoes which annoyed us after sunset, were then benumbed; and although the sun rose with the full intensity of its heat, it was not so inconvenient in the early morn as to induce us to look for shade. Not a breath was stirring; and the notes of the laughing jackass and some few small birds, alone showed that there were other beings enjoying the beauty of this august solitude.

Oct. 12.--We proceeded three or four miles up the creek, and found a crossing at a fishing place of the natives; in an old camping place near this fishery, I saw a long funnel-shaped fish trap, made of the flexible stem of Flagellaria. Hence we travelled about north-west by west, towards a fine mountain range, which yesterday bore W. N. W. After six miles of undulating scrubby country, and broad-leaved tea-tree forest, we arrived at a creek with a fine pool of water, which, notwithstanding its Nymphaeas, Charas, and Typhas, was slightly brackish and bitter. Limnaea, and two species of Melania, were found in it; the one species, with a long sharp spire, had been found in a reedy brook, at the upper Burdekin. Limmen Bight river was not half a mile from our camp; and I now hoped that we should soon be out of the system of salt-water creeks joining it from the southward.

Our lat. was 15 degrees 13 minutes (?) and longitude, according to reckoning, 135 degrees 30 minutes. We had left the stiff grasses of the coast, and the pasture was fast improving. John Murphy shot the Torres Straits pigeon (Carpophaga luctuosa, GOULD) which we had once before observed; but it was exceedingly shy and rare, and only seen in pairs.

Oct. 13.--We travelled about sixteen miles to the southward, to lat. 15 degrees 29 minutes 10 seconds, following the river, and heading several salt water creeks, which prolonged our journey very much. Stony hills and ranges frequently approached the river, and rendered our travelling difficult and fatiguing. They were composed of baked sandstone, and white and blue indurated clay, the strata of which dipped at a very small angle to the southward, and the strike from east to west. The flats between the ranges, and along the river and creeks, were openly timbered and well grassed; and, at the head of a salt-water creek, we found deep ponds of constant water covered with Nymphaeas, and surrounded with Typhas and drooping tea-trees. Towards the end of the stage, where the high rocky hills formed deep declivities into the river, we had to ascend them, and to travel along their summits. A good sized creek joined the river at their southern slopes, which, though salt below, contained some good pools of fresh water higher up. To the southward of this creek, there were four very remarkable flat-topped cones of sandstone, which appeared like a plateau cut into four detached masses. These I called the "Four Archers," in honour of my excellent hosts Messrs. David, Charles, John, and Thomas Archer of Moreton Bay. From the eastern one, I enjoyed a fine view, and distinguished distant ranges broken by a gap to the southward, and detached long-stretched ridges to the westward.

I went with Charley to examine the river, in order to find a fording place, in which we succeeded at about four miles south-west from our camp, in lat. 15 degrees 30 minutes 31 seconds; where a stony bar crossed the salt water, leaving a small channel in which the tide formed a shallow stream. The bed of the river became very broad and sandy, covered with shrubs like those of the Lynd and most of the other rivers we had passed.

Oct. 14.--We crossed the river, and travelled about ten miles north-west, over a succession of stony ridges, separated by fine open tea-tree and box flats. Some fine shallow sandy watercourses, quite dry, went down to the north by east. At the end of the stage, the uniform colour of the country was interrupted by the green line of a river-bed, so pleasing and so refreshing to the eye, with the rich verdure of its drooping tea-trees and myrtles, interspersed with the silver leaves of Acacia neurocarpa and Grevillea chrysodendron. The river was formed by two broad sandy beds, separated by a high bergue, and was full 700 yards from bank to bank. It contained large detached water-pools fringed with Pandanus, which were very probably connected by a stream filtering through the sands, I called it the "Wickham," in honour of Captain Wickham, R.N. of Moreton Bay, who had recently commanded a survey of the north-west coast of New Holland, in H.M.S. Beagle.

The red wallabi (Halmaturus agilis, GOULD) was very numerous along the gullies of the river: and we started a flock of red foresters (Osphranter Antilopinus, GOULD) out of a patch of scrub on the brow of a stony hill. Charley and Brown, accompanied by Spring, pursued them, and killed a fine young male. I had promised my companions that, whenever a kangaroo was caught again, it should be roasted whole, whatever its size might be. We had consequently a roasted Red Forester for supper, and we never rolled ourselves up in our blankets more satisfied with a repast.

Brown found a Eugenia, with large white blossoms and large coriaceous oblong lanceolate shining leaves; it was a tree of thirty or forty feet high, with a grey bark, and a good hard wood. It was growing at the upper part of the creek on which we were encamped last night. Its fruit was two inches in diameter, with longitudinal ribs, scarlet red, and very eatable when dropt from the tree, but when gathered on the tree, it had an aromatic pungency. This tree was very common along the well watered creeks of Arnheim's Land; particularly along the South Alligator River, and at Raffles Bay. Brown brought from the same locality a Melastoma, which, according to him, was a shrub, three or four feet high.

Oct. 15.--We continued our journey in a north-west direction. The first five or

228

six miles was over a succession of very lightly timbered box-flats, alternating with small plains. They were bounded by scrubs and ranges, which we crossed, and from the top of one obtained the view of a remarkable system of parallel ranges, all steep mountain walls of a white colour indicating the nature of their rock, and separated from each other by perfectly level flats covered with broad leaved tea-tree forest. At their foot a richer tree vegetation existed, principally composed of the leguminous Ironbark, Blood-wood, and Pandanus. The darker verdure of these trees, which we also observed at the foot of the most distant range, made us believe that a river was near it. After travelling about five miles over a flat, we crossed a broad sandy creek, which we did not follow, although beaten foot-paths of the natives led down it, as we firmly believed that a river was before us. At five miles farther, we came to the foot of the range, which rose suddenly from the level country, and, although a small watercourse existed in the tea-tree flat, our anticipated river proved to be like the Dutchman's "Cape Fly-away." In ascending the range, our poor bullocks suffered severely, and, when we reached the summit, they stood panting with their tongues hanging out of their mouths; I therefore halted a short time, to allow them to recover. The east slopes of all these ranges were steep, but to the north-west they were very gentle, and covered with stringy-bark forest. A long succession of similar ranges was seen to the north-west. A small watercourse brought us to a creek containing large but dry water-holes. Finding that it turned to the eastward, round the range we had just crossed, and that it almost disappeared in the scrubby tea-tree flats, we turned to the northward, passed several more ridges, and encamped long after sunset, near a dry but promising creek, without water. I immediately sent Mr. Calvert and Charley down the creek, in search of water, and they returned, towards midnight, with the welcome intelligence that they had found some fine pools.

I had been absent during the latter part of the stage, and most unfortunately our kangaroo dog had been left behind, whereby this most valuable animal was lost. He had been the means of our obtaining so much, and indeed the greatest part of our game, that his loss was severely felt by us.

Our lat. was 15 degrees 10 minutes.

Oct. 16.--We travelled down to the water, about four miles north-east along the creek, which was covered with Cypress pine thickets, and tea-tree scrub. Mr. Calvert and Charley returned on our tracks to endeavour to recover our poor dog. They found him almost dead,--stretched out in the deep cattle track, which he seemed not to have quitted, even to find a shady place. They brought him to the camp; and I put his whole body, with the exception of his head, under water, and bled him; he lived six hours longer, when he began to bark, as if raving, and to move his legs slightly, as dogs do when dreaming. It seemed that he died of inflammation of the brain. If we become naturally fond of animals which share with us the comforts of life, and become the cheerful companions of our leisure hours, our attachment becomes still greater when they not only share in our sufferings, but aid greatly to alleviate them. The little world of animated beings, with which we moved on, was constantly before our eyes; and each individual the constant object of our attention. We became so familiar with every one of them, that the slightest change in their walk, or in their looks was readily observed; and the state of their health anxiously interpreted. Every bullock, every horse, had its peculiar character, its well defined individuality, which formed the frequent topic of our conversation, in which we all most willingly joined, because every one was equally interested. My readers will, therefore, easily understand my deep distress when I saw myself, on recent occasions, compelled to kill two of our favourite bullocks long before their time; and when our poor dog died, which we all had fondly hoped to bring to the end of our journey. Brown had, either by accident, or influenced by an unconscious feeling of melancholy, fallen into the habit of almost constantly whistling and humming the soldier's death march, which had such a singularly depressing effect on my feelings, that I was frequently constrained to request him to change his tune.

Oct. 17.--We travelled about eighteen miles N. N. W. over an undulating country, in which Cypress-pine thickets alternated with scrubby stringy-bark forest, and some tea-tree flats. After seven miles, we crossed a large dry creek, which went to the eastward; and, eight miles further, we entered upon a fine box-flat, with hills to the north and north-west. We followed a very promising Pandanus creek, in which the presence of Typha (flag, or bulrush) and a new species of Sesbania indicated the recent presence of water. Mr. Roper having ascended one of the hills, and seen a green valley with a rich vegetation about three miles to the northward, we in consequence left the creek, which turned to the eastward; and, after passing several miles of most wretched scrub, came into an open country, with scattered groves of trees. As the sun was setting, I resolved upon encamping in an open plain, although without water, except what we carried in our large stew-pot. Charley, who had been sent forward, had not yet joined us; I, therefore, ordered two guns to be fired, to let him know where we were; he immediately answered us from a short distance, where he lighted up a cheerful fire. After some time, during which misfortune and carelessness had played us the trick of upsetting our waterpot, Charley arrived with the welcome news that he had found some water-holes in a small creek; we therefore, at moonrise, again saddled our tired animals, and repaired thither.

The day had been exceedingly hot; but the passing shadows of cumuli which formed in the afternoon, occasionally afforded us a delightful relief. The sea breeze was strong, particularly towards evening; but the dense scrub and forest kept it from us during the day.

Oct. 18.--I stopped at the water-holes, to allow our cattle to recover. It was a lovely place. The country around us was very open, and agreeably diversified by small clusters of the raspberry-jam tree. Salicornia and Binoe's Trichinium indicated the neighbourhood of salt water; but the grass was good and mostly young. The creek was shaded by drooping tea-trees and the broad-leaved Terminalia, which also grew scattered over the flats. The water-hole on which we were encamped was about four feet deep, and contained a great number of guard-fish, which, in the morning, kept incessantly springing from the water. A small broad fish with sharp belly, and a long ray behind the dorsal fin, was also caught. It was highly amusing to watch the swarms of little finches, of doves, and Ptilotis, which came during the heat of the day to drink from our water hole. Grallina australis, Crows, Kites, Bronze-winged and Harlequin pigeons, (Peristera histrionica, GOULD), the Rose cockatoo (Cocatua Eos), the Betshiregah (Melopsittacus undulatus), and Trichoglossus versicolor, GOULD, were also visitors to the water-hole, or were seen on the plains. The day was oppressively hot; and neither the drooping tea-trees, nor our blankets, of which we had made a shade, afforded us much relief Clouds gathered, however, in the afternoon, and we had a few drops of rain in the course of the night and following morning. Charley and John had gone out on horseback to obtain some emus, with which the country seemed to abound; they returned, however, at night, without any emus, but brought in about twenty-two whistling and black ducks, one goose and several waders, which they had obtained at a lagoon which was several miles in length, and varied from 50 to 300 yards in breadth, covered with Nymphaeas, and fringed with a dense vegetation; it was surrounded by fine pasture. Never, as they described, had they seen so many ducks and geese together; when they rose, their numbers darkened the air, and their noise was deafening. They had observed a wooden post, cut with an iron tomahawk, rammed in the ground and propped with several large stones; which seemed to be the work either of white men or Malays.

Oct. 19.--We travelled about four miles north 30 degrees west, over plains and an open undulating box and raspberry jam tree country, to the lagoon which my companions had discovered. They had not exaggerated their account, neither of the beauty of the country, nor of the size of the lagoon, nor of the exuberance of animal life on it. It was indeed quite a novel spectacle to us to see such myriads of ducks and geese rise and fly up and down the lagoon, as we travelled along. Casuarinas, drooping tea-trees, the mangrove myrtle (Stravadium) and raspberry-jam trees, grew either on the flats, or formed open groves along the banks; and Polygonums covered the water's edge. When we

231

came to the end of the lagoon, which was bounded on the left by a stony rise of flaggy Psammite, I observed a green belt of trees scarcely 300 yards to the northward; and on riding towards it, I found myself on the banks of a large fresh water river from 500 to 800 yards broad, with not very high banks, densely covered with salt water Hibiscus (Paritium), with a small rubiaceous tree (Pavetta?), which filled the air with the jasmine-like fragrance of its blossoms; with Flagellaria, water Pandanus, and a leguminous climber with bunches of large green blossoms (Mucuna?--D.C. Pr.). The water was slightly muddy, as if a fresh had come down the river; and the tide rose full three feet. It was the river Mr. Roper had seen two days before, and I named it after him, as I had promised to do. The country along its left bank was well-grassed and openly timbered with box; hills were on the opposite side. Its course was from north-west to south-east; but this seemed to be rather local. Natives seemed to be numerous; for their foot-path along the lagoon was well beaten; we passed several of their fisheries, and observed long fishtraps made of Flagellaria (rattan). All the cuts on various trees were made with an iron tomahawk. Natives, crows, and kites were always the indications of a good country. Charley, Brown, and John, who had been left at the lagoon to shoot waterfowl, returned with twenty ducks for luncheon, and went out again during the afternoon to procure more for dinner and breakfast. They succeeded in shooting thirty-one ducks and two geese; so that we had fifty-one ducks and two geese for the three meals; and they were all eaten, with the exception of a few bony remains, which some of the party carried to the next camp. If we had had a hundred ducks, they would have been eaten quite as readily, if such an extravagant feast had been permitted.

Oct. 20.--We travelled about ten miles N. 60 degrees W. up the river; and I was fortunate enough to determine my latitude by an observation of Alpheratz, which cloudy nights had prevented me from obtaining since the 15th October: it was 14 degrees 47 minutes; my longitude, according to reckoning, was 135 degrees 10 minutes. The river continued equally broad, with a fine open box-tree country on its right, whilst a range of hills with several bluff breaks extended along the left side, interrupted occasionally by some openings of small creeks, and, in one place, by the valley of a small river, which Brown saw joining it from the northward.

We followed a broad foot-path of the natives, which cut the angles of the river, and passed along several large lagoons at the foot of some low sandstone ridges, that occasionally approached the river, which was joined by some brushy creeks, one of which was of a considerable size. The box-trees were of stunted growth, but the raspberry-jam trees were still abundant and larger than usual. The grass was plentiful, but old and dry. The lagoons were covered with ducks, geese, and pelicans; and native companions were strutting about on the patches of fresh burnt grass. Brown pursued two emus, and caught one of them. Wallabies were numerous; two bustards, and even a crocodile were seen. A small lizard or newt was observed on the mud between high and low water marks. The green ant of the Lynd inhabited the shady trees of the brushy banks; and, in the forest, brick coloured and black ants were numerous and troublesome.

A strong easterly wind was blowing during the day, and no cumuli formed.

Camps of the natives were frequent, and fresh burnings and fresh mussel-shells showed that they had been lately at the lagoons. But, on the river, the camps were older and not so numerous, and no burnings had lately taken place.

Oct. 21.--After waiting a very long time for our horses, Charley came and brought the dismal tidings that three of the most vigorous of them were drowned, at the junction of the creek with the river. Although the banks of the Roper were steep and muddy, the large creek we had passed was scarcely two miles distant, and offered an easy approach to the water on a rocky bed. It remained, therefore, inexplicable to us how the accident could have happened.

This disastrous event staggered me, and for a moment I turned almost giddy; but there was no help. Unable to increase the load of my bullocks, I was obliged to leave that part of my botanical collection which had been carried by one of the horses. The fruit of many a day's work was consigned to the fire; and tears were in my eyes when I saw one of the most interesting results of my expedition vanish into smoke. Mr. Gilbert's small collection of plants, which I had carefully retained hitherto, shared the same fate. But they were of less value, as they were mostly in a bad state of preservation, from being too much crowded. My collection had the great advantage of being almost complete in blossoms, fruit, and seed, which I was enabled to ensure in consequence of the long duration of our expedition, and of the comparative uniformity of the Australian Flora.

I left the unfortunate place, and travelled about six miles up the river, which kept a W. N. W. course. Open box-flats were bounded by ridges two or three miles from the river. At the opposite side, ranges were seen with some rocky bluff hills. Charley shot a bustard.

Oct. 22.--We travelled about seven miles to the westward, when we came to a broad creek, which compelled us to go five miles to the southward in order to cross it. The country was still a succession of box-flats along the river, with rocky barren ranges in the distance; the latter, however, approached so near the creek, that we found it difficult to pass along. About two miles and a-half

233

from our last camp, we had to cross a running Casuarina brook, which, though very small, was so boggy, that two of our horses were again in great danger of being lost.

Last night we heard the calls of natives at the opposite side of the river. As soon as they saw us, they crossed the river, and came pretty close to us: the discharge of our guns, however, kept them at a distance. Several of our party, during their watches saw them moving with fire sticks on the other side of the river. In the morning, three of them came boldly up; so I went to them with some presents, and they became very friendly indeed. Presents were exchanged; and they invited us in the most pressing manner to accompany them to their camp; and were evidently disappointed in finding that we could not swim. I gave them horse-nails, and they asked me to bend them into fish-hooks. They had doubtless seen or heard of white people before; but of our horses and bullocks they were much afraid, and asked me whether they could bite: they accompanied me, however, pretty near to the camp; but kept their arms round my waist, to be sure of not being bitten. As we proceeded on our journey, they followed us for a long distance, and offered Charley and Brown a gin, if we would go to their camp. They were circumcised, and two front teeth had been knocked out; they had horizontal scars on their chests.

A great number of flying-foxes (Pteropus) were in the river brush, and Brown shot three of them.

The days were cloudless and very hot; the east wind was strong during the afternoon; the nights very cool and pleasant, but without dew.

Oct. 23.--This morning, our sable friends came again to our camp; they made their approach known by a slight whistling. We invited them to come nearer, and many new faces were introduced to us. Of three young people, one was called "Gnangball," the other "Odall," and a boy "Nmamball." These three names were given to many others, and probably distinguished three different tribes or families. We gave them sheets of paper on which the figures of kangaroos, emus, and fish were drawn. When we were loading our bullocks, a whole mob came up with great noise; and one of them danced and jumped about with incessant vociferations, flourishing his wommerah, crowned with a tuft of opossum's hair, like a Drum-major; I put a broken girth round his waist, which seemed to tranquillize him wonderfully. In drinking water out of my pot, I offered it to my friend; but he hesitated to follow my example, until he applied to an elderly, bearded, serious-looking man, who sipped of it, and then my friend ventured to taste its contents. When we started on our journey they followed us with many remarks for a very long way, until we came again to the river; when their appetites probably compelled them to return to their camp; but not before inviting us to accompany them thither, and giving us to understand that they had plenty to eat. On leaving us, they pointed down the river, and repeated the word "Aroma!" "Aroma!"

About three miles to the westward of our camp, the water ceased, and the creek formed a dry sandy bed, covered with Casuarinas; it was joined by two Pandanus creeks with steep deep channels, and well provided with water-holes. I had to go down the creek four miles, in order to avoid some steep rocky ranges; but we turned afterwards to the northward, and travelled, over an open well-grassed country, to the river: it was, however, full of melon-holes and very stony. Ranges and high rocky ridges were seen in every direction. From one of them a pillar of smoke was rising, like a signal fire. The extensive burnings, and the number of our sable visitors, showed that the country was well inhabited. About four or five miles from the last creek,-- which I shall call "Hodgson's Creek," in honour of Pemberton Hodgson, Esq.--the river divided into two almost equal branches, one coming from the northward, and the other from north-west by west. I named the river from the northward the "Wilton," after the Rev. Mr. Wilton of Newcastle, who kindly favoured my expedition. Its latitude was about 14 degrees 45 minutes.

About three miles above the junction of the Wilton with the Roper, we again encamped on the steep banks of the latter, at a spot which I thought would allow our horses and cattle to approach in safety. One unfortunate animal, however, slipped into the water, and every effort to get him out was made in vain. Its constant attempts to scramble up the boggy banks only tired it, and as night advanced, we had to wait until the tide rose again. I watched by him the whole night, and at high water we succeeded in getting him out of the water; but he began to plunge again, and unfortunately broke the tether which had kept his forequarters up, and fell back into the river. At last I found a tolerable landing place about fifty yards higher up; but, as I was swimming with him up to it, and trying to lead him clear of the stumps of trees, he became entangled in the tether rope by which I guided him, rolled over, and was immediately drowned. This reduced our number of horses to nine. When the other horses were brought to the camp, another rushed into the water, but I swam with him at once to the good landing place, and we succeeded in saving him.

I. started late on the 24th Oct. and travelled over a country similar to that of our late stages. About a mile up the river, a ledge of rocks crossed the bed, over which a considerable stream formed a small fall and rapids; above this was a fine sheet of water, overhung with shady tea-trees, Casuarinas, and Pandanus, which made this crossing place extremely lovely. My grief at having lost an excellent horse which I had ridden for the greatest part of the journey, was increased by now knowing that one mile more travelling would have saved him to me. The northern banks of the river were at first open: but they soon became bounded either by isolated, or chains of, rocky hills. These hills separated the valley of the river from an open well grassed, but extremely stony back country; from which creeks carried the water down to the river, through gaps and openings between the hills. To the northward of this back country, other ranges ran parallel to those along the river, from northwest by west to south-east by east, and shorter ranges joined them occasionally. The whole country was composed of sandstone and indurated clay, with very distinct stratification. The layers of clay were white, grey, or slate-coloured; with many shining leaflets of mica.

The days were very hot; the east-breeze very strong during the afternoon, and particularly towards sunset; the nights were warm, clear, and without dew.

Some sheldrakes and wallabies were seen, and a bustard was shot by Charley: large fish were splashing in the water. I gathered the large vine-bean, with green blossoms, which had thick pods containing from one to five seeds. Its hard covering, by roasting, became very brittle; and I pounded the cotyledons, and boiled them for several hours. This softened them, and made a sort of porridge, which, at all events, was very satisfying. Judging by the appearance of large stones which were frequently found, in the camps of the natives, still covered with the mealy particles of some seed which had been pounded upon them, it would seem that the natives used the same bean; but I could not ascertain how they were able to soften them. It did not make good coffee; and, when boiled in an iron pot, the water became very dark. Our latitude was 14 degrees 44 seconds.

Oct. 25.--We travelled about seven miles northwest to lat. 14 degrees 39 minutes, following the river in its various windings over more than twelve miles. The country was well grassed, and openly timbered with white gum, box, and leguminous Ironbark; but occasionally broken by deep gullies, which were fringed with the articulate-podded Acacia (Inga moniliformis), and the broad-leaved Terminalia. Several ranges with rocky slopes approached or bounded the river; and three remarkable bluff hills, two on its right, and one on its left side, formed characteristic landmarks. Their summits were surrounded by perpendicular precipices, from the foot of which steep rocky, but uniform slopes went down to the level country. Thick high reeds covered the approaches of the river, and the lower parts of the gullies; and noble Casuarinas rivalled the drooping tea-tree in beauty. Grevillea pungens (R. Br.) was observed on the hills; it is, therefore, not particular to the coast scrub. A species of native tobacco, with smaller blossoms than that of the Hunter, and with its radical leaves spreading close over the ground, was growing on the open spaces round the water-holes. The river was well supplied with long reaches of water connected by a small stream.

236

In the morning, we had a pleasant westerly breeze, which veered to the north-west and northward; the regular sea breeze set in from the northeast in the afternoon; the night was hot and sultry; but the weather during the day was cooler than that we experienced for the last week.

The red wallabies were very numerous, particularly in the kind of jungle along the river. Sheldrakes and Ibises abounded at the water-holes. Charley shot two wallabies.

Oct. 26.--We enjoyed most gratefully our two wallabies, which were stewed, and to which I had added some green hide to render the broth more substantial. This hide was almost five months old, and had served as a case to my botanical collection, which, unfortunately, I had been compelled to leave behind. It required, however, a little longer stewing than a fresh hide, and was rather tasteless.

We accomplished about eight miles in a straight line to the westward, but went over a much greater extent of ground; as I mistook a large though dry creek from the northward for the river, and followed it about four miles; when, finding my mistake, I crossed about four or five miles of rich treeless plains, and reached the river again at the foot of a long high range to the westward. Other ranges appeared to the eastward and northward. As we approached the river, we passed some sandstone hills covered with a dense scrub exactly like that of the sea coast south of Limmen Bight. It was principally composed of several species of Acacia of Grevillea chrysodendron (R. Br.), and of the Bossiaea with broad stem. All along the outside of the scrub, we observed old camps of the natives; several of whom were seen crossing the plains.

The bed of the river became excessively wild: the Pandanus channel was still full of water, and running; but the dry bed was full of rocky water-holes or chains of them, composed of, and scattered over with blocks of sandstone; and overgrown with most magnificent Casuarinas, with tea-trees and flooded-gum (or its representative).

Large camps of the natives were full of the shells of lately roasted mussels (Unios), the posterior part of which appeared to be much broader, and more sinuated, than those we had hitherto seen. John and Charley found the head of an alligator; and the former caught the broad-scaled fish of the Mackenzie (Osteoglossum), which weighed four pounds. The mosquitoes, and a little black ant, were very annoying during the warm but slightly dewy night.

As we were slowly winding our way among the loose rocks, Brown's horse got knocked up, and we were compelled to encamp. After the disasters which had lately befallen us, I became more alive to the chances to which we were exposed, even more so than after Mr. Gilbert's death; up to which time we had travelled more than a thousand miles, without any great misfortune. At the commencement of our journey, the cooee of my companions, who were driving the bullocks and horses after me, had generally called me back to assist in re-loading one of our restive beasts, or to mend a broken packsaddle, and to look for the scattered straps. This was certainly very disagreeable and fatiguing; but it was rather in consequence of an exuberance of animal spirits, and did not interfere with the hope of a prosperous progress: but, since leaving the Seven Emu River, these calls invariably acquainted me with the failing strength of our poor brutes; and knowing only too well the state of exhaustion in which they were, I was almost constantly expecting to be reminded of it, as I was riding along, which rendered me extremely nervous and restless. The death of our spare horses did not allow us any more to relieve the others by alternate rests, and we became soon aware of their increasing weakness. This was considerably aggravated by the necessity under which we were of keeping two horses tethered near the camp, not only to facilitate the finding of the others in the morning, but to form a defence against a possible attack of the natives.

Oct. 27.--We travelled about seven miles up the river, to lat. 14 degrees 40 minutes in a W.S.W. course: and to long. 134 degrees 16 minutes, according to my reckoning. The range still continued along the right bank of the river; and, at length, when it ceased, another range commenced at the left bank. Here the aspect of the country changed very agreeably. Fine, well grassed plains of moderate size extended along the river, and between its numerous anabranches: for the river divided into several Pandanus channels, either running or with chains of water-holes. These plains were bounded by a range trending east and west, about two or three miles from the left bank of the river. Smoke was seen beyond it. Mr. Roper met and spoke with three natives, who did not appear to be afraid of him. Another of our horses became knocked up, and compelled us to encamp very early in the day, and, as they were all much exhausted, I allowed them to feed at large, without taking the usual precaution of keeping two tethered, in the event of being surprised by the natives. That this was intentionally taken advantage of seemed probable; for, after night-fall, at the commencement of Charley's watch, four natives sneaked up to the camp, and were preparing to throw their spears, when they were seen by Charley, who immediately gave the alarm. We got up instantly, but they had disappeared, and no one but Charley saw anything of them. I should have been inclined to consider it a hoax, had I not heard their distant cooees as late as 9 o'clock, when I silenced them by the discharge of a gun.

Oct. 28.--We travelled ten miles in a north-west direction, to lat. 14 degrees 33 minutes. When we had followed the green belt of the river near four miles, Charley, who had been sent to shoot some ducks, returned, and reported that

238

we were near the head of the river; and that he had discovered water bubbling out of the ground at the foot of a slight rise. We now followed the direction of some smoke which rose behind a large mountain; passing on our way, over an undulating country clothed with a forest of the broad-leaved tea-tree; and a scrubby flat with large melon-holes fringed with raspberry-jam trees; and through a gap between two high ranges, in which there was a small dry creek that turned to the north-east. From a large Polygonum water-hole which had recently become dry, a swarm of whistling ducks rose, probably scared by our approach. Two bustards were also seen. About three miles farther, we came to a good-sized creek, up which we proceeded until we found a small pool of water, which, after some digging, gave us a good supply. Charley had found a fine pool about four miles higher up.

At this time, I was suffering from a great irritability of the skin, and was covered all over with a prickly heat; the slightest pressure or rubbing produced inflammation and boils, particularly about the knees: and Mr. Phillips suffered in the same way, at the arm and elbow. Mr. Gilbert had been subject to these boils when we were travelling at Peak Range, and along the Isaacs; but, since that time until now, none of the party had been inconvenienced by them.

Oct. 29.--We travelled about twelve miles N.N.W., and followed the creek about four miles, to allow our cattle and horses to drink freely at the water-hole discovered by Charley the day before. We passed some plains, and through a broad-leaved tea-tree forest, and then skirted a thick scrub, which covered the approaches of a range. After seven miles travelling, we came to an immense flat lightly timbered with box and broad-leaved tea-tree, and surrounded on every side, except the S.S.E., by high ranges, protruding like headlands into the plain. Upon passing them afterwards, I found them to form undulating chains of baked sandstone hills.

We crossed several small watercourses going to the north-east and east, and came to a considerable creek, near which basalt cropped out. This was the first igneous rock of more recent date, that we had met with since leaving Separation Creek, and the upper Lynd. Even my Blackfellows recognized at once the rock of Darling Downs; and we hailed it as the harbinger of western waters. The whole country up the creek had been lately burned, which induced me to follow it towards its head, in hope of finding the place where the natives had procured water. The bed was filled with basaltic boulders, as were also its dry holes, from one of which the Grallina australis rose, and for the first time deceived our expectations. In a wider part of the valley, I observed wells of the natives dug in the creek, which we enlarged in the hope of their yielding a sufficient supply of water; but in this we were mistaken, as barely enough was obtained to quench our own thirst. Charley, however, in a search up the creek, and after a long ramble, found a small pond and a spring

239

in a narrow mountain gorge, to which he had been guided by a beaten track of Wallurus. Our horses and bullocks, which were crowding impatiently round the little hole we had dug, were immediately harnessed, and we proceeded about three miles in a north direction to the head of a rocky valley, where our cattle were enabled at least to drink, but all the grass had been consumed by a late bush fire.

The Acacia of Expedition Range was plentiful in the large flat and at the wells of the natives, and formed a fine tree: its seeds, however, were shed, and had been roasted by the late bush fire. Mr. Phillips (who was always desirous of discovering substitutes for coffee, and to whom we owed the use of the river-bean of the Mackenzie) collected these seeds, and pounded and boiled them, and gave me the fluid to taste, which I found so peculiarly bitter that I cautioned him against drinking it; his natural desire, however, for warm beverage, which had been increased by a whole day's travelling, induced him to swallow about a pint of it, which made him very sick, and produced violent vomiting and purging during the whole afternoon and night. The little I had tasted acted on me as a lenient purgative, but Mr. Calvert, who had taken rather more than I did, felt very sick. The gum of this Acacia was slightly acid, and very harmless.

Oct. 30.--We travelled about four miles to the N.W. and N.N.W. along the summit of rocky ranges, when a large valley bounded by high ranges to the north and north-west, burst upon us. We descended into it by a steep and rocky basaltic slope, and followed a creek which held a very tortuous course to the south-west; we had travelled along it about seven miles, when Charley was attracted by a green belt of trees, and by the late burnings of the natives, and discovered a running rivulet, coming from the N.N.W. It was fringed with Pandanus, Acacia (Inga monilifornis) and with an arborescent Vitex, with ternate leaves. The flats were well grassed, and lightly timbered with box and white-gum. On the flat summit of the sandstone ranges, we observed the Melaleuca gum, the rusty gum, the mountain Acacia, and Persoonia falcata, (R. Br.) The basaltic rock was apparently confined to the upper part of the valley, where it had broken through the sandstone, which composed all the ranges round our camp, the latitude of which I observed to be 14 degrees 23 minutes 55 seconds. At our last camp, I observed a Platycercus, of the size of the Moreton Bay Rosella, with blackfront, yellow shoulders, and sea-green body; the female had not the showy colours of the male, and the young ones were more speckled on the back. I believe it to be the Platycercus Brownii, GOULD. A black and white Ptilotis, the only stuffed specimen of which was taken by a kite almost out of Mr. Gilbert's hand, was very frequent at the wells of the natives.

During the night, a great number of flying-foxes came to revel in the honey of the blossoms of the gum trees. Charley shot three, and we made a late but welcome supper of them. They were not so fat as those we had eaten before, and tasted a little strong; but, in messes made at night, it was always difficult to find out the cause of any particular taste, as Master Brown wished to get as quickly as possible over his work, and was not over particular in cleaning them. Platycercus versicolor (the Port Essington Parrakeet) visited, in large flocks, the blossoms of the gum trees, and was quite as noisy through the day, as the flying-fox was during the night.

Oct. 31.--When we were going to start, Brown's old horse was absent, and after much searching, the poor brute was found lying at the opposite side of the creek, with its back down the slope, and unable to move. We succeeded in turning him, and helping him to rise, but he was so weak, as to be scarcely able to stand: indeed all our cattle were tired and foot-sore, in consequence of several days travelling over rocky ranges, and required rest. I therefore determined on remaining here a day, as no place could be better suited for their recovery. The grass was young and various, the water delightfully cool, and the scattered trees were large and shady. Numerous birds frequented the water; a species of Ptilotis, with its cheerful and pleasing note, entertained us at daybreak, as the Leatherhead with its constantly changing call and whistling did during the day. Dacelo cervina, GOULD, (the small laughing Jackass) was not heard so frequently nor so regularly as its representative of the east coast. I found a species of fern (Taeniopsis) along the creek, and a species of Mimosa about three feet high had been observed on the plains and the flats of the Roper. Charley and Brown went to shoot flying-foxes, and returned at luncheon with twelve; during the afternoon, they went again and brought in thirty more; having left about fifty hanging, wounded, on the trees. They had been at a large swamp and a pond, connected with the creek, in which Charley declared that he had seen a strange animal "with two horns," and which had deterred him from going into the water. As Brown, on the following day, saw a crocodile in the same pond, Charley's imagination had very probably added two horns to his wonderful animal.

CHAPTER XIV

INTERVIEW WITH A NATIVE
DISTRESSING HEAT
A HORSE STAKED: IT DIES
MYRIADS OF FLYING-FOXES
MAGNIFICENT VALLEY
FRIENDLY NATIVES
SHOT EXHAUSTED
INSTINCT OF BULLOCKS
SOUTH ALLIGATOR RIVER
FRIENDLY NATIVES WITH AN ENGLISH HANDKERCHIEF, AND
ACQUAINTED WITH FIRE-ARMS
THEIR LANGUAGE
MIRAGE.

Nov. 1.--We reached lat. 14 degrees 16 minutes 17 seconds, having travelled about nine miles north-west by north. A range composed of baked sandstone, approached so close to the banks of "Flying-Fox Creek," that we were obliged to cross the range; to the east-ward of which tea-tree flats extended, with many deep but dry water-holes, fringed with fine drooping tea-trees. The country farther on, was well grassed and lightly timbered. Winding round isolated ranges on a N.N.W. course, we came again on the Pandanus creek, which we followed. This creek was joined by several other sandy creeks, also by dry channels fringed with Pandanus, and by chains of water-holes, in which Typhas (bullrush) indicated the underground moisture. Some long-stretched detached hills were seen to the northward, and a long range to the eastward, trending from south to north. The flat valley between them was scattered over with groves of Pandanus. A high stiff grass covered the approaches of the creeks, and long tracts, which had been burnt some time ago, were now covered with delightful verdure. This, with the dark green belt of trees which marked the meanderings of several creeks, gave to this beautiful country the aspect of a large park. I was following one of the sandy creeks, when Mr. Calvert called my attention to a distant belt of Pandanus, which he supposed to be a river; I sent Mr. Roper to examine it; and, when the discharge of his rifle apprized us that he had met with water, we followed him. It was a broad creek, with a stream about three feet deep, and from seven to ten yards wide, with a firm and sandy bed; its banks were shaded by large gum-trees, and

Sarcocephalus; and thick reeds, and a stiff blady grass fringed its waters. The frequent smoke which rose from every part of the valley, showed that it was well inhabited. Brown met two natives, with their gins and children, but they ran away as soon as they saw him. At sunset, a great number of them had collected near our camp, and set fire to the grass, which illumined the sky, as it spread in every direction. They tried to frighten us, by imitating a howling chorus of native dogs; but withdrew, when they saw it was of no avail; at all events, they left us undisturbed during the night--except by one of their dogs, which had been attracted probably by the scent of our flying-fox supper. John and Charley had remained behind to shoot flying-foxes, and they returned at sunset, with twenty-nine; which furnished us with a good breakfast and dinner. The night was clear, and a strong warm breeze set in at a quarter to nine, from the N.N.E. It was as full and steady as those winds we had experienced at Peak Range, and at the Mackenzie. Although we had seen the heads of only one branch of the Roper, I feel convinced that this creek, which was no doubt joined by that at which we encamped the day before, belonged equally to that river.

Nov. 2.--We travelled about eight miles and a half north 30 degrees west along the creek, cutting however one of its bends by crossing some basaltic ridges with a flat summit; from which two almost parallel ranges were seen to the westward, one near, and the other blue in the distance. To the northward, two mountains appeared, from which the creek seemed to take its principal rise. The creek wound between baked sandstone hills, and was alternately enlarging into Nymphaea ponds, and running in a small stream over a pebbly or sandy bed. Pandanus, drooping tea-trees, Terminalias, Acacias, and Sarcocephalus gave it a rich green appearance. The apple-gum and Eugenia, with ribbed scarlet fruit, grew on the flats. Methorium Endl. was found, in leaf and size resembling the hazel-nut; it had showy red and white blossoms. The clustered fig-tree was abundant along the creek; but its ripe fruits were rare at this time of the year.

A small fish, a species of Gristes, about six inches long, was seen in the Nymphaea ponds, but we could not induce it to bite.

At 9 o'clock P.M. we felt again a strong warm breeze from north by east; but at 2 o'clock in the morning, a fine cool breeze, quite bracing and refreshing, blew from the westward.

A flight of wild geese came down the creek, at about 2 o'clock in the morning, which made me suppose that the creek was an outlet of some large lagoons, like those in the valley of the Burdekin.

Nov. 3.--We continued our course up the creek, for nine or ten miles, to lat. 14 degrees 2 minutes 46 seconds. Its stream still continued; but the valley became narrower, and the Pandanus and drooping tea-trees rarer. Ponds and water-holes extended along the foot of the ridges, in a direction parallel to the creek. The broad-leaved Terminalia was in blossom. Polyphragmon, which was first met with at the upper Lynd; Careya arborea, Hakea arborescens, and Coniogeton arborescens, were observed. White cockatoos were numerous, but shy. A pale green horse-fly annoyed us as well as our horses.

The ridges were not very high, and all were composed of baked sandstone; at the left side of the creek, near our camp, there was a chain of conical hills.

As we were travelling along, a native suddenly emerged from the banks of the creek, and, crossing our line of march, walked down to a Nymphaea pond, where he seemed inclined to hide himself until we had passed. I cooeed to him; at which he looked up, but seemed to be at a loss what to do or say. I then dismounted, and made signs to show my friendly disposition: then he began to call out, but, seeing that I motioned away my companions with the horses and bullocks, as I moved towards him, and that I held out presents to him, he became more assured of his safety, and allowed me to come near and put some brass buttons into his hand. I understood him to ask whether we were following the creek, and I answered "Brrrrrr aroma aroma!!" pointing at the same time with a long sweep to the northward. As, however, we were equally unintelligible to each other, and he did not appear to be very communicative, I mounted my cream-coloured horse, and left him staring at me in silence until I was out of sight. We encamped at noon, under two wide-spreading Sarcocephalus trees, whose grateful shade offered us a shelter from the scorching sun. But, as the sun got low, the shades of the oval crown of the trees drew rapidly off, and we had to lean against the shady side of the butt to obtain relief from the heat, which had so enervating an effect upon us that the slightest exertion was painful. After sunset, however, in the comparative coolness of the evening, our animal spirits revived; and it was only during that part of the day, and in the early morning before sunrise, that I felt inclined to attend to any business that required much bodily exertion. It was a great enjoyment indeed to lie devoid of any covering on our couch, and watch the fading tints of sunset. The usual, and therefore expected, night breeze did not set in; but, about half-past 10 o'clock P.M., there was a slight stir in the atmosphere, accompanied with a sense of moisture, as if a distant thunder-storm had occurred, and interrupted the usual progress of the breeze.

Nov. 4.--We travelled about seven miles, north-west by north, to lat. 13 degrees 56 minutes 46 seconds. After following the creek about a mile, it turned so far to the westward that I left it, and with much difficulty ascended the ranges to the northward: from their highest elevation, I saw that a high range, trending from south-east to north-west, bounded the valley of the creek I had left; another fine range was seen to the eastward. Following a gully, we descended into the valley of a creek flowing to the southward, and which probably joined the creek I had left below the place of our last encampment. In the lower part of the gully, we came upon some fine Nymphaea ponds and springs surrounded by ferns. The whole valley, though narrow, was beautifully grassed. Trichodesma, Grewia, Crinum, and the trefoil of the Suttor, grew on the flats; the apple-gum, rusty-gum, the mountain Acacia and Fusanus, the last in blossom, grew on the ridges.

The rock was a baked sandstone; in the pebbles of the creek I found the impressions of bivalves (one ribbed like Cardium).

Our bullocks had become so foot-sore, and were so oppressed by the excessive heat, that it was with the greatest difficulty we could prevent them from rushing into the water with their loads. One of them--that which carried the remainder of my botanical collection--watched his opportunity, and plunged into a deep pond, where he was quietly swimming about and enjoying himself, whilst I was almost crying with vexation at seeing all my plants thoroughly soaked.

Nov. 5.--We travelled in all about eleven miles N. 55 degrees W. to latitude 13 degrees 50 minutes. After following the creek, on which we had encamped, to its head, we passed over a scrubby stringy-bark forest; and, whenever we came to watercourses going to the eastward, we turned to the north-west and westward. We passed several sandstone hills and ridges rising out of this sandy table land, and attempted to cross one of them, but our path was intercepted by precipices and chasms, forming an insurmountable barrier to our cattle. We, therefore, followed a watercourse to the southward, winding between two ranges to the westward and southward, and continued again to the north-west, which brought us to a tributary of the creek we had just left, and in which we found large water-holes covered with Nymphaeas and Villarsias.

The strata of the range which we ascended, dipped to the south-west; in which direction I saw a high range, probably the continuation of the one I had observed at yesterday's stage along Roper's Creek.

The Melaleuca-gum, the Cypress-pine, Fusanus and Banksia abounded in the stringy-bark forest, and along the creeks; and the flats round the water-holes were covered with a dark green sedge, which, however, our cattle did not relish so much as, from its inviting verdure, I had anticipated would have been the case. The remains of fresh-water turtles were frequently noticed in the camps of the natives; and Mr. Calvert had seen one depicted with red ochre on the rocks. It is probable that this animal forms a considerable part of the food of the natives. John Murphy reported that he had seen a hut of the

245

natives constructed of sheets of stringy-bark, and spacious enough to receive our whole party; the huts which I had observed were also very spacious, but covered with tea-tree bark. Smoke from the natives' fires was seen from the range in every direction, and their burnings invariably led us to creeks.

Charley shot a rock wallabi of a different species from any we had previously seen: it was of a light grey colour; the tail was smooth, and its black tip was more bushy than in other species; there were two white spots on the shoulder; it was smaller than those of Ruined Castle Creek, and the red wallabies of the Mitchell and of the shores of the gulf. John shot a large Iguana of remarkably bright colours, which were perhaps owing to a late desquamation of the skin.

Nov. 6.--We travelled fourteen miles N. 30 degrees W. to latitude 13 degrees 38 minutes 28 seconds, and encamped in a little creek, at the head of which was a grassy drooping tea-tree swamp. We left all the eastern water-courses to the right, and followed several which went down to the southward, up to their heads. The country, with the exception of the ridges which bounded the narrow valleys of watercourses, was a sandy level stringy-bark forest, interspersed with Melaleuca-gum and leguminous Ironbark; saplings of which formed large tracts of a low open under-wood. We had passed a large but dry swamp, having no outlet, and surrounded with Pandanus, when Brown called my attention to an opening in the forest, and to a certain dim appearance of the atmosphere peculiar to extensive plains and valleys. Travelling in that direction we soon found ourselves at the margin of the sandy table-land, from which we overlooked a large valley bounded by high ranges to the westward. We then followed a very rocky creek, in its various windings, in search of water; Grallina australis called four times, and deceived us each time; and cockatoos, and pigeons, and finches, all proved false prophets. However, about five miles farther, we found a small pool, at which natives had very recently encamped, and, three miles farther, two fine water-holes fringed with Pandanus.

Our bullocks and horses were very foot-sore, and could scarcely move over the rocky ground.

The ridges at the head of this western creek were covered with an arborescent Capparis, the ripe fruit of which tasted very like strawberries; but those which were not ripe were very pungent. Another little tree, belonging to the Hamelieae D.C., with large white fragrant blossoms, and fruit about two inches long and one broad, with numerous seeds nestling in a pulpy substance, was very abundant. In its ripe state, the pulp turned black; I ate some of it, but although it proved to be harmless, it was not good. The little bread-fruit of the upper Lynd, no doubt belonged to the same class of plants.

I believe that all the creeks which we passed since leaving the Roper, still belonged to that river; and that the western creek and all the western waters we met, until reaching the South Alligator river, belonged to the system of the latter. The division of the eastern and western waters was, according to my reckoning, in longitude 133 degrees 35 minutes.

Nov. 7.--We followed the creek for about four or five miles, and halted at a well-grassed spot with good water-holes, in order to kill one of our bullocks, and allow the other two and the horses to recover. The poor brute was fairly knocked up and incapable of going any farther, even without a load. Some of my readers may wonder that our bullocks should suffer so much when travelling through a country both well grassed and well watered, and by such short stages; but they should consider the climate in which we travelled, and the excessive heat to which we were exposed. The rocky nature of the ground contributed no less to their foot-weariness and exhaustion. If I could have rested two or three days out of seven, the animals would have had time to recover, and would have done comparatively well. But, independent of the fatigues of travelling, the relaxing and enervating influence of the climate was as visible in our cattle as in ourselves.

The apple-gum, a bloodwood, and the poplar-gum(?) grew round our camp; the grasses were tender, but formed distinct tufts; Crinum was plentiful.

The night breeze set in at a quarter to 9 o'clock from north-east, or north by east, strong, full and warm; there was a slight moisture in the air before daybreak, which rendered our almost dry meat a little damp again.

We were occupied during the 8th Nov. in drying our meat, mending and washing our things, and arranging the few loads which were left.

Nov. 9.--We travelled down the creek in a south-west course, for about nine miles. Low sandstone ranges bounded its valley to the southward and south-east; stony ridges with stunted trees and Cypress-pine extended to the north-west. The banks of the creek, which I called "Snowdrop's Creek," after the bullock we had killed, were grassy and open; it was well provided with water. A pretty little Sida, a Convolvolus, and Grewia, were growing amongst the young grass. Mr. Calvert saw the Livistona palm.

We felt a breeze from the eastward during the afternoon, as usual, and the strong night breeze from north and north-east; but, in the morning, a wind from north-west and west, which belonged probably to another system of atmospherical movements.

A swarm of whistling ducks (Leptotarsis Eytoni, GOULD.) passed during the night from down the creek to the eastward, which made me suppose that Snowdrop's Creek was either joined by large creeks with water, or that itself joined a larger river. The black Ibis was frequent at the water-hole.

Nov. 10.--We travelled about six miles and a half N. N. W. The creek turned so far to the westward and southward, that I left it, and crossed some ridges, beyond which a very rocky creek going down to Snowdrop's Creek, intercepted our course. Having crossed it with great difficulty, we travelled through a scrubby forest, and came to the heads of the same creek, several of which were formed by swamps. Here the drooping tea-tree, growing in a sandy peat, attained a stately height. The sandy slopes around the swamps were covered with Banksia, the Melaleuca gum, and Pandanus, and a rich profusion of grasses and low sedges surrounded the deep pools of spring water. These spots, which bore the marks of being much visited by the natives, were like oases in the dry, dull, sandy forest, and formed delightful shady groves, pleasing to every sense. Kangaroos and various birds, particularly the white cockatoo, were numerous; and the little bees came like flies on our hands, on my paper, and on our soup plates, and indicated abundance of honey; a small species of Cicada had risen from its slumbers, and was singing most cheerfully. One of our horses was seriously staked in the belly, by some unaccountable accident; I drew a seton through the large swelling, although, considering its exhausted state, I entertained but a slight hope of its recovery.

Nov. 11.--We accomplished about ten miles in a direct line, but on a long and fatiguing circuitous course. Starting in a northerly direction, we passed over some rocky ground, but soon entered into a sandy level, covered with scrubby, stringy-bark forest, intermixed with Melaleuca gum. At the distance of four miles I came to a rocky creek going to the westward, which I followed. From one of the hills which bounded its narrow valley, I had a most disheartening, sickening view over a tremendously rocky country. A high land, composed of horizontal strata of sandstone, seemed to be literally hashed, leaving the remaining blocks in fantastic figures of every shape; and a green vegetation, crowding deceitfully within their fissures and gullies, and covering half of the difficulties which awaited us on our attempt to travel over it. The creek, in and along the bed of which we wound slowly down, was frequently covered with large loose boulders, between which our horses and cattle often slipped. A precipice, and perpendicular rocks on both sides, compelled us to leave it; and following one of its tributary creeks to its head, to the northward, we came to another, which led us down to a river running to the west by south. With the greatest difficulty we went down its steep slopes, and established our camp at a large water-hole in its bed. The longitude of the river was, according to my reckoning, 133 degrees 6 minutes.

A new species of rock pigeon (Petrophassa, GOULD.) with a dark brown body, primaries light brown without any white, and with the tail feathers rather worn, lived in pairs and small flocks like Geophaps, and flew out of the shade of overhanging rocks, or from the moist wells which the natives had dug in the bed of the creek, around which they clustered like flies round a drop of syrup. A fine shady Eucalyptus, with a short barrel, but large spreading branches, and with the grey bark of the box, grew between the rocks along the creek.

Nov. 12.--We had been compelled to leave the injured horse behind, and upon going this morning with Charley to fetch it to the camp, we found the poor brute dead. On our return to the camp, we followed another creek to the northward, which also joined the river, about eight miles to the eastward of our camp. The river was densely covered with scrub, and almost perpendicular cliffs bounded its valley on both sides. Myriads of flying-foxes were here suspended in thick clusters on the highest trees in the most shady and rather moist parts of the valley. They started as we passed, and the flapping of their large membranous wings produced a sound like that of a hail-storm.

Nov. 13.--The two horses ridden by Charley and myself yesterday, had suffered so severely, that I had to allow them a day of rest to recover. In the mean time, I went with Charley and Brown to the spot where we had seen the greatest number of flying-foxes, and, whilst I was examining the neighbouring trees, my companions shot sixty-seven, of which fifty-five were brought to our camp; which served for dinner, breakfast, and luncheon, each individual receiving eight. The flying-fox lived here on a small, blue, oval stone-fruit, of an acid taste, with a bitter kernel; it grew on a tree of moderate size. Very small specimens of the Seaforthia palm were here observed for the first time; and the large scarlet fruit of Eugenia was found.

During the night, we heard the first grumbling of thunder since many months.

Nov. 14.--We travelled about twelve miles north by west. After crossing the river, we followed a rocky creek to its head, and passed over ten miles of level sandy country of stringy-bark forest, with Melalcuca gum and Banksia, interrupted only by a small Pandanus creek. At the end of the stage, we came to rocky creeks, one of which headed in a drooping tea-tree swamp, with rich vegetation, but without water. The creek, which we followed down for two miles, there changed its character, and meandered through sandy, well-grassed flats, and contained some good water-holes, on which we encamped. John told me that he had found the ripe fruit of Exocarpus cupressiformis; which I doubted very much, as I had not seen the slightest trace of it since we left the Dawson, although Exocarpus latifolia was very frequent all over the sandy table-land. But we gathered and ate a great quantity of gibong (the ripe fruit of Persoonia falcata), and some small yellow figs of the glossy-leaved fig-tree. I observed a Eucalyptus of rather stunted growth, with broad, almost oval

249

leaves, and long, narrow seed-vessels.

During the night, thunder clouds and lightning were seen in every direction; and the whole atmosphere appeared to be in a state of fermentation. Heavy showers poured down upon us; and our tarpaulings, which had been torn to pieces in travelling through the scrub, were scarcely sufficient to keep ourselves and our things dry. But in the morning of the 15th, all nature seemed refreshed; and my depressed spirits rose quickly, under the influence of that sweet breath of vegetation, which is so remarkably experienced in Australia, where the numerous Myrtle family, and even their dead leaves, contribute so largely to the general fragrance. This day we travelled about six miles to the W. N. W.

Our course, however, was for three miles to the northward, over a sandy level forest, intercepted by several rocky creeks. The third which we came to, I followed down to the westward, and came to a large creek, which soon joined a still larger one from the eastward. Both were well provided with water; and we encamped at a very large hole under a ledge of rock across the bed of the creek; and which probably formed a fine waterfall during the rainy season.

Thunder-storms formed to the southward and northward; but we had only a few drops of rain. It was remarkable to observe that those to the southward vered round to the south-west by west, whereas those to the northward vered round to the north-east and east.

Nov. 16.--We travelled nine miles north-west by north; crossed numerous rocky creeks, and some undulating country; and had a most distressing passage over exceedingly rocky ranges. At the end of the stage, we came to a large Pandanus creek, which we followed until we found some fine pools of water in its bed. My companions had, for several days past, gathered the unripe fruits of Coniogeton arborescens, Br.; which, when boiled, imparted an agreeable acidity to the water, and when thus prepared tasted tolerable well. When ripe, they became sweet and pulpy, like gooseberries, although their rind was not very thick. This resemblance induced us to call the tree "The little Gooseberry tree." At the table land, and along the upper South Alligator River, it was a tree from twenty-five to thirty feet high, with a fresh green shady foliage; but, at the Cobourg Peninsula, it dwindled into a low shrub. The fruit was much esteemed there by the natives; for, although the tree was of smaller size, the fruit was equally large and fine.

Nov. 17.--We travelled four or five miles through Banksia, and Melaleuca-gum forest, crossed several rocky creeks; and followed down the largest of them; which in its whole extent was exceedingly rocky. The rock was generally in horizontal layers. There were many high falls in the bed, which compelled me to leave the creek, and proceed on the rising ground along its banks, when suddenly the extensive view of a magnificent valley opened before us. We stood with our whole train on the brink of a deep precipice, of perhaps 1800 feet descent, which seemed to extend far to the eastward. A large river, joined by many tributary creeks coming from east, south-east, south-west and west, meandered through the valley; which was bounded by high, though less precipitous ranges to the westward and south-west from our position; and other ranges rose to the northward. I went on foot to the mouth of the creek; but the precipice prevented my moving any farther; another small creek was examined, but with the same result. We were compelled to move back, and thence to reconnoitre for a favourable descent. Fortunately the late thunderstorms had filled a great number of small rocky basins in the bed of the creek; and, although there was only a scanty supply of a stiff grass, our cattle had filled themselves sufficiently the previous night to bear a day's privation. In the afternoon, Charley accompanied me on foot in a northerly direction (for no horse could move between the large loose sandstone blocks), and we examined several gullies and watercourses, all of a wild and rocky character, and found it impossible to descend, in that direction, into the valley. Charley shot a Wallooroo just as it was leaping, frightened by our footsteps, out of its shady retreat to a pointed rock. Whilst on this expedition, we observed a great number of grasshoppers, of a bright brick colour dotted with blue: the posterior part of the corselet, and the wings were blue; it was two inches long, and its antennae three quarters of an inch.

Nov. 18.--We returned to the creek in which we had encamped on the 16th, and pitched our tents a little lower down, where some rich feed promised our cattle a good treat. Immediately after luncheon, I started again with Charley down the creek, myself on horseback, but my companion on foot. It soon became very rocky, with gullies joining it from both sides; but, after two miles, it opened again into fine well-grassed lightly timbered flats, and terminated in a precipice, as the others had done. A great number of tributary creeks joined it in its course, but all formed gullies and precipices. Many of these gullies were gently sloping hollows, filled with a rich black soil, and covered with an open brush vegetation at their upper part; but, lower down, large rocks protruded, until the narrow gully, with perpendicular walls, sunk rapidly into the deep chasm, down which the boldest chamois hunter would not have dared to descend. I now determined to examine the country to the southward; and, as it was late and my horse very foot-sore, I remained for the night at the next grassy flat, and sent Charley back to order my companions to remove the camp next morning as far down the creek as possible, in order to facilitate the examination, which, on foot, in this climate, was exceedingly exhausting.

Nov. 19.--I appeased my craving hunger, which had been well tried for twenty hours, on the small fruit of a species of Acmena which grew near the rocks that bounded the sandy flats, until my companions brought my share of stewed green hide. We went about three miles farther down the creek, and encamped in the dense shade of a wide spreading Rock box, a tree which I mentioned a few days since. From this place I started with Brown in one direction, and Charley in another, to find a passage through the labyrinth of rocks. After a most fatiguing scramble up and down rocky gullies, we again found ourselves at the brink of that beautiful valley, which lay before us like a promised land. We had now a more extensive view of its eastern outline, and saw extending far to our right a perpendicular wall, cut by many narrow fissures, the outlet of as many gullies; the same wall continued to the left, but interrupted by a steep slope; to which we directed our steps, and after many windings succeeded in finding it. It was indeed very steep. Its higher part was composed of sandstone and conglomerate; but a coarse-grained granite, with much quartz and felspar, but little mica and accidental hornblende, was below. The size of its elements had rendered it more liable to decomposition, and had probably been the cause of the formation of the slope. In the valley, the creek murmured over a pebbly bed, and enlarged from time to time, into fine sheets of water. We rested ourselves in the shade of its drooping tea-trees; and, observing another slope about two miles farther, went to examine it, but finding that its sandstone crest was too steep for our purpose, we returned to mark a line of road from the first slope to our camp. For this purpose I had taken a tomahawk with me, well knowing how little I could rely on Brown for finding his old tracks; but, with the tomahawk, he succeeded very well; for his quick eye discovered, from afar, the practicability of the road. We succeeded at last, and, after many windings, reached our camp, even quicker than we had anticipated. Charley returned next morning, and reported that he had found a descent, but very far off. This "very far off" of Charley was full of meaning which I well understood.

During the night we had a very heavy thunder-storm which filled our creek and made its numerous waterfalls roar.

Nov. 20.--We proceeded on our tree-marked line to the slope, and descending, arrived, after some difficulty, safe and sound in the valley. Our horses and cattle were, however, in a distressing condition. The passage along rocky creeks, between the loose blocks of which their feet were constantly slipping, had rendered them very foot-sore, and had covered their legs with sores. The feed had latterly consisted either of coarse grasses, or a small sedge, which they did not like. But, in the valley, all the tender grasses reappeared in the utmost profusion, on which horses and bullocks fed most greedily during the short rest I allowed them after reaching the foot of the slope. The creek formed a fine waterfall of very great height, like a silver belt between rich green vegetation, behind which the bare mountain walls alone were visible. I proceeded down the creek about three miles to the north-west, when it joined a larger creek from the south-west. Here one of our two remaining bullocks refused to go any further; and as our meat bags were empty, I decided upon stopping in this favourable spot to kill the bullock.

Careya arborea, the broad-leaved Terminalia, Coniogeton arborescens, an umbrageous white-gum tree, and Pandanus, together with the luxuriant young grass, gave to the country a most pleasing aspect. But the late thunder-storm had rendered the ground very damp, and that with the mawkish smell of our drying meat, soon made our camp very disagreeable. In the rocky gullies of the table land, we had observed a great number of shrubs, amongst which a species of Pleurandra, a dwarf Calythrix, a prostrate woolly Grevillea, and a red Melaleuca, were the most interesting. Near the slope by which we entered the valley, a species of Achras was found, but with a much smaller fruit than that of Port Jackson.

The melodious whistle of a bird was frequently heard in the most rocky and wretched spots of the table land. It raised its voice, a slow full whistle, by five or six successive half-notes; which was very pleasing, and frequently the only relief while passing through this most perplexing country. The bullock was killed in the afternoon of the 20th, and on the 21st the meat was cut up and put out to dry; the afternoon was very favourable for this purpose; but, at night rain set in, and with the sultry weather rendered the meat very bad. The mornings were generally sultry and cloudy; during the afternoon the clouds cleared off with the sea-breeze: and towards sunset thunder-storms rose, and the nights were rainy, which prevented me from making observations to ascertain my latitude. The longitude of the descent, was, according to reckoning, 132 degrees 50 minutes. A little before sunset of the 21st four natives came to our camp; they made us presents of red ochre, which they seemed to value highly, of a spear and a spear's head made of baked sandstone (GRES LUSTRE). In return I gave them a few nails; and as I was under the necessity of parting with every thing heavy which was not of immediate use for our support, I also gave them my geological hammer. One of the natives was a tall, but slim man; the others were of smaller size, but all had a mild and pleasing expression of countenance.

Large fish betrayed their presence in the deep water by splashing during the night: and Charley asserted that he had seen the tracks of a crocodile. Swarms of whistling ducks occupied the large ponds in the creek: but our shot was all used, and the small iron-pebbles which were used as a substitute, were not heavy enough to kill even a duck. Some balls, however, were still left, but these we kept for occasions of urgent necessity.

Nov. 22.--As our meat was not sufficiently dry for packing we remained here the whole of this day; but, at night, the heaviest thunder-storm we perhaps had ever experienced, poured down and again wetted it; we succeeded, however, notwithstanding this interruption, in drying it without much taint; but its soft state enabled the maggots to nestle in it; and the rain to which it had been exposed, rendered it very insipid.

Poor Redmond, the last of our bullocks, came frequently to the spot where his late companion had been killed; but finding that he was gone, he returned to his abundant feed, and when I loaded him to continue our journey down the river he was full and sleek. It was interesting to observe how the bullocks on all previous occasions, almost invariably took cognizance of the place where one of their number had been killed. They would visit it either during the night or the next day, walk round the spot, lift their tails, snuff the air with an occasional shake of their horns, and sometimes, set off in a gallop.

Nov. 23.--We travelled about eight miles north-west over an equally fine country. A high range of Pegmatite descended from the table land far into the valley, from east to west; and an isolated peak was seen to the west of it at the left bank of the river.

The Eugenia with scarlet fruit, and another species with rose-coloured fruit, of most exquisite taste--particularly when the seed was abortive, and the pericarp more developed--were abundant on the flats of the river; and Aemena?, with smaller fruit and thin acidulous rind, grew straggling on the ridges.

A thunder-storm from the north-east, compelled us to hasten into camp; and we had scarcely housed our luggage, when heavy rain set in and continued to fall during the first part of the night.

Nov. 24.--We travelled about nine miles to the north-west, to lat. 13 degrees 5 minutes 49 seconds, which a clear night enabled me to observe by a meridian altitude of Castor. We were, according to my latitude, and to my course, at the South Alligator River, about sixty miles from its mouth, and about one hundred and forty miles from Port Essington.

The river gradually increased in size, and its bed became densely fringed with Pandanus; the hollows and flats were covered with groves of drooping tea-trees. Ridges of sandstone and conglomerate approached the river in several places, and at their base were seen some fine reedy and rushy lagoons, teeming with water-fowl. A flock of black Ibises rose from a moist hollow; white and black cockatoos, were seen and heard frequently. At day-break, I was struck with the sweet song of Rhipidura flaviventris, GOULD.

The natives cooeed from the other side of the river, probably to ascertain whether we were friendly or hostile; but did not show themselves any farther.

254

They were Unio eaters to a great extent, judging from the heaps of shells we saw along the river; the species of Unio on which they lived, was much smaller than that we had observed on the Roper. John and Charley saw a native in the bed of the river, busily employed in beating a species of bark, very probably to use its fibres to strain honey. He did not interrupt his work, and either did not see them, or wished to ignore their presence. The horse flies began to be very troublesome, but the mosquitoes fortunately did not annoy us, notwithstanding the neighbourhood of the river, and the late rains. Charley and Brown shot five geese, which gave us a good breakfast and luncheon.

A strong breeze from the northward set in late every afternoon, since we had descended into the valley of the South Alligator River.

Nov. 25.--We travelled about seven miles and a half N.W. by W., to lat. 13 degrees 0 minutes 56 seconds. I intended to follow the sandy bergue of the river, but a dense Pandanus brush soon compelled us to return, and to head several grassy and sedgy swamps like those we passed on the last stage. Chains of small water-holes, and Nymphaea ponds, ran parallel to the river; and very extensive swamps filled the intervals between rather densely wooded ironstone ridges, which seemed to be spurs of a more hilly country, protruding into the valley of the river. Some of these swamps were dry, and had a sound bottom, allowing our cattle to pass without difficulty. Others, however, were exceedingly boggy, and dangerous for both horse and man; for Charley was almost suffocated in the mud, in attempting to procure a goose he had shot. The swamps narrowed towards the river, and formed large and frequently rocky water-holes, in a well defined channel, which, however, became broad and deep where it communicated with the river, and which in many places rivalled it in size. A belt of drooping tea-trees surrounded the swamps, whilst their outlets were densely fringed with Pandanus. The Livistona palm and Cochlospermum gossypium grew on the ridges; the tea-tree, the stringy-bark, the leguminous Ironbark and Eugenia were useful timber. The whole country was most magnificently grassed.

A Porphyritic sienite cropped out at the head of the first swamp, about a mile from our last camp.

We had cut our rifle balls into slugs, with which Charley and Brown shot three geese (Anseranus melanoleuca, GOULD).

A low range was seen at the south-east end of the large swamp on which we encamped.

Nov. 26.--We travelled about nine miles and a half N.N.W. to lat. 12 degrees 51 minutes 56 seconds. After having once more seen the river, where it was joined by the broad outlet of a swamp, I turned to the northward, and passed over closely-wooded and scrubby ridges of ironstone and conglomerate, with pebbles and pieces of quartz covering the ground. Livistona inermis, R. Br. formed small groves; and Pandanus covered the hollows and banks of two small creeks with rocky water-holes going to the westward. About six miles from our last camp, an immense plain opened before us, at the west side of which we recognized the green line of the river. We crossed the plain to find water, but the approaches of the river were formed by tea-tree hollows, and by thick vine brush, at the outside of which noble bouquets of Bamboo and stately Corypha palms attracted our attention. In skirting the brush, we came to a salt-water creek (the first seen by us on the north-west coast), when we immediately returned to the ridges, where we met with a well-beaten foot-path of the natives, which led us along brush, teeming with wallabies, and through undulating scrubby forest ground to another large plain. Here the noise of clouds of water-fowl, probably rising at the approach of some natives, betrayed to us the presence of water. We encamped at the outskirts of the forest, at a great distance from the large but shallow pools, which had been formed by the late thunder-showers. The water had received a disagreeable sour aluminous taste from the soil, and from the dung of innumerable geese, ducks, native companions, white cranes, and various other water-fowl. The boggy nature of the ground prevented our horses and the bullock from approaching it; and they consequently strayed very far in search of water. In the forest land, the Torres Straits pigeon (Carpophaga luctuosa, GOULD,) was numerous. At sunset, Charley returned to the camp, accompanied by a whole tribe of natives. They were armed with small goose spears, and with flat wommalas; but, although they were extremely noisy, they did not show the slightest hostile intention. One of them had a shawl and neckerchief of English manufacture: and another carried an iron tomahawk, which he said he got from north-west by north. They knew Pichenelumbo (Van Diemen's Gulf), and pointed to the north-west by north, when we asked for it. I made them various presents: and they gave us some of their ornaments and bunches of goose feathers in return, but showed the greatest reluctance in parting with their throwing sticks (wommalas.) They were inclined to theft, and I had to mount Brown on horseback to keep them out of our camp.

Nov. 27.--The natives returned very early to our camp, and took the greatest notice of what we were eating, but would not taste anything we offered them. When Brown returned with our bullock, the beast rushed at them, and pursued them for a great distance, almost goring one of their number.

We travelled about three miles and a half north-east, but had to go fairly over ten miles of ground. We followed the foot-path of the natives for about two miles, passing over some scrubby ridges into a series of plains, which seemed

256

to be boundless to the N.W. and N.N.W. A broad deep channel of fresh water covered with Nymphaeas and fringed with Pandanus, intercepted our course; and I soon found that it formed the outlet of one of those remarkable swamps which I have described on the preceding stages. We turned to the E. and E.S.E. following its outline, in order either to find a crossing place, or to head it. The natives were very numerous, and employing themselves either in fishing or burning the grass on the plains, or digging for roots. I saw here a noble fig-tree, under the shade of which seemed to have been the camping place of the natives for the last century. It was growing at the place where we first came to the broad outlet of the swamp. About two miles to the eastward, this swamp extended beyond the reach of sight, and seemed to form the whole country, of the remarkable and picturesque character of which it will be difficult to convey a correct idea to the reader. Its level bed was composed of a stiff bluish clay, without vegetation, mostly dry, and cracked by the heat of the sun; but its depressions were still moist, and treacherously boggy; in many parts of this extensive level, rose isolated patches, or larger island-like groves of Pandanus intermixed with drooping tea-trees, and interwoven with Ipomaeas, or long belts of drooping tea-trees, in the shade of which reaches of shallow water, surrounded by a rich sward of grasses of the most delicate verdure, had remained. Thousands of ducks and geese occupied these pools, and the latter fed as they waded through the grass. We travelled for a long time through groves of drooping tea-trees, which grew along the outline of the swamps, but using great caution in consequence of its boggy nature. Several times I wished to communicate with the natives who followed us, but, every time I turned my horse's head, they ran away; however, finding my difficulties increased, whilst attempting to cross the swamp, I dismounted and walked up to one of them, and taking his hand, gave him a sheet of paper, on which I wrote some words, giving him to understand, as well as I could, that he had nothing to fear as long as he carried the paper. By this means I induced him to walk with me, but considerably in advance of my train, and especially of the bullock; he kept manfully near me, and pointed out the sounder parts of the swamp, until we came to a large pool, on which were a great number of geese, when he gave me to understand that he wished Brown to go and shoot them; for these natives, as well as those who visited us last night, were well acquainted with the effects of fire arms.

We encamped at this pool, and the natives flocked round us from every direction. Boys of every age, lads, young men and old men too, came, every one armed with his bundle of goose spears, and his throwing stick. They observed, with curious eye, everything we did, and made long explanations to each other of the various objects presented to their gaze. Our eating, drinking, dress, skin, combing, boiling, our blankets, straps, horses, everything, in short, was new to them, and was earnestly discussed, particularly by one of the old

257

men, who amused us with his drollery and good humour in trying to persuade each of us to give him something. They continually used the words "Perikot, Nokot, Mankiterre, Lumbo Lumbo, Nana Nana Nana," all of which we did not understand till after our arrival at Port Essington, where we learned that they meant "Very good, no good, Malays very far." Their intonation was extremely melodious, some other words, the meaning of which we could not make out, were "Kelengeli, Kongurr, Verritimba, Vanganbarr, Nangemong, Maralikilla;" the accent being always on the first syllable of the word, and all the vowels short.

Nov. 28.--Our good friends, the natives, were with us again very early in the morning; they approached us in long file, incessantly repeating the words above mentioned, Perikot, Nokot, etc. which they seemed to consider a kind of introduction. After having guided us over the remaining part of the swamp to the firm land, during which they gave us the most evident proofs of their skill in spearing geese--they took their leave of us and returned; when I again resumed my course to the northward. I understood from the natives that a large lake, or deep water, existed at the head of the swamp, far to the east and north-east. We travelled about nine miles north by east, to lat. 12 degrees 38 minutes 41 seconds.

A foot-path of the natives led us through an intricate tea-tree swamp, in which the rush of waters had uprooted the trees, and left them strewed in every direction, which rendered the passage exceedingly difficult. In the middle of the swamp we saw a fine camp of oven like huts, covered with tea-tree bark. After crossing some scrubby sandstone ridges, we came to a sandy creek, up which we proceeded until we found a small water-hole, which had been filled by the late thunder-storms, where we encamped.

The weather had been very favourable since we left the upper South Alligator River. It was evident from the appearance of the creek and the swamps, that the rains had been less abundant here. Cumuli formed here regularly during the afternoon, with the setting in of the north-west sea breeze, but dispersed at sunset, and during the first part of the night. Thunder clouds were seen in the distance, but none reached us. The clear nights were generally dewy.

The country was most beautifully grassed: and a new species of Crinum, and several leguminous plants, diversified with their pretty blossoms the pleasing green of the flats and the forest.

Since the 23rd of November, not a night had passed without long files and phalanxes of geese taking their flight up and down the river, and they often passed so low, that the heavy flapping of their wings was distinctly heard. Whistling ducks, in close flocks, flew generally much higher, and with great rapidity. No part of the country we had passed, was so well provided with game as this; and of which we could have easily obtained an abundance, had not our shot been all expended. The cackling of geese, the quacking of ducks, the sonorous note of the native companion, and the noises of black and white cockatoos, and a great variety of other birds, gave to the country, both night and day, an extraordinary appearance of animation. We started two large native dogs, from the small pool at which we encamped; a flock of kites indicated to me the presence of a larger pool which I chose for our use; and here we should have been tolerably comfortable, but for a large green-eyed horse-fly, which was extremely troublesome to us, and which scarcely allowed our poor animals to feed.

We had a heavy thunder-storm from the north-east, which, however, soon passed off.

Nov. 29.--We travelled about twelve miles to the northward to lat. 12 degrees 26 minutes 41 seconds, over ironstone and baked sandstone ridges, densely wooded and often scrubby. The first part of the stage was more hilly, and intersected by a greater number of creeks, going down to west and north-west, than the latter part, which was a sandy, level forest of stringy-bark and Melaleuca gum. The little gooseberry-tree (Coniogeton arborescens, D.C.) the leguminous Ironbark, a smooth, broad-leaved Terminalia, Calythrix, and the apple-gum, were plentiful. Livistona inermis, R. Br. grew from twenty to thirty feet high, with a very slender stem and small crown, and formed large groves in the stringy-bark forest. A grass, well known at the Hunter by its scent resembling that of crushed ants, was here scentless; a little plant, with large, white, tubular, sweet-scented flowers, grew sociably in the forest, and received the name of "native primrose;" a species of Commelyna, and a prostrate malvaceous plant with red flowers, and a species of Oxystelma, contributed by their beauty and variety to render the country interesting.

Nov. 30.--The lower part of the creek on which we were encamped was covered with a thicket of Pandanus; but its upper part was surrounded by groves of the Livistona palm. As our horses had been driven far from the camp by the grey horse-fly and by a large brown fly with green eyes, which annoyed us particularly before sunset, and shortly after sunrise, we had to wait a long time for them, and employed ourselves, in the meanwhile, with cutting and eating the tops of Livistona. Many were in blossom, others were in fruit; the latter is an oblong little stone fruit of very bitter taste. Only the lowest part of the young shoots is eatable, the remainder being too bitter. I think they affected the bowels even more than the shoots of the Corypha palm.

We made a short Sunday stage through a fine forest, in which Livistona became more and more frequent. We crossed several creeks going to the westward; the country became more hilly, and we followed a large creek with a good supply of rainwater, until it turned too much to the westward, when we encamped. The clear night enabled me to make my latitude, by an observation of Castor, to be 12 degrees 21 minutes 49 seconds. We had accomplished about five miles to the northward.

We saw two emus, and Charley was fortunate enough to shoot one of them; it was the fattest we had met with round the gulf. During the clear, dewy night, flocks of geese and ducks passed from the west to the north-east, and I anticipated that the next stage would bring us again to large swamps. The bed of the creek on which we encamped was composed of granitic rock.

CHAPTER XV

JOY AT MEETING NATIVES SPEAKING SOME ENGLISH
THEY ARE VERY FRIENDLY
ALLAMURR
DISCERNMENT OF NATIVE SINCERITY
EAST ALLIGATOR RIVER
CLOUDS OF DUST MISTAKEN FOR SMOKE
IMPATIENCE TO REACH THE END OF THE JOURNEY
NATIVES STILL MORE INTELLIGENT
NYUALL
BUFFALOES; SOURCE FROM WHICH THEY SPRUNG
NATIVE GUIDES ENGAGED; BUT THEY DESERT US
MOUNT MORRIS BAY
RAFFLES BAY
LEAVE THE PACKHORSE AND BULLOCK BEHIND
BILL WHITE
ARRIVE AT PORT ESSINGTON
VOYAGE TO SYDNEY.

Dec. 1.--We travelled about eleven or twelve miles to the northward, for the greater part through forest land, large tracts of which were occupied solely by Livistona. A species of Acacia and stringy-bark saplings formed a thick underwood. The open lawns were adorned by various plants, amongst which we noticed a species of Drosera, with white and red blossoms? a Mitrasacme; a narrow-leaved Ruellia, the white primrose, the red prostrate malvaceous plant, a low shrubby Pleurandra, and an orchideous plant--one of the few representatives of this family in the Australian tropics; the most interesting, however, was a prostrate Grevillea, with oblong smooth leaves, and with thyrsi of fine scarlet flowers; which I consider to be Grevillea Goodii, R. Br.

We crossed two small creeks, and, at the end of three miles, we came to a Pandanus brook, the murmuring of whose waters over a rocky pebbly bed was heard by us at a considerable distance. A broad foot-path of the natives led along its banks, probably to large lagoons, of which it might be the outlet. The country became flatter, more densely wooded, and gently sloping to the northward, when we entered a tea-tree hollow, through which the mirage indicated the presence of an immense plain, which we all mistook for the Ocean. We crossed over it to a belt of trees, which I thought to be its northern boundary. The part of the plain next to the forest-land was composed of a loose black soil, with excellent grass; farther on it was a cold clay, either covered with a stiff, dry grass, apparently laid down by the rush of water, or forming flats bare of vegetation, which seemed to have been occasionally washed by the tide. Finding that the belt of trees was a thicket of mangroves along a salt-water creek, I returned to some shallow lagoons near the forest, the water of which was drinkable, though brackish and aluminous. To the westward of the plains, we saw no other limit than two very distant hills, which I took to be the two hills marked to the southward of the embouchure of the South Alligator River. To the eastward, we saw another narrow belt of trees; beyond which, however, the plain evidently continued. Numerous pillars of smoke were seen to the westward.

A fine north-west breeze set in at three o'clock in the afternoon, and refreshed us, as well as the cattle, which were suffering most severely from heat and fatigue.

Dec. 2.--Whilst we were waiting for our bullock, which had returned to the running brook, a fine native stepped out of the forest with the ease and grace of an Apollo, with a smiling countenance, and with the confidence of a man to whom the white face was perfectly familiar. He was unarmed, but a great number of his companions were keeping back to watch the reception he should meet with. We received him, of course, most cordially; and upon being joined by another good-looking little man, we heard him utter distinctly the words, "Commandant!" "come here!!" "very good!!!" "what's your name? !!!!" If my readers have at all identified themselves with my feelings throughout this trying journey; if they have only imagined a tithe of the difficulties we have encountered, they will readily imagine the startling effect which these, as it were, magic words produced--we were electrified--our joy knew no limits, and I was ready to embrace the fellows, who, seeing the happiness with which they inspired us, joined, with a most merry grin, in the loud expression of our feelings. We gave them various presents, particularly leather belts, and received in return a great number of bunches of goose feathers, which the natives use to brush away the flies. They knew the white people of Victoria, and called them Balanda, which is nothing more than "Hollanders;" a name used by the Malays, from whom they received it. We had most fortunately a small collection of words, made by Mr. Gilbert when at Port Essington; so that we were enabled to ask for water (obert); for the road (allun); for Limbo cardja, which was the name of the Harbour. I wished very much to induce them to become our guides; and the two principal men, Eooanberry and Minorelli, promised to accompany us, but they afterwards changed their minds.

My first object was to find good water, and our sable friends guided us with the greatest care, pointing out to us the most shady road, to some wells surrounded with ferns, which were situated in some tea-tree hollows at the confines of the plains and the forest. These wells, however, were so small that our horses could not approach to drink, so that we had to go to another set of wells; where I was obliged to stop, as one of our horses refused to go any farther. This place was about four miles E.N.E. from our last camp. The wells were about six or eight feet deep, and dug through a sandy clay to a stiff bed of clay, on which the water collected. It would appear that the stiff clay of the plains had been covered by the sandy detritus of the ridges, from which the water slowly drained to the wells. It was evident, from the pains which the natives had taken in digging them, that the supply of fresh water was very precarious. In many instances, however, I observed that they had been induced to do so, simply by the want of surface water in the immediate neighbourhood of places where they obtained their principal supply of food. This was particularly the case near the sea-coast, where no surface water is found; whilst the various fish, and even vegetable productions, attract the natives, who will, in such a case, even contract the habit of going the longest possible time without water, or, at least, with very little, as is well shown in Mr. Eyre's journey round the Australian Bight. We had to water our horses and the bullock with the stew pot; and had to hobble the latter, to prevent his straying, and attacking the natives.

The natives were remarkably kind and attentive, and offered us the rind of the rose-coloured Eugenia apple, the cabbage of the Seaforthia palm, a fruit which I did not know, and the nut-like swelling of the rhizoma of either a grass or a sedge. The last had a sweet taste, was very mealy and nourishing, and the best article of the food of the natives we had yet tasted. They called it "Allamurr" (the natives of Port Essington, "Murnatt"), and were extremely fond of it. The plant grew in depressions of the plains, where the boys and young men were occupied the whole day in digging for it. The women went in search of other food; either to the sea-coast to collect shell-fish,--and many were the broad paths which led across the plains from the forest land to the salt-water--or to the brushes to gather the fruits of the season, and the cabbage of the palms. The men armed with a wommala, and with a bundle of goose spears, made of a strong reed or bamboo (?), gave up their time to hunting. It seemed that they speared the geese only when flying; and would crouch down whenever they saw a flight of them approaching: the geese, however, knew their enemies so well, that they immediately turned upon seeing a native rise to put his spear into the throwing stick. Some of my companions asserted that they had seen them hit their object at the almost incredible distance of 200 yards: but, making all due allowance for the guess, I could not help thinking how formidable they would have been had they been enemies instead of friends. They remained with us the whole afternoon; all the tribe and many visitors, in all about seventy persons, squatting down with crossed legs in the narrow shades of the trunks of trees, and shifting their position as the sun advanced. Their wives were out in search of food; but many of their children were with them, which they duly introduced to us. They were fine, stout, well made men, with pleasing and intelligent countenances. One or two attempts were made to rob us of some trifles; but I was careful; and we avoided the unpleasant necessity of showing any discontent on that head. As it grew late, and they became hungry, they rose, and explained that they were under the necessity of leaving us, to go and satisfy their hunger; but that they would shortly return, and admire, and talk again. They went to the digging ground, about half a mile in the plain, where the boys were collecting Allamurr, and brought us a good supply of it; in return for which various presents were made to them. We became very fond of this little tuber: and I dare say the feast of Allamurr with Eooanberry's and Minorelli's tribe will long remain in the recollection of my companions. They brought us also a thin grey snake, about four feet long, which they put on the coals and roasted. It was poisonous, and was called "Yullo." At nightfall, after filling their koolimans with water, there being none at their camp, they took their leave, and retired to their camping place on the opposite hill where a plentiful dinner awaited them. They were very urgent in inviting us to accompany them, and by way of inducement, most unequivocally offered us their sable partners. We had to take great care of our bullock, as the beast invariably charged the natives whenever he obtained a sight of them, and he would alone have prevented their attacking us; for the whole tribe were so much afraid of him, that, upon our calling out "the bullock," they were immediately ready to bolt; with the exception of Eooanberry and Minorelli, who looked to us for protection. I had not, however, the slightest fear and apprehension of any treachery on the part of the natives; for my frequent intercourse with the natives of Australia had taught me to distinguish easily between the smooth tongue of deceit, with which they try to ensnare their victim, and the open expression of kind and friendly feelings, or those of confidence and respect. I remember several instances of the most cold-blooded smooth-tongued treachery, and of the most extraordinary gullibility of the natives; but I am sure that a careful observer is more than a match for these simple children of nature, and that he can easily read the bad intention in their unsteady, greedy, glistening eyes.

Dec. 3.--The natives visited us very early in the morning, with their wives and children, whom they introduced to us. There could not have been less than 200 of them present; they were all well made, active, generally well-looking, with an intelligent countenance: they had in fact all the characters of the coast blacks of a good country; but without their treacherous dispositions. I started in a north-east direction; and as we were accompanied by the natives, I led our bullock, by the noserope, behind my horse. After crossing a plain, we were stopped by a large sheet of salt-water, about three or four miles broad, at the opposite side of which a low range was visible; when Eooanberry explained that we had to go far to the south-east and south, before we could cross the river, and that we had to follow it down again at the other side. He expressed his great attachment to his wife and child, and obtained leave of us to return to his tribe, which had already retired before him. Seeing the necessity of heading the river, which I considered to be the East Alligator; the longitude of which was, where we first came to it, 132 degrees 40 minutes according to reckoning; I returned to the forest land, and travelled along its belt of Pandanus, to obtain a better ground for our cattle, and to avoid the scorching heat of the forenoon sun. Observing some singularly formed mountains rising abruptly out of the plains and many pillars of smoke behind them, I tried to get to them, but was again prevented by the broad salt water. We now steered for a distant smoke to the south-east by east, and had travelled fully seventeen miles on, or along extensive plains, when we perceived seven natives returning on a beaten foot-path, from the salt water to the forest. We cooeed--they ran! But when we had passed, and Charley stopped behind alone, they came up to him, and, having received some presents, they showed us some miserable wells between two tea-tree groves; after which they hastened home. Our cattle were tired and thirsty, but we could give them nothing to drink, except about six quarts of brackish water; which fell to the share of our bullock. The feed, however, was rich and young, and during the night a heavy dew was deposited, Many flocks of geese came flying low over the plains, which made us hope that water was not very distant. Whilst we were passing the head of a small Mangrove creek, four native dogs, started out of a shady hole; but we looked in vain for fresh water. The plains, which were very level, with a few melon-holes, were scattered all over with dead Limnaeas, which showed evidently, that fresh, or slightly brackish water, covered them occasionally, and for some length of time. Since we first entered upon the large plains of the Alligator Rivers, we had seen myriads of the small cockatoo (Cocatua sanguinea, GOULD), which retired towards night, in long flights from the plains, to the shade of the drooping tea-trees near the shallow pools of water on which we encamped. We had also observed several retreats of flying-foxes in the most shady parts of the Pandanus groves, receiving frequently the first indication of them by the peculiar odour of the animal.

Cumuli formed very early in the morning, and increased during the day, sending down showers of rain all round the horizon. The sea breeze set in at 3 o'clock; and the weather cleared up at sunset, and during the first part of the night; but after 1 o'clock A. M. became cloudy again, with inclination to rain; heavy dew fell during the clear part of the night.

Dec. 4.--The natives returned very early to our camp. I went up to them and made them some presents; in return for which they offered me bunches of goose feathers, and the roasted leg of a goose, which they were pleased to see me eat with a voracious appetite. I asked for Allamurr, and they expressed themselves sorry in not having any left, and gave us to understand that they would supply us, if we would stay a day. Neither these natives nor the tribe of Eooanberry would touch our green hide or meat: they took it, but could not overcome their repugnance, and tried to drop it without being seen by us. Poor fellows! they did not know how gladly we should have received it back! They were the stoutest and fattest men we had met.

We travelled at first to the east, in the direction from which the geese had come last night, but, arriving at ridges covered with scrubby forest, we turned to the north-east, and continued in that direction about seven miles and a half, over iron-stone ridges, when we again entered upon the plains of the river. Mountains and columns of smoke were seen all along its northern banks; but we afterwards found that most of those supposed columns of smoke were dust raised by whirlwinds. We now followed the river until a vine brush approached close to its bank, into the cool shade of which our bullock rushed and lay down, refusing to go any farther; our packhorse and most of our riding horses were also equally tired. The bed of the river had become very narrow, and the water was not quite brine, which made me hope that we should soon come to fresh water. Charley, Brown, and John, had gone into the brush to a camp of flying-foxes, and returned with twelve, which we prepared for luncheon, which allowed our bullock time to recover. They gave an almost incredible account of the enormous numbers of flying-foxes, all clustering round the branches of low trees, which drooped by the weight so near to the ground that the animals could easily be killed with endgels. The Seaforthia palm raised its elegant crown far above the patches of vine brush which we passed at the river side of the ridges.

After a delay of two hours, we again started, and travelled in a due south direction towards some thick smoke rising between two steep and apparently isolated rocky hills: they were about four miles distant, and, when we arrived at their base, we enjoyed the pleasing sight of large lagoons, surrounded with mangrove myrtles (Stravadium), with Pandanus, and with a belt of reeds and

Nelumbiums. Man, horse, and bullock, rushed most eagerly into the fine water, determined to make up for the privation and suffering of the three last days. The lagoons were crowded with geese, and, as the close vegetation allowed a near approach, Brown made good use of the few slugs that were still left, and shot ten of them, which allowed a goose to every man; a great treat to my hungry party.

Dec. 5.--I determined upon stopping for a day, to allow our cattle to recover. Every body was anxious to procure geese or flying-foxes; and, whilst three of my companions went to the flying-fox camp which we had visited yesterday, loaded with ironstone pebbles for shot, and full of the most sanguine expectations, Brown was busy at the lagoons, and even Mr. Roper stirred to try his good luck. The two met with a party of natives, who immediately retreated at sight of Mr. Roper; but during the afternoon they came to the other side of the lagoon opposite to our camp, and offered us some fish, a Silurus (Mao) and a tench (?) which they had speared in the lagoons. I made a sign for them to come over and to receive, as presents in exchange, some small pieces of iron, tin canisters, and leather belts; which they did; but they became exceedingly noisy, and one of them, an old rogue, tried to possess himself quietly and openly of every thing he saw, from my red blanket to the spade and stew-pot. I consequently sent Brown for a horse, whose appearance quickly sent them to the other side of the lagoon, where they remained until night-fall. Brown offered them half a goose, which, however, they refused; probably because it was not prepared by themselves, as they were very desirous of getting some of the geese which we had not yet cooked. Brown had shot nine geese, and our fox hunters returned with forty-four of the small species.

When the natives became hungry, they ate the lower part of the leaf-stalks of Nelumbium, after stripping off the external skin. They threw a great number of them over to us, and I could not help making a rather ridiculous comparison of our situation, and our hosts, with that of the English ambassador in China, who was treated also with Nelumbium by its rich Mandarins.

The natives seemed to speak a less melodious language, which might be ascribed to the mountainous character of their country. I collected the following names: Kobboyakka, Nobungop, Kanbinycx, Manguradja, Apirk (Apek), Yaganyin, Kolar, Kadgupa, Gnanga Gnanga. Ayir meant stone spear; Ekolpen, jagged fish-spear.

I made the latitude of these lagoons, by an observation of Castor, 12 degrees 23 minutes 19 seconds.

Dec. 6.--The natives visited us again this morning, and it was evident that they

266

had not been with their gins. They invited us to come to their camp; but I wished to find a crossing place, and, after having tried in vain to pass at the foot of the rocky hills, we found a passage between the lagoons, and entered into a most beautiful valley, bounded on the west, east, and south by abrupt hills, ranges, and rocks rising abruptly out of an almost treeless plain clothed with the most luxuriant verdure, and diversified by large Nymphaea lagoons, and a belt of trees along the creek which meandered through it. The natives now became our guides, and pointed out to us a sound crossing place of the creek, which proved to be the head of the salt-water branch of the East Alligator River. We observed a great number of long conical fish and crab traps at the crossing place of the creek and in many of the tributary salt-water channels; they were made apparently of Flagellaria. Here I took leave of our guides: the leader of whom appeared to be "Apirk," a young and slender, but an intelligent and most active man. We now travelled again to the northward, following the outline of the rocky ridges at the right side of the creek; and, having again entered upon the plains, we encamped at a very broad, shallow, sedgy, boggy lagoon, surrounded with Typhas, and crowded with ducks and geese, of which Brown shot four. It was about four miles east of our yesterday's camp. Numerous flocks of the Harlequin pigeon (Peristera histrionica, GOULD) came to drink at this lagoon; and innumerable geese alighted towards the evening on the plain, and fed on the young grass, moistened by the rain. The number of kites was in a fair proportion to that of the geese; and dozens of them were watching us from the neighbouring trees.

We found a new Eugenia, a tree of rather stunted growth, with broad opposite leaves, and fruit of the size of an apple, of a delicate rose-colour, and when ripe, a most delicious refreshment during a hot day. We had frequently met with this tree on sandstone ridges, and in sandy soils, but had never before found it in fruit. The day was distressingly hot, but we had several light showers during the afternoon.

Dec. 7.--"Apirk," with seven other natives, visited us again in the morning, and it seemed that they had examined the camp we had last left. They gave us to understand that we could travel safely to the northward, without meeting any other creek. Apirk carried a little pointed stick, and a flat piece of wood with a small hole in it, for the purpose of obtaining fire. I directed my course to a distant mountain, due north from the camp, and travelled seven or eight miles over a large plain, which was composed of a rich dark soil, and clothed with a great variety of excellent grasses. We saw many columns of dust raised by whirlwinds; and again mistook them for the smoke of so many fires of the natives. But we soon observed that they moved in a certain direction, and that new columns rose as those already formed drew off; and when we came nearer, and passed between them, it seemed as if the giant spirits of the plain were holding a stately corrobori around us. They originated on a patch of ground divested of its vegetation by a late fire. There was a belt of forest to the northward, and the current of the sea-breeze coming up the valley of the river from N.N.W. seemed to eddy round the forest, and to whirl the unsheltered loose earth into the air.

Towards the river, now to the west of our course, peaks, razor-backed hills, and tents, similar to those we had observed when travelling at the west side of the river on the 3rd December (and probably the same), reappeared. To the east of the mountain, towards which we were travelling, several bluff mountains appeared, which probably bounded the valley of a river flowing to the northward, and disemboguing between the Liverpool and Mount Morris Bay. For the last five miles of the stage, our route lay through forest land; and we crossed two creeks going to the east, and then came to rocky sandstone hills, with horizontal stratification, at the foot of which we met with a rocky creek, in the bed of which, after following it for a few miles, we found water. The supply was small; but we enlarged it with the spade, and obtained a sufficient supply for the night. A thunder-storm formed to the northward, which drew off to the westward; but another to the north-east gave us a fine shower, and added to the contents of our water-hole. A well-beaten foot-path of the natives went down the creek to the south-east. My latitude, according to an observation of Castor, was 12 degrees 11 minutes.

We saw the Torres Strait pigeon; a Wallooroo and a red kangaroo (Osphranter Antilopinus, GOULD). The old camps of the natives, which we passed in the forest, were strewed with the shells of goose eggs, which showed what an important article these birds formed in the culinary department of the natives; and, whilst their meat and eggs served them for food, their feathers afforded them a protection against the flies which swarmed round their bodies during the day.

The arborescent Vitex with ternate leaves, which I had first met with at the Flying-Fox Creek of the Roper, was also observed here.

At this time we were all sadly distressed with boils, and with a prickly heat; early lancing of the former saved much pain: the cuts and sores on the hands festered quickly; but this depended much more on the want of cleanliness than any thing else. A most dangerous enemy grew up amongst us in the irresistible impatience to come to the end of our journey; and I cannot help considering it a great blessing that we did not meet with natives who knew the settlement of Port Essington at an earlier part of our journey, or I am afraid we should have been exposed to the greatest misery, if not destruction, by an inconsiderate, thoughtless desire of pushing onward.

Dec. 8.--I went to the westward, to avoid the rocky ground, and if possible to come into the valley of the East Alligator River, if the country should not open and allow me a passage to the northward, which direction I took whenever the nature of the country permitted. After crossing the heads of several easterly creeks, we came upon a large foot-path of the natives, which I determined to follow. It was, in all probability, the same which went down the creek on which we had encamped last night: it descended through a narrow rocky gully, down which I found great difficulty in bringing the horses; and afterwards wound through a fine forest land, avoiding the rocky hills, and touching the heads of westerly creeks, which were well supplied with rocky basins of water. It then followed a creek down into swampy lagoons, which joined the broad irregular sandy bed of a river containing large pools and reaches of water, lined with Pandanus and drooping tea-trees. This river came from the eastward, and was probably the principal branch of the East Alligator River, which joined the salt-water branch we had crossed in latitude about 12 degrees 6 minutes. We met another foot-path at its northern bank, which led us between the river and ranges of rocky hills, over a country abounding with the scarlet Eugenia, of which we made a rich harvest. We encamped at a fine lagoon, occupied, as usual, with geese and ducks, and teeming with large fish, which were splashing about during the whole night. The situation of these lagoons was, by an observation of Castor, in lat. 12 degrees 6 minutes 2 seconds; and about nine miles north-west from our last camp.

Immediately after our arrival, Brown went to shoot some geese, and met with two natives who were cooking some roots, but they withdrew in great haste as soon as they saw him. Soon afterwards, however, a great number of them came to the opposite side of the lagoon, and requested a parley. I went down to them with some presents, and a young man came over in a canoe to met me. I gave him a tin canister, and was agreeably surprised to find that the stock of English words increased considerably; that very few things we had were new to him, and that he himself had been at the settlement. His name was "Bilge." He called me Commandant, and presented several old men to me under the same title. Several natives joined us, either using the canoe, or swimming across the lagoon, and, after having been duly introduced to me, I took four of them to the camp, where they examined everything with great intelligence, without expressing the least desire of possessing it. They were the most confiding, intelligent, inquisitive natives I had ever met before. Bilge himself took me by the hand and went to the different horses, and to the bullock and asked their names and who rode them. The natives had always been very curious to know the names of our horses, and repeated "Jim Crow," "Flourbag," "Caleb," "Irongrey," as well as they could, with the greatest merriment. Bilge frequently mentioned "Devil devil," in referring to the bullock, and I think he alluded to the wild buffaloes, the tracks of which we

269

soon afterwards saw. We asked him for "Allamurr;" and they expressed their readiness to bring it, as soon as the children and women, who both went under the denomination of Piccaninies, returned to the camp. The day being far advanced, and their camp a good way off, they left us, after inviting us to accompany them: but this I declined. About 10 o'clock at night, three lads came to us with Allamurr; but they were very near suffering for their kindness and confidence, as the alarm of "blackfellows" at night was a call to immediate and desperate defence. Suspecting, however, the true cause of this untimely visit, I walked up to them, and led them into the camp, where I divided their Allamurr between us; allowing them a place of honour on a tarpauling near me for the remainder of the night, with which attention they appeared highly pleased. The night was clear and dewy, but became cloudy with the setting of the moon.

Dec. 9.--The natives came to our camp at break of day, and Bilge introduced several old warriors of a different tribe, adding always the number of piccaninies that each of them had; they appeared very particular about the latter, and one of the gentlemen corrected Bilge very seriously when he mentioned only two instead of three. Bilge had promised to go with us to Balanda, but, having probably talked the matter over during the night, with his wife, he changed his intentions; but invited us in the most urgent manner, to stay a day at their camp. Although no place could be found more favourable for feed and water, and a day's rest would have proved very beneficial to our cattle, yet our meat bags, on which we now solely depended, were so much reduced, that every day of travelling was of the greatest importance; as the natives told us that four days would bring us to the Peninsula, and two more to Balanda. We crossed the plain to the westward, in order to avoid the low rocks and rocky walls which bounded this fine country to the north and east. After about three miles, however, we turned to the northward, and travelled with ease through an open undulating forest, interrupted by some tea-tree hollows. Just before entering the forest, Brown observed the track of a buffalo on the rich grassy inlets between the rocks. After proceeding about five miles we crossed a chain of fine Nymphaea ponds; and, at five miles farther, we came upon a path of the natives, which we followed to the eastward, along a drooping tea-tree swamp, in the outlet of which we found good water. Our lat. was 11 degrees 56 minutes; about ten miles and a half north by east, from Bilge's lagoon. Mitrasacme elata, and all the other little plants I have before mentioned, were growing in the stringy-bark forest. A flight of whistling ducks came at night, and alighted on the ground near our camp; but departed as soon as they saw us moving. Tracks of buffaloes were again observed by Charley. The night was clear and very dry.

Dec. 10.--We travelled about seven miles to the northward; but kept for the first three miles in a N.N.W. direction from our camp, when we came to a small plain, with a Mangrove creek going to the westward; scarcely two miles farther, we crossed a drooping tea-tree swamp, of which a Pandanus creek formed the outlet; and, two miles farther still, a large plain opened upon us, in which we saw a great number of natives occupied in burning the grass, and digging for roots. All the country intervening between the creeks and the plain was undulating stringy-bark forest. I left my companions in the shady belt of drooping tea-trees, and rode with Charley towards the natives, in order to obtain information. They were, however, only women and children, and they withdrew at my approach, although I had dismounted and left my horse far behind with Charley. They had, however, allowed me to come near enough to make them understand my incessant calls for "obeit," water, adding occasionally "Balanda; very good; no good." When they had disappeared in the forest, Charley came with the horse, and we reconnoitred along the boundaries of the plain to find water, but not succeeding, we returned; and, when opposite to the place where I had left my companions, I cooeed for them to come over to me. My cooee was answered by natives within the forest, and, shortly afterwards four men came running out of it, and approached us most familiarly. They spoke English tolerably, knew the pipe, tobacco, bread, rice, ponies, guns, etc.; and guided us to a fine lagoon, which I named after the leading man of their tribe, "Nyuall's Lagoon." Two of them promised to pilot us to Balanda and to "Rambal," which meant houses. They were very confiding, and women and children entered for the first time freely into our camp.

They examined every thing, but made not the slightest attempt to rob us even of a trifle. When the women returned at night, they did not bring "Allamurr," or, as it was here called, "Murnatt," but plenty of "Imberbi," the root of Convolvolus, which grow abundantly in the plain: they gave us a very seasonable supply of it, but would not taste our dried beef, which they turned, broke, smelled, and then with a feeling of pity and disgust returned to us. Nyuall gave an amusing account of our state: "You no bread, no flour, no rice, no backi--you no good! Balanda plenty bread, plenty flour, plenty rice, plenty backi! Balanda very good!"

He, Gnarrangan, and Carbaret, promised to go with us; and the first intended to take his wife with him. They imitated with surprising accuracy the noises of the various domesticated animals they had seen at the settlement; and it was amusing to hear the crowing of the cock, the cackling of the hens, the quacking of ducks, grunting of pigs, mewing of the cat, etc. evident proofs that these natives had been in Victoria.

A heavy thunder-storm passed over at 6 o'clock P. M. and the natives either crowded into my tent, or covered their backs with sheets of tea-tree bark, turning them to the storm, like a herd of horses or cattle surprised by a heavy shower in the middle of a plain. Imaru lay close to me during the night, and, in order to keep entire possession of my blanket, I had to allow him a tarpauling.

Dec. 11.--We travelled about seven miles N.N.W. over an immense plain, with forest land and rising ground to the eastward, in which direction four prominent hills were seen, one of which had the abrupt peak form of Biroa in Moreton Bay. The plain appeared to be unbounded to the westward. When we approached the forest, several tracts of buffaloes were seen; and, upon the natives conducting us along a small creek which came into the plain from the N.N.E., we found a well beaten path and several places where these animals were accustomed to camp. We encamped at a good-sized water-hole in the bed of this creek, the water of which was covered with a green scum. As the dung and tracks of the buffaloes were fresh, Charley went to track them, whilst Brown tried to shoot some Ibises, which had been at the water and were now perched on a tree about 300 yards off. At the discharge of the gun a buffalo started out of a thicket, but did not seem inclined to go far; Brown returned, loaded his gun with ball, went after the buffalo and wounded him in the shoulder. When Charley came back to the camp, he, Brown and Mr. Roper pursued the buffalo on horseback, and after a long run, and some charges, succeeded in killing it. It was a young bull, about three years old, and in most excellent condition. This was a great, a most fortunate event for us; for our meat bags were almost empty, and, as we did not wish to kill Redmond, our good companion, we had the prospect of some days of starvation before us. We could now share freely with our black friends, and they had not the slightest objection to eat the fresh meat, after baking it in their usual manner. They called the buffalo "Anaborro;" and stated that the country before us was full of them. These buffaloes are the offspring of the stock which had either strayed from the settlement at Raffles Bay, or had been left behind when that establishment was broken up. They were originally introduced from the Malay islands. I was struck with the remarkable thickness of their skin, (almost an inch) and with the solidity of their bones, which contained little marrow; but that little was extremely savoury.

We had a heavy thunder-storm at 10 o'clock at night from the southward.

Dec. 12.--Part of the meat was cut up and dried, and part of it was roasted to take with us; a great part of it was given to the natives, who were baking and eating the whole day; and when they could eat no more meat, they went into the plains to collect "Imberbi" and Murnatt, to add the necessary quantum of vegetable matter to their diet. The sultry weather, however, caused a great part of the meat to become tainted and maggotty. Our friend Nyuall became ill, and complained of a violent headache, which he tried to cure by tying a string tightly round his head.

The black ibis, cocatua, kites, crows, and a small black and white species of heron, frequented our water-hole.

The night was extremely close, and, to find some relief, I took a bath; which gave me, however, a very annoying inflammation of the eyes.

Dec. 13.--At day break, an old man, whom Nyuall introduced to us as Commandant, came with his gin, and invited us to his camp, about two miles off. We went to it with the intention of continuing our journey, and found a great number of women and children collected in very spacious huts or sheds, probably with the intention of seeing us pass. They had a domestic dog, which seemed very ferocious. A little farther on, we came to a small creek, with good water-holes, and our guides wished us to stop; but, when I told them that we were desirous of reaching Balanda as soon as possible, and added to my promise of giving them a blanket and a tomahawk, that of a pint pot, Gnarrangan and Cabaret again volunteered, and pursuaded a third, of the name of Malarang, to join them. For some miles, we followed a beaten foot-path, which skirted the large plain, and then entered the forest, which was composed of rusty-gum, leguminous Ironbark, Cochlospermum gossypium, and a small apocynaceous tree (Balfouria, Br.); we crossed several salt-water creeks which went down to Van Diemen's Gulf. The country near these creeks, was more undulating, the soil sandy and mixed with small ironstone pebbles; fine tea-tree flats with excellent grass, on which the buffaloes fed, were frequent. Along the plain, small clusters of brush protruded into it from the forest, or covered low mounts of sea shells, mixed with a black soil. Amongst these copses, the tracks of buffaloes were very numerous.

We travelled about ten miles north-west by north, and encamped at a small pool of water in a creek, in which the clayey ironstone cropped out. Its water was so impregnated with the astringent properties of the gum-trees, that Mr. Phillips boiled and drank it like tea. Before arriving at this creek, we had a thunder-storm, with heavy rain, from the northward. After pitching our tents, our guides went out, and returned with a small Iguana (Vergar), and with pods of the rose-coloured Sterculia, which they roasted on the coals. I succeeded in saving a great part of our meat by smoking it.

Our horses were greatly distressed by large horse-flies, and every now and then the poor brutes would come and stand in the smoke of our fires to rid themselves of their persevering tormentors. This want of rest during the night contributed very much to their increasing weakness; though most of them were severely galled besides, which was prevented only in two by the most careful attention, and daily washing of their backs. On this stage we again passed one of those oven-like huts of the natives, thatched with grass, which I have mentioned several times, and which Nyuall's tribe called "Corambal." At the place where we encamped, the ruins of a very large hut were still visible, which indicated that the natives had profited by their long intercourse with the Malays and Europeans, in the construction of their habitations.

Dec. 14.--When we started, intending to follow the foot-path, our native guides remained behind; and, when I had proceeded two or three miles, my companions came up to me and stated, that the natives had left us, but that they had given them to understand that the foot-path would conduct us safely to Balanda. They had attempted to keep the large tomahawk, but had given it up when Brown asked them for it. I was very sorry at their having left us, as the cloudy sky had prevented me for several days from taking any latitude, and determining my position. We crossed a great number of small creeks, coming from the eastward, and draining the ridges of the neck of the Peninsula. Scattered Pandanus and drooping tea-trees grew on their banks as far as the fresh water extended; when they were succeeded by the salt-water tea-tree and the mangrove, covering and fringing their beds, which enlarged into stiff plains, without vegetation, or into mangrove swamps. The latter were composed of Aegiceras, Bruguiera, and Pemphis. The tracks of the buffaloes increased in number as we advanced, and formed broad paths, leading in various directions, and made me frequently mistake them for the foot-path of the natives, which I eventually lost. A course north 30 degrees west, brought us to easterly creeks, one of which I followed down, when Brown called out that he saw the sea. We, therefore, went to the sea-side, and found ourselves at the head of a large bay, with an island to the north-east, and with headlands stretching far into the ocean, which was open and boundless to the northward. It was Mount Morris Bay, with Valentia and Crocker's islands; the latter, however, appeared to us to be a continuation of the main land. We now went to the north-west and westward, until we came again on westerly waters. The country in the centre of the neck of the Peninsula, was very hilly, and some of the ridges rose, perhaps, from one hundred and fifty to two hundred feet above the level of the sea; one or two hills were still higher. They were all composed of a clayey ironstone, and clothed with patches of scrub, formed principally of Calythrix, and with a more open forest of Cypress pine, white-gum, tea-trees, bloodwood, Livistona palms, Pandanus, with shrubby Terminalias and Coniogetons. The grass was dry, but high and dense; and buffalo tracks spread in every direction, particularly down the creeks, both to the eastward and westward.

We followed a westerly creek in all its windings, in order to detect water in one of its rocky water-holes. The rock was shaly, of a greyish colour, like the clay shale of Newcastle above the layers of the coal, but more indurated. Patches

274

of vine brush grew along the banks, and their verdure led me frequently to expect the presence of water. We met, however, only with salt-water, where the mangroves commenced, and had consequently to continue our journey. Here we again came on the foot-path of the natives, which skirted the mangrove swamps, and I followed it for about three miles farther, crossed several dry watercourses, and at last found some pools of rain water, in a small creek. I was fortunate enough to make my latitude by an observation of Regulus, 11 degrees 32 minutes 11 seconds.

Dec. 15.--I followed the foot-path of the natives, with the intention of continuing on it, until I came in sight of Mounts Bedwell and Roe. If I had done so, much trouble would have been saved. But, after we had travelled more than three hours, the country became very hilly and ridgy, and I supposed that we were close to those mountains, but were prevented, by the ridges, from seeing them. We went consequently to the northward, and after an hour's riding over a hilly, but openly timbered country, came to an easterly creek, which we followed down, until we found an abundance of water. The upper part of this creek was very scrubby, and with but little grass. I imagined that we had arrived at the west side of Port Essington, and that the creek on which we encamped was probably the Warvi. To ascertain this, I rode down the creek with Charley: it became more open; limited flats of sandy alluvium were clothed with the refreshing verdure of young grass, and with groves of Banksias; its hollows were fringed with large drooping tea-trees. The creek itself was a succession of shady water-holes, out of which, at our approach dashed buffaloes, three and four at a time, shaking their muddy heads, as they scrambled up the steep banks, and galloped to the neighbouring thickets. The stiff sedges of the salt-water, and the salt-water tea-trees, made their appearance about three miles from our camp; and it is probable that the sea was scarcely half a mile farther. High hills rose to the northward, openly timbered, but at their base with patches of scrub, and very stony. Here we heard the distant cooees of natives, which we answered, going in their direction, until we came to a camp, in which we found an old lame man, "Baki Baki," and a short sturdy fellow, "Rambo Rambo;" both of whom knew a great number of English words, and were quite familiar with the settlement, and knew the Commandant, Mr. Macarthur. They promised the guide us the next morning to Balanda, after having made many inquiries about our stock of provisions and of tobacco. I made my latitude 11 degrees 26 minutes 18 seconds, by an observation of Regulus; which, allowing a possible error of a few miles, confirmed me in my belief, that we were at the head of the harbour; particularly as Baki Baki had told me that he had come this very morning from the settlement.

Dec. 16.--When we arrived with our whole train at the camp of the natives, their behaviour was quite altered, and they now showed as little inclination to guide us to the settlement, as they had been eager last night to do so. I persuaded Baki Baki, however, to go, at least part of the way; and, when we saw that he became tired, we mounted him on one of the horses, and led it by the bridle. He pointed to the W.N.W. as the direction in which the settlement lay. We travelled about five miles over stony ironstone ridges, with extensive groves of Livistona palm covering their slopes. Here Baki Baki desired to dismount; and, telling us that it was a very good road to Balanda, took his leave and returned. Soon after we came to a large creek full of water, running to the eastward, which we followed up for a long distance, before we were able to cross. Our pack-horse became bogged, and as it was so weak that it would not even make an effort to extricate itself, and as I supposed that we were near the settlement, we took off its pack-saddle and load, and left it behind. We crossed two or three more watercourses; and continued the course pointed out by the native, until it became very late, and I found myself compelled to look for water; particularly as our bullock showed evident symptoms of becoming knocked up. I therefore followed the fall of the country to the north-east; and, in a short time, came to the sea-side. We compared our little map of the harbour of Port Essington with the configuration of the bay before us, but nothing would agree exactly, although it bore a general resemblance to Raffles Bay.

A narrow belt of brush covered the approaches to the water; but the scarlet Eugenia grew on the sandy flats towards the hilly forest; where we also found a new tree, a species of Anacardium, which the natives called "Lugula;" it bore a red succulent fruit, formed by the enlargement of the stalk, with a greyish one-seeded nut outside, like Exocarpus. The fruit was extremely refreshing; the envelope, however, contained such an acrid juice that it ate into and discoloured my skin, and raised blisters wherever it touched it: these blisters were not only followed by a simple excoriation, but by a deep and painful ulceration. In the forest, we met with some few small Seaforthia palms, the young shoots of which we obtained with great difficulty, not then knowing how easily the natives strip them of the surrounding leaves and leafstalks. I followed a a well beaten foot-path of the natives to the northward, crossed a creek, in the mangrove swamp of which another horse was bogged, which we extricated after great exertion; and, after two or three miles, came to a large fresh-water swamp (Marair) on which we encamped. The sun had long set, and our cattle, as well as ourselves, were miserably tired. We were here visited by a tribe of natives, who were well acquainted with the settlement; they were all friendly, and willing to assist us; and many of them spoke very tolerable English. One of them, apparently the chief of the tribe, though a hunchback, named "Bill White," promised to guide us to the settlement. He gave us to understand that we had come too far to the northward, and that we had to go to the south-west, in order to head Port Essington, and to follow its west coast, in order to arrive at Victoria. We were, in fact, at Raffles Bay. The natives knew every body in Victoria, and did not cease to give us all the news; to which we most willingly listened. They fetched water for us from a great distance, and gave us some Murnatt, which was extremely welcome. Perceiving the state of exhaustion and depression in which we were, they tried to cheer us with their corrobori songs, which they accompanied on the Eboro, a long tube of bamboo, by means of which they variously modulated their voices. I may mention that we experienced a heavy thunder-storm during the afternoon.

Dec. 17.--We started, with a willing guide, for the goal of our journey, and travelled to the south-west over a hilly country, covered with groves of the Livistona palm, which, as we proceeded became mixed with Seaforthia (the real cabbage-palm). A fine large creek, containing a chain of large water-holes went to the north-east, and disembogued probably into Bremer's Bay. We followed it for three or four miles towards its head; and, when crossing it, we had a very heavy thunder-storm; at the earliest hour we had ever witnessed one. The Seaforthia palm because very abundant, and at last the forest was formed entirely of it, with trees of every size. Our guide showed us how we could easily obtain the young shoots, by splitting the leaves and leafstalks; and we enjoyed a fine meal of the cabbage. Our bullock refused to go any farther, and, as I then knew that the settlement was not very distant, I unloaded him, and covered his packsaddle and load with tarpaulings, and left him to recruit for a few days; when I intended to send for him. As we approached the harbour, the cabbage palm became rarer, and entirely disappeared at the head of it. We crossed several creeks running into the harbour, until we arrived at the Matunna, a dry creek, at which the foot-path from Pitchenelumbo (Van Diomen's Gulf) touched the harbour, and on which we should have come last night. We followed it now, crossed the Warvi, the Wainunmema, and the Vollir--all which enlarged into shallow lagoons or swamps, before they were lost between the mangrove thickets. At the banks of the Vollir, some constant springs exist, which induced Sir Gordon Bremer to choose that place for a settlement, and on which Victoria at present stands. All these creeks were separated from each other by a hilly forest land; but small fertile flats of sandy alluvium, clothed with young grass, and bordered by Banksias, extended along their banks. The forest was principally composed of stringy-bark, the leguminous Ironbark, Melaleuca-gum, with underwood of Acacias, Coniogeton, Pachynemas, Pultenaeas? and Careya? A tree very much resembling the real Ironbark (Eucalyptus resinifera) was observed at the Warvi; but I expect it will be found entirely different. The stringy-bark and the drooping tea-tree were the only useful timber near the settlement. The Cypress-pine (Callitris) could, however, be obtained without any great difficulty from Mount Morris Bay, or Van Diemen's Gulf. On the Vollir, we came on a cart road which wound round the foot of a high hill; and, having passed the garden, with its fine Cocoa-nut palms, the white houses, and a row of snug thatched cottages burst suddenly upon us; the house of the Commandant being to the right and separate from the rest. We were most kindly received by Captain Macarthur, the Commandant of Port Essington, and by the other officers, who, with the greatest kindness and attention, supplied us with every thing we wanted. I was deeply affected in finding myself again in civilized society, and could scarcely speak, the words growing big with tears and emotion; and, even now, when considering with what small means the Almighty had enabled me to perform such a long journey, my heart thrills in grateful acknowledgement of his infinite kindness.

After a month's stay at Port Essington, the schooner Heroine, Captain Mackenzie, arrived from Bally, on her voyage to Sydney, via Torres Strait and the Inner Barrier, a route only once before attempted with success. We embarked in this vessel, and arrived safely in Sydney, on the 29th of March. To the generous attentions of Captain Mackenzie our party owe much; and, at his hospitable table, we soon forgot the privations of our late journey. At Sydney, a reception awaited us, the warmth and kindness of which, it is out of my power to describe. All classes pressed forward to testify their joy at our reappearance, which, we found, had been long despaired of, and to offer their aid in supplying our wants. A public subscription was set on foot, which, in a very few weeks, by the liberal contributions which flowed in from all parts of the Colony, amounted to upwards of Fifteen Hundred pounds; and in the Legislative Council, a motion was brought forward, which, by the unanimous vote of that House, and the ready concurrence of His Excellency, Sir George Gipps, the Governor, devoted a Thousand Pounds out of the Public Revenue to our use. In the Appendix to this volume, will be found the very handsome letter, in which the Hon. Mr. E. Deas Thomson, the Colonial Secretary, conveyed to me this resolution of the Government; and an account of the proceedings taken at the School of Arts, on the 21st September, when His Honor, The Speaker, Dr. C. Nicholson, presented me with that portion of the public subscription, which the Committee of the Subscribers had awarded. In laying these documents before the Public, I will leave it to be supposed how vain would be any attempt of mine to express my gratitude to that generous people to whom I have inscribed this humble narrative.

APPENDIX.

LETTER FROM THE COLONIAL SECRETARY TO DR. LEICHHARDT.

Colonial Secretary's Office,
Sydney, 25th June, 1846.

Sir,--I do myself the honour to inform you that the Auditor General has been requested to prepare a warrant for the payment, out of the Crown Revenue, of a gratuity of 1000 pounds to yourself and party which accompanied you in your recent expedition to Port Essington; in consideration of the successful issue of that very perilous enterprise; the fortitude and perseverance displayed by the persons engaged in it; and the advantages derived from it to the Colony; and I beg to add, that it is with much gratification that I make this communication to you.

The money is to be divided in the manner stated below, which the Governor has considered reasonable, after weighing all the circumstances of the case, and advising with the gentleman who waited on His Excellency on Friday the 11th instant, and who formed a deputation from the Committee, who have superintended the collection and distribution of the money (1400 pounds.) raised in Sydney by voluntary subscription, in testimony of the services rendered to the Colony by you and your companions, viz.

Dr. Leichhardt	600 pounds	
Mr. Calvert	125	
Mr. Roper	125	
John Murphy	70	
W. Phillips, who has already received from the Government a pardon		30
The two aboriginal natives, Charles Fisher and Harry Brown		50

	1000	

The 50 pounds for the two Blacks will be lodged in the Savings' Bank, and will not be drawn out without the approval of the Vice President of that Institution. I have the honour to be, Sir,

Your most obedient Servant,
(Signed) E. DEAS THOMSON,
COLONIAL SECRETARY.

* * * * *

THE LEICHHARDT TESTIMONIAL.

[Extract from the Sydney Herald, Sept. 22, 1846.]

Yesterday afternoon, a meeting of the subscribers to the Leichhardt Testimonial was held in the School of Arts.

At half-past three o'clock the Honourable the Speaker of the Legislative Council entered the room with Dr. Leichhardt, who was received with loud applause.

As soon as silence was restored, the Speaker rose and addressed Dr. Leichhardt. He said, The duty has been assigned to me of presenting to you, on behalf of a numerous body of colonists, an acknowledgment of the grateful sense they entertain of the services rendered by you to the cause of science and to the interests of this colony. Whilst I fully participate in the admiration with which your merits are universally acknowledged, I confess that I shrink from the task now imposed upon me, from a sense of my inability to do justice to it in language commensurate with the occasion. For indeed it would be difficult to employ any terms that might be considered as exaggerated, in acknowledging the enthusiasm, the perseverance, and the talent which prompted you to undertake, and enabled you successfully to prosecute, your late perilous journey through a portion of the hitherto untrodden wilds of Australia. An enthusiasm undaunted by every discouragement, a perseverance unextinguished by trials and hardships which ordinary minds would have despaired of surmounting, a talent which guided and led you on to the full and final achievement of your first and original design.

It is needless for me to recall to the recollection of those around me, the circumstances under which the project of undertaking an overland journey to Port Essington was formed. The smallness of your party, and the scantiness of its equipment, the length and unknown character of the country proposed to be traversed, induced many to regard the scheme as one characterised by rashness, and the means employed as wholly inadequate towards carrying out the object in view. Many withheld their support from a dread lest they might be held as chargeable with that result which their sinister forebodings told them was all but inevitable with a small but adventurous band. You nevertheless plunged into the unknown regions that lay before you. After the lapse of a few months without any tidings of your progress or fate, the notion became generally entertained that your party had fallen victims to some one of the many dangers it had been your lot to encounter; that you had perished by the hands of the hostile natives of the interior; that want of water or exposure to tropical climate were even but a few of the many evils to which you had rendered yourself liable, and to the influence of some one or more of which it was but too probable you had fallen a prey. Two parties successively went out with the hope of overtaking you, or at least of ascertaining some particulars of your fate. The result of these efforts was, however, fruitless, and but few were so sanguine as to believe in the possibility of you or your comrades being still in existence. I need not recall to the recollection of those here present, the surprise, the enthusiasm, and the delight, with which your sudden appearance in Sydney was hailed, about six months ago. The surprise was about equal to what might be felt at seeing one who had risen from the tomb; a surprise, however, that was equalled by the warm and cordial welcome with which you were embraced by every colonist; and when we listened to the narrative of your long and dreary journey--the hardships you had endured, the dangers you had braved, the difficulties you had surmounted--the feeling with which your return amongst us was greeted, became one of universal enthusiasm. For it would indeed be difficult to point out, in the career of any traveller, the accomplishment of an equally arduous undertaking, or one pregnant with more important results, whether we contemplate them in a scientific, an economical, or a political point of view. The traversing, for the first time by civilised man, of so large a portion of the surface of this island, could not fail to be attended with many discoveries deeply interesting to the scientific inquirer, in botany, geology, and zoology. Your contributions to each of these departments of knowledge have consequently been equally novel and valuable. In a social and economical point of view, it is difficult, if not impossible, to over-estimate the importance of the discovery recently made of an all but boundless extent of fertile country, extending to the north, soon to be covered with countless flocks and herds, and calculated to become the abode of civilized man. In its political aspect, the possession of an immense territory, now for the first time discovered to be replete with all those gifts of nature which are necessary for the establishment and growth of a civilized community, cannot be regarded as a fact of small importance; nor the possession of a continuous tract of fine and fertile land, that connects us with the shores of the Indian ocean, and which would appear to render the Australian continent a mere extension of the Anglo-Indian empire as a matter of indifference. It would be almost impossible to exaggerate the importance of these considerations; I shall, however, abstain from occupying your time by dwelling upon what must be so obvious to all. The Colonists of New South Wales, Dr. Leichhardt, have been anxious to evince their gratitude to you for all that you have done in behalf of this their adopted country. As soon as your return was announced, subscriptions were entered into for the purpose of presenting to you a suitable testimonial. To the fund raised for this purpose persons of all classes, and from every quarter of the colony, have contributed. The sum that has been raised amounts to 1518 pounds 18 shillings 6 pence. The Executive, with a laudable emulation, have presented you a sum of 1000 pounds from the Crown revenue. Gratifying as this demonstration must doubtlessly prove to your feelings, it is unquestionably beneath your deserts; and the substantial reward due to your past exertions will be found in the undying glory of having your name enrolled amongst those of the great men whose genius and enterprise have impelled them to seek for fame in the prosecution of geographical science--with those of Niebuhr, Burckhardt, Park, Clapperton, Lander, and, in Australian geography, with those of Oxley, Cunningham, Sturt, Eyre, and Mitchell. In these days of universal knowledge, when there are so many competitors for distinction in every department of science, few attain the desired goal of scientific eminence. Perhaps no one has so fair a chance of giving immortality to his name as he who has first planted his foot where civilized man had never before trodden. The first chapter in the history of Australia, some thousand years hence, will present a narration of those adventurous spirits--of the exploits of those who may fairly be considered its first conquerors, and by whose peaceful triumphs an empire had been added to the parent state. I cannot close this brief address without indulging in an aspiration for the safety and success of one now engaged in an enterprise similar to that from which you hate earned so much honour. I allude to Sir T. Mitchell. To enter upon any eulogium of the character or abilities of that distinguished officer on the present occasion, is uncalled for; the enterprise in which he is engaged must command the sympathy of every person here present, and I am sure of no one more than of yourself. In enterprises such as those in which both he and yourself are engaged, it may fairly be said the harvest is plentiful, the labourers are few--a kindred taste and zeal in the pursuit of a common object can be attended with no other than a worthy and generous emulation. It only remains for me to add one word to what I have already said--you have disclosed your intention of starting within a few weeks from the present time on another exploratory expedition. From your past career we may all safely indulge in sanguine anticipations as to your future success. That Providence may guide you in your wanderings and crown your future labours with new laurels is the ardent wish of all on whose behalf I now address you. Let me, however, beg that you will guard, against any unnecessary exposure to risk, that life in the preservation of which we all feel so deep a concern. With the assurance of the gratitude, esteem, and admiration of my brother colonists, permit me now to present you with 854 pounds, being the proportion of the public subscription awarded to you.

Dr. LEICHHARDT (who was evidently deeply affected) said: Mr. Chairman and Gentlemen, I thank you for the munificent gift with which you have honoured me--I thank you for the congratulations for the past--for your kind wishes for my approaching expedition. [Note. 1] I feel the more the weight of your generous liberality, as I am conscious how much your kindness has overvalued my deserts; but I shall try to render myself worthy of it; and I hope that the Almighty, who has so mercifully taken care of me on my former expedition, will grant me skill and strength to continue my explorations, and will render them equally successful and beneficial to this colony. May his blessings attend the generous people who have shown, by the honours they have done me, how great an interest they take in the advancement of discovery.

Mr. C. COWPER then moved a vote of thanks to the Committee and their Secretary, which was acknowledged by Mr. R. GRAHAM, when the business of the meeting closed.

Those who appreciate the value of Dr. Leichhardt's scientific exploration of the country from Moreton Bay to Port Essington, and who feel any interest in his record of the difficulties of his enterprise, will be glad to learn that the Royal Geographical Society of London has recently awarded him the Queen's Gold Medal, in acknowledgment of his services; and that the Royal Geographical Society of Paris has likewise adjudged him its Gold Medal of this year.

[Note 1. The object of the new Expedition here alluded to, Is to explore the Interior of Australia, to discover the extent of Sturt's Desert and the character of the Western and North-Western Coast, and to observe the gradual change in vegetation and animal life from one side of the Continent to the other.

Dr. Leichhardt does not expect to be able to accomplish this overland journey to Swan River, in less than two years and a half. According to a letter written by him on the eve of his departure (Dec. 6, 1846); his party consisted of six whites, and two blacks; he had purchased thirteen mules, twelve horses, and two hundred and seventy goats; and bad received forty oxen, three mules, and two horses, as presents. He then purposed to travel over his old route, as far as Peak Range, and then to shape his course westwards; but thought it not impossible, as his course depends on water, that be should be obliged to reach the Gulf of Carpentaria, and then to follow up some river to its source.--Ed.]

The End

Made in the USA
Coppell, TX
02 August 2024

35494710R00157